THE INSIDERS' GUIDE ®

TO

Greater Richmond

Including Chesterfield, Hanover and Henrico Counties

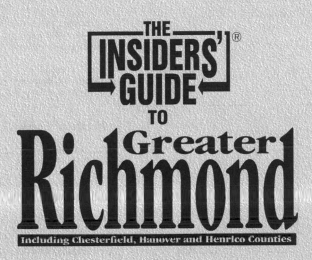

THE INSIDERS' GUIDE TO
Greater Richmond

Including Chesterfield, Hanover and Henrico Counties

by

Paula Kripaitis Neely

and

David M. Clinger

The Insiders' Guides Inc.

Co-published and marketed by:
Richmond Newspapers, Inc.
333 East Grace Street
Richmond, VA 23219

Co-published and distributed by:
The Insiders' Guides Inc.
The Waterfront • Suites 12 &13
P.O. 2057
Manteo, NC 27954
(919) 473-6100

•

FOURTH EDITION
1st printing

•

Copyright ©1995
by *Richmond Newspapers, Inc.*

•

Printed in the United States
of America

•

ISBN 0-912367-75-X

Richmond Newspapers
Supplementary Publications

Director
Jim Boyle

Manager
Ernie Chenault

Account Executive
Heidi Crandall
Mike Morrison
Adair Frayser-Roper

Artists
**Sean Contreras, Ronnie Johnson,
Susan Reilly and Ben Schulte**

The Insiders' Guides® Inc.

Publisher/Editor-in-Chief
Beth P. Storie

President/General Manager
Michael McOwen

Vice President/Advertising
Murray Kasmenn

Partnership Services Director
Giles Bissonnette

Creative Services Director
Mike Lay

Online Services Director
David Haynes

Sales and Marketing Director
Julie Ross

Managing Editor
Theresa Chavez

Project Editor
Dan DeGregory

Project Artist
Mel Dorsey

Fulfillment Director
Gina Twiford

Controller
Claudette Forney

On the cover:
Skyline photo by Jonathan Swift

Preface

If you're a newcomer or a visitor, we hope this book will help you discover our city with the ease and confidence of a longtime resident. If you've lived here long enough to be an Insider, you may find, as we did, that the sections will give you a more complete understanding of the city and all that it offers. Some sections may even help put current events in better perspective. This guide is also handy to have when you aren't entertaining guests from out of town.

As we researched this book, we found that there were many things about Richmond we didn't know. And, even though we've both lived here for more than 20 years, we learned that there's a lot more going on in Richmond than we realized.

Although we tried to include everything that we thought should be included in this book, we were quickly overwhelmed by the volume of what we wanted to mention. So, if you don't see your favorite place or event listed here, it may be because we had to make some tough choices about what to include. When we publish the next edition, we will undoubtedly include some different places, and we welcome your ideas about what you would like to see in these pages. Just send us a letter and let us know who we should contact for more information.

The Museum and White House of the Confederacy contains the world's largest collection of Confederate artifacts and documents.

About the Authors

Paula Kripaitis Neely is a free-lance writer and public relations consultant who has lived in Richmond since 1972. Her work has appeared in numerous regional and national publications, and she's received a string of awards from Press Women International, the International Association of Business Communicators and the Virginia Public Relations Association. A graduate of Virginia Commonwealth University, she has held marketing and public relations positions with the Science Museum of Virginia and the Virginia Department of Motor Vehicles. A Delaware native, she enjoys living in the Old Church area of Hanover County with her children — Brian, Laura and Sarah — and her husband Richard, a native Richmonder, whose considerable knowledge about the area helped make this book possible.

David M. Clinger arrived in Richmond in 1956, fresh out of Washington and Lee University, as a reporter for the *Richmond Times-Dispatch*. His subsequent career in corporate public relations included an extensive stint as director of corporate and financial information for Reynolds Metals Company, one of the Fortune 500 companies headquartered in Richmond. He was one of the founders of the Public Relations Council, Inc., a major Virginia public relations firm based in Richmond, and today is its managing partner. He writes about the Richmond area for national magazines and served on the staff of The Metro Chamber's "Focus On Our Future" initiative. He has lived north of the river and south of the river and today is a city dweller in a high-rise on Franklin Street.

Acknowledgments

Elizabeth C. Akers;
John Albers, City of Richmond;
Ann C. Andrews;
Arts Council of Richmond;
Barbara Batson;
William H. Baxter, Retail Merchants
  Association of Greater Richmond;
Sue Brinkerhoff Bland, Virginia
  Tourism Development Group;
Betty Booker;
LuAnne Brannen, Metro Richmond
  Convention and Visitors Bureau;
John I. Carrington;
Chesterfield County Economic
  Development Office;
Virginius Dabney's *Richmond: The Story
  of a City*;
George and Teresa Davis;
Bill and Rosemary Dietrick;
Phil DuHamel;
Nancy Finch;
Ann Freeman, Henrico County Schools;
Mildred Gatewood;
Greater Richmond Chamber of Commerce;
Greater Richmond Partnership, Inc.;
Hanover County Economic
  Development Office;
Henrico County Economic Development
  Office;
Hugh Gouldthorpe, Owens & Minor;
Historic Richmond Foundation;
Neville C. Johnson;
Carolyn and Robert Kripaitis;
Barbara Lee Kruger, Capital Area Agency
  on Aging;
Anne Louise Maliff;

John Markon;
Michael McGrann, Valentine Museum;
Lucy Meade, Downtown Richmond, Inc.;
Pamela Michael;
Tyler C. Millner;
Pauline Mitchell, retired from
  Chesterfield County;
Ethel and Richard Neely;
Richard, Brian, Laura and Sarah Neely;
Ashley Neville;
Margaret Peters, Virginia Department of
  Historic Resources;
George Peyton, Retail Merchants
  Association of Greater Richmond;
Steve Row;
Sarah C. Ruffin;
James K. Sanford's *Richmond: Her
  Triumphs, Tragedies & Growth*;
Charles Saunders and Staff, Richmond
  Newspapers Library;
James K. Schultz's *Richmond: A River
  City Reborn*;
David Slonaker, Hanover County Schools;
Lillie Stratton;
Harry Ward's *Richmond: An Illustrated
  History*;
Hermion White;
Greg Wingfield;
Gene Winter;
And various other trusted friends and
  confidants.
Thanks also to these departments of
  Richmond Newspapers, Inc.:
  Creative Services, Retail Advertising
  and Classified Advertising.

Credit: Metro Richmond Convention and Visitors Bureau

Virginia's State Capitol is located in Richmond.

Table of Contents

Directory of Maps

Richmond

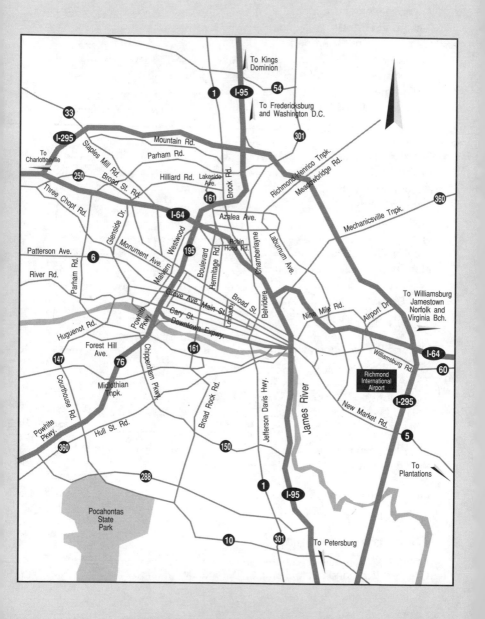

Greater Richmond

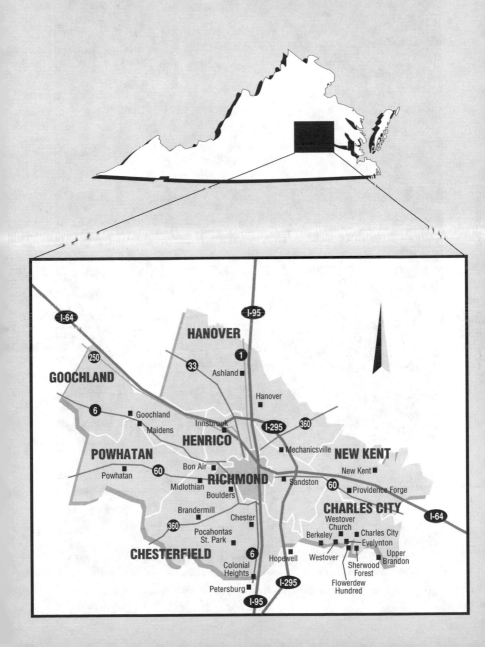

A little girl waves from the carousel ride at Valentine Riverside.

Inside
Richmond History

It used to be said that Richmond, like Rome, was built on seven hills.

You don't hear this much anymore, maybe because no one could ever agree on what hills were supposed to be part of this comparison with the Eternal City.

Among those most frequently mentioned are nine: Church Hill, Gamble's Hill, Oregon Hill, Shockoe Hill, Libby Hill, Chimborazo Hill, Navy Hill, Union Hill and Maddox Hill.

Perhaps the comparison developed because sitting atop one of the hills and dominating the skyline in early lithographs was a building of Roman Imperial architecture, the State Capitol.

Its architect, Thomas Jefferson, modeled it after Maison Carree, a Roman temple at Nimes, France, which he found to be "one of the most beautiful, if not the most beautiful and precious morsel of architecture left to us by antiquity." His only change from the original was to make the Capitol's columns Ionic instead of Corinthian.

Charles Dickens, when he visited in 1842, counted neither seven nor nine hills, but eight. "We rode and walked about the town, which is delightfully situated on eight hills, overhanging the James River; a sparkling stream, studded here and there with bright islands, or brawling over rocks," he later wrote in his *American Notes*.

It may be the city's enduring physical beauty, to which Dickens alludes, that has given it such eternal appeal.

The thing that strikes most visitors is the number of trees and parks, of which Richmond has an exceedingly large measure. Then there is the city's human scale and its easygoing lifestyle, things it has managed to retain along with an architectural treasure-trove that makes every walking tour a delight. History plays its role at every turn and, like many Richmonders, you soon may find yourself talking about epic events of the past almost as if they happened yesterday.

The beauty of the city's public places is something to enjoy, and Richmonders make the most of it with street festivals, outdoor concerts, baseball at The Diamond, arts in the parks and white-water rafting on the James. This leads into a cultural world that is packed with symphony, ballet, opera, galleries, theater, museums, impromptu performances, food festivals, garden and flower shows, spring and holiday house tours and so many other offerings that *Style Weekly*, the local arts and cultural journal, once was led to headline: "Lordy, Lordy, So Much To Do, So Little Time!"

It has been estimated that one out of every five people living in the Richmond area today didn't live here three years ago. Some came with the avalanche of new companies that now call Richmond home. Some came here to study at colleges and universities, and then decided to stay. Others have simply come, often without jobs, seeking a haven that, as an Old World exchange student said, "has a certain continuum about it."

This influx of new blood has generated an energy that is enhanced by Richmond's position as an urban center at the heart of what's described as an emerging Golden Crescent stretching from Baltimore and Washington south to the bustling ports of Hampton Roads.

Richmond today ranks among the nation's 14 largest Fortune 500 corporate headquarters centers. It is a major financial center, buoyed by the presence of the headquarters of the Fifth Federal Reserve District, a host of regional banks, big accounting firms and of a vast array of securities and investment firms.

Two major law firms, one with almost 500 lawyers, are headquartered here, putting Richmond in a megafirm league that is outdistanced only by New York, Los Angeles, Houston and Chicago. Five members of the New York Stock Exchange are headquartered in Richmond; only six cities in the nation have five or more.

A major medical center, with one of the top research universities in the nation, Richmond is the home of the Biotechnology Institute of Virginia's Center for Innovative Technology and is a growing hub for biomed/biotech firms. To build on these strengths, a new Virginia Biotechnology Research Park has been established on 22 acres adjacent to the downtown campus of Virginia Commonwealth University's Medical College of Virginia.

Crisscrossed by north-south and east-west interstates and rail lines, with its own deepwater port and perhaps the nation's fastest-growing air cargo facilities, Richmond has become an important distribution center.

Businesses like Richmond because it's the kind of place that helps attract and keep good people. Its work stoppage rates are among the lowest in the nation, and Richmond-area manufacturing workers are 85 percent more productive per worker hour than the United States as a whole, based on U.S. Department of Commerce figures.

Tobacco, the staple of the economy in years gone by, now shares the spotlight with aluminum, chemicals, paper, electronics, industrial equipment, prepared foods, plastics, energy, transportation services, high-tech fibers, pharmaceuticals, discount retailing, recreational products, publishing, financial services and national customer service operations.

Richmond, the historic city, actually traces its origins to massive rock formations, visible amid rapids in the James River, that once were part of Africa.

Recent discoveries place the Richmond Basin in a geological period called Triassic, about 210 million years ago, when the North American and African continents on their separate tectonic plates were welded together and beginning to pull apart, creating the Atlantic Ocean. The African plate was pushed and pulled down into the earth's mantle, and as the rock heated from the friction and pressure, sediments of the African crust melted and squeezed upward into the crust of the North American plate through deep faults or cracks.

In cutting across this rock "fall zone," the James River drops some 100 feet in 7 miles, reaching sea level at Richmond's 14th Street bridge. It is here that the character of the river changes from rapids, which at times are robust enough for Class V white-water rafting, to a meandering tidal estuary.

It is this natural, geological feature that attracted Native Americans and their settlement of Powhatan Village on what is today Fulton Hill.

It was this same feature that attracted the first English explorers in 1607, less than 10 days after they landed at Jamestown. They had sailed up the James looking for a route to the East India Sea. Here, at the falls of the James, they were struck by the potential of the rapids to operate water wheels. Grist and flour mills were vital to the economy of the time, as were sawmills, and the first report by Capt. Christopher Newport to King James emphasized the possibilities of harnessing the power of the rapids. The river also offered a navigable route from the Atlantic Ocean to the interior of the new land, and easy transport for goods produced along the river's edge.

Richmond thus became the site of one of the first English settlements in America. It was here that the first hospital in America was established and that plans were laid for a great university, although it was never built. The first tobacco, iron and coal produced in America, as well as timber, formed the backbone of the economy.

Great plantation homes, many still standing today, were built along the James, and present-day Richmond was laid out in 1737 — named for Richmond-on-the-Thames in Surrey County, England. French Huguenots had settled in the area earlier, and in the late 1730s there was an effort to attract German immigrants. One, Jacob Ege, a Wurttemberger, built a stone house, the oldest building still standing in Richmond, on Main Street between 19th and 20th streets.

It was on Church Hill, at St. John's Church, before an assembly that included George Washington and Thomas Jefferson, that Patrick Henry spoke 47 unforgettable words: "Why stand we here idle? Is life so dear and peace so sweet as to be purchased at the price of chains and slavery? Forbid it, Almighty God! I know not what course others may take; but as for me, give me liberty or give me death!"

The shot heard round the world was fired 30 days later at Concord, Massachusetts.

As the Revolutionary War took shape, plans were made to use tobacco in Richmond warehouses as money, and the cannon factory at Westham, 6 miles to the west, was busy turning out guns. Richmond's Chatham Rope Yard was making rigging for ships, and the Bellona Works across the river in Chesterfield was manufacturing powder. Public records from the state capital at Williamsburg were brought to Richmond for safekeeping from the British, and the capital was moved to Richmond permanently in 1780.

But the British, nevertheless, were coming.

In January, 1781, Richmond was occupied and burned by three British armies under Benedict Arnold. Continental Army troops under the Marquis de Lafayette and Baron von Steuben thwarted a second attack. But British forces under Cornwallis occupied the town again in June, burning tobacco and other stores in the streets. En route to Richmond, Cornwallis made his headquarters for 18 days at Hanover Tavern, still standing and now a dinner theater in Hanover County. Local lore says he left without paying his bill.

Lafayette and Colonel Anthony Wayne pursued the British down the

James, and the British surrendered at Yorktown four months later.

As the young United States looked westward for growing room, no one was more aware of the significance of the James River than was George Washington. On November 15, 1784, he appeared before the Virginia General Assembly in Richmond to promote the formation of a company "for clearing and extending the navigation of the James River from tidewater up to the highest parts practicable on the main branch thereof," according to one historian.

The first Richmond sections of the canal were completed in 1789 and 1794, and water was let into the Richmond basin between Eighth, 11th, Canal and Cary streets in 1800. The "Great Waterway to the West," what was to become the James River and Kanawha Canal, helped open up America's heartland for trade to and from points abroad and transformed Richmond into an important trading center.

As the early 1800s unfolded, Richmond was beginning to realize its great potential for economic development. Tobacco production was firmly established; the Richmond area was a major exporter of American coal; four iron works were in operation; Richmond was a major flour-milling center; and manufacturing plants were busy turning out furniture, glass, books, textiles and refined sugar.

The Richmond, Fredericksburg and Potomac Railroad Company was chartered in 1834, and within the next 20 years Richmond became a major railroad center, served by 20 lines. Richmond College, now the University of Richmond, was chartered in 1840, and Richmond's Medical College of Virginia was incorporated in 1854. Interestingly enough, the city had a German-language newspaper, and 25 percent of the white population in those days was German.

Mounting intersectional animosities and tension over the slavery issue increased with John Brown's raid on Harpers Ferry.

Virginia overwhelmingly opposed secession and breakup of the Union and even attempted to call all states to a peace conference in Washington. But the die was cast after seven Southern states seceded from the Union and President Lincoln called for troops from Virginia to help suppress the rebellion in the Deep South. The Virginia Convention, meeting in Richmond, voted almost 2-to-1 in favor of withdrawing from the Union.

Thus Richmond, for the second time, was thrust into a war of secession. The city became the capital of the Confederate States of America and its principal manufacturing, supply and hospital center.

"On to Richmond!" became the battle cry of Federal troops, with the city as their primary objective for four years. Seven military drives were hurled at the city. In one, the Battle of Cold Harbor, the Union army suffered 7,000 casualties in less than 30 minutes.

Insiders' Tips

Richmond is the only city in America burned in two wars — the Revolutionary War and the Civil War.

During the war years bacon went from 12¢ a pound to $8 a pound and butter from 25¢ a pound to $25 a pound. Lack of meat led Confederate President Jefferson Davis to recommend rats as being "as good as squirrels." Rats sold in some places for $2.50 each, and the superintendent of a local military hospital made available a recipe for cleaning, basting and roasting the rodents.

Word of Petersburg's fall came to Confederate President Davis on Palm Sunday, 1865, while he was attending services at St. Paul's Church. It was now clear that Richmond could no longer be defended, and warehouses and stores were set afire. Nine hundred buildings were burned during the evacuation fire, including almost everything in the area bounded by Main, Fourth, 15th and the James River. With fires raging out of control, the city's surrender took place the next day.

When President Lincoln arrived unexpectedly, and somewhat unceremoniously, on April 4, the smoke from the devastated business and commercial district still lingered. From Rocketts Landing he walked up Main Street and then to the White House of the Confederacy.

It would be five years before Virginia would be readmitted to the Union, during which time it underwent Reconstruction, including two years of military rule. Yet, almost phoenix-like, Richmond's economy rebounded, and the city entered an energetic period of industrialization and urbanization.

By the 1890s and the turn of the century, the economy was booming: iron, tobacco, flour, paper, brick, woolens, locomotives, shipbuilding, fertilizer, carriages, soap, spices. Richmond's Bessemer works was the third largest in the South. Truly, Richmond exemplified the New South.

In 1903 Maggie L. Walker, the daughter of a former slave, founded what is now Consolidated Bank and Trust Company, making her the nation's first female bank president.

In 1914 Richmond was chosen as the site for the headquarters of the Fifth Federal Reserve District, making it the focal point of finance for much of the Southeast. For this and other reasons, the city came out of World War I with enhanced business prestige. From 1910 to 1920 the population jumped 34.5 percent.

Richmond weathered The Great Depression better than most because of the depression-resistant tobacco base of its economy.

It even saw another building boom in the late 1930s. But then, through World War II, and for the next two decades, things remained fairly status quo.

The opening of Reynolds Metals Company's new corporate headquarters building in the late 1950s, the founding of the fledgling James River Corporation in 1969, and the completion in 1978 of the downtown riverfront headquarters of the Federal Reserve Bank designed by Minoru Yamasaki set the stage for the explosive era of growth that dramatically changed the face of the city.

In the 1980s, with strong regional government cooperation, a massive expansionary period began — industrial and office investment doubled year to year to a rate of $1 billion annually. It was during this period that Richmond became firmly established as a major corporate center, as well as a U.S. beachhead for several Japanese and European companies, and the area grew into a major distribution and financial center.

It was also during this period that local residents within 60 days raised $8 million for The Diamond, a showcase minor league baseball stadium with skyboxes, a restaurant and all of the amenities. A $22 million expansion of the Virginia Museum of Fine Arts doubled gallery space and gained the museum international acclaim. The first phase of the $450 million James Center was completed. And the $200 million Tobacco Row project — covering 15 contiguous city blocks, the largest historic renovation project in the nation and an important boost for downtown housing — got under way.

Partners for Livable Places named the Richmond area one of the dozen or so "most livable and innovative" metropolitan areas in the nation. *Inc.* magazine picked it as one of the top 30 "Hot Spots" for new and expanding business. *Health* magazine ranked the Richmond area No. 1 among "America's Ten Healthiest Cities." And *City & State* magazine placed Richmond's government among the nation's top 10, based on financial health and management.

Famous sons and daughters include Pocahontas, the Indian princess; Nancy Langhorne, who later became Lady Astor, the first woman elected to the British House of Commons, and her sister, Irene, the famous Gibson Girl of the 1890s; Edgar Allan Poe, the father of the mystery story, and other writers such as Mary Johnston, Ellen Glasgow, James Branch Cabell, and today's Tom Wolfe and Patricia Cornwell; George W. Goethals, chief engineer of the Panama Canal; former U.S. Supreme Court Justice Lewis F. Powell Jr.; tennis, football and golf greats like Arthur Ashe Jr., Willie Lanier, Lanny Wadkins, Bobby Wadkins and Vinny Giles; and entertainers like Shirley MacLaine, Warren Beatty and the late Bill "Bojangles" Robinson. In addition,

Richmond Firsts

With a colonial history going back to the early 1600s, Richmond has had plenty of opportunity to pioneer a number of "firsts." They include:

First Hospital
America's first hospital, a "guest house for sick people," was built in 1611 at Henricus, the first major English settlement in the Richmond area.

First Tobacco
After observing Native Americans cultivating tobacco, John Rolfe in 1612 followed their example and planted a crop just east of Richmond in the area he named Varina after a variety of Spanish tobacco. The popularity of the "noxious weed" in England convinced colonists that if money didn't grow on trees, then it most certainly grew on tobacco plants.

First Iron and Coal
America's first ironworks were established in 1619 at Falling Creek in Chesterfield County where there were heavy outcroppings of ore. The first coal mining in the New World began in the Richmond area in the mid-1700s, and by the 1790s accounted for a healthy share of the area's exports.

First Thanksgiving

The first Thanksgiving in America took place at Berkeley Plantation in 1619, a year before the Pilgrims landed at Plymouth Rock.

Oldest Medical College Building in South

The Egyptian Building (1845) of Virginia Commonwealth University's Medical College of Virginia is the oldest medical college building in the South and is considered the finest example of Egyptian Revival architecture in America. The building was remodeled in 1939 with funds given by Bernard Baruch, the New York financier, in honor of his father, Simon Baruch, who was an MCV graduate and the father of modern hydrotherapy.

First Military Aircraft

It was in Civil War military campaigns around Richmond that the first military "aircraft" — tethered balloons — were used for aerial reconnaissance.

First Electric Streetcar

The first commercial streetcar system powered by overhead electric lines from a central station was put into operation in Richmond in 1888 by Julian Frank Sprague after he was unable to persuade New York to accept the idea. Sprague was a former assistant to Thomas A. Edison.

First Female Bank President

The first female bank president in the U.S. was Maggie L. Walker, daughter of a former slave, who organized St. Luke's Penny Savings Bank in Richmond in 1903. The bank of which she was president is now part of Richmond's Consolidated Bank & Trust Company, the oldest African-American-owned bank in the nation.

First Cellophane

The first Cellophane in the U.S. was produced in Richmond in 1930 by DuPont. Today Kevlar fiber, pound-for-pound rated five times stronger than steel and used in bulletproof vests, is made exclusively in Richmond by DuPont, as are other high-tech fibers tradenamed Nomex, Teflon and Tyvek.

First Canned Beer

The first beer in the United States in tin-plated steel cans — Krueger Ale, produced by the Krueger Brewery of Newark — was test-marketed in Richmond beginning on January 24, 1935. The conservative Richmond market was a favorite for new-product tests; "if it sells in Richmond, it will sell anyplace." The 1935 innovation that made beer packaging history was eclipsed by a better container, the recyclable all-aluminum can, developed in Richmond in 1963 by Reynolds Metals Company.

First Household Foil
Reynolds Wrap household foil, produced by Richmond-based Reynolds Metals Company, was pioneered in test markets in Richmond in 1947.

First Tamari Brewery Outside of Japan
Tamari, the soy seasoning of choice in the elite circles from the tables of shoguns to the Ginza's best restaurants, was brewed exclusively in Japan for centuries — until 1987 when San-Jurushi of Japan chose Richmond as the home of its first international brewery.

First ISDN Phone Service
In the forefront of telecommunications development, C&P Telephone (Bell Atlantic-Virginia), headquartered in Richmond, pioneered the nation's first commercial (non-trial) Integrated Services Digital Network (ISDN) in 1988.

professional careers launched here include those of Pulitzer Prize-winning editorial cartoonist Jeff MacNelly, TV commentator Roger Mudd and musician Bruce Springsteen.

Says the meeting planners guide of the Metropolitan Richmond Convention & Visitors Bureau: "Virginia's capital is like no other . . . . Its architect was Thomas Jefferson. Its spokesman was Patrick Henry. Its lawmaker, John Marshall. Its poet, Edgar Allan Poe. And its general, Robert E. Lee."

A more contemporary addition to this who's who lineup is Oliver Hill, the civil rights lawyer who played a key role in the Brown vs. the Board of Education decision. In addition, the city has been blessed with risk-takers and corporate visionaries like the Gottwalds of Ethyl, Brent Halsey and Bob Williams of James River Corporation, Jim Wheat of Wheat First Butcher Singer, the Reynoldses of Reynolds Met-

als, Claiborne Robins of A.H. Robins, J. Harwood Cochrane of Overnite Transportation and subsequently of Highway Express, the Bryans of Media General, the Lewises of Best Products, the Wurtzels of Circuit City Stores, and a host of other business and community leaders who have helped make Richmond what it is today.

Modern-day Richmond — something people refuse to believe until they see it — is described by Pulitzer Prize-winning editor and historian Virginius Dabney as an "intriguing blend of the old and the new — of Charleston and Savannah on one hand, and Atlanta and Dallas on the other. While showing the élan and drive in business and industrial realms, the city clings — a bit precariously at times — to its distinctive 18th- and 19th-century heritage."

In trying to describe in a few words what today's Richmond is all about, this is probably the closest you can get.

Inside
Getting Around Richmond

The Richmond area has a very well-designed, well-maintained street and expressway system. Local governments and the Virginia Department of Transportation have done a good job of anticipating urban growth, and new and expanded roads usually are put in place before there is a heavy need for them.

Rush-hour bottlenecks do occur at toll booths on the Downtown and Powhite expressways. But the rush-hour backups usually are of relatively short and predictable duration.

Inclement weather, especially snow, brings traffic to a painfully slow crawl. Richmonders don't see a lot of snow and don't have much experience driving in it. This results in some serious fender benders, which complicate matters. The best advice is to allow yourself a little extra time on bad-weather days, be patient and move cautiously with the flow.

A number of wide, new bridges have been completed across the James River in recent years. This makes river crossings much less of a problem than they used to be, save for those who insist on using the Huguenot Bridge to avoid paying expressway tolls.

Before you buy a house, rent an apartment, or select an office site, you might want to experiment at rush hour with sev-

Until recently Richmond's motorized trackless trolleys served the downtown area.

Credit: Greater Richmond Transit Authority

eral alternate routes (and bridges, if you are looking at a home on one side of the river and an office on the other).

Even then, if you're used to L.A., Washington, Houston, Charlotte or Atlanta, you might wonder if Richmonders know what the word bottleneck really means. The automobile is the favored mode of transport in Richmond, and highway planners and builders have placed high priority on being sure local residents can use personal vehicles with as little encumbrance as possible.

Easy Access to Recreation Areas

Richmond's location at the intersection of north-south I-95 and east-west I-64, and at the junction of other major highways, places it within easy reach of resort, vacation and recreation areas in all directions. In just an hour or two you can travel east or southeast to the Chesapeake Bay, or one of the many rivers that flow into this giant estuary; to Virginia Beach; or you can be well on your way to North Carolina's Outer Banks. An hour or so to the west lie the Blue Ridge Mountains with ample opportunities for camping, hiking, backpacking and skiing. Within the same amount of time, in any direction, you'll find history — Colonial Williamsburg, Fredericksburg, Petersburg, Jefferson's Charlottesville — as well as the museums and cultural offerings of Washington, D.C.

Traffic Patterns

Unless there is a sign forbidding it, you can turn right at a red light providing there is no oncoming traffic. The same holds true for left turns from a one-way street onto another one-way street.

Right of way in traffic circles is for the most part as you would expect, with traffic in the circle having preference. One of the major exceptions is the circle around the Lee Monument on Monument Avenue. In this case through traffic on Monument has the primary right of way, so great care must be taken if you are moving around the circle or if you are crossing it via Allen Avenue.

The system of street numbering and naming generally is pretty sane. If someone gives you an address on a numbered street between First and 40th, you do have to double check to see if this is in the East End (Church Hill and Shockoe Bottom) or on the South Side (Forest Hill and Bainbridge); similar street designations exist in both places. Few streets change their names, although Malvern does become Westwood as it crosses Broad Street, and Monument Avenue and W. Franklin Street exchange names at Stuart Circle. Boulevard (actually the name of a major thoroughfare) going north flows into Hermitage. Boulevard south takes you onto Westover Hills Boulevard after you cross the river, and Westover Hills Boulevard south flows into Belt Boulevard.

Buses

The Greater Richmond Transit Co. (GRTC) is the local public bus system. Equipment is modern and comfortable — but under-utilized by most Richmonders. The basic rate is $1.25, although you can buy a book of 10 "Super Saver" tickets that will allow you to ride for just $1 or less ($10 per book, or $5 per book if you are a senior citizen or are disabled). Transfers cost 15¢, but are just 10¢ with "Super Saver" tickets and are free for senior citizens and the disabled. A book of 20 school tickets for students in high school or below may be purchased for $12.50. Routes cover the City of Richmond and extend into Henrico County. Daily service on most routes begins at 5:30 AM and ends at midnight. Route information is available by calling 358-GRTC.

Park and Ride

Park and ride service is available in the following locations: U.S. 1 at John Tyler Community College (100 spaces), U.S. 360 and Route 653 at Rockwood Park (150 spaces), I-64 and Route 623 (30 spaces), I-64 and Route 617 at Oilville (15 spaces), U.S. 360 at Mechanicsville (109 spaces), U.S. 60 at Bottoms Bridge (40 spaces).

Greater Richmond Transit Co. (GRTC) bus service is available at peak hours from these locations: I-64 at Airport Drive (305 spaces), Parham and Fordson roads (352 spaces), Glenside Drive near Staples Mill Road (480 spaces), and Gaskins Road at Mayland (399 spaces).

Ridesharing

The Commuter Center operated by Ridefinders coordinates ridesharing by bus, car pool and van pool. If you are interested in finding a bus route, car pool partner or van pool group to get to and from work, you should first seek out your company's Employee Transportation Coordinator (ETC) who, in turn, has an established relationship with Ridefinders and the Greater Richmond Transit Company. If your company does not have an ETC, then you should contact The Commuter Center directly by phone (643-RIDE), or by facsimile transmission (649-2513). If you rideshare at least three days a week, you'll be entitled to a Guaranteed Ride Home, a service operated by Ridefinders for regular bus riders and carpoolers. The service provides a ride if you have a midday emergency, miss your bus or if you unexpectedly have to work late.

Photo: Richmond Newspapers

Swift Creek Resevoir is one of several large bodies of water near Richmond.

Parking

Observe parking signs and parking meter regulations carefully. In Richmond they mean what they say. The police department has a good supply of parking tickets, and they are doled out liberally. Towing is down to a science along streets where early-morning and late-afternoon rush-hour parking is prohibited.

Property owners also are quick to tow vehicles left in private parking places. Also, city law requires cars to be towed if there are three or more delinquent parking tickets on record. If your car is towed from the street you'll need to call police information at 233-7956 or 780-5100 to retrieve it.

Parking lots and decks downtown are plentiful, and they are fairly well dispersed throughout different areas of the center city. In fact, for the first time in Richmond's history, there are probably too many parking decks. This has put some pressure on monthly rates, so you'll be wise to shop around. Rates range from $20 a month in peripheral areas to $125 monthly in top-line office buildings. Hourly rates range from 50¢ to $2.50, depending on location.

Taxis

Taxis can be hailed on the street, but don't expect to snag one. Taxis moving on the street usually already have a fare or are in the process of responding to a pickup call. The best thing is to call one of the 30 cab companies listed in the Yellow Pages or ask the receptionist at the office or hotel you are visiting to make arrangements for you. It takes cabs time to respond to pickup calls, so be sure to factor this into your planning and make your arrangements early.

Uniform taxi rates are set by Richmond City Council and by county boards of supervisors. They are $1.50 for the first $1/5$ mile, 30¢ for each additional $1/5$ mile, and 30¢ for each minute of delay. There is an extra charge of $1 each for additional passengers older than 6 years. A $1 surcharge may be added between 9 PM and 6 AM. All tolls are charged to the passenger. At the driver's discretion, riders 65 years of age and older are eligible for a 20 percent discount off meter fare. Riders may request and receive an estimate of fare before the trip begins and a written receipt upon arrival at the destination. Comments and suggestions about taxi service are welcomed by the Taxicab Services Coordinator, Richmond Regional Planning District Commission, by phone at 359-TAXI or by facsimile transmission at 358-5386.

Washington Airport Shuttle

Richmond is fortunate in that residents can take advantage of air service in and out of Washington, D.C. One convenient way to do this is to utilize ground transportation to and from Washington National Airport provided by Groome Transportation. The cost of the minibus shuttle is $27. Weekday departures begin at 6:30 AM at Richmond International Airport, with a stop 30 minutes later at the Holiday Inn-Crossroads on Staples Mill Road near Broad Street. The last departure from Richmond leaves the airport at 3:30 PM and the Holiday Inn-Crossroads at 4 PM. Reservations are not required. The weekend schedule differs. For information, call 222-7222 or (800) 552-7911. Groome also provides charter service and door-to-airport limousine service in the greater Richmond area. For charter service, call 222-7226.

Intercity Ground Travel and Charters

Greyhound Bus Lines is a nation-wide bus service offering regularly scheduled as well as charter service. The station is at 2910 N. Boulevard, across from The Diamond and just a few blocks off of Broad Street. Fare and schedule information may be obtained by calling 254-5938 or (800) 231-2222. Charter service can be arranged by calling (800) 454-2487.

Capitol City Travel Agency and Virginia Tours, Inc. offer round-trip bus service to Atlantic City. Buses leave Southside Plaza at 5:45 AM, the site of the former John Marshall Hotel at 6 AM, and the library on Brook Road at 6:15 AM. Buses normally return about 2 AM. The service is not offered on Mondays unless there is sufficient interest. Information may be obtained by calling 644-2901 or 359-1112.

Winn Transportation/Winning Tours Inc. is a full-service charter bus travel service. It makes one scheduled round trip to Williamsburg on Mondays, with stops at the Pottery, the outlet shopping center, Busch Gardens and in the historic area of Colonial Williamsburg. Service departs the bus line office at 1831 Westwood Avenue at 8:10 AM and returns at 6:30 PM. Information on fares and charter service is available by calling 358-6666 or (800) 296-9466.

James River Bus Lines has regularly scheduled round-trip service on Wednesdays and Sundays to the Charles Town, West Virginia, racetrack. On Sundays, service also is offered to points south including Petersburg, Suffolk, Portsmouth, Norfolk and Virginia Beach. Sunday buses depart the Greyhound terminal at 8 AM, and returning buses depart Virginia Beach at 7 PM. It also has a regular run to Atlantic City every Wednesday and

Credit: Richmond Newspapers

One of the easiest and most efficient ways to get around Richmond is on GRTCs buses.

Saturday, departing from Azalea Mall at 6 AM and returning at 3 AM. Information may be obtained by calling 321-7661.

Amtrak provides passenger rail service on main north-south routes and to the east, as well as connecting service to the west. Northern destinations include Washington, Philadelphia, Atlantic City, New York and Boston. Southern stops include Raleigh, Charlotte, Columbia (S.C.), Tampa and Miami. One train goes to Newport News daily. The train station is at 7519 Staples Mill Road, just a short distance off of I-64 W. The station is a modern, one-level structure with barrier-free access for wheelchairs and is open 24 hours a day. Requests for general information and reservations may be made by calling (800) 872-7245. The number for package express is 264-9194 and the local sales office number is 262-2031.

Some of the most commodious charter buses in town are available from Tourtime America, and information on rates may be obtained by calling 550-1287. Excellent bus charter service also is available from Greyhound Bus Lines (as noted above), Groome Transportation at 222-7226, James River Bus Lines at 321-7661, Winn Transportation/Winning Tours, Inc. (buses, limousines and executive sedans) at 358-6666 or (800) 296-9466 and from Virginia Overland Charters at 233-1152. Information on charters of trolleys is available from the Greater Richmond Transit Company at 358-3871. Daily guided van tours of the city and of Civil War sites are offered by Historic Richmond Foundation at 780-0107.

If You Want Something Different

For a slow and romantic tour of downtown, including the Capitol Square and Shockoe Slip, try a horse-drawn carriage. The carriage operates in warm-weather months from 8 PM to 2 AM Friday and Saturday beginning at 12th and Cary streets. A half-hour costs $25, a full hour $50. No reservations are necessary. If you need more information, the person to call is Sam Slate at 749-3322.

For other occasions, call Jim Hundley of Hundley's Horse-Drawn Carriage Service at 743-9233. He offers a wide range of antique carriages, all presented with traditional elegance and charm for business functions, birthdays, weddings, anniversaries, promotions and nights on the town.

Or, try a hot-air balloon. Charters are available from Barnstormer Air Shows at 798-8830 or Balloons Over Virginia at 730-3814.

You might also take a genuine London cab. London Transport of Richmond at 343-4343 operates these vehicles. They're great for impressing business visitors and are popular for weddings and special events.

Inside
The Civil War

Richmond in 1860 was overwhelmingly opposed to secession. Virginia's governor, a strong Unionist, urged a national convention to calm mounting intersectional animosities. Even the decision by seven Deep South states to leave the Union and the firing on Fort Sumter did not sway Virginia's position. Meeting in Richmond, the Virginia General Assembly issued an invitation to the then 34 states of the Union to attend a peace conference in Washington, and a delegation of Virginians was sent to meet with President Lincoln in hopes of averting the looming catastrophe.

But public opinion shifted radically on April 15, 1861, when President Lincoln called for 75,000 volunteers, including 8,000 from Virginia, to quell the rebellion in the Deep South. Delegates who just a few days earlier had voted 88 to 45 against secession now voted 88 to 55 in favor of it. When a statewide referendum was held on the action the following month, the vote was 4-to-1 for secession, with only four Richmonders voting against it.

Richmond moved quickly to a war footing. It became the principal training, hospital, armament and munitions center for the new Confederacy, as well as its capital city. From all over the South young men came to train under the supervision of Robert E. Lee, a former U.S.

Credit: Richmond National Battlefield Park

Gaines Mill is just one of the many Civil War battlefields in the Richmond area.

Army colonel who had just declined an offer to command the Northern armies, a man who owned not a single slave, but a man who could not turn his back on his native Virginia.

Belle Isle, under today's Lee Bridge, became an overcrowded prison camp for Union enlisted men. A warehouse and ship chandlery at 20th and E. Cary streets was hastily converted into a prison for Federal officers — the infamous Libby Prison. The Tredegar Iron Works at the foot of 7th Street and local arsenals and armories turned out artillery, muskets, ammunition, mines, railroad iron, plate for ironclads and other matériel needed to wage battle on land and sea.

It is not surprising, then, that "On to Richmond!" became the rallying cry of Union troops, with the city their primary objective for four years, or that one-fourth of the Civil War's battles and 60 percent of its casualties occurred within a 75-mile radius of the city.

Seven military drives were hurled against the beleaguered city. Two, Gen. George McClellan's Peninsula Campaign of 1862 and Gen. Ulysses S. Grant's devastating assault in 1864, brought Union troops within sight of the Capitol. Richmonders became accustomed to the "eternal cannonade" as guns on nearby front lines blasted away night and day.

Richmond-area Civil War battlefields and sites — including Cold Harbor where 7,000 Federal troops fell in a hailstorm of bullets in 30 minutes — abound. A good way to become more familiar with this epic period of Richmond's history is to visit the **Chimborazo Visitor Center** (on the site of the Civil War's Chimborazo General Hospital, the largest in the world at the time), 3215 East Broad Street, 226-1981. The center has exhibits, an audiovisual presentation on the battlefields around Richmond, a 30-minute film, *Richmond Remembered*, and battlefield tour maps, as well as an audio tape (for rent or purchase) that will lead you on a 4-hour tour of area battlefields and parks.

The center is operated by Richmond National Battlefield Park, which contains 10 park units. Each unit of the park is interpreted by National Park Service historical markers and some sites, such as Fort Harrison and Drewry's Bluff, have short hiking or self-guided trails. Picnic facilities are available at Fort Harrison and at the Cold Harbor Visitor Center.

An essential part of any Civil War tour also is a visit to the Museum of the Confederacy at 12th and E. Clay streets.

Here's an overview of some of the area's most famous Civil War sites listed by chronological significance:

DREWRY'S BLUFF

Federal gun boats, including the ironclad *Monitor*, were repulsed by Confederate firepower commanding the bluff just below Richmond on May 15, 1862. The fort was never captured during the war.

SEVEN PINES

It was here, just 7 miles east of Richmond, that Confederate forces under

There are 35 Civil War battlefields in the Richmond area.

Gen. Joseph E. Johnston assaulted positions of Union forces advancing on the city on May 31, 1862. Johnston was badly wounded.

CHICKAHOMINY BLUFF

From this vantage point, Gen. Robert E. Lee, who replaced the wounded Johnston, observed Union troop movements prior to what was to become known as the Seven Days Battle in late June, 1862. Lee's brilliant strategy and tactics in a series of desperate encounters over the next week forced McClellan's retreat and saved Richmond for the moment.

BEAVER DAM CREEK

It was here, in a pleasant little creek valley near the intersection of routes 156 and 360 (Mechanicsville Turnpike), that the first encounter of the Seven Days Battle took place on June 10, 1862. Confederate troops under Lee's command attempted to break the Union lines by fording the creek and millrace, waist deep in water and under fire from Federal troops on higher ground to the west.

GAINES MILL

It was during the second of the Seven Days, here in the fields around the Watt House, that troops from Texas and Georgia finally broke the strong Union defensive position and sent the Federals retreating across the Chickahominy River.

SAVAGE'S STATION

Confederate forces here attempted unsuccessfully to disrupt the Union withdrawal toward the James River on June 29.

WHITE OAK SWAMP

Using artillery, a Union rear guard fought a successful delaying action that allowed the main body of the Union army to move closer to the James and to the protection of Federal gunboats on June 30.

MALVERN HILL

This was the final engagement of the Seven Days Battles. Retreating Union troops under McClellan, with the Confederates in hot pursuit, stopped here to make a stand on July 1, 1862. Confederate troops threw assault after assault up the open slopes of Malvern Hill against massed artillery and infantry fire. All of the assaults proved futile. According to one Confederate officer: "It was not war — it was murder." McClellan continued to retreat to the safety of Harrison's Landing at Berkeley Plantation and thence to Alexandria.

BERKELEY PLANTATION

During the Peninsula Campaign in 1862 it was at Berkeley Plantation that aerial reconnaissance was first employed, with observations balloons used to direct artillery fire. This is the place, also, while it was a Union army base in 1862, that the plaintive notes of "Taps" were composed.

YELLOW TAVERN

Two years later, on May 4, 1864, Union forces crossed the Rapidan River and began their final massive assault on Richmond. Confederate cavalry hero J.E.B. Stuart was mortally wounded in fierce fighting on May 11 at Yellow Tavern, located almost precisely where I-95 and I-295 cross paths between Richmond and Ashland today.

HANOVER JUNCTION

Opposing forces met at Hanover Junction, the crossroads of two ma-

Drewry's Bluff, located south of Richmond, was one of the many Confederate Civil War strongholds.

Credit: Richmond National Battlefield Park

jor Confederate rail supply lines, on May 23.

HAW'S SHOP

The Union and Confederate cavalry engagement on May 28 here on the grounds of Enon Church was one of the larger cavalry battles of the war.

COLD HARBOR

It was here that Confederate troops had dug in, ready for the oncoming Grant. With Lee thus blocking the entrance to Richmond, Grant ordered massive as-saults. They were among the most intense of the war. Grant's effort, from May 31 to June 2, was unsuccessful and costly, with thousands of dead and wounded lying unattended for days in a no-man's land before a truce could be arranged. Grant would later call the final assault at Cold Harbor his greatest mistake. But Richmond, again, had been saved.

HOWLETT LINE AND BERMUDA HUNDRED LINE

Meanwhile, to the south of Richmond at Bermuda Hundred Neck on the James

More major Civil War battles were fought in Virginia than in any other state.

River, a Federal force under Gen. Benjamin Butler had come ashore. Confederate forces built a 3-mile-long entrenchment line running from the James to the Appomattox River and in May and June, 1864, effectively bottled up Butler's army for the remainder of the war.

RIVER ROAD

Coming through what is today's West End, Union Col. Ulrich Dahlgren led several hundred handpicked cavalrymen down River Road to attack the city in 1864 in an attempt to free prisoners on Belle Isle. He was repelled by the Home Guard on the outskirts of town on what is today's Cary Street. Veering around Richmond, Dahlgren was killed and his men captured when they encountered units of the 9th Virginia Cavalry.

FORT HARRISON

To the southeast between State Route 5 and the James River, and originally part of the outer ring of defenses around Richmond, Fort Harrison remained in Con-

federate hands until the latter days of the war. It was finally captured by Grant's troops in action from September 29 through 30, 1864. Other forts, many within shouting distance of Fort Harrison, managed to ward off the attackers, and Lee made an attempt to recapture some forts in early October.

Richmond would hold out for six more months, until Palm Sunday, April 2, 1865.

It was on that day at St. Paul's Church that Confederate President Jefferson Davis received word that the Union army had breached the main lines at Petersburg, that Lee was retreating toward Danville and that Richmond no longer could be defended.

Confederate warships, riding at anchor in the James River with their magazines loaded, were blown up by their officers. Approximately 900 downtown buildings were burned in the Evacuation Fire after warehouses were set ablaze to keep their contents from falling into enemy hands.

The Fan District features turn-of-the-century townhouses on streets
that spread westward in the shape of a fan.

METRO RICHMOND'S

Premier Communities And Builders

RICHMOND'S DESIGN LEADER

Better Not Wait To Buy A Home In FoxHall

Our Energy Saver Homes by Colonial Homecrafters, Ltd. on lots 1C4 & B87 are designed for year-round comfort and energy savings

EQUAL HOUSING
OPPORTUNITY

With a brand new section of homesites just opening there's never been a better time to buy a home in FoxHall. The new 3600 square foot clubhouse is the center of the neighborhood's recreational amenities, in cluding pools, tennis courts, a playground, picnic pavilion and a soccer field.

With new companies location in Richmond, the homes in FoxHall won't last long. Ride through our serene, secure neighborhood and visit our furnished model open 2 5 weekdays and 12-5 weekends. Don't miss your opportunity to live in this beautiful West End neighborhood surrounded by the best recreational facilities you could ever want.

ENERGY SAVER HOME®

METROPOLITAN
REAL ESTATE
INCORPORATED
804 741-4108

Dramatic from Any Angle

ight from the entrance foyer, the views are dramatic in Dumont's newest furnished model, **The St. Ives**.

An abundance of light, graceful arches and classic details leave a lasting impression of the skillful construction evident in Dumont's latest model.

Come visit the St. Ives at Bellgrade, the Information Center for Dumont Homes in the Richmond area, and stop in across the street at our other decorated model, **The Bordeaux**. You'll see first hand why Dumont has been the name known for excellence in home building for more than 20 years.

Distinctive Custom Homes from $150,000 To $1 Million

Visit the St. Ives and the Bordeaux Decorated Models 1 p.m.- 5 p.m. Monday-Thursday, Saturday and Sunday, or by appointment.

MIKE DUMONT
CONSTRUCTION COMPANY, INC.

apple Door Systems
Virginia's Garage Door Headquarters Since 1973

Mary Crostic, Sales Mgr.
(804) 379-9141 ◆ (804) 379-3161 (Model)

To visit, go South from the Parham-Chippenham Extension to Huguenot and Robious Roads.

Dumont Construction Company uses quality Apple garage doors.

EQUAL HOUSING OPPORTUNITY

Introducing Six Of Our Model Neighbors.

Teal Building Corporation
"The Sterling"

Each has a character all its own with inspired designs that feature high-tech work-saving kitchens and living spaces that are openly inviting. And all are built in the finest home-building tradition by such names as Tomac Corporation, D.O. Allen Homes Inc., Byrd Construction Co., Teal Building Corporation, C. Richard Dobson Builders Inc., and Parker-Lancaster Corporation.

Byrd Construction Co.
"Chatham"

Tour our Hanover Collection of furnished model homes — the area's largest — from 11 a.m. until 5:30 p.m. daily.

D.O. Allen Homes Inc.
"The Carrington"

- Neighborhood homes range from the mid $130,000s to over $250,000.
- Amenities include clubhouse, two recreation centers, tennis courts, biking and jogging trails, and community activties.

C. Richard Dobson Builders Inc.
"The Regent"

Parker-Lancaster Corporation
"Kirkwood II"

KINGS CHARTER

Tomac Corporation
"The Paxton"

For more information, call Kings Charter Realty at (804) 550-2001.
Take I-95 North to the Atlee Elmont Exit. Bear right on Sliding Hill Road.
Right again on Kings Charter Drive to the Kings Charter sales center.

RICHMOND NOW HAS A PERSONAL BUILDER.

If you thought you'd seen all there is to see in new home design, take a look at Regency. You'll find a builder with more than just an award-winning reputation. You'll also find refreshing new designs made especially for Richmond... in any of our fine communities, a golf course setting or on a site that you choose. At Regency, our success is directly attributed to our commitment to giving homebuyers the services they need. From our own mortgage company to assistance in selling your existing home. We even offer custom designs, with prices starting from just the $180s.

And we've designed special programs specifically for the realtor community. Regency. We're one of the Mid-Atlantic region's leading builders and we've come home to you... in Richmond. Call us today at (804) 643-0296... and find out what it really means to have a "personal builder". Look for Regency in these fine communities:

Birkdale - phone Donna Rivers-Owens at (804) 639-1500.
Foxcroft - phone East West Realty at (804) 739-0700.
Or, for *Regency Custom Homes*, phone Mary Sue Wilson at (804) 751-4583.

REGENCY

MAKE US YOUR PERSONAL BUILDER.

The New Neighborhood Traffic in Riverlake Colony

You will enjoy living in this established River Road community of custom built residences, located just minutes from the best public and private schools, shopping areas and businesses. Spacious and flexible living spaces, distinctive front elevations and innovative features distinguish the homes in Riverlake Colony. But most memorable of all will be the families you will meet along the peaceful streets that wind through this elegant neighborhood. It's a great place to call home.

From Cary Street, Parham or Gaskins Road, go west on River Road 1/2 mile past Gaskins Road, turn right onto Colony Lake Drive.

Our Energy Saver Homes by Colonial Homecrafters, Ltd. and R&N Construction on lots 7AA and 23FA are designed for year-round comfort and energy savings.

ENERGY SAVER HOME®

EQUAL HOUSING OPPORTUNITY

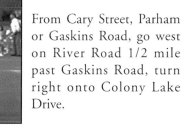

METROPOLITAN
REAL ESTATE
INCORPORATED
(804) 741-4108

This message is sponsored in part by Virginia Power

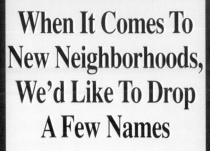

When It Comes To New Neighborhoods, We'd Like To Drop A Few Names

Shadow Creek, Greywalls, Westbury, The Grange, Norwood Creek, Sherwood, Woolridge, Chatsworth at Millquarter, Wythe Trace, Rockstone.

For information on one of the subdivisions that Napier, Old Colony Realtors represents, call us at (804) 794-4531 or 1-800-966-7669

NAPIER
OLD COLONY REALTORS®

EQUAL HOUSING OPPORTUNITY

Introducing The Reed's Landing Corporation Development of

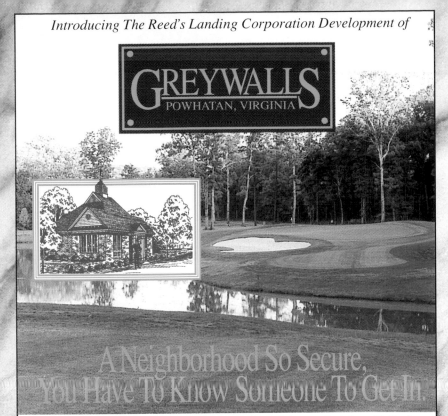

GREYWALLS
POWHATAN, VIRGINIA

A Neighborhood So Secure, You Have To Know Someone To Get In.

In most neighborhoods, security is not a planned priority. Greywalls is different. Its design includes a security easement as well as a gatehouse located at a single entrance. There are plans to man this gate house 24 hours a day. The result is a neighborhood that is quiet, secure and totally private.

But security is only part of what makes Greywalls so unusual. Homesites, averaging more than two acres in size, have been carefully laid out to accommodate even the largest homes and still leave enough room for a formal garden, a dramatic entrance, a tennis court, or your own private pool. The property itself is magnificent.

The Homes Will Be Spacious and Elegant in Every Detail.

The homes at Greywalls will feature classic architectural styles that have been specifically adapted for this neighborhood. Individual homes will be available for purchase this summer, starting at $450,000. For those who prefer to custom build, homesites are also available.

The Neighborhood Is Located In Powhatan County, Just 15 Minutes From Chesterfield Towne Center.

Greywalls is conveniently located in Powhatan County on Huguenot Trail. The neighborhood is near the historic Foundry site overlooking Fine Creek. It is convenient to schools, shopping, churches, recreation and it's just 15 minutes from the busy Chesterfield Towne Center.

Only a limited number of homes and homesites will be developed each year. If you would like more information about the unique neighborhood, or would like to make an appointment to see the property, please call The Reed's Landing Corporation at **(804) 598-5959.**

EQUAL HOUSING OPPORTUNITY

598-5959 • Powhatan, Virginia

Compare Our Standards To Yours.

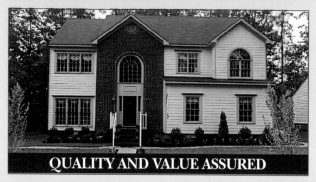

QUALITY AND VALUE ASSURED

You may be surprised at the number of extras you'll see when you walk into a model home built by Byrd Construction Co., Inc. You'll see 9-foot ceilings, triple crown molding in the formal rooms, oak flooring, 2-story areas, sunken living rooms, kitchen bay windows, trey ceilings, and luxurious master baths with ceramic tile flooring, skylights and jacuzzi. You'll be even more surprised to know that **these extras ares STANDARD in most Byrd homes.** Visit one of our furnished models today. We build Energy Saver Homes designed for year-round comfort and energy savings.

ARBOR LANDING-CHESTERFIELD

KINGS CHARTER-HANOVER

SHADOW CREEK-POWHATAN

ENERGY SAVER HOME®

Let us build a Byrd home for you. We will build on your lot or ours/your plan or ours. Call us today.

EQUAL HOUSING OPPORTUNITY

BCC Byrd Construction Co., Inc.
(804) 378-0531

THE ART
OF HOMEBUILDING

1995 DESIGN TRADITION Reprinted w/Permission

WINNER OF THE 1994 WYNDHAM
BUILDER CUSTOMER SERVICE AWARD

J.R. WALKER
& Company

804-672-0857

**ENERGY
SAVER
HOME**®

The classic homes built by J.R. Walker &
Company provide the perfect living environment with meticulously designed light-
filled interiors and quietly elegant exterior
elevations. An experienced professional staff
known for exceptional craftsmanship and
attention to detail distinguished J.R. Walker
& Company as a builder of the area's finest
custom homes found in Richmond's best
neighborhoods; or, if you prefer, we can
build on a homesite of your selection

Visit our homes in Chatsworth Landing and
Hardwick at Wyndham and see first hand
the timeless appeal of a J.R. Walker home.

This Message is sponsored in part by Virginia Power.
Our Energy Saver Homes on Lots 2 and 29 are designed
for year-round comfort and energy savings.

**EQUAL HOUSING
OPPORTUNITY**

IMPROVING YOUR STROKE.

IT MEANS MANY DIFFERENT THINGS TO THE FAMILIES OF RIVER'S BEND.

Golf. Tennis. Swimming. Boating. Whatever your pleasure, get more strokes in at River's Bend.

Located just 20 minutes from downtown and 15 minutes to the airport, this riverfront community offers the convenience of an easy commute with all the lifestyle amenities you're looking for.

Here you'll find graceful, elegant homes situated along the historic James River. And with home prices from the $180's to

over $400,000 - you're sure to find a home style to suit your active lifestyle.

If you've been looking far and wide for a place to call home, visit River's Bend today. You may find the way to improve your stroke is just around the bend.

Travel 2 1/2 miles from I-95 (Exit 61-A) on Route 10 East. 1/2 mile from I-295, Chester Exit.

EQUAL HOUSING OPPORTUNITY

EAST WEST REALTY

748-3316 **530-1041**
from Richmond *from Tri-Cities*

RIVER'S BEND
❖ ON · THE · JAMES ❖

THE HIGHLANDS

Route 10 to Beach Road.
Left on Nash Road
2 1/2 Miles on left
HIGHLANDS REALTY
748-7361

**1-5 Acres Lots •18 Hole Golf Course
150 Acres of Lakes • Community Pool
Estate Size Lots on Lake and Golf Course
Neighborhoods from $150's to $400+**

YES, Please send me more information on homes
and amenities in THE HIGHLANDS

NAME_____

ADDRESS_____

CITY_____

Mail To: Highlands Realty
P.O. Box 1096 Chester, VA 23831

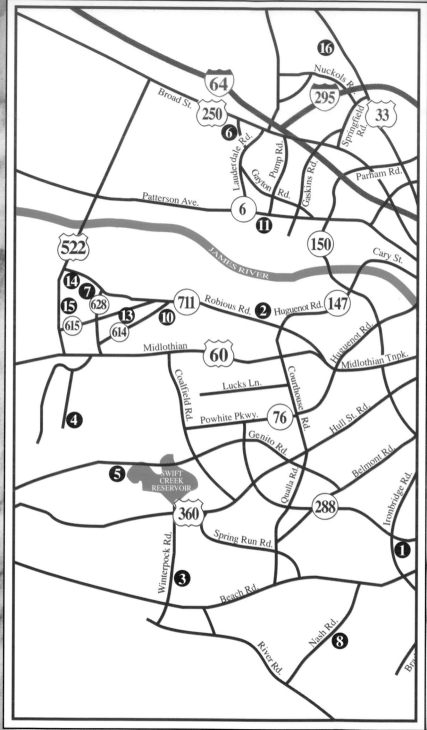

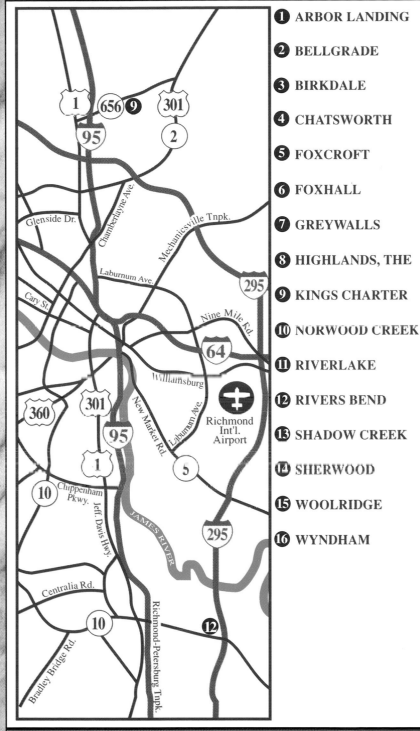

1. ARBOR LANDING
2. BELLGRADE
3. BIRKDALE
4. CHATSWORTH
5. FOXCROFT
6. FOXHALL
7. GREYWALLS
8. HIGHLANDS, THE
9. KINGS CHARTER
10. NORWOOD CREEK
11. RIVERLAKE
12. RIVERS BEND
13. SHADOW CREEK
14. SHERWOOD
15. WOOLRIDGE
16. WYNDHAM

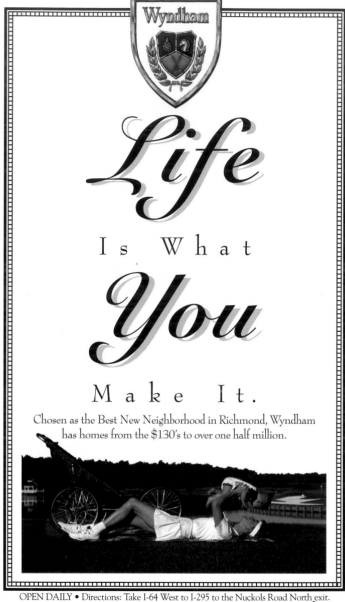

Life

I s   W h a t

You

M a k e   I t.

Chosen as the Best New Neighborhood in Richmond, Wyndham
has homes from the $130's to over one half million.

OPEN DAILY • Directions: Take I-64 West to I-295 to the Nuckols Road North exit.
Represented by Snyder Hunt Realty, (804) 360-1100 • (800) 360-1113.
A **SNYDER HUNT** Community.

Inside
Neighborhoods

Richmond has all the cultural amenities and attractions of a growing metropolitan area, yet it also has the charm and intimacy of a small town. From the city to the suburbs to the rural countryside, it's a metropolitan area that's rich with a diversity of neighborhoods that have their own unique personalities and traditions. That may be why so many people who live here never move away, and why so many families think it's a great place to live. In fact, Richmond has been identified as one of "50 Fabulous Places to Raise Your Family," by the authors of a book by the same name. Richmond was chosen for its "cuburban" way of live — "part country, part urban, part suburban."

You'll find historic antebellum and turn-of-the-century homes, contemporary homes, colonial homes, multimillion-dollar estates and working farms. You'll also find a lot of involved people. Many neighborhoods have active community associations that organize Neighborhood Watch programs, sponsor social activities and unite over zoning issues.

Richmond also enjoys a renewed interest in city living, and we're very proud of our restored neighborhoods near downtown. There has already been a great deal of renovation in the Fan and Church Hill. Renovation efforts are also under way in Jackson Ward, Oregon Hill, Shockoe Slip and Shockoe Bottom.

To help you get your bearings, we've organized information in this section to correspond with the way Insiders talk about the area — by neighborhoods and sections of town.

Historic City Neighborhoods

The Fan

This historic neighborhood just west of downtown derives its name from the way the streets fan out from Monroe Park at Belvidere Street to the Boulevard. The Fan includes the famous Monument Avenue with its gracious mansions that sell for as much as $1 million and turn-of-the-century townhouses that range upwards in price from $65,000, depending on their condition and how much renovation has been done. Fan renovation efforts became popular in the 1960s, and most of the homes here have been at least partially renovated.

Tree-lined parks and streets, beautifully landscaped courtyards, rooftop gardens, cobblestone alleys, brick sidewalks and numerous neighborhood restaurants and pubs add to the charm of the area. Many of Richmond's historic and cultural attractions and parks are just minutes away.

Most of the people who live here enjoy a casual, active lifestyle. Residents include students and faculty from nearby Virginia Commonwealth University, as well as families, singles and professionals from diverse social, economic and ethnic backgrounds.

Church Hill

Overlooking Shockoe Bottom, Shockoe Slip and downtown, Church Hill is Richmond's first historic district and includes St. John's Church where Patrick Henry made his famous liberty speech. The area around the church is the oldest intact residential district in the city and features restored antebellum homes ranging from modest Federal cottages to major Greek Revival structures. The neighborhood also includes 19th-century Victorians.

Several parks offer attractive green spaces, and thanks to the hilly location, many homes have views of the river or city skyline. Gas street lamps and brick sidewalks add to the historic ambiance. High on the Hog is a popular annual neighborhood event open to the public, with bands, beer and barbecue.

Homes that need renovation range from about $50,000 to more than $100,000. Renovated homes cost from about $110,000 to more than $300,000. Homes nearby range from gutted frame houses at bargain prices to $130,000 homes that are fully renovated.

Oregon Hill

Next to the Fan, Oregon Hill has relatively smaller townhouses that range from about $20,000 to more than $100,000, depending on how much renovation is needed. Hollywood Cemetery and the James River Park surround two sides of this small neighborhood that was origi-

nally known as Sydney. People who lived here usually worked at nearby foundries, armories and mills.

Jackson Ward

In the heart of downtown north of Broad Street, Jackson Ward includes historic 2nd Street, the Maggie Walker House and the Bojangles Statue. The Richmond Coliseum and 6th Street Marketplace are nearby.

The neighborhood has a variety of 19th- and early 20th-century urban row houses that range in price from $20,000 to more than $150,000, depending on how much renovation is needed or has been done. A majority of the city's cast iron porches are found in this neighborhood and reflect the influence of the European craftspeople who lived here.

Shockoe Slip/ Shockoe Bottom

Just east of downtown near the river, Shockoe Slip was once the commercial center of Richmond. This quaint area features cobblestone streets, restaurants, shops, hotels, nightlife and apartments in renovated 19th-century warehouses and buildings.

Shockoe Bottom is down the hill from the Slip. This trendy neighborhood near Dock Street includes the colorful and historic Farmers Market and the Edgar Allan Poe Museum. It's the home of art studios and galleries, apartments and restaurants, all housed in renovated buildings.

Tobacco Row

About 15 city blocks between 22nd and Pear streets along the riverfront are included in the Tobacco Row project east of downtown. There was a concentration of manufacturers in this area, and the architectural styles range from the 1840s to the 1930s. Currently two old warehouse buildings have been renovated and transformed into apartment houses where monthly rent averages around $600. Development began in the mid-1980s and is expected to continue for a few more years. The first phase includes more than two million square feet of office, retail and residential space. Tobacco Row is considered to be one of the country's most ambitious redevelopment projects and is the single largest economic recovery tax-act project in the United States.

West End

Often called the "fashionable" or "trendy" West End, this area is generally thought of as the area that stretches west from the Boulevard and includes part of Richmond and part of Henrico County. The area between the Boulevard and Thompson Street is called West of the Boulevard; the area west of Parham Road is the Far West End.

The elite Country Club of Virginia, the University of Richmond and the exclusive neighborhoods of Windsor Farms, Westhampton and Westmoreland Place lend prestige to the area. River Road, with its stately old homes overlooking the river, adds an air of charming elegance.

Windsor Farms stretches from Portland Place to Locke Lane and from Cary Street to the James River. It includes two of Richmond's most significant historical attractions, Agecroft Hall and the Virginia House. Many of the estate homes here have spectacular views of the James River and are worth millions of dollars. Other homes in this planned community vary in size and feature Georgian style architecture. The streets circle outward from the Grace Baptist Church and common area in the center of the neighborhood. Originally, Windsor Farms was the 500-acre estate of Thomas C. Williams Jr. It was subdivided in 1926.

Relatively new developments include Lockgreen on the James River near Windsor Farms, and Kanawha Trace, perched on a bluff overlooking the river near Maymont, Dogwood Dell and Byrd Park. **Kanawha Trace** features contemporary condominiums and townhouses starting at $75,000. **Lockgreen** offers a collection of luxurious townhouses and single family residences off Old Locke Lane in a variety of prices ranging up to several million dollars.

West Enders enjoy convenient access to gourmet restaurants, such as duJour and The Butlery, and several fashionable shopping areas — Regency Square, The Shops at Libbie and Grove, and River Road Shopping Center. Henrico County schools as well as a number of private schools in the area are considered excellent. West End residents are served by numerous churches and two of the best hospitals in the area, St. Mary's and Henrico Doctors Hospital.

Far West End

People mean many different things when they say the Far West End, but we think they usually mean the rapidly growing suburban area of Henrico County west of Parham Road. New developments include Foxhall, Morgan Run, Wyndham (a golf course community), Wellesley with lakeside, single-family homes and townhouse communities, and the "dream houses" of Windsor on the James, off scenic River Road.

Residents here enjoy the lake, playing fields, soccer, hiking, jogging at Deep Run Park and excellent educational opportunities at reputable public and private schools in the area.

There are hundreds of subdivisions, townhouse communities and apartment complexes throughout the West End and the Far West End, with homes that start around $80,000 and range upward to a million dollars. Home and condominium architectural styles include colonial, Victorian, contemporary, transitional and Georgian.

Northside

Northside usually refers to the area of the city north of Broad Street where you'll find the State Fairgrounds, The Diamond, the Arthur Ashe Center, Bryan Park, the A.P. Hill Monument, Virginia Union University, Presbyterian School of Christian Education and the Union Theological Seminary. Neighborhoods such as Bellevue, Ginter Park and Highland Park help define the diversity of the residents who live here.

Ginter Park, developed by Maj. Lewis Ginter in 1892, was one of the first planned communities in the area. A designated historical area, Ginter Park includes restored Victorian-style homes and turn-of-the century mansions ranging from about $100,000 to more than $300,000. According to local legend, Maj. Ginter wanted to develop a neighborhood on the north side of Richmond so that the sun would not be in his eyes going to or from work.

Bellevue, is another old established neighborhood with an arched entranceway off Hermitage Road that features spacious homes built in the '20s and '30s when people had large families. The neighborhood extends to Brook Road where residents swap stories at the local drugstore.

Highland Park is a neighborhood with unrestored turn-of-the-century houses, just south of the State Fairgrounds and the Richmond International Raceway. Efforts to restore the neighborhood are under way.

Northern Henrico County

Northern Henrico County is a growing suburban and rural area that includes Glen Allen, Lakeside, Chamberlayne Farms and Chamberlayne Heights neighborhoods. Interstates 295, 95 and 64 provide fast, convenient access to any destination in the metropolitan area.

Glen Allen, an old rural community, is enjoying rapid growth now and includes a variety of single-family homes ranging in price from about $100,000 to more than $200,000. This is the area that includes the Innsbrook residential and office park development, historic Meadow Farm and Crump Park, the Crossings Golf Course and the new Virginia Center Commons shopping mall.

Closer to Richmond, **Lakeside** and **Dumbarton** are major established Northside neighborhoods with economically-priced single family residences,

Homes in the Ivy Bend section of Wyndam in Henrico offer many amenities.

apartment complexes and numerous small businesses. Bryan Park is famous for its azalea displays, the Lewis Ginter Botanical Gardens, Belmont Golf Course and Jefferson Lakeside Country Club. Homes range from about $70,000 to more than $100,000.

Chamberlayne Farms and **Chamberlayne Heights** were two of Richmond's first middle-class suburban neighborhoods that began developing in the mid-'50s. Homes here are priced from about $90,000 to $145,000.

East End

Eastern Henrico County is usually referred to as the East End and includes the Highland Springs, Sandston and Varina areas near the Richmond International Airport and the Richmond Industrial Park. The East End offers economical housing in a rural setting. Prices range from $30,000 to $100,000 or more. A number of commercial warehouses and light industrial parks have also developed here recently.

Residents have convenient access to Dorey Park, a popular new recreational area with a fishing lake, playing fields, picnic areas, tennis courts and trails. The Glenwood Country Club is also nearby.

South Side

South Side is everything on the southside of the James River, which includes South Richmond and Powhatan and Chesterfield counties.

People who live in South Side have access to downtown and areas north of the river via the Powhite Parkway Bridge, Edward Willey Memorial Bridge, Huguenot Bridge, Nickel Bridge, Robert E. Lee Bridge, Manchester Bridge and the I-95 bridge. The new Chippenham Parkway Connector and a sophisticated system of roads keeps traffic moving quickly and smoothly most of the time to destinations throughout the metropolitan area.

South Richmond

In South Richmond, you'll find major sections of the James River Park System, beautiful old Forest Hill Park, Wil-

• **27**

low Oaks Country Club and the established neighborhoods of Westover Hills, Stratford Hills and Forest Hill. South Side is also home to McGuire Veterans Hospital, Philip Morris (one of the world's largest cigarette manufacturers) and Deepwater Terminal — the Port of Richmond.

There's a variety of homes here for every budget and lifestyle including the Bluffs at Stony Point condominium community and the prestigious cliffside homes that wind along Riverside Drive high above the James River.

Chesterfield County

Chesterfield is the largest county in the metropolitan area, and it's grown so rapidly, the population has doubled in the last 10 years. It's saturated with new developments and subdivisions, and miles of shopping centers and office complexes along Midlothian Turnpike (U.S. 60).

Residents enjoy an excellent county school system that is building new schools as fast as it can to catch up with the growth. There are also numerous recreational opportunities and parks, including Pocahontas State Park and Rockwood Park.

Chesterfield is the home of several commercial parks including the Arboretum, Center Pointe, the Commonwealth Center, the Acropolis, Moorefield and Waterford.

Shoppers will find a large selection of stores at Cloverleaf Mall and Chesterfield Towne Center, the largest mall in the area. Sycamore Square offers unusual boutiques and great restaurants in a quaint village setting.

People who live in Chesterfield County receive excellent medical care at Chippenham Hospital.

Historic Bon Air and the award-winning communities of Brandermill and Woodlake are among the most well-known Chesterfield neighborhoods. Salisbury and River's Bend on the James are two other talked-about communities known for their luxury homes and excellent golf courses.

Bon Air, the "good air" community, got its name years ago when Richmonders used to travel here by train to stay in their summer or weekend homes to escape the coal smoke in the city. Some of the old Victorian inns are still standing, and the neighborhood features a variety of Victorian-style homes, especially along Buford Road. This old established community is just across the Huguenot Bridge from the West End.

Chester is another old established community that developed just before the Civil War as a popular summer resort for Richmonders. According to legend, after the Civil War Northern treasure hunters rushed to Chester to look for $800,000 in military money that a general supposedly buried here. The treasure has yet to be found. The older sections of Chester are known for their quiet village character. Home prices here range from about $100,000 to $150,000. In the newer developments prices begin around $200,000.

Brandermill and **Woodlake**, developed by East West Partners of Virginia, are planned communities in the western part of the county surrounding Swift Creek Reservoir. Their designs are very similar. Brandermill is the oldest and includes cluster homes, condominiums, golf course homes and lakefront homes. It's a complete community with shops, restaurants, tennis courts, waterfront parks, boat landings, jogging and walking trails, fishing docks, swimming and windsurfing. Residents also enjoy the amenities of the

Brandermill Inn and Conference Center. Together the communities have more than 5,500 homes that vary in style form colonial to contemporary and in price from the $90s to more than $500,000. Thanks to the new Powhite Extension and Route 288, people who live here can drive to downtown or the West End in about 20 minutes.

Foxcroft, developed by Delmarva Properties, Inc., is adjacent to Woodlake in western Chesterfield County. Homes here range from the $150s to more than $300,000. Home styles encompass Victorian, traditional and transitional. Amenities include a swimming pool, tennis courts, clubhouse, bike trails and playground. The commute to downtown Richmond is about 30 minutes.

The **Salisbury** community in the western part of the county is built around the 40-acre lake and the Salisbury Country Club, which has one of the best golf courses in the area. Estate homes surround the site of the country home where Patrick Henry lived while he was governor of Virginia. Salisbury was also one of the first coal mining communities in the country. Most of the homes in the community are colonials. Townhouses that back up to the golf course are among the newest additions.

River's Bend on the James was the first planned community in Chesterfield County to be built on the James River. Luxury homes here range from about $160,000 to $1 million. A challenging 18-hole PGA golf course with beautiful views of the river is a focal point of this new community.

Powhatan County

Powhatan County is just south of the James River and west of Chesterfield County. This once-rural county is now home to many families who enjoy its relaxed atmosphere and large home sites. Powhatan's major thoroughfares allow for an easy commute to Metropolitan Richmond: East-west U.S. 60 bisects the county and connects with major roadways such as Route 288; Route 711 (Huguenot Trail) follows the James River from Huguenot Road to Route 522, the major north-south artery between Powhatan and Goochland counties.

Beautiful plantation homes and his-

The Hanover Tomato

For as long as local farmers can remember, the Hanover tomato (grown in eastern Hanover County) has been the queen of locally grown produce. Year after year, taste test after taste test, the Hanover lives up to its reputation as the tastiest tomato in this part of the country.

In fact, it's become so popular that some people from out-of-state drive hours just to buy some of the lush red fruit at roadside produce stands.

There doesn't seem to be any logical reason why Hanover tomatoes should taste better than other tomatoes. They just do. Some say the magic is in the dirt — sandy, loamy coastal plain soil. But extension service officials say the same type of soil is found in parts of King William, New Kent and King and Queen counties. So why aren't tomatoes grown there considered as special?

Even when people transplant Hanover-grown tomato plants in similar soil, their tomatoes just don't taste as good as Hanover tomatoes. Any way you slice it, the Hanover tomato is still the best.

After a few hot summer nights, Hanover tomatoes are also some of the first locally grown tomatoes to hit the market. Watch for them at roadside produce stands and in grocery stores around the Fourth of July.

As its reputation has spread, the tomato also has become cause for celebration. Annual tributes include the Black Creek Fire Department's Tomato Festival, held in eastern Hanover County at Battlefield Park Elementary School on U.S. 360. Sponsored by the fire department on the first Saturday after the Fourth of July, this festival attracts thousands of people and features bacon, lettuce and tomato sandwiches, tomato cooking contests, tomato eating contests, crafts, demonstrations, live music, a variety of games and a parade.

An even larger Tomato Festival is held in late July at the 17th Street Farmer's Market in Shockoe Bottom. Sponsored by the Richmond Department of Parks and Recreation and Downtown Presents, this festival attracts 10,000 to 12,000 people with live country and bluegrass music, square dancers, cloggers, children's activities, historical tours and more.

toric churches, some of which date back to the 1700s, reflect Powhatan's rich heritage. The scenic Huguenot Trail has been enjoyed by travellers since Robert E. Lee ventured along the route to visit his brother on the return trip to Richmond following his surrender at Appomattox. Today the route passes remaining old homes, churches and open landscape.

The development evident today began in the late 1970s north of U.S. 60 in the county's eastern portion. **King William Woods** and **Country Town** were among Powhatan's first subdivisions to offer new homes and one-acre, zoned-residential lots. Newer developments along Huguenot Trail, such as **Shadow Creek**, **Sherwood** and **Norwood Creek**, offer building sites between one and three acres. The new 160-acre **Greywalls** community, a Reeds Landing Corporation project, is nestled amid horse farms, James River plantations and the private Foundry Golf Club. To maintain a pastoral feel in this controlled-access community, the integrity of the natural surroundings is considered throughout the building process. Two-acre home sites with fairway frontage start at $475,000. Another residential option for the golf enthusiast is **Chatsworth @ Millquarter** which fronts the public Millquarter Golf Course.

In Powhatan's western and southern areas, farms dot the countryside. Here, west of the Courthouse, you'll find the history-laden villages of Macon, Mosely, Ballsville, Tobaccoville and Cartersville.

Recreational opportunities abound in Powhatan. County residents and neighbors frequent the boat landings and the wildlife preserve. On any given weekend you'll find families fishing, power boating and canoeing around Watkins and Maidens landings on the James River. The Appomattox River is another recreational mecca.

Powhatan County's citizens reputedly are dedicated to preserving their rural atmosphere, quality developments, excellent schools and rich history.

Hanover County

Hanover County offers world famous tomatoes and relaxed "country" living in an area that's rich with Civil War battlefields and history. It's the second largest county in the metropolitan area, but it has the fewest people, and most of them would like to keep it that way. They unite frequently over zoning issues and oppose any development that doesn't adhere to the comprehensive plan.

The county is usually divided into areas referred to as eastern Hanover, western Hanover and the Hanover Courthouse area.

In eastern Hanover just off U.S. 360, you'll find the town of **Mechanicsville**, with its landmark windmill bank building and proliferation of independent, family-owned businesses. Cherrydale is an older established neighborhood here, and Battlefield Green is a popular new one with condominiums and single-family homes.

The nearby Cold Harbor area is included in the Richmond National Battlefield Park System and is famous for its battlefields and Civil War sites. There's a variety of housing and subdivisions throughout the area.

Farther east is the area known as **Old Church**, named after an Anglican church established in 1718. The old Immanuel Episcopal Church on Route 606, built in 1853, is the successor to the first church building. This rural area includes several historic estates and plantations, and contemporary new homes on the Pamunkey River. People who live out here think nothing of driving 10 or more miles to the nearest country store. There are numerous farms but only a few planned neighborhoods such as Pine Knoll and Sinclair Manor. Lake Idylwilde, featuring 10 acre lots on a wooded lake, is one of the newest communities. The Mattaponi and Pamunkey Indian reservations are nearby.

North on U.S. 301 is the Hanover Courthouse area, named after the historic Hanover Courthouse built in 1735. This is the center of the county government, and it's also the site of the historic Hanover Tavern and Barksdale Dinner Theatre.

Richmond Newspapers' new production facility and Hanover Airport, a popular takeoff site for hot-air balloons, are nearby. On a pleasant day, it's not unusual to see several hot-air balloons drifting above the fields and trees.

Kings Charter was the first planned community and has received several design awards. It features a variety of homes centered around a restored historic mansion that now serves as a community building. There are two lakes, a country club, tennis courts, jogging and bike trails and a fitness center. Ash Creek is one of the newest developments with homes ranging from $130,000 to $275,000.

The Houndstooth Cafe and Thyme and Sage are popular area restaurants. Antique shops abound on U.S. 301, and Virginia Center Commons is the nearest and newest place to shop.

Western Hanover includes Montpelier and Beaverdam. It's mostly rural and very scenic with views of the South Anna and North Anna rivers. Overhill Lake is a popular recreation and swimming area, and the Up and Away Dude Ranch is the site of many outdoor picnics and barbecues.

Ashland

Popularly known as "the center of the universe," Ashland is the home of Randolph-Macon College, founded in 1830. Residents love the small college-town atmosphere and beautiful 18th-century Victorian homes with their wraparound porches and generous lawns.

Bounded by suburban and rural areas in Hanover County, Ashland is close to **Scotchtown**, the pre-revolutionary home of Patrick Henry, the Ashland Berry Farm, Paramount's Kings Dominion amusement park and the historic Hanover Tavern and Barksdale Dinner Theatre. The Smokey Pig, the Ironhorse

and Homemades By Suzanne are popular restaurants in the area.

Ashland was originally developed as a summer community for the Richmond, Fredericksburg and Potomac Railroad. A commuter rail line connecting Ashland to Richmond opened around 1900 but was discontinued in the 1930s.

People who live here tend to be very active in local politics and are doing a good job of balancing the small-town character of the area with growth and development.

Neighboring Areas

Many people who work in Richmond live in Goochland, King William and New Kent counties. If you don't mind a 30- to 60-minute commute to downtown Richmond, these rural areas offer quiet, relaxed country living and more home for your dollar.

South of Richmond is the Tri-Cities Area, which includes Hopewell, a scenic town overlooking the James and Appomattox rivers, Colonial Heights and **Petersburg**, small cities on the Appomattox River. Petersburg is the largest and has many historic and Civil War attractions and restored areas.

Fort Lee is here, so many area residents are involved with the military. Virginia State University is nearby in Ettrick, and there are historic plantations on both sides of the James River on state routes 5 and 10. There's more information about Petersburg attractions in the chapter on daytrips. Southpark Mall, one of the largest and most beautiful new shopping malls in the area, has spectacular holiday exhibits that attract people from throughout the Richmond area, as well as shoppers from out of state.

Inside
Government

For voter registration information and to find out who represents your district, contact your local registrar's office — Richmond, 780-5950; Henrico, 672-4347; Chesterfield, 748-1471; or Hanover, 537-6080.

Richmond representatives in the Virginia General Assembly are Senators Benedetti, Lambert and Marsh, and Delegates Ball, Cantor, Cunningham, Hall, Jones and Rhodes.

Chesterfield representatives are Senators Benedetti, Marsh and Martin, and Delegates Cox, DeBoer, Ingram, Nixon, Reid and Watkins.

Henrico representatives are Senators Benedetti, Lambert, Marsh and Stosch, and Delegates Ball, Barlow, Cantor, Cunningham, Grayson, Jones, Reid and Rhodes.

Hanover representatives are Senator Cross and Delegate Hargrove.

State Government

Elected Officials

The Governor of Virginia is Republican George F. Allen. Democrat Donald S. Beyer, Jr. is the Lt. Governor, and Republican James S. Gilmore, III is the Attorney General.

State Senate

Joseph Benedetti (R)
10th Senate District, 600 E. Main Street, 20th Floor, Richmond 23219, 780-0505.

The General Assembly's House of Delegates at the State Capitol.

Benjamin J. Lambert III (D)
9th Senate District, 904 N. First Street, Richmond 23219, 643-3534.

Walter A. Stosch (R)
12th Senate District, Markel Building at Innsbrook, 4551 Cox Road, Suite 110, Glen Allen 23060, 527-7735.

Steve Martin (R)
11th Senate District, P.O. Box 36147, Richmond 23235, 674-0242.

Henry L. Marsh III (D)
16th Senate District, 509 N. 3rd Street, Richmond 23219, 648-9073.

Elmo G. Cross Jr. (D)
4th Senate District, 7277 Hanover Green Drive, Mechanicsville 23111, 746-4621.

House of Delegates

Robert B. Ball Sr. (D)
74th District, 827 E. Parham Road, Richmond 23227, 262-1861.

William K. Barlow (D)
64th District, P.O. Box 190, Smithfield 23430, 357-9720.

Eric I. Cantor (R)
73rd District, 2500 E. Parham Road, Suite 4, Richmond 23228, 266-6100.

M. Kirkland Cox (R)
66th District, 3236 Longhorn Drive, Colonial Heights 23834, 526-5135.

Jean W. Cunningham (D)
71st District, P.O. Box 542, Richmond 23204, 343-7588.

Jay W. DeBoer (D)
63rd District, 16 E. Tabb Street, Petersburg 23803, 861-4310.

George W. Grayson (D)
97th District, P.O. Box 1969, Williamsburg, 23187, 253-0553.

Franklin P. Hall, (D)
69th District, Bon Air Professional Building, 2800 Buford Road, Suite 202, Richmond, 23235, 272-1515.

Frank D. Hargrove Sr. (R)
55th District, 10321 Washington Highway, Glen Allen 23059, 550-3000.

Riley E. Ingram (R)
62nd District, 3302 Oaklawn Boulevard, Hopewell 23860, 458-9873.

Dwight C. Jones (D)
70th District, 2000 Riverside Drive, Apt. #11P, Richmond 23225, 649-8683.

Samuel A. Nixon Jr. (R)
27th District, 7412 Barkbridge Road, Chesterfield 23832, 743-7773.

Insiders' Tips

Harry S Truman loved shirts and pajamas made by Creery Shirtmakers in Richmond. The firm dusted off the 33rd president's patterns and favorite swatches to fill a last order — for the Truman Library and Museum in Independence, Missouri.

John F. Reid (R)
72nd District, P.O. Box 29566, Richmond 23242, 226-3713.

Anne G. Rhodes (R)
68th District, P.O. Box 14569, Richmond 23221, 285-2718.

John Watkins (R)
65th District, P.O. Box 159, Midlothian 23113, 379-2063.

U.S. Congress

Senators

John W. Warner (R)
225 Russell Senate Office Building, Washington, D.C. 20510, (202) 224-2023, or 1100 E. Main Street, Richmond 23219, 771-2579.

Charles S. Robb (D)
493 Russell Senate Office Building, Washington, D.C. 20510, (202) 224-4024, or 1001 E. Broad Street, Richmond 23219, 771-2221.

Representatives

Herbert H. Bateman (R)
1st District, Room 2350 Rayburn House Office Building, Washington, D.C. 20515, (202) 225-4261, or 4712 Southpoint Parkway, Fredericksburg 22407.

Thomas J. Bliley Jr. (R)
7th District, 2448 Rayburn House Office Building, Washington, D.C. 20515, (202) 225-2815 or 4914 Fitzhugh Avenue, Suite 101, Richmond 23230, 771-2809.

Robert C. Scott (D)
3rd District, 501 Cannon House Office Building, Washington, D.C. 20515, (202) 225-8351, or Jackson Center, 501 N. Second Street, Richmond 23219, (804) 644-4845.

Norman Sisisky (D)
4th District, 2371 Rayburn House Office Building, Washington, D.C. 20515, (202) 225-6365, or 43 Rives Road, Petersburg 23805, (804) 732-2544.

Local Government

The City of Richmond, the town of Ashland and each of the surrounding counties have separate forms of government and locally elected officials. If you want to get involved, you may want to join any of a number of active citizens organizations.

Richmond

Richmond became a town in 1742 and the state capital in 1781. Today, it's home to about 203,000 residents.

Richmond has a well-balanced economy and is continually developing ways to attract and keep businesses in the downtown area. Like most cities, Richmond is also concentrating its efforts on reducing crime.

The City Council meets at 6 PM the second and fourth Monday of each month except August, in the council chamber on the second floor of City Hall, 900 E. Broad Street. Council members are elected to serve two-year terms. They elect the mayor and vice-mayor from among themselves and appoint the city manager.

City services include a police department, sheriff's department, fire department, water and sewer, gas, weekly trash pickup and parks and recreation.

City offices are in downtown Richmond at City Hall, 900 E. Broad Street. For more information call 780-7000.

Chesterfield County

Chesterfield County was formed from Henrico County in 1749. It's the second largest county in the area, covering about 450 square miles. The population has almost doubled in the past 10 years, and the county is coping with the challenges of rapid growth. The population is currently about 233,000.

The five-member Board of Supervisors usually meets at 3 PM and 7 PM the second and fourth Wednesday of each month in the public meeting room at the County Courthouse on Ironbridge Road. Services include a police department, sheriff's department, fire department, refuse disposal, water and sewer, and parks and recreation.

County offices are at 9901 Lori Road, 748-1211.

Hanover County

Hanover County was formed from New Kent County in 1720. It's the area's largest county with more than 470 square miles, but it has the smallest population — about 70,000. Residents here enjoy rural living with easy access to the city, and they actively oppose rapid, unplanned growth.

The Board of Supervisors meets at 7 PM on the second Wednesday of each month, and at 2 PM on the fourth Wednesday of each month in the Wickham Building at the Hanover Government Center on U.S. 301. Board members are elected for four-year terms.

Hanover provides a sheriff's department, landfills and recycling containers and a parks and recreation department. Water and sewer service is provided in the more urban areas of the county and in the area from Hanover Industrial Air Park to Va. 156 south of Mechanicsville. Fire and rescue services are provided by volunteer departments.

County offices are on U.S. 301 at Hanover Courthouse. Phone numbers vary — 537-6000, 730-6000 (Old Church and Ashland) and 798-6160 (Rockville).

Henrico County

Formed in 1634, Henrico County was one of Virginia's original shires. Since then, 10 counties have been carved from it. Today, this well-planned county encompasses 244 square miles and has a population of 230,729, the largest in the area.

The five-member board of supervisors meets at 7 PM on the second and fourth Wednesday of each month at the government building on Parham Road.

Henrico services include a police department, sheriff's department, fire department, water and sewer, trash collection, landfills and a parks and recreation department.

The phone number for the county administrative offices on Parham Road is 672-4206.

Ashland

The town of Ashland, in Hanover County, is the home of Randolph-Macon College. In the early 1900s through the 1930s, a railroad commuter line connected Ashland to Richmond. Easy access to Richmond by U.S. 1 and I-95 also contributed to the town's development. Today, about 6,000 residents call Ashland home.

The town council meets at 7:30 PM on the second and fourth Tuesday of each month in the Municipal Building at 101 Thompson Street. Council members are elected for four-year terms.

Ashland has a police force and provides refuse disposal, sewer and water service. Residents pay county and town taxes. The phone number for the administrative offices is 798-9219.

Political Parties and Organizations

RICHMOND CRUSADE FOR VOTERS
2600 Brook Rd.
Richmond   329-9429 or 321-1203
This nonprofit, nonpartisan political organization was founded in 1956 to fight Jim Crow laws and get African-Americans more involved in the political pro-

cess. Today, it advocates bottom-up grass roots political action. Members must be registered voters and pay annual dues of $10. Willie Williams III is the president.

REPUBLICAN PARTY OF VIRGINIA
115 E. Grace St.
Richmond   780-0111
The state chairman is Patrick McSweeney.

DEMOCRATIC STATE HEADQUARTERS
1108 E. Main St., Second Floor
Richmond   644-1966
The state chairman is Mark R. Warner.

AMERICAN PARTY IN VIRGINIA
P.O. Box 86
Mechanicsville 23111   746-3910
The state chairman is Al Moore.

LIBERTARIAN PARTY
P.O. Box 17474
Arlington 22216   (800) 619-1776
The state chairman is Rick Sincere.

INDEDEPENDENT | SCHOOLS

LANDMARK CHRISTIAN SCHOOL

A QUALITY EDUCATION = ARMOUR FOR FUTURE

- K-5 through 12th grade
- ABEKA Curriculum
- Modest tuition rates
- Christ-centered environment
- 28 Years of Quality Education
- College preparatory
- Music & Sports Programs
- Ministry of Landmark Baptist Church

**4000 Creighton Road
Richmond Virginia 23223
(804) 644-5550**

28 Years of Quality Education

The Stony Point School

Jr. Kindergarten Through 7th Grade

28 acre campus
10:1 student ratio
Personalized Instruction
Extended Day Program

3400 Stony Point Road
272-1341

Admission without regard to race, creed
or ethnic origin

Good Shepherd Episcopal School

- Pre K through 7th grade
- 10:1 Student teacher ratio
- small classes
- modest tuition rates
- spanish for all grades
- state-of-the-art computers
- intramural & interscholastic athletic programs
- church-centered environment
- convenient location
- strong fine arts program
- 5 minutes to downtown
- extended day program
- fully accredited by the Virginia Assoc. of Independent Schools

**4207 Forest Hill Avenue
Richmond, Virginia 23225
231-1452**

RICHMOND MONTESSORI SCHOOL
499 Parham Road, Richmond

" One of the 10 best preschools in America"

Child Magazine, August 1993

See how this excellence extends from pre-school through middle school.

Schedule a visit today:
741-0040

RMS is an accredited school welcoming students regardless of race, religion, national origin.

Inside
Schools and Child Care

Excellent public schools and numerous private schools offer a variety of educational choices for area residents. Blessed by a high degree of business and parental involvement, area schools maintain high standards of quality and have a national reputation for developing innovative programs.

Cooperative efforts among the schools are ongoing. For example, the resources and programs of the Mathematics-Science Center are funded locally and shared by five area school systems; Thomas Jefferson High School is a regional Governor's School; Henrico televises classes to more than 30 school divisions throughout the state; and students throughout the area have access to the MCI Hotline, staffed by teachers who help with homework assignments. The area schools also participate in a Cultural Relations Fellowship Program, an exchange program for area students and students from Germany that gives them an opportunity to live, work and attend school in a foreign country.

Each county and the City of Richmond has its own unique school system. An overview of each is included in this chapter followed by a sampling of private schools and child-care providers in the area.

Richmond Public Schools

Amid the challenges faced by most urban school systems, Richmond has

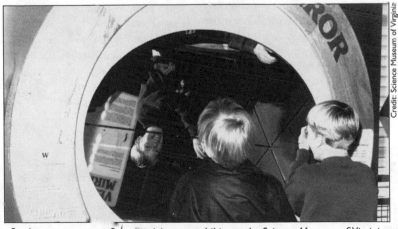

Credit: Science Museum of Virginia

Students try out one of the participatory exhibits at the Science Museum of Virginia.

gained a reputation for its diversity of award-winning programs for gifted and talented students, advanced placement studies, technical and vocational schools, and magnet and model schools.

The system serves more than 28,000 students and operates 31 elementary schools, eight middle schools, nine high schools, seven exceptional education facilities, three vocational educational schools and a nationally recognized arts and humanities center.

Beginning with early childhood and continuing through adult education, Richmond's public schools offer expansive instructional programs and a variety of learning environments to meet the needs of all students, regardless of age or ability. Exemplary schools based on model and magnet instructional themes exist at all grade levels. Richmond's public schools are recognized nationally for programs in early childhood, exceptional and vocational education. Both students and faculty have earned regional, state and national honors.

Gifted Students

Accelerated learning environments are provided for students in kindergarten through 12th grade. Academically advanced secondary students may enroll in advanced placement or honors classes in all subject areas. High school-age students identified as academically gifted or potentially gifted may choose to attend alternative high school programs at Richmond Community High or Open High. For more information, call 780-7805.

Exceptional Education Programs

Students with special needs between the ages of 2 and 22 are provided with classroom environments ranging from resource rooms to special schools that best meet their needs. Richmond's exceptional education program includes nationally recognized facilities such as the Richmond Cerebral Palsy Center and classes for hearing impaired students.

The school system includes a vocational program for trainable mentally retarded and severely handicapped students. The program is community-based and includes hands-on vocational training for students at local businesses and public workplaces. For more information call 780-7312.

Richmond Technical Center

Since opening in 1968, the Richmond Technical Center has been one of the state's premiere regional vocational education centers, serving Richmond, Charles City, Hanover, King William and New Kent. More than 20 technical, trade and business courses are taught here to prepare students for entry level jobs. An evening program for adults is also available.

Insiders' Tips

The Franklin Military School at 1611 N. 31st Street was the first and is one of the few public military schools in the country.

The center offers flexible hours, after-school courses and site-based instruction. Courses include computer-assisted drafting and design, pre-engineering and management information technology, masonry, cabinetmaking, carpentry, electrical trades, printing, commercial art, auto mechanics, auto body repair, graphics communication, cosmetology, practical nursing, commercial foods, machine trades, welding and electronics.

Arts and Humanities Center

In the Mosby Building at 1002 Mosby Street, the center's specialists serve as resource teachers in all areas of the arts. As part of the Artists in the Schools and Writers in the Schools programs, the center also sponsors visual artists, quilters, sculptors, painters, potters and other artists who visit middle and high school art classes to discuss their techniques, philosophies and educational backgrounds.

Enrollment Procedures

Some elementary and middle schools have open enrollment policies, but students who live in a school's attendance zone are usually given first priority for enrollment.

At the magnet high schools the first priority is given to students who live in the school's residential area. If a student wishes to attend a magnet program outside their residential area, they must apply to the school.

To apply for a magnet or a model school, parents and their children must first choose which learning environment will best meet their needs and interests. Model elementary schools are divided into three attendance zones to provide par-

ents with a choice of programs. Call or visit the school of your choice and ask for details.

Students entering school for the first time, or those new to the division, must provide the following information at the time of registration: birth certificate, immunization record, Social Security number and a recently completed physical examination report. For further details call Pupil Placement at 780-7811.

Bus Transportation

Bus transportation is provided for elementary students who live more than a mile from their schools and for secondary students who live more than 1.5 miles from their schools. For information call 780-6166.

Volunteers In Public Schools

Richmond also has a successful Volunteers in Public Schools program that attracts more than 5,000 volunteers a year from all walks of life who serve as lunch buddies, mentors and tutors. To find out more about volunteering call 780-7779.

School-Business Partnership

This program links schools with area corporations to provide students with academic and cultural enrichment activities and organizations. It motivates them to stay in school, expands their knowledge of career options and provides mentors and role models to help build students' self-esteem.

Several hundred businesses including large corporations, government agencies and small businesses participate in the program. For more information call 780-7711.

Richmond School Board

The Richmond City School Board is an elected body responsible for setting policy and ensuring that the school system follows state and federal guidelines. Meetings are held twice a month in the Board room on the 17th floor of City Hall. Citizens are invited to address the Board during a 30-minute public information period at each meeting. If you wish to speak, you must register by 10 AM on the day before the meeting. Certain guidelines and restrictions apply to speakers. For more information, call 780-7719.

Elementary Schools

The elementary education program is designed to strengthen students' academics, enrich their cultural experiences and build their self-esteem. Emphasis is placed on reading and communication skills, mathematics and number concepts, and an understanding of history and how it shaped the present.

There are 31 elementary schools including 12 model schools listed below which offer a thematic-based instructional approach. Gifted and talented students are challenged through the SPACE (Special Program for Academic and Creative Excellence Program). For more information contact the director of elementary

education, 780-7777 or call the following schools:

BELLEVUE MODEL SCHOOL
Academic Enrichment Through Visual and Performing Arts
2301 E. Grace St.   780-4417

BLACKWELL MODEL SCHOOL
Family and Community Education Center
1600 Everett St.   780-5078

JOHN B. CARY MODEL SCHOOL
Quality Education
3021 Maplewood Ave.   780-6252

J.B. FISHER MODEL SCHOOL
Critical and Creative Thinking
3701 Garden Rd.   320-2491

WILLIAM FOX MODEL SCHOOL
Creative and Innovative Thinking
2300 Hanover Ave.   780-6259

GINTER PARK MODEL SCHOOL
International Studies
3817 Chamberlayne Ave.   780-8193

MARY MUNFORD MODEL SCHOOL
International Studies
211 Westmoreland Ave.   780-6267

SOUTHAMPTON MODEL SCHOOL
Environmental Science
3333 Cheverly Rd.   320-2434

SWANSBORO MODEL SCHOOL
Creative Writing
3160 Midlothian Tnpk.   780-5030

WESTOVER HILLS MODEL SCHOOL
Communications and Technology
1211 Jahnke Rd.   780-5002

Insiders' Tips

Richmonders like each year's first snowfall because it gives them a chance to stock up on everything as if they're preparing for the Blizzard of 1888.

WHITCOMB COURT MODEL SCHOOL
Technology and the Basics
2100 Sussex St.   780-4318

WOODVILLE MODEL SCHOOL
Performing and Visual Arts
2000 N. 28th St.   780-4821

Middle Schools

For students in the 6th through 8th grades, the middle school curriculum is designed to help students master basic skills, understand concepts and problem-solving, and explore various electives such as foreign languages, computer technology, fine arts and vocational education.

State-designated vanguard, model and thematic-based schools offer instruction in areas such as creative arts, academic enrichment, international studies and technology to provide middle school students with a range of educational settings. All schools offer an academic core of communicative arts, mathematics, science and social studies.

Programs for gifted and talented students, extracurricular opportunities, mentorships and partnership initiatives with area corporations and universities, and activities designed to promote self-esteem and healthy lifestyles are an integral part of the middle school curriculum.

For more information, call 780-7788.

High Schools

Students in the 9th through 12th grades can participate in college preparatory, vocational, technical training and work-study programs. For advanced students, an honors program offers the opportunity to take a number of college-level courses while still in high school.

Richmond offers a variety of high school settings including alternative schools for academically gifted and talented students, one of the nation's few public military high schools, a regional Governor's School, plus magnet programs in teacher training, life sciences, international studies, business enterprise systems, the arts, math, science and technology, and vocational/technical studies.

For more information contact the Director of Secondary Education, 780-7788.

ARMSTRONG
Professional Development Teacher Academy
1611 N. 31st St.   780-4017

Through a joint effort with Richmond Public Schools, the University of Richmond, Virginia Commonwealth University, Virginia State University and Virginia Union University, prospective teachers observe classrooms and implement innovative instructional approaches designed to meet the needs of urban students.

FRANKLIN MILITARY
1611 N. 31st St.   780-8526

This is the first and one of the few public military schools in the country.

HUGUENOT
Life Sciences
7945 Forest Hill Ave.   320-7967

This school prepares students for both entry-level careers and higher education in the health professions. Members of health care organizations and medical and dental societies provide assistance as program consultants and guest lecturers.

THOMAS JEFFERSON
International and Governmental Studies
4100 W. Grace St.   780-6028

The Thomas Jefferson magnet program offers international and governmental studies, concentrating in areas such as International Business and Technology, Diplomacy and Governmental Relations and International Cultures and Law.

JOHN F. KENNEDY
Math, Science and Computer Technology
2300 Cool Ln.   *780-4449*

This school offers pre-engineering and pre-technical sequences. Courses include computer-assisted design (CAD) and programming, biology, chemistry, physics and accelerated math courses.

JOHN MARSHALL
Business Enterprise Systems
4225 Old Brook Rd.   *780-6052*

Students here learn skills in business management, information systems, business writing and speaking and economics. Courses are offered in computer concepts, business communications, marketing, international business information systems and financial management. Local businesses provide resources, mentoring and shadowing experiences.

OPEN HIGH
600 S. Pine St.   *780-4661*

At Open High, students engage in college preparatory course work at various locations throughout the community. The school emphasizes independent thinking and community involvement. Internships, university study and mentorships are part of the unique individualized curriculum.

RICHMOND COMMUNITY
5800 Patterson Ave.   *285-1015*

At Richmond Community High, students study a college preparatory curriculum that features advanced placement courses, "minimesters," opportunities to combine study and travel, and enroll in classes at area universities.

GEORGE WYTHE
High School for the Arts
4314 Crutchfield St.   *780-5037*

George Wythe High School for the Arts opened in 1990 as the area's only public high school program for students interested in studying the visual and performing arts. The school offers courses in theater, dance, drama, visual arts and arts technology. Practicing artists visit the school regularly to provide demonstrations, master classes and career guidance. The school system's Arts and Humanities Center is here.

Chesterfield County Schools

Chesterfield County operates the largest school system in the Richmond area and the third largest in Virginia. The county has 55 schools, including the Chesterfield Technical Center, nine high schools, 11 middle schools and 34 elementary schools. In spite of crowded facilities, Chesterfield continues to enjoy a reputation for excellence in education. The dropout rate is only about 3 percent and about 75 percent of its students go on to colleges or technical schools.

Chesterfield County students also consistently score higher than the state average on standardized tests, and their SAT scores are higher than the state and national averages. Statistics on test scores and other measurements are available from the Chesterfield County Public Schools Superintendent's Office, 748-1559.

To prepare students for life in the 21st century, the school system is changing the way it operates and to some extent, the way students are educated. Schools are taking a more hands-on approach to learning, and a curriculum council is looking for ways to integrate subject areas and develop an interdisciplinary approach to learning. The county aims to ensure that all students are competent not only in subject matter, but also in the technological and life-coping skills necessary to be productive citizens.

How to accommodate the rapid growth in the schools has dominated budget and planning discussions. Plans have been developed based on recommendations from consultants and the results of nine community forums.

Enrollment

Transfer students should register during school office hours at the school they will attend. For attendance zone information, call 748-1666. Proof of county residency is required, and it's helpful to bring a report card from the previous school. The Chesterfield school will request a transfer of records from the previous school.

Each student enrolling in a Virginia public school for the first time must provide a birth certificate, Social Security number and a medical record of immunizations. Elementary students must also have a physical examination within 12 months of the school year. For a list of schools and general information, contact the superintendent's office, 748-1411.

Kindergarten

Children must be 5 years old by September 30 of the school year to enroll in kindergarten. A full-day kindergarten program is offered. Chesterfield also offers a preschool program for children with disabilities who must be 2 years old by September 30.

Middle Schools

All of the middle schools are making changes that reflect reforms being made nationally in middle school education. The Manchester Middle School includes a center-based gifted program as well as a program for students to progress through studies toward a high school diploma in an alternative setting.

High Schools

A special program for mathematics and science is offered at Clover Hill High School for selected students from all county high schools who are highly gifted in mathematics and science. Communities in Schools, a public/private partnership, supports alternative programs at all levels to keep students from dropping out. Students may work toward receiving a high school diploma at several alternative settings or academies.

Gifted and Talented

The county provides services for students identified as gifted. There is an elementary center-based gifted program at Henning Elementary School that serves students from 11 other schools that don't have school-based programs. In 1992, the county began a middle school center-based gifted program at Manchester Middle School, and there is a special mathematics and science program at Clover Hill High School for selected county students. Honors and advanced placement courses are offered to secondary students.

Special Education

The county provides a full range of special education programs for students with special needs from birth through age 21. Programs and services are for students who are learning disabled, emotionally disturbed, mentally retarded, multihandicapped, visually impaired, hearing impaired and speech and language impaired.

Chesterfield County Technical Center

The center offers more than 23 career programs including data processing, electronics, auto mechanics and licensed practical nursing. The Second School Day program offers high school credit courses at night at the center.

Administration

Chesterfield's five-member School Board is the official governing body for the school system. A.S. "Art" Warren is the Chairman. Thomas R. Fulgham is the Superintendent.

The school board meets twice a month except in July, August, November and December when it meets once. Unless otherwise announced, meetings are usually held in the county administration public meeting room, 9901 Lori Road, in the Courthouse complex. They are open to the public unless otherwise specified by law. You may also see them on a live broadcast aired on Storer Cable Channel 6.

Public participation is encouraged at every level in the school system. The School Board policy manual and School Board meeting agendas are available for inspection at each school and the School Administration Building, 9900 Krause Road.

Business and Industry Partnerships

Chesterfield has a variety of partnerships with businesses and industries including Project Awareness, a cooperative effort with Philip Morris, the Chesterfield Technical Center and Thomas Dale High School. The project is designed to help close the gap between classroom preparation and job application. The schools work with Philip Morris to recommend changes in the curriculum.

The Business Exchange program offers teachers and principals exposure to management training and other programs offered by business and industry. Participating companies include DuPont, Virginia Power, Ukrops, Signet Bank, Philip Morris and First Virginia Bank.

Hanover County Schools

Hanover County enjoys a growing reputation for excellent schools and innovative programs including School Renewal, a school-based management program that provides continuous improvement in school climate, planning, curriculum and instruction, staff development and communication.

Students in Hanover County have consistently scored above state and national averages on standardized achievement tests. About 84 percent of the students plan to continue their education after high school.

Schools, students and teachers are frequently recognized throughout the state for excellence. Liberty and Chickahominy Middle Schools recently were selected as two of seven exemplary middle schools in Virginia and were nominated by the State Department of Education to participate in the U.S. Secondary School Recognition Program.

Special enrichment programs include an Artist-in-Residence, Writer-in-Residence, Musician-in-Residence and Storyteller-in-Residence. Students explore mathematics and science topics at the Mathematics-Science Center, a resource shared by schools in the metropolitan area. They also participate in the annual Festival of the Arts and Sciences each spring and numerous competitions such as Odyssey of the Mind, Young Authors, a county spelling bee and Virginia Junior Academy of Sciences.

Hanover County operates 11 elementary schools, three middle schools and three high schools. The Lee-Davis and Patrick Henry High Schools were recently expanded and renovated. Another elementary school is planned for 1997-98 to meet expected growth. For a list of schools and more information about curricula or enrollment, contact your school or the Hanover County Public Schools, 752-6000.

Classroom Snapshot

All Hanover County schools offer parents a unique voice mail communication system which enables them to listen to a message recorded by their child's teacher, 24 hours a day. The message summarizes the day's activities, explains homework assignments and includes announcements. Parents may also listen to messages from the principal, general school information and school menus.

Hanover schools were the first in Virginia to use this type of voice-mail communication system.

Early Childhood Programs

Hanover operates three federally funded preschool programs — Early Childhood Special Education, Chapter I and Head Start.

Early Childhood Special Education Programs serve infants and toddlers with developmental delays. Services may be provided in the home, in a day-care setting or in a small group setting. When the children begin school programs at age 3, services are available at several schools or from local community service organizations (or a combination of both), depending on the child's needs.

Chapter I preschool programs are at South Anna, Henry Clay, Elmont and Mechanicsville elementary schools. Children attend a full day of school Monday through Thursday. Fridays are devoted to home visits and parent participation. Transportation is provided.

Head Start programs are offered at Beaverdam, John M. Gandy, Rural Point and Cold Harbor Elementary Schools. Children who will be 4 years of age by September 30 of the school year may apply. Children attend a full day of school Monday through Thursday. Fridays are devoted to home visits. Transportation is provided.

Elementary Schools

The curriculum for kindergarten through 5th grade provides varied educational experiences for students to develop their maximum physical, social, emotional and cognitive potential through programs in language arts, mathematics, social studies, health, science, physical education, art and music. Other integral parts of the elementary curriculum include Writing-to-Read, Writing-to-Write, summer school, computer education, Chapter 1/Reading Recovery and computer assisted instruction.

Middle Schools

Students in the 6th through 8th grades take a rigorous academic curriculum that includes language arts, mathematics, science, social studies and health/physical education. An alternate day block schedule provides options for students to select art, band, chorus, forensics, gifted/talented resource, computer concepts, teen living, theater arts and structured science research. Individual needs are met through a Gifted/Talented Program, the Special Education Program and tutorial assistance. Unique features of the curriculum include accelerated learning opportunities for students to receive high school credit in mathematics, science, foreign language, agriculture and technology. Each grade level contains faculty serving on interdisciplinary teams led by a senior teacher who serves as the curriculum and instructional leader/coordinator for the grade.

Senior High Schools

Students in the 9th through 12th grades may pursue the state's standard or advanced studies diploma. Students may also earn the Hanover County Seal of Excellence or an Honors Diploma.

Flexible use of time such as the Alternate Day Block Schedule, used in all six secondary schools, allows students to take advantage of options such as college courses, mentorships, apprenticeships and independent study. Enrollment in college dual-credit courses and area tech-nical programs is offered to rising juniors and seniors in a variety of campus and community settings. Students who are at least age 16 may participate in Youth Apprenticeships — a collaborative effort with the Virginia Department of Labor and Industry, Hanover business and industry leaders and the county schools.

Alternative programs for advanced students include independent study, enrollment in local college courses and mentorships. Advanced placement courses are offered in English, foreign languages, biology, chemistry, physics, calculus, American history, European history and computer science.

Special Education Programs

A county-wide advisory committee with representatives from all the schools meets bimonthly to promote collaboration and integrated educational opportunities for all students. Schools also have site teams that meet periodically to plan for the needs of the students, teachers, staff and parents. Hanover CARES is a related project designed to improve direct, comprehensive services for infants and toddlers with developmental delays as well as their families. Hanover also provides a resource center for parents of students with disabilities. Parents may receive copies of information, videotapes and books on topics such as ADHD and Helping with Homework.

Special education services are provided to identified students with disabilities from ages 2 through 21. Programs and services are available for students who are learning disabled, emotionally disturbed, mentally retarded, multi-handicapped, visually impaired, hearing impaired, or speech and language impaired.

A concrete pipe makes a great fort for these preschoolers.

Related services such as physical and occupational therapy, adaptive physical education and special transportation are provided when appropriate.

Gifted and Talented

This program serves about 2,000 students who are identified as gifted and talented. Elementary students receive differentiated classroom instruction and enrichment programs. They also participate in a resource program provided by full-time specialists in gifted and talented education. Middle schools are served by full-time specialists, and gifted and talented resources and seminars are offered as electives to 6th through 8th grade students. In secondary schools, academically gifted students are encouraged to enroll in advanced courses and advanced placement courses. Students talented in art, creative writing and music are encouraged to enroll in elective courses in their talent areas. Each high school has a specialist who coordinates enrichment activities. Mentorships are available, and rising jun-

iors and seniors may be selected to participate in the Governor's School for the Gifted, a four-week summer program at area colleges and universities.

An advisory committee composed of parents, teachers, administrators, students and community representatives is appointed by the school board and meets quarterly. Parents are invited to attend orientation meetings and county-wide workshops and seminars. They also receive school-based and county newsletters.

Vocational Education

Students are encouraged to plan a program of studies within an occupational theme such as business/finance, marketing, engineering/technology, health/human services, agriculture/natural resources and fine arts/media. Juniors and seniors may enroll in selected technical courses at Highland Springs Technical Center, Richmond Technical Center and J. Sargeant Reynolds Community College. Classes taken at J. Sargeant Reynolds

Community College earn both high school and college credit. Tech Prep programs and Youth Apprenticeships are also available.

Adopt-a-School Partners in Education Programs

Hanover has partnerships with more than 100 area businesses, agencies and civic associations that share resources, personnel and services with the school. In return, schools provide businesses with the use of school facilities, equipment and student decorative projects.

In the Effective Communication for Employment program, more than 92 representatives from area businesses teach 10th and 11th grade students job-seeking and performance skills such as telephone etiquette, interviewing and how to complete applications.

Adult Education

The Adult Education Department offers preparatory classes for the General Educational Development (GED) exam, Adult Basic Education (ABE), adult literacy, courses for high school credit and classes for enrichment and skills improvement.

Administration

A school board member from each of Hanover's seven magisterial districts is appointed to a four-year term by the board of supervisors.

Monthly meetings are held at 7:30 PM on the second Tuesday of the each month (first Tuesday in December) in the school board office at 200 Berkley Street in Ashland. The public is encouraged to attend meetings and participate. Closed sessions are held occasionally, as provided by law, to permit the board to discuss privately matters such as personnel, land acquisition, legal counsel and student hearings.

The school board appoints the Superintendent, who acts as the chief administrator and executive officer of county schools.

Henrico County Schools

Henrico County has one of the state's largest school systems and has always had a strong academic program. About 90 percent of Henrico's graduates continue their education after high school. About a fourth of the students earned a "B" average or better, and about half of the students earned advanced studies diplomas. Henrico County Public Schools operates 37 elementary schools, seven middle schools and eight high schools.

Recently developed high school specialty centers offer concentrated studies in specific areas including alternative studies; engineering, design and future transportation; the arts; foreign language immersion; science, mathematics and technology; humanities; communications; leadership, government and global economics, and the international baccalaureate.

School division people and programs have earned state and national recognition. The Henrico County School Board received the 1993 Kennedy Center/National School Boards Association Award for its support of the arts in education. Art specialist George "Bucky" Wise was named the 1994 National Art Educator of the Year by the National Art Education Association. The U.S. Department of Education has recognized several

Henrico schools as national Blue Ribbon schools, including Douglas Freeman High School, Hermitage High School, Godwin High School, Brookland Middle School and Longan Elementary School. Glen Allen and Seven Pines Elementary Schools were finalists in the 1994 Blue Ribbon competition.

Outstanding and new programs include the aviation program, Students Understanding Neighbors Program, Japanese foreign language courses, Ameurop Cultural Relations Program, the Humanities Center, a Peer Advisor program and a vocational program in which students build houses to sell. Henrico has also established a partnership program with the International School in Hamburg, Germany, and with a school in Bogota, Columbia.

Business and community involvement is encouraged through the Lay Advisory Committee, Community Council Program, Golden Age Program and a number of advisory committees. The Henrico Education Foundation was established in 1991 and is led by area business people to provide opportunities for students and teachers beyond those available in the school system.

Enrollment Procedures

General information about Henrico schools is available from the public information office, 226-3727. To find out which school your child will attend, call the research and planning office, 226-3829. Then, contact the principal at the school. If you are transferring from another school division, you will need to provide a birth certificate, proof of residency, an immunization record, Social Security number, withdrawal papers from the last school attended and a copy of the last report card. The new school will send for a transcript of records.

Kindergarten registration is held each spring on publicized dates. Call the principal of the school your child will attend for more information.

Kindergarten

Kindergarten in Henrico is a half-day program with emphasis on activities that promote reading and math readiness. The morning program is from 7:55 AM until 11:05 AM. The afternoon program is from 11:05 AM until 2:10 PM.

Elementary

Elementary schools include kindergarten through the 5th grade. An integrated curriculum helps students understand how different areas of study relate, while reinforcing the importance of language and communication skills. Weekly art and music instruction as well as physical fitness classes are included as part of the regular elementary program. Through the Students Understanding Neighbors (SUN) program, students in kindergarten through 5th grade learn to speak Spanish, French and Japanese, while studying the cultures of Canada, Mexico and Japan. Beginning in 1995, a $10 million elementary school computer initiative program, funded by the county, will provide one computer for every four to five students.

Middle Schools

Academic requirements in middle school (6th through 8th grades) include English, mathematics, science and social studies. Students may also choose exploratory subjects. Henrico middle schools provide a gradual transition from elementary school to high school. Students progress from team teaching in the 6th grade to changing classes in the 8th grade.

Moody Middle School has been designated as the first middle school specialty center for the pre-international baccalaureate program. The core of the program is rigorous academic study that moves beyond the requirements of a traditional middle school.

An alternative middle school in the former Mount Vernon Baptist Church on W. Broad Street near Parham Road is an option for students who are not achieving up to expectations in regular classroom settings or who need special disciplinary or academic attention. Students must adhere to a dress code and develop a strong work ethic, responsibility and respect for others.

High Schools

The curriculum for the 9th through 12th grades includes college preparatory, work/study programs, and vocational and technical training that provide entry-level job skills. Five foreign languages are taught including Japanese. Honors and advanced placement courses are offered for students who demonstrate the ability and desire for indepth study.

The Virginia E. Randolph Community High School offers an alternative approach to earning a diploma for students who are not performing to their potential.

Adult Education

This program offers adults three ways to complete high school: General Edu-

cational Development classes and testing, an External Diploma program and an Adult High School program. English as a Second Language is also available to adults. Henrico also offers dozens of special interest courses such as furniture upholstering and boating, as well as marketing, management, investment and real estate classes and seminars. A schedule of classes is mailed to county residents twice a year.

An adult education center in Highland Springs includes administrative offices, classrooms and laboratories. Through the Golden Age Program, senior citizens age 60 and older do not have to pay tuition for adult education classes; they also receive free admission to school athletic events and musical productions. For more information call 226-3780.

Special Education

Henrico offers special education programs to children from ages 2 to 21. Programs are designed to meet individual handicapping conditions through the development of an individual educational program. Whenever possible, students attend regular classrooms. A Parent Resource Center, 261-5069, at the Crestview Annex provides information and training for parents of special-education students.

Technical Education

Vocational education students choose from a variety of opportunities. They may build houses or fly airplanes, or they may choose to take courses in marketing, home economics, business, agriculture, health occupations, technology or trade and industrial education. Students attend a half-day at their home school and a half-day at either the Hermitage or the Highland Springs Technical Centers. Through the Ameurop Cultural Relations Program, vocational education students may spend 10 week apprenticeships in West Germany.

Humanities Center

This center, at 2401 Hartman Street, provides enrichment programs and experiences to all students by bringing professional visual and performing artists into each school. Local opera, theater and ballet companies and nationally known artists visit and perform throughout the year. The center also sponsors summer performing arts workshops, after-school arts workshops and drama and oratorical contests.

Gifted Program

Students in kindergarten through the 12th grade who are identified as gifted may participate in a variety of academic, creative and community programs.

Special Needs

Henrico offers a Head Start program at several elementary schools, a Chapter 1 program, and remedial and tutorial assistance programs, including PRIME. The county also offers the English as a Second Language program.

Administration

The five-member board is elected from the magisterial districts of the county. The public is encouraged to attend the board meetings that are held each month on the fourth Thursday at 8 PM in the Glen Echo Building, 3810 Nine Mile Road, unless otherwise announced. The administration building is in the Henrico Eastern Government Center, 3820 Nine Mile Road.

School-Business Partnerships

In this partnership program, businesses and schools sign an agreement to share resources. For more information, call 226-3713.

Private Schools

Private schools in the Richmond area offer a variety of traditional curricula as well as ungraded and other nontraditional learning environments. Some schools have special programs for gifted students or learning disabled and emotionally disturbed students. Day care and before- and after-school care are also available through some of the schools. Tuition fees vary and may change periodically.

Private schools in Virginia have their own accreditation system that is overseen by the Virginia Council for Private Education. Schools that receive VCPE accreditation are recognized by the State Board of Education.

If you're interested in enrolling your child in a private school, the Virginia Association of Independent Schools suggests that you begin your search in the fall a year before you want your child to be enrolled. Ask for catalogues and contact the admissions office to schedule an interview about admissions procedures. You should also visit the school when it's in session. Tours, class visits and informal meetings with students, faculty and administrators are generally available.

Here's a sampling of the private schools in the area. This list is not meant to be all-inclusive, but is sufficiently complete to start you out well on your search.

ALL SAINTS CATHOLIC SCHOOL
3418 Noble Ave.   *329-7524*

About 230 students are enrolled in this school which offers instruction for preschool to 8th grade. There is also an after-school program. Tuition for preschool is $2,500, and $2,150 for kindergarten through 8th grade.

BENEDICTINE HIGH SCHOOL
304 N. Sheppard St.   *355-8679*

This boys-only Catholic school is run by the Benedictine Monks and offers college preparatory instruction from 9th through 12th grade. About 200 students are enrolled. The student body is diverse and represents a variety of neighborhoods, faiths and ethnic groups. Tuition costs about $4,900 and includes a uniform. JROTC is required of all students to promote citizenship and leadership.

COLLEGIATE SCHOOLS
N. Mooreland Rd.   *741-9722*

This school in the far West End offers instruction for kindergarten through the 12th grade. About 1,300 students are enrolled. Tuition varies. Kindergarten costs about $5,930 for a half-day, and a full-day for 1st through 4th grade costs $6,465. Grades 5 through 8 cost $7,425; and grades 9 through 12 cost $8,050. An after-school program is available daily until 6 PM. The school is open year round. Some financial assistance is available.

FORK UNION MILITARY ACADEMY
Fork Union   *842-3212*

Though not in Richmond proper, this private boys' school has been educating Richmond youths since 1898, so it can claim its place here. Fork Union is about 50 miles west of Richmond and is a nonprofit institution affiliated with the Baptist General Association of Virginia. It is a college preparatory school with more than 90 percent of its graduates going on to higher education. Comprised of a junior school for grades 7, 8 and 9, and an upper school for 10th through 12th graders, the Academy uses a basic military system to promote structure and organization for its students. The present student body has boys from 35 states and 15 countries. Call for tuition and other information.

GOOD SHEPHERD EPISCOPAL SCHOOL
4207 Forest Hill Ave.   *231-1452*

This coed school enrolls about 175 students in pre-kindergarten through grade 7. Children age 3 and older are admitted. Extended day care from 7 AM until 6 PM is available. Tuition for pre-kindergarten is $1,650, and $2,600 for kindergarten. Tuition for grades one through seven is $3,250.

HANOVER ACADEMY
115 Frances Rd.
Ashland   *798-8413*

This school serves about 130 students in kindergarten through the 8th grade. A preschool, nursery, transportation and day-care services are also available. Tuition costs are $2,070 for kindergarten, $2,190 for 1st through 2nd grade, $2,210 for 3rd through 4th grade, and $2,250 for 5th through 8th grade. All teachers are state-certified.

HUGUENOT ACADEMY
2501 Academy Rd.   *598-4211*

Huguenot is a co-educational college preparatory, non-sectarian, independent school. This Powhatan County school currently enrolls approximately 250 students from seven surronding counties and Richmond, for grades pre-K through 12. Transportation is provided from and to specific areas. Tuition ranges from $2800 to $5225, and discounts are available if more than one child per family is enrolled. Community relations are emphasized, as evidenced by the Big Brother/Big Sister program in which lower school students interact with high school students.

JEWISH COMMUNITY DAY SCHOOL OF CENTRAL VIRGINIA
501 Parham Rd. 965-0862

About 40 students are enrolled in this school. Instruction is offered for kindergarten through 5th grade. Tuition for kindergarten is $3,900, and $4,250 for 1st through 5th grade.

LANDMARK CHRISTIAN SCHOOL
4000 Creighton Rd. 644-5550

This school offers kindergarten for 4- and 5-year-olds and instruction for 1st through 12th grade. About 320 students are enrolled. Tuition for kindergarten is $1,250 for a half-day and $1,350 for a full-day. Tuition is $1,350 for grades 1 through 6, $1,400 for grades 7 through 8, and $1,500 for grades 9 through 12. There are additional fees for application and registration. Transportation costs $500 to $650 a year.

LIBERTY CHRISTIAN SCHOOL
U.S. 360
Mechanicsville 746-3062

About 2,000 students are enrolled here

in kindergarten though 9th grade. Day care is also available. Monthly tuition is $168 (K), $194 (1st through 5th) and $214 (6th through 9th). Discounts are available if more than one child in a family is enrolled. There are additional fees for registration, books and transportation.

RICHMOND MONTESSORI SCHOOL
499 Parham Rd. 741-0040

About 200 students from ages 2½ to 14 attend this school's ungraded, individualized alternative education program. An extended school day program is available year round. Tuition varies from $1,425 to $9,295, depending on the program you select.

RUDLIN TORAH ACADEMY
6801 Patterson Ave. 288-7610

This coed school teaches secular and Judah studies and enrolls about 120 students in grades K through 8. Some tuition assistance is available. Full-day kindergarten is available. Tuition is $4,300 (K), $4,600 (1st through 4th) and $4,800 (5th through 8th). Books and supply fees are not included.

ST. ANDREW'S PAROCHIAL SCHOOL
227 S. Cherry St. 648-4545

About 100 students in kindergarten through 5th grade attend this school. The school is open primarily for children living in Oregon Hill but admits others as capacity permits. There is no tuition fee. The school operates on an endowment. There is a $30 supply fee.

Eat Virginia-grown peanuts and ham — the saltier the better.

Insiders' Tips

St. Benedict School
3100 Grove Ave.   254-8850

About 265 students in grades K through eight attend this Catholic school. Tuition for parishioners is $1,495 (K through 8th). Tuition for non-parishioners is $2,235 (K through 8). Discounts are available for more than one child in a family. After-school care is available.

St. Bridget's School
6011 York Rd.   288-1994

About 480 students in grades K through 8 attend this coed Catholic school. Tuition for parishioners is $1,810 (K) and $1,910 (1st through 8th). Tuition for Catholic non-parishioners is $2,110 (K) and $2,710 (1st through 8th). Non-Catholics pay $2,160 (K) and $2,980 (1st through 8th). Discounts are available for more than one child in a family. After-school care is also available.

St. Catherine's School
6001 Grove Ave.   288-2804

About 725 students attend this girls-only, independent college preparatory Episcopal school for grades junior kindergarten through 12th grade. An optional residential boarding program is offered for grades 9 through 12. Advanced placement courses and extracurricular sports and arts programs are also available. Courses are coordinated with St. Christopher's in grades 9 through 12. Day tuition ranges from about $6,840 to $8,870. Boarding school tuition including room and board is about $18,950.

St. Christopher's School
711 St. Christopher's Rd.   282-3185

About 800 students attend this boys-only, independent college preparatory Episcopal school for junior kindergarten through grade 12. The high school division is coordinated with St. Catherine's School. Tuition ranges from $6,595 to $8,695. Day care is available for St. Catherine's and St. Christopher's students in grades JK through 7.

Saint Gertrude High School
3215 Stuart Ave.   358-9114

About 214 students are enrolled in this girls-only Catholic school for grades 9 through 12. The emphasis of the educational program is college preparatory with many honors and advanced placement courses offered. Tuition is about $4,825 a year.

St. Michael's Episcopal School
8706 Quaker Ln.   272-3514

This coed school enrolls about 370 students in grades K through 8. Tuition is $3,200 for kindergarten, $3,400 (1st through 5th) and $3,600 (6th through 8th).

The Steward School
Gayton and Ryandale Rds.   740-3394

This coed school enrolls about 230 students from kindergarten through grade 12. This is a small school with an average student-teacher ratio of about 12 to 1. Before- and after-school care is available. Tuition ranges from $6,350 (K through 5th), $7,250 (6th through 8th) and $7,875 (9th through 12th).

Stony Point School
3400 Stony Point Rd.   272-1341

About 60 students in junior kindergarten through 8th grade attend this coed school. Classes are small, with one teacher for about every 10 students. Tuition is $2,750 (JK), $3,270 (K), $3,450 (1st), $3,600 (2nd), $3,775 (3rd), $3,925 (4th),

$4,075 (5th), $4,225 (6th), and $4,375 (7th and 8th). Discounts are available for families who have more than one child enrolled in the school.

TRINITY EPISCOPAL SCHOOL
3850 Pittaway Rd. 272-5864
About 270 students in grades 8 through 12 attend this coed college preparatory day school. Tuition is $6,625 (8th) and $6,975 (9th through 12th).

Private Schools Offering Special Education Programs

DOOLEY SCHOOL
8000 Brook Rd. 262-1663
At St. Joseph's Villa, this school enrolls about 40 students and provides a psychoeducational treatment program for exceptional adolescents ages 6 through 19 who are emotionally disturbed, learning disabled, mentally retarded or behaviorally disordered. Day and residential programs are available. Students must be referred through schools, courts or social services.

NEW COMMUNITY SCHOOL
4211 Hermitage Rd. 266-2494
About 55 students with dyslexia learning disability are enrolled here in grades 6 through 12. Tuition is $11,900 (grades 6 through 8) and $12,850 (grades 9 through 12).

RIVERSIDE SCHOOL, INC.
2110 McRae Rd.
Bon Air 320-3465
About 50 students are enrolled in this nonsectarian elementary and intermediate school for children with learning disabilities, especially dyslexia. One-on-one tutoring sessions are provided daily. Tuition is $7,000.

Educational Organizations

VIRGINIA ASSOCIATION OF INDEPENDENT SCHOOLS
101 N. Mooreland Rd. 282-3592
This statewide organization, established in 1973, provides its members with a school evaluation and accreditation process recognized by the Virginia Board of Education, professional development opportunities, professional services and networks and comparative surveys on member school operations. VAIS also monitors state and federal legislation. More than 60 independent schools are members of VAIS. Member schools must have been in operation for at least five years and have an accredited academic program at least through the 2nd grade.

VIRGINIA COUNCIL FOR PRIVATE EDUCATION
101 N. Mooreland Rd. 282-3592
VCPE was organized in 1974 as a Virginia affiliate of the National Council for American Private Education (CAPE). Its comprised of more than 12 different associations, and each represents academic institutions. All VCPE members must be not-for-profit and have a racially nondiscriminatory enrollment policy. VCPE acts as a liaison to the State Department of Education and provides an accrediting process for members. Call for information about accredited private schools.

Child Care

If you have children, you'll probably need to find a good source for child care whether you're working full-time, part-time, at home or just need a break.

As in most metropolitan areas, there are a number of options to consider before you decide what type of child care service is best for your situation. There are home-based child care providers, child care centers, church and community organization services, employer-based child care, au pairs, nannies and live-in services.

If you prefer a family setting for your child, and you want a home-based child care provider, we recommend that you talk to other mothers, child-care centers and people at your church for information about reputable caregivers in your area. You can also check the newspaper ads or use the assistance of a child-care referral service that keeps lists of caregivers who have vacancies. The weekly cost for full-time care is about $45 to $100. Hourly rates start at about $1.50 to $2. Infants cost more than toddlers and preschoolers.

The Virginia Department of Social Services can provide you with a list of licensed home day caregivers, but there are many excellent home-based caregivers who do not have licenses. There are many licensing requirements, but basically, if you keep fewer than six children, you do not need a license.

The Department of Social Services can also provide you with a list of licensed day care centers. Usually, day care centers provide care for children ages 2 through 12. Most of the centers require that children be potty-trained before they are accepted. You'll find that most day care for infants is provided by individuals; fewer than 20 percent of the centers offer infant care. Rates range from about $56 to $125 a week, depending on the age of the child.

Before- and after-school care is available through many day care centers, the YMCA, home-based caregivers and some area schools.

There are also caregivers who will come to your home and do "light" housekeeping. You'll find these individuals through personal referrals and newspaper ads. Rates start at about $40 a day.

You may also want to consider a nanny. There are several nanny referral services in the area. One is also a training center that serves as a placement agency for graduates. Weekly rates range from about $200 to $300.

If you need day care on a part-time basis or just occasionally, many churches in the area sponsor Mothers' Morning Out Programs, which typically operate as a parent cooperative effort, with minimal or no fees. Some of the schools in the area also offer day-care services as part of home economics or vocational training courses to give students an opportunity to work with children. The YMCA, recreation centers, churches and other community centers may also be good sources for other temporary or short-term care such as after-school care.

VIRGINIA DEPARTMENT OF SOCIAL SERVICES LICENSING DIVISION

1603 Santa Rosa Rd.   662-9078
(Tyler Building)

The state Department of Social Services serves as a regulatory and licensing agency for child-care centers and providers. The department provides free lists of licensed centers and family home-care providers in the Richmond area, as well as brochures with helpful suggestions about how to find quality child care.

The department also maintains records on religiously exempt facilities and investigates complaints about licensed facilities. The department will provide some information about the number and type of complaints filed against providers and centers and whether complaints were valid or not. Sometimes the information can be provided by phone.

COUNCIL ON EARLY CHILDHOOD AND CHILDHOOD AND DAY CARE PROGRAMS
371-8603

This state council monitors the availability and affordability of child care especially for at-risk 4-year-olds and other at-risk preschoolers. The council also administers federal grants including subsidies for programs like Head Start for low-income working parents. It also provides support for state Head Start programs.

Additionally, the council works with employers who want to provide child-care benefits to employees, such as tax advantages or research and referral services, as well as on-site child care.

HEAD START

Information on Head Start programs for at-risk preschoolers is available through the Richmond Community Action Program or area schools.

Research and Referral Services

KIDCARE
5001 W. Broad St., Ste. 217   649-0219

This is a child-care referral service for the Richmond area that was established in 1986 by the Memorial Child Guidance Clinic as a counseling agency for children. KidCare maintains a list of about 400 day care providers and 350 day care centers with information about locations, fees, schools, bus-lines and services. If your child needs a special service or a special kind of care, the staff will give you information about providers who offer those services.

KidCare makes certain that providers have up-to-date health records, and it checks criminal records and child-abuse histories. It also provides training courses in safety and child development and helps individuals set up family home child-care services.

Providers pay a small fee to be listed, and parents pay about $15 for each ZIP code area listing of providers. Lists include registered providers and most of the church-exempt providers. Some employers offer the referral service as an employee benefit.

NANNIES BY KIDCARE
5001 W. Broad St.   282-6085

This nanny school and placement service was founded by Beverley Evert, a trained British nanny who worked for several Richmond families and another placement service before starting this business in the late 1980s. Previously known as New World Nannies, the business is now owned by KidCare and continues to offer much the same services as before.

Referrals are provided for full-time, part-time and live-in nannies for permanent or temporary situations of at least 4 month's duration. About 125 nannies are placed in permanent situations each year.

Nannies listed with the service must provide character and child-care references in addition to any mothering experience they may have had. The agency checks child abuse, criminal and driving records, provides an employment verification check and requests medical and health information. The staff also conducts personal interviews that include child-care scenario questions about nutrition, discipline, play and emergency care.

There is a one-time $75 retaining fee for permanent placement services, plus a $500 placement fee for full-time nannies, a $350 placement fee for part-time nannies, and a $700 fee for live-in nannies. Families receive a complimentary booklet on interviewing, hiring and keeping a nanny. It also includes tax information, sample contracts and problem-solving advice. Placement usually takes an average of four to six weeks. Salaries range from $200 to $300 a week or $6 an hour.

The academy is the only nanny school in Richmond. The three-month work/study program is certified by the Department of Education. Courses are held in the evenings and on weekends at training locations throughout the area. Students learn CPR, first-aid, child safety, child development, creative play and learning, child health, child education and cognitive learning, as well as professionalism and interpersonal communication skills. Instructors include KidCare staff members and other child-care professionals in the area. Call the school for enrollment information.

CHRISTIAN NANNIES
530 E. Main St.   *649-8268*

This service provides referrals for nannies in the Richmond area who demonstrate Christian values to the children they care for, regardless of denomination. Nannies are available to work on a live-in, full-time, part-time, summer-only or temporary basis.

The agency conducts a screening process that includes a statement of health, referrals, DMV and criminal record checks. The staff also conducts an extensive interview and provides drug screening, AIDS tests and employment verification on request.

Red Cross classes and courses in child care and safety are offered as well as STEP classes.

The agency lists an average of 130 nannies actively seeking positions. Placement fees vary — a part-time nanny is $255, full-time is $460 and live-in is $600.

The average placement time is four to six weeks.

CARE "4" KIDS
530 E. Main St.   *649-8804*

Care "4" Kids is a nonprofit organization that provides referrals for family day-care providers, special schools and day-care centers. Child-care training and educational classes are also offered for parents and providers.

The staff visits each provider who is registered and conducts medical, DMV and criminal checks. Referral fees are based on a graduated scale up to $60 a year. Providers are screened in advance, so referral lists include only providers with vacancies who are interested.

Care "4" Kids also offers a consultation service for businesses that want to start an in-house day-care service for their employees and a contractual service to help businesses assist their employees with day-care issues.

THE NANNY CONNECTION
1519 Huguenot Rd.   *379-9314*

This company provides a complete range of in-home child-care service, nannies, parent helpers and sitters for live-in, full-time or part-time work. They also provide au pair referrals and overnight, emergency and sick child care. They even provide baby-sitters or nannies for out-of-town hotel guests. Established in 1987, this is Richmond's first and oldest nanny service.

The agency verifies and talks to references, conducts personal interviews, checks criminal records, child-abuse histories and driving records. Nannies must also be CPR certified and have at least a high school education and a minimum of one year's experience in child care or an educational background in early childhood.

Placement fees vary depending on the type of service you need from about $750 for a live-in nanny to $525 for a full-time nanny to $325 for a part-time nanny. Part-time nannies are usually paid $6 per hour, and full-time experienced nannies earn about $200 to $300 a week. Placement usually takes about four to six weeks.

AuPair Care
(800) 4AuPair

Headquartered in San Francisco, this company provides European nannies to families around the country. The women and men are between the ages of 18 and 25 and are thoroughly interviewed and screened by the company. While living with the family as a family member, participating in everyday events, the au pair provides an average of 45 hours per week of child care. The cultural exchange aspect of the program is a wonderful advantage of this type of care, according to families who currently participate. The au pairs are in the country on a 13-month visa and are overseen while here by a community counselor who provides emotional and practical support for both the au pair and the family. Cost, regardless of the number of children you have, averages $185 a week.

Students chat between classes at Randolph-Macon College.

Inside
Colleges and Universities

Richmond has one of the top-ranked and most heavily endowed private universities in the nation, one of the country's most historic African-American universities and one of the nation's top public research universities.

All told, there are 10 institutions of higher learning in the Richmond area; they are an enormous cultural and educational resource for the community and provide broad opportunities for continuing education for residents.

The following information is brief, especially in terms of available continuing education opportunities. For more detailed information, call the phone numbers listed. For information on the various spectator sports associated with many of these institutions, see our Sports chapter.

RANDOLPH-MACON COLLEGE
Ashland   752-7305

Randolph-Macon, with an enrollment of about 1,100, is a classic liberal arts co-educational college located in a small-town environment. It is among a select group of only 10 percent of colleges and universities with a Phi Beta Kappa chapter. Along with colleges and universities such as Amherst, Williams, Smith, Wellesley, Swathmore, Davidson and Oberlin, it ranks as a "Liberal Arts I" institution in a Carnegie Commission study.

The college offers 28 majors in areas of study including arts management, biology, business, chemistry, the classics, computer science, economics, English, environmental science, fine arts, French, German, history, international studies, mathematics, philosophy, physics, political science, psychology, religious studies, romance languages, sociology and Spanish.

Particular strengths are the natural and physical sciences and premedical studies. The school offers study-abroad programs in Spain, France, Germany, Italy, Great Britain, Japan and Korea.

UNIVERSITY OF RICHMOND
University of Richmond   289-8640

The University of Richmond, one of the nation's most heavily endowed private universities, for a number of years has ranked among "America's Best Colleges" in the annual list compiled by *U.S. News & World Report*. For three consecutive years it also placed second in the South with a 95.9 out of 100 rating. A recent guidebook written by Princeton University students ranks the University of Richmond's campus as one of the five most beautiful in the nation. The guidebook also concludes that UR's students are America's second best looking.

The university, founded in 1830, is coeducational and enrolls about 2,900 full-time undergraduate students and about 500 full-time graduate and law students from 40 states and 17 foreign countries. Thirty-five percent of the freshmen rank in the top 10 percent of their respective secondary school classes.

Located in the West End on a 350-acre campus that includes a 10-acre lake, the University of Richmond includes **Richmond College**, the residential college for undergraduate men in liberal arts and sciences, and **Westhampton College**, the residential college for undergraduate women in liberal arts and sciences. It also includes the **E. Claiborne Robins School of Business**, with its Richard S. Reynolds graduate division, the **T. C. Williams School of Law**, a graduate school for arts and sciences and the **University College** which includes the summer and evening schools and continuing education programs.

The university's new **Jepson School of Leadership Studies** is the first in the nation to offer a bachelor's degree in this important field.

An executive master of business administration degree program is designed for those who wish to pursue part-time academic study of management and who already hold baccalaureate degrees and management positions. Its Women's Resource Center involves more than 6,000 men and women in self-improvement classes, life-planning seminars, support groups and job and career counseling. Evening classes are offered for four majors, and noncredit classes are offered in a variety of fields.

VIRGINIA COMMONWEALTH UNIVERSITY
821 W. Franklin St.   828-1222
1101 E. Marshall St. (MCV)   828-0488
Virginia Commonwealth University, in center city, is the state's largest urban university (22,000 students), is one of the nation's top public research universities and has the nation's largest evening school program. It offers 42 degree programs that are not available at any other institution in Virginia, and about 80 percent of faculty members hold the highest degree in their fields of study.

It has two campuses: the academic campus in the Fan District and the **Medical College of Virginia** campus, or east campus, downtown. The university is co-educational, state-supported, offers 142 degree programs and traces its history back to the founding of the Medical College of Virginia in 1838.

VCU's east campus is the site of the Medical College of Virginia Hospitals, one of the largest and most active university-affiliated health care centers in the United States. This campus houses the divisions of allied health professions, dentistry, medicine, nursing, pharmacy and basic sciences as well as the School of Graduate Studies and the Division of Continuing Studies and Public Service. All of this makes VCU one of only 20 universities in the nation with a school in every health-related discipline.

The academic campus is the home of the colleges and schools of the arts, business, community and public affairs, education, humanities and sciences, and social work. The **School of the Arts** is one of the largest in the nation. The **School of Business** is one of only three in the nation with a chair in real estate, and the Management Center offers more than 200 programs a year for private industry and government. Engineers and other professionals with strong science backgrounds can pursue graduate engineering degrees through fully accredited courses offered at VCU by Virginia Polytechnic Institute & State University and the University of

Virginia. A new School of Engineering is under construction and will begin enrolling students in 1996.

VCU also offers opportunities for study abroad through its **Center for International Programs**, 828-8471.

VIRGINIA STATE UNIVERSITY
Ettrick   *524-5902*

Virginia State University, founded in 1882, is a state-supported coeducational institution with an enrollment of about 4,000 students. It is located in Chesterfield County in the town of Ettrick near Petersburg.

Degrees are awarded from the School of Agriculture and Applied Sciences, School of Business, School of Education, School of Natural Sciences and School of Humanities and Social Sciences.

Graduate degrees are offered by the School of Graduate Studies and the School of Continuing Studies. The latter program is designed for people interested in pursuing advanced education without seeking a degree. At the same time, an interdisciplinary degree is available from the school.

The university operates a 416-acre agricultural research farm a mile from its 236-acre campus. Virginia State also offers innovative degree programs in hotel/restaurant management, public administration and engineering technology.

VIRGINIA UNION UNIVERSITY
1500 N. Lombardy St.   *257-5881*

Virginia Union University is among the nation's finest traditionally African-American institutions of higher learning and has been a powerful force in shaping the history of Richmond. In the process it has educated many of the city's and the state's leaders.

It offers 22 undergraduate liberal arts and business majors as well as graduate degrees in theology. Majors with the highest enrollment are business administration, accounting and history.

Its core liberal arts curricula is augmented by specialized programs such as a dual-degree engineering program in conjunction with the University of Michigan, the University of Iowa and Howard University in Washington, D.C. and a joint-degree program in law with St. John's University School of Law in New York.

The Sydney Lewis School of Business Administration at Virginia Union offers undergraduate degrees in business, with majors in accounting, business administration and business education.

Virginia Union attracts students from all over the United States and from abroad, and its undergraduate student body of about 1,500 students represents 28 states and eight foreign countries.

J. SARGEANT REYNOLDS COMMUNITY COLLEGE

1701 E. Parham Rd.   *371-3676*

J. Sargeant Reynolds Community College enrolls about 25,000 full- and part-time students on three campuses: downtown at 700 E. Jackson Street, in Henrico County on Parham Road one mile west of U.S. 1 and I-95, and in Goochland County on State Route 6 near the courthouse.

The college is the third largest in the Virginia Community College System and offers college transfer classes as well as more than 40 career-specific programs. Developmental studies in math and English are offered to those who are not yet qualified to enroll in a program.

A specialty of the downtown campus near the Medical College of Virginia is health career training. Popular programs at the Parham Road campus are those in engineering and electronics. Agricultural and automotive/diesel programs are those with heaviest student involvement at the western campus.

Both the Parham Road and downtown campuses offer free career counseling and placement offices that are open to the public. Programs to help women entering or returning to the job market are also offered. At the downtown campus, the Center for the Deaf helps deaf and hard-of-hearing students enter the educational programs of the college.

Studies can lead to an associate in applied science degree, diploma or certificate, an associate of arts or science degree in liberal arts, engineering or education, or certification in areas including computer technology and hotel and restaurant management.

In addition to the main telephone number listed above, the downtown campus can be reached directly at 786-6791, the Parham Road campus at 371-3270, and the western campus at 786-3316 from Richmond, at 556-4663 from Goochland, and at 598-2595 from Powhatan.

JOHN TYLER COMMUNITY COLLEGE

13101 Jefferson Davis Hwy.   *796-4000*

John Tyler Community College enrolls about 10,000 students annually in credit courses at three locations: the Chester Campus, the Midlothian Campus and the Fort Lee Center. Studies at John Tyler lead to associate in applied science degrees, associate in arts and sciences for transfer degrees and certificates and career studies certificates in vocational and technical subjects.

The most sought after curricula are

liberal arts for transfer to four-year colleges and universities, business management and administration, computer information systems, electronics, nursing, physical therapist assistant and police science. New programs include an associate in applied science degree in early childhood development and a certificate in fine arts that parallels the first year of art foundation studies at Virginia Commonwealth University. John Tyler is the only college in Virginia that offers a funeral service program.

The Division of Continuing Education offers credit and noncredit training both on and off campus to meet the professional development needs of individuals and area businesses and organizations. The Business, Industry and Government Services Center offers noncredit instruction in a variety of subjects including the latest computer software programs, office management and supervisory skills and total quality management. The Department of Community Education offers non credit courses of personal and recreational interest.

BAPTIST THEOLOGICAL SEMINARY AT RICHMOND

1204 Palmyra Ave.   *355-8135*

This seminary, established in 1991-92, is supported by The Baptist General Association of Virginia and by Baptist churches and organizations. It prepares men and women for careers in churches and other organizations and offers the master of divinity, a three-year basic preparatory degree for a variety of fields of ministry. It participates with three other local institutions in the Richmond Theological Consortium: Union Theological Seminary, Presbyterian School of Christian Education and Virginia Union University's School of Theology.

UNION THEOLOGICAL SEMINARY IN VIRGINIA
3401 Brook Rd. 355-0671

Located on Richmond's north side, Union Theological Seminary is recognized for its vigorous academic program and its pioneering work in field education and student-in-ministry experiences. Its excellent library of about 250,000 volumes and its audiovisual, closed-circuit television and other electronic teaching aids provide special learning opportunities.

A seminary of the Presbyterian Church (USA), the institution offers doctor of ministry, master of divinity, doctor of philosophy and master of theology degree programs. It also offers a dual degree program (master of divinity/master of arts in Christian Education) in cooperation with the Presbyterian School of Christian Education.

PRESBYTERIAN SCHOOL OF CHRISTIAN EDUCATION
1205 Palmyra Ave. 254-8042

The Presbyterian School of Christian Education offers two master's programs and a program leading to a doctorate. It is the only one of 11 theological institutions of the Presbyterian Church (USA) to specialize solely in training for Christian education.

A master of arts program is the basic part of the curricula and takes about two years to complete. A master of arts degree program that combines Christian education with social work is offered in cooperation with Virginia Commonwealth University. Also available is a program leading to a doctorate in education.

UNIVERSITY OF VIRGINIA
Richmond Center
7740 Shrader Rd., Ste. E 662-7464

The Richmond Center is operated by the Division of Continuing Education of the University of Virginia, Charlottesville. It offers programs in the arts and sciences, publishing and communications, business management, engineering, environmental studies, computer studies, education and nursing. Its Engineering Review courses prepare individuals for the state examination.

Inside
Shopping

Shockoe Slip, Carytown and the Shops at Libbie and Grove offer a diversity of boutiques, restaurants and specialty shops in unique shopping areas that are fun to explore. Richmond also has numerous shopping malls anchored by one or more of the area's major department stores, Leggett, Hecht's, Peebles, Proffitt's, JCPenney and Sears.

In addition to the malls and shopping areas, there are specialty stores to please almost every shopper looking for everything from designer clothes to exotic foods. And, if you can't find what you need in the Richmond area, you will probably find it in Washington, D.C., just two hours away.

Bargain shoppers will discover that Richmond has its share of discount stores from electronics to shoes, and there are a number of vintage clothing and consignment stores where you can find everything from retro fashions to baby clothes in like-new condition for a fraction of the original cost. You'll also find great deals on everything from designer clothes to housewares and pottery at the outlet shops in Williamsburg, just 45 minutes east of Richmond.

For groceries, we think you'll find the some of the best service and produce in town at **Ukrops**, a local, family-owned grocery chain, where they treat customers like guests. Employees go out of their

6th Street Marketplace is adjacent to the Coliseum and the Richmond Marriott.

way to make sure you have an enjoyable shopping experience, and it's not unusual to see the owners greeting customers. Just about everyone in town has a story about Ukrops to tell. They've completely redefined the grocery shopping experience.

For those who like poking around in dusty old antique stores, you'll be delighted to know that Richmond has a wealth of shops in the metropolitan area and surrounding counties. You can go on a number of antiquing expeditions without seeing the same store twice.

We also have several excellent craft shows at the Richmond Centre, Strawberry Hill and at the Showplace where you can buy items directly from the artisans. See the Annual Events chapter for information about upcoming exhibits.

If you're looking for unusual or distinctive gifts, you'll find out-of-the-ordinary items at the gift shops at the Science Museum of Virginia, the Richmond Children's Museum, the Museum and White House of the Confederacy, the Valentine Museum, Valentine Riverside, the Virginia Museum of Fine Arts, Maymont and the Lewis Ginter Botanical Gardens.

In this chapter we explain what you can expect to find at the major shopping areas and at a few of our special shops.

Unique Shopping Areas

CARYTOWN

Cary St. from the Boulevard to the RMA

You'll be surprised at the unusual variety of shops, boutiques, restaurants and food stores in this nine-block shopping area just west of the Fan District that extends from the Boulevard to the RMA beltline. There are more than 250 stores and professional offices lining both sides of the one-way street, in shopping courts, alleys and along side streets. It's also the

site of the Byrd Theatre, a national historic landmark, which still operates as a movie and entertainment theater.

Carytown began in the 1930s with the construction of the Cary Court Shopping Center, and it's been growing ever since. The old First Baptist Church has been renovated for retail use and includes **Annette Dean's** (men's and women's fashions), **Simon's Cafe**, **Martin Furnishings** (interior design) and **Karina's Hair**.

You'll also find Oriental rug dealers, art galleries, florists, card and party shops, bakeries, seafood stores, wine and cheese shops, antique stores, fine furniture stores, clothing and lingerie stores, a pet shop, a bicycle shop, a kitchen shop and piano shops. The shops seem to have developed spontaneously in no particular order, so you might be in an Oriental rug store one minute and a pet store the next. Shopping here is truly a unique experience and a lot of fun on a pleasant day.

Carytown stores include **Schwarzschild Jewelers**, **Tiffany's** (bridal wear and consulting), **Old Dominion Camera Shop**, **Jean Jacques Bakery**, **Bangles & Beads** (costume jewelry and supplies), **Lorraine Hardware**, **Silk Jungle** (silk plants and arrangements), **Bleums** (florist), **Amazing Pets**, **Two Wheel Travel** (bicycle shop), **Carytown Coffee & Tea**, **Tobacco House**, **Mongrel's** (unusual and creative cards, stationery and party supplies), **Ellman's Dancewear** (since 1948), **Premiere** (costumes, theatrical accessories), **For the Love of Chocolate** (everything chocolate), **Cabbage Rose** (gifts and florals), **City Shoes**, **Childrens Market Exchange**, **Skirt and Shirt** (clothing), **Gourmet Delights**, **Louis Briel** (portrait artist), **Zarouhi's Trove** (antiques and collectibles), **Just the Right Thing** (contemporary jewelry), **Plan 9 Records**, **The**

Phoenix (Southwestern attire and paraphernalia), **Narcissus** (women's accessories), **Sorrell King Outlet** (Richmond designer of women's and children's clothing), **Pink** (fashionable clothing, cards, gifts and jewelry with a New York flair), **But is it Art?, Du Soleil, Second Time Around** (antiques and collectibles), **Martha's Mixture** (antiques), **Lane-Sanson** (international gifts, jewelry and furnishings), **Narnia** (children's books), **The Compleat Gourmet,** (kitchen equipment and accessories), **Garden Designs** (planters and garden accessories), **Road Runner** (running supplies), **House of Lighting,** the **Mill End Shop** (fabric, draperies, slip covers), **Richmond Piano** and **The Hall Tree** (consignment clothing). There's also a Ukrops and The Grocery Store

On side streets you'll find **Owen Suter's Fine Furniture,** Annette Dean Consignments, The Art & Frame Shop, **Incredible Edibles** and **Niblick and Cleek** (golf clothing).

If you want to see it all, allow yourself plenty of time, park and walk up one side and down the other. There are more than 27 places to eat, so you can stop for lunch or refreshments if you get tired. Popular restaurants are Gourmet Delights, Josie's Cafe, the New York Deli, The Track, Chopsticks and Amici's. (See the Restaurants chapter for more information.) There are also a number of sidewalk cafes that are perfect for people-watching.

You may also want to visit the annual Carytown Watermelon Festival in August, when the merchants association sponsors a weekend street party with special activities.

Parking is available along Cary Street, side streets or at free parking decks at Crenshaw and Dooley, and at Sheppard

and Colonial. Shop hours vary. Most of the stores are open from 10 AM to 5:30 PM, Monday through Saturday. Some stay open later depending on the season, and a few stores are also open on Sunday.

SHOCKOE SLIP
Cary St. From 10th to 13th Sts.

Near downtown, historic Shockoe Slip offers cobblestone streets, restaurants, hotels, boutiques, art galleries, antique shops and clothing stores in a quaint three-block area of Cary Street known for its renovated tobacco buildings and warehouses.

Special shops here include **Tudor Gallery** (estate jewelry), **Hurah** (folk art gallery), **Shockoe Espresso** (coffee house), **D.M. Williams, Ltd.** (fine leathers and men's and women's apparel), **Beecroft & Bull, Ltd.** (fine men's clothing and furnishings), **The Toymaker of Williamsburg, Dransfield Jewelry** (creative fine jewelry by design) and **Antiques Boutique** (heirlooms, accessories, unusual gifts, jewelry). You'll also find **My Romance** (unusual gifts), **The Fountain Bookstore, Glass Reunions** (specializing in blown and stained glass) **The Virginia Shop** (Virginia-made products), **Cudahy's** (art and fine crafts), the **Valentine Riverside Museum Shop** and a number of other clothing, jewelry and antique shops.

Be sure to allow time for lunch, dinner or drinks while you're here. Shockoe Slip has earned a reputation for having excellent restaurants and clubs with live music, comedy and dancing. See the Restaurants and Nightlife chapters for more details.

Shockoe Slip is also fun to visit during many special events in the downtown area such as the Tour DuPont and the

Halloween Pumpkin Party sponsored by the merchant's association. Christmas brings a bustle of activity, special shows and events, twinkling lights and a sense of magic to the Slip.

Street parking is limited, but there are several parking lots around the area within easy walking distance. Most of the stores open at 10 AM Monday through Saturday and stay open until 5 PM or 6 PM. Some stay open later on Friday and Saturday nights, and a few stores are open on Sunday.

THE SHOPS OF LIBBIE AND GROVE "ON THE AVENUES"
Libbie and Grove Aves.

This charming shopping area in the West End might remind you of an exclusive boutique area in a small resort town. About 45 specialty shops and restaurants line both sides of the street in one- and two-story buildings and Victorian-style homes with awnings, friendly porches and sidewalk cafes. Attorneys, doctors, Realtors, interior designers and travel agents have also set up shop here, renovating old buildings and adding to the neighborly ambiance. Shops begin on Libbie Avenue within about two blocks of Grove Avenue and continue on Grove Avenue for a block or two on either side of the intersection.

The Arcade on Grove is one of the newest additions to the shops here. Modeled after a European-style shopping arcade with a gazebo and handpainted wall murals, The Arcade on Grove offers a collection of specialty shops unlike any other place in Richmond. Shops include **Morning Glory** (garden pots, tools and accessories), **Market Place** (gifts), **Open House** (gifts for the kitchen and home) and **Homemades by Suzanne** (lunch, carry-out dinners and catering).

Other new shops include **John Barber Art Ltd.** (original maritime paintings and lithographs), **The Stepping Stone Gallery** (contemporary crafts and fine art), **Grove Avenue Coffee & Tea** (coffees from the world, salads and sandwiches), **Granger's** (women's apparel and accessories), **Frillseekers** (unusual home fashions, furniture and jewelry) and **Kim Faison Antiques** (European and continental).

Walk a block in any direction and you'll find a variety of specialty shops offering women's fashions, jewelry, baskets and plants, fabrics, antiques, home fashion accessories, gifts, country crafts and decorative items, art galleries, children's clothing, books and more. Because the shops are owned by local merchants, you'll also enjoy personalized service and attention.

Other shops here include **Thistle's** (fine leather goods, gifts and accessories), Monkey's (designer dresses, sportswear and accessories), **Madelyn's** (ladies' apparel, shoes and accessories), **Cabell Shop** (classic ladies' clothing), **Victoria Charles Ltd.** (designer and estate jewelry), **Carreras Ltd.** (fine jewelry), **J. Taylor Hogan** (interior design, gifts and bridal registry), **Hampton House** (fine gifts and English antiques), **Country Charm** (country crafts, antiques and accessories), **The Flag Center, Chadwick Antiques, Ltd.** (fine furniture, accessories and gifts), **Didgies** (children's fashions), **Fisher Pewter** (pewter and sterling), **IBIS** (hair salon), **Peter Blair** (men's clothing), **Bartleby's-Eton** (classic clothing for men and boys), **The Knitting Basket** (knitting supplies including imported yarns), Cachet, Ltd., (delightful gifts and decorative accents for memorable interiors), **Paper Plus** (wedding invitations, writing paper and gifts), **Mary Anne & Co.** (an-

libbie&grove

ON · THE AVENUES

Experience Richmond's Finest Shopping

Jeanne's
Cards & Collectibles

A member of the
Richmond Ornaments Collector's Club

Invites You to Join

Hallmark   *and*   ENESCO

National Ornament Clubs

(804) 285-5558
5811 Grove Avenue • "On the Avenues"
We ship UPS worldwide

Jeanne Walls

PETER·BLAIR

Fine men's clothing, gifts & accessories

HAND PICKED TIES & DRESS SHIRTS
•
SPECIALTY SPORT COATS & TROUSERS
•
SUITS & FORMAL WEAR BY SPECIAL ORDER

Dick Fowlkes • 5718 Grove Ave.
288 • 8123

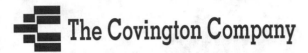

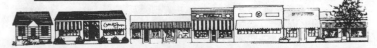

tiques and interior design services) and **Ardley** (women's fashions).

Combine your shopping with lunch, or visit the avenues in the evening for a movie at the Westhampton Theatre and dinner at duJour or the Peking. DuJour was voted the best neighborhood cafe and specializes in fresh, innovative cuisine. You can relax and dine at the sidewalk cafe when the weather permits. The Peking is a well-established restaurant, specializing in authentic Szechuan and Mandarin cuisine.

On the corner of Grove and Maple Avenues, check out **Jeanne's Cards & Collectibles**. If you work up an appetite perusing Jeanne's selection, step up to the counter of Bill's BBQ.

Free parking is available along the streets or in parking lots behind the shops — use the entrance from Libbie Avenue or behind Bill's BBQ on Maple Avenue.

Store hours vary from about 9 AM to 5 PM, Monday through Saturday.

6TH STREET MARKETPLACE
550 E. Marshall St.   *648-6600*

You'll find a number of specialty boutiques and restaurants at this unique downtown marketplace between the Carpenter Center on Grace Street and the Marriott on Broad Street. The narrow, two-level center is probably best known among locals for its ornate walkway that spans Broad Street.

Built in 1987, 6th Street Marketplace caters mainly to downtown office workers at lunch time and to visitors attending conferences and events at the Richmond Centre and the Coliseum. Festival Park, an open area between the marketplace and the Coliseum, is also the site of many special events including the Friday Cheers concert series sponsored by Downtown Presents. . . .

Some of the shops here include **Second Glance** (cards and gifts), **Gerri's Gifts** (country crafts and gifts), **Bridges** (authentic African goods), **New Attitudes** (women's shoes), **Shingar** (international clothing for women), **20 Below** (women's fashions for $20 or less), **Heritage Gallery** (prints and frames), **Footlocker** (athletic shoes) and **Radio Shack** (audio, video and other home electronics).

You'll also find numerous fast food places in the food court and several restaurants including Blue Point Seafood, Mulligan's (sports bar) and The Market Place Cafe (seafood). See the Restaurants and Nightlife chapters for more details.

Free validated parking is available from participating merchants with a $10 purchase. Shops are open 10 AM to 6 PM, Monday through Saturday; 12:30 PM to 5:30 PM on Sunday.

SYCAMORE SQUARE SHOPPING VILLAGE
Midlothian Tnpk.,
Sycamore Square and
Crowder Drs.   *320-7600*

This quaint shopping village in Chesterfield County will remind you of Williamsburg with its Colonial-style buildings and high-pitched cedar shake roofs. There are numerous shops, specialty boutiques, art galleries, professional offices and a Ukrops arranged in clusters to resemble a small town. Crab Louie's, a popular seafood restaurant, is also here, as well as the Italian Cafe. See the Restaurants chapter for more information.

Specialty shops include **Sycamore Pewtersmith, D'Ors, Ltd.** (women's fashions), **Down the Garden Path** (garden shop), **Ginni's Decorating & Gifts** (interior decorating and gifts), **R.S.V.P.** (party services and gifts) and **The Toy Shoppe**. **Talbot's** (women's apparel) is also nearby.

Shops are open from 10 AM to 5 PM, Monday through Saturday. Some are open earlier or later, and they are all closed on Sunday.

Major Shopping Malls and Centers

CHESTERFIELD TOWNE CENTER

Huguenot Rd. and
Midlothian Tnpk.   794-4660

Decorated with palm trees and skylights throughout, this mall has the ambiance of a tropical paradise, especially on a sunny day. This South Side mall is the largest in the area, with more than 140 shops and restaurants including **Leggett, Hecht's** and **Proffitt's**. Sears will also open a store here soon. At Chesterfield Towne Center, you'll find stores that are unlike any in the area has, including **Gantos** (stylish women's fashions), **Northern Reflections** (casual wear for men and women), **San Rio Surprises** (a children's accessory store), **Accessory Lady** and **Charter Club** (traditional clothing for women). Other popular stores here include **Structure, Ann Taylor, Compagnie Express Internationale, Eddie Bauer, Cocoanut Jewelry** and the **Santa Fe Traders**. There's also a nine-screen movie theater, plenty of fast food restaurants in the Palm Court and Spinnaker's Restaurant.

At the customer service desk, in the Palm Court, you can borrow a free stroller or wheelchair, get a free shopping bag or buy gift certificates.

The mall also offers **Club Mom** in cooperation with WWBT 12, B103.7-FM, Commonwealth Parenting Center and Chippenham Medical Center. The club features special seminars, workshops, fashion events and provides discounts for members. To register, just visit the Palm Court. The mall also sponsors holiday and community events and a mall walker program. Frequent walkers receive awards such as T-shirts and warm-up jackets based on the number of miles they walk.

Stores are open 10 AM until 9 PM, Monday through Saturday and 12:30 PM to 5:30 PM on Sunday.

CLOVERLEAF MALL

7201 Midlothian Tnpk. at
Chippenham Pkwy.   276-8650

The South Side's Cloverleaf Mall opened in 1972 and has been a favorite mall of Richmond shoppers for more than 20 years. Anchored by **Hecht's, JCPenney** and **Sears**, the mall offers more than 90 stores and services arranged in a complex that makes shopping easy and quick. In addition to its user-friendly layout, Cloverleaf also has stores with moderately priced merchandise which make it more value-oriented than other shopping centers.

In 1987, the mall added the food court and a movie theater building and completed significant renovations.

Some favorite stores here include **Petite Sophisticate** (clothing for petite women), **Victoria's Secret** (lingerie), **Limited Express** (women's fashions), **Sea Dream Leather** (leather boots, bags, belts and accessories), **Ingle's Nook** (country and classic home decorations and accessories), **Babbage's** (computer software and Nintendo), **Cavalier** (popular young men's fashions), **Limited Express** (popular young women's fashions), **San Francisco Music Box** (musical gifts), **Things Remembered** (engravable gifts for home, office, weddings, etc.) and **Nature's Elements**.

While you're here, you can enjoy a snack or a meal at numerous fast food restaurants in the food court or you can visit Andy's Barbecue & Ribs, the Piccadilly Cafeteria or Ruby Tuesday Restaurant. You can also see a movie at the NEI Cloverleaf Cinema. Family-oriented events and community activities are also held here frequently.

If you want to shop the whole mall, we suggest that you park in the back of the mall near **Hecht's** and **JCPenney** and enter through the food court. For shopping bags, gift certificates, strollers, wheelchairs, stamps and gift wrapping, visit the information booth near the center of the mall.

Store hours are 10 AM to 9 PM, Monday through Saturday; 12:30 PM to 5:30 PM on Sunday.

FAIRFIELD COMMONS
Nine Mile Rd. at
Laburnum Ave. 222-4167

This mall opened in 1967 as Eastgate Mall and became Fairfield Commons in 1990 when the mall was sold to Interstate Properties, a New Jersey-based shopping center owner. Anchored by **Peebles, G.C. Murphy's** and **CVS Pharmacy**, the mall has a pleasant, airy look.

Other stores here include **Kay-Bee Toys & Hobbies, Footlocker** and **FootAction** (athletic shoes and clothes), **B. Dalton Booksellers, Afterthoughts** (accessories), **Thom McAn, Radio Shack, Whitney & Whitney Plus** (women's apparel), **The Timing** (popular women's fashions), **Genie of Oakton** (women's career fashions), **Kid City** (children's fashions), **JW** (contemporary young men's fashions), **Ragtime** (young women's fashions), **Payless Shoes, Sam Goody, General Nutrition Center** (a.k.a. GNC) and **Galeski Optical.**

Restaurants include Shoney's, Empire Szechuan Gourmet and the Mixing Bowl, located inside Peebles. Frozen treats from **Freshens Yogurt** help keep the little ones happy.

Near the Richmond International Airport, the mall serves shoppers in eastern Henrico and Hanover, Charles City and New Kent counties. Wheelchairs, strollers, shopping bags and information are available at the Security/Information desk. A 24-hour information line, 222-4167, provides recorded information about mall stores and events such as community, school and cultural programs sponsored by the mall.

Store hours are 10 AM to 9 PM, Monday through Saturday; 12:30 PM to 5:30 PM on Sunday.

GAYTON CROSSING
Gayton, Gaskins and Quioccasin Rds.

This West End strip center is one of the largest in the entire metropolitan area. Anchored by both The **Grocery Store** and **Ukrops** supermarket, the shopping mix includes home furnishings and entertainment, men's, women's and children's apparel and shoes, restaurants, pet care, health and beauty products, gifts and miscellaneous services.

Some of the more interesting shops include **Arts Limited** (artwork, framing and supplies), **Carol Pipes Interior Design** (commercial and residential interior design), **Lamp Emporium** (lamps, chandeliers, prints, mirrors, shades and gift items), **Shoe Trends** (women's fashion shoes), **Jos. A Bank Clothiers** (traditional clothing for men and women), **Kids Unlimited** (clothing and accessories for girls and boys), **Melting Pot Restaurant, Pat's** (women's specialty clothing), **Plaid Racket** (tennis rackets, accessories and clothing for the entire family), **Canine Design** (dog and cat grooming and tattooing), **Family Pet Center** (dogs, cats, fish, birds and a complete line of pet supplies), **Gayton Animal Hospital** (specialized medical care for pets), **Mail Boxes, Etc.** (postal, business and communication services), **Travel Agents International** (business and vacation travel agency), Frenchy's Bakery (homemade breads, rolls and assorted specialties), Karen's Homemades (homemade breads, sandwiches, salads and vegetarian products), Peter Pizza Plus (pizza and other Italian specialties), **Book Gallery** (full service bookstore and gourmet gifts), **Gayton Flowers** (fresh flowers, silk and dried arrangements, balloons and wedding consultation), **Jessie's Hallmark** (cards and gifts), **Paper & Party** (cards, balloons and other party supplies), **Shir-Rudolf's Collectibles and Gifts**, Sycamore **Pewtersmith** (quality gifts and housewares), **Wild Bird Center** (bird feeders and accessories) and **Toys That Teach** (children's creative learning toys).

INNSBROOK SHOPPES
W. Broad St. at Cox Rd.

As part of the Far West End's most prestigious office development, this strip center faces W. Broad Street near the intersection of I-64. It boasts some of the area's best restaurants, DeFazio's and Dakotas, as well as the popular nightspot Mulligan's Grill and Pub. (See the Restaurants and Nightlife chapters). Because of its comfortable and elegant courtyard and pavilion, the center plays host to a summer-long series of Wednesday night musical events known as Innsbrook After Hours.

But if you're in the mood for shopping, you won't be disappointed. You will find a variety of specialty shops and boutiques here. Some of the shops include **By Invitation Only** (a bridal boutique offering everything from tuxedos to linge-

rie), **Pip Printing**, **High Cotton** (women's career and sportswear boutique), **Salon Duvall** (hair salon), **Mark and Co. Jewelers**, **Breakers at DeFazio's** (billiards and dart parlor), **Shady Grove YMCA at Innsbrook** (exercise club) and **Innsbrook Cellular** (cellular phones and service). For takeout and cafe-style lunches, try World Cup Coffee (coffee, tea and cafe), Boychik's Deli, Manhattan Bagel (bagels and cafe), Hickory Hams (glazed hams, turkeys and deli) or the Dairy Queen.

REGENCY SQUARE
Parham and Quioccasin Rds.   740-7467

Anchored by Hecht's, JCPenney and Sears, Regency Square lives up to its reputation for being one of "the" places to shop in Richmond. All of the department stores are the largest in the area, with unmatched merchandise selection and quantities. Many a label of the stores can only be found in Richmond at Regency Square. Some of the newest shops in this West End mall include **Warner Bros. Studio Store**, **The Disney Store**, **Banana Republic** (men's and women's apparel), **Natural Wonders** (gift items related to nature and science), **Brooks Brothers** (traditional men's and women's apparel), **Circuit City Express** (unique state-of-the-art personal electronic equipment and gifts), **Wentworth Gallery** (an exclusive art gallery), **Eddie Bauer** (casual apparel for men and women), **Caché** (unique women's clothing and accessories), **Guess** (men's and women's clothing, shoes and accessories), **Deck the Walls** (print and frame shop), **Bath & Body Works** (bath and body products), **Nine West** (women's shoes) and **The Body Shop** (bath, body and cosmetics).

Other popular stores include **Ann**

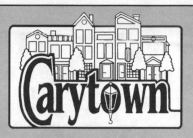

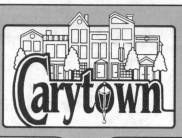

Taylor, Laura Ashley, Laura Ashley Child, The GAP/GAP Kids, Gymboree, The Limited, Sea Dream Leather, Britches of Georgetowne (exclusive men's clothing) and Brentano's (unique book store).

While you're here, you can order a fresh cup of gourmet coffee from The Coffee Beanery, Ltd. — the aroma is irresistible, and you can grab a quick bite to eat or a frozen yogurt at numerous fast food restaurants in The Food Court. If you prefer a more leisurely lunch or dinner, try Applebee's.

If you want to combine a movie with your shopping trip, the Ridge Theatre is just a few blocks away across Parham Road.

For shoppers' convenience, the mall offers "Regency Services" at the Concierge Desk. If you can't find something, or you're not sure if the mall has it, the staff will use a computerized listing of merchandise and services available in all of the mall's stores to help you locate it. Just call or Fax them a note, 740-SHOP or (800) 431-SHOP. Strollers, wheelchairs, coat check, gift registry, gift certificates, shopping bags, even disposable diapers for emergencies are available at the Concierge Desk on the upper level.

Mall hours are 10 AM until 9 PM, Monday through Saturday; and 12:30 PM to 5:30 PM on Sunday.

RIVER ROAD SHOPPING CENTER
6200 River Rd. at Huguenot Rd.

If you're looking for designer fashions for women, this is the place to shop. In the West End, the River Road Shopping Center features **Frances Kahn**, **Copeland's** and **Talbot's**.

The center also includes the **Kellog Collection** (home furnishings and accessories), Azzurro (Italian restaurant) and

The Butler's Pantry (takeout food, bakery and gourmet store). See the Restaurants chapter for more information.

Shop hours vary, but most are open 10 AM to 5:30 PM Monday through Saturday.

SHOPS AT WILLOW LAWN
5000 W. Broad St. at Willow Lawn Dr. 282-5198

At the intersection of Broad Street and Willow Lawn Drive near Staples Mill Road, Willow Lawn was a popular strip shopping center for many years and was remodeled several years ago to include an enclosed mall area and a food court.

Anchored by **Leggett**, **Tower Records and Video**, and **Barnes and Noble Bookstore**, Willow Lawn features more than 100 stores including **Chimney Corner** (bridal registry, fine furnishings and gifts), **Kitchen Kuisine** (Virginia products and wines, fine kitchen wares, gift baskets), **Britches Great Outdoors** and **Structure** (men's casual wear), **The Limited** (popular women's fashions), **Cocoanut Jewelry** (unique jewelry), **Kay-Bee Toys**, **Victoria's Secret**, **Rack Room Shoes** (variety of shoes for men, women and children), **The Nature Company** (ecological and earth gifts), **The Bombay Company** (classic home accessories and furnishings), **Picture Parts** (for framing and art) and **Lillian Vernon** (retail version of the catalogue operation).

The Food Court offers a dozen international eateries including the Seattle favorite Starbucks Coffee. While you're there, take a few minutes to watch the Cinnabon employees make fresh cinnamon buns. For a lively bar or a great salad, visit Ruby Tuesday Restaurant. You'll also find Belle Kuisine, Padow's Hams and Deli, and Chesapeake Bagel Bakery. There's also a four-screen movie theater here.

METRO RICHMOND

Shopping Spots

Advertising Supplement

Libbie & Grove

"On the Avenues"

Libbie & Grove

the very best of Richmond

CHESTERFIELD TOWNE CENTER

Hecht's, Leggett, Profitts and over 140 shops, services, and restaurants. Open daily 10-9, Sunday 12:30-5:30, Midlothian Turnpike at Huguenot Road, **794-4660.**

where good values are in the bag

Cloverleaf Mall

In Richmond, smart shoppers choose Cloverleaf. Where dozens of Richmond's favorite stores offer you quality merchandise at a reasonable price. And you don't have to walk miles to find just what you're looking for. There's also a food court and movie theater for your entertainment. When you add it all up, you'll see Cloverleaf's got good values in the bag.

JCPenney, Sears, Hecht's and over 80 shops and services.
Midlothian Tnpk. at Chippenham Pkwy. 276-8650
Open 10:00 - 9:00 Mon.-Sat., 12:30 - 5:30 Sun.

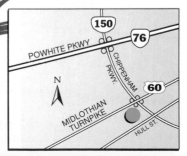

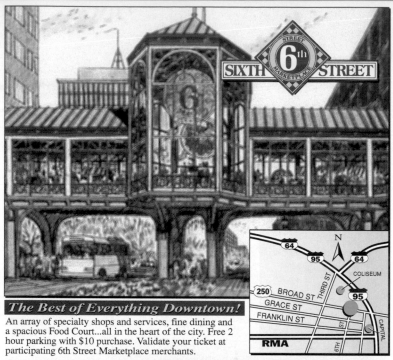

The Best of Everything Downtown!

An array of specialty shops and services, fine dining and a spacious Food Court...all in the heart of the city. Free 2 hour parking with $10 purchase. Validate your ticket at participating 6th Street Marketplace merchants.

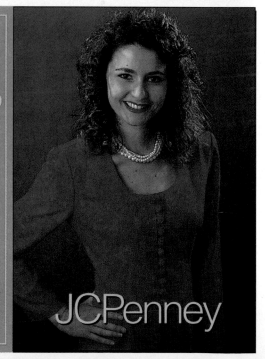

in Rome it's Via Veneto... in Beverly Hills it's Rodeo Drive...in Richmond it's Carytown

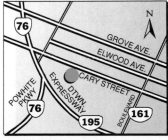

Carytown is unlike <u>any</u> other shopping experience in Richmond. No where else can you find the variety of shops and services in one place. So if you're tired of the same old mall scene, come to the truly different shopping alternative– Carytown!

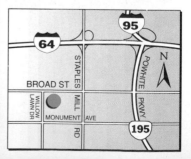

"*Willow Lawn Has Stores Like These?*"

If I'd Only Known...

IF YOU HAVEN'T BEEN TO WILLOW LAWN RECENTLY, YOU DON'T KNOW WHAT YOU'RE MISSING. WE'VE GOT EVERYTHING FROM FASHIONS TO RESTAURANTS TO PERSONAL SERVICES. WITH EASY ACCESS AND AMPLE, CONVENIENT PARKING. NOW THAT YOU KNOW, SHOP THE SHOPS AT WILLOW LAWN.

THE · SHOPS · AT
WILLOW LAWN

Open Monday - Saturday 10am to 9pm, Sunday 12:30 to 5:30 pm
West Broad Street and Willow Lawn Drive
(804)-282-5198

Barnes & Noble	Cocoanut Jewelry	Garden Botanika	Leggett	Native Cotton	Picture Parts	Structure
Belle Kuisine	CVS Pharmacy	GNC	Lechter's Housewares	Nature Company	Rack Room Shoes	Starbucks Coffee
The Bombay Company	the eagle's eye	Gloria Jean's Coffee Beans	Lillian Vernon	Order from Horder	Radio Shack	Tower Records & Video
Britches Great Outdoors	Express, Inc. Foot Locker	Kay-Bee Toys	The Limited Matthew's Hallmark		Ruby Tuesday Sassafras	Victoria's Secret

THE · SHOPS · AT
WILLOW LAWN

for
Fast, Fresh, Fun Eating...
Ukrop's
Carryout
cafe

At Ukrop's Westpark, Harbour Pointe, Ashland, Fountain Square, Chesterfield Meadows, Stony Point, Brook Run, Mechanicsville, Sycamore Square, The Village or Fresh Express downtown.

See our article in this Restaurant Section for addresses and phone numbers.

Store hours are 10 AM until 9 PM, Monday through Saturday; 12:30 PM to 5:30 PM on Sunday.

VIRGINIA CENTER COMMONS
10101 Brook Rd.
Glen Allen   266-9000

On U.S. 1 about a half-mile north of I-295, Virginia Center Commons is the area's newest shopping mall. Anchored by JCPenney, Profitt's, Leggett, Hecht's and Sears, the mall offers a growing number of popular shops, but it's not as crowded as some of the others in more populated areas.

Situated in a spacious open area of Glen Allen, the mall features terrazzo tile floors, brick columns, palm trees and sky lights. There are more than 80 stores here including Ingle's Nook (home accessories and gifts), Tailors Row (men's fashions), The GAP/GAP Kids (cotton clothing for all ages), Finish Line (value-priced sportswear and shoes), The Coffee Beanery (coffee shop), The Limited, The Limited Express, Structure, Bath & Body Works, Athlete's Foot (athletic shoes), Sea Dream Leather (leather clothes and accessories), Rees Jewelers (independently owned jewelry store), Things Remembered (keepsakes and gifts) and T-Shirts Plus (custom designed T-shirts).

Ruby Tuesday, the mall's full-service restaurant, is so popular that the average waiting time for a table is about an hour. There are also numerous fast food restaurants in the Food Court. Kids of all ages like to visit the Candy Express and Fun-N-Games arcade.

Virginia Center Commons also offers special events and family entertainment nearly every weekend, including the magical Santa's Castle, a favorite among children at Christmas. Frequent shoppers may participate in valuable prize drawings and receive a free gift when they spend $50 or more at the mall. The mall is also home to the Bear Footers, a walking club sponsored by Henrico Doctor's Hospital. All registered walkers may walk the mall from 7:30 AM until 10 AM Monday through Friday. Gift certificates, shopping bags and wheelchairs are also available. Ask for more information at the customer service booth.

Stores are open 10 AM to 9 PM, Monday through Saturday; 12:30 PM until 5:30 PM on Sunday.

Nearby Shopping

SOUTH PARK MALL
230 Southpark Cir.
Colonial Heights   *526-3900*
This beautiful shopping mall south of Richmond in Colonial Heights opened in 1989 and has grown so rapidly that it's known by some as a shopper's paradise. Anchored by **Hecht's**, **Leggett**, **JCPenney** and **Sears**, the mall offers about 90 stores and services. Restaurants include Morrison's Cafeteria and Spinnakers. There are also several fast food restaurants.

In addition to the 800,000-square-foot center, the Southpark complex includes two large strip shopping centers, Southpark Crossing and Southpark Square, plus ParkSouth, an office/service specialty center, and other outparcels that include **Wal-Mart**, a bank, restaurants and a building supplies store.

Southpark has a reputation for spectacular Easter and Christmas displays and attracts shoppers from out-of-state during these seasons. At Christmas, a special train transports visitors through a winter wonderland including an elves' workshop, a gold mine and caves. There's also a 32-foot-tall Christmas tree that stretches

high into the sky dome and Santa's house built into the side of a snow mountain. At Easter, the mall offers a similar train ride through seasonal exhibits.

Southpark is conveniently located directly off I-95 S. at Exit 54 (Temple Avenue). Stores are open 10 AM to 9 PM, Monday through Saturday; 12:30 PM to 5:30 PM on Sunday.

MASSAPONAX OUTLET CENTER
904 Princess Anne St.
Fredericksburg   *(703) 373-8853*
About 45 minutes north of Richmond at the intersection of I-95 and U.S. 1, the Massaponax Outlet Center opened in 1990 and offers about 30 brand name stores including **Springmaid/Wamsutta** (linens), **Bass Company Store** (shoes and apparel), **Izod** (men's and women's apparel), **Sassafras** (women's apparel), **Corning** (dishes and cookware), **Oneida** (silver), **Van Heusen** (men's and women's apparel) and **Kitchen Collection** (accessories). The area also includes a mini-golf course, a Comfort Inn and the Spotsylvania County Visitor's Center. Hungry shoppers will find a Cracker Barrel Restaurant, Aunt Sarah's Restaurant and a food court in the outlet center. Stores are open 10 AM until 9 PM, Monday through Saturday; noon to 6 PM, Sunday.

Williamsburg

There are many unique and special places to shop and browse in Williamsburg for clothing, crafts, home accessories, furniture, gifts and the like. The discount outlets are especially popular.

At **Berkeley Commons Outlet Center**, 5699 Richmond Road, you'll find top designer and fine name brand

clothing and other products at 20 to 70 percent off the usual market price.

At the **Williamsburg Outlet Mall**, U.S. 60 W. in Lightfoot, you'll find more than 60 factory outlet stores and food courts. Shops here also offer 20 to 70 percent off retail prices.

The **Williamsburg Pottery Factory**, on U.S. 60 about 5 miles west of Williamsburg, is a sprawling complex of 32 Quonset-style huts, outbuildings and warehouses with 8,000 parking places. It's not so much a factory as it is an international array of goods displayed along miles of shelves. You'll find pottery, but you'll also find fine crystal, plants, dried and silk flowers, baskets, microwave ovenware, folk art, woodwork, lamps, home accessories, glassware and more. People come here by the busload to shop 'til they drop.

Antiques

There are literally hundreds of antique stores within an hour's radius of the Richmond metropolitan area, and there are numerous weekend auctions where you might find a good deal. There are two areas in Richmond that are especially well known for their antique shops — downtown and U.S. 301 north of Richmond. Other popular antique areas include Carytown and U.S. 1 north of the city.

In the 300 block of Broad Street in downtown Richmond, you'll find **Gaslight Antiques** (unusual Victorian antiques), **Stuckey's Antique Emporium** (furniture, glassware, military items and jewelry), and **Berry's Antiques** (variety of antiques and collectibles). There's also a **Collectors' Old Book Shop** at 15 S. Fifth Street that sells out-of-print and rare books, and there are many more shops

nearby and throughout the downtown area. Contact Downtown Richmond, Inc., for a free brochure, 643-2824.

If you head north on U.S. 301, you'll find numerous antique stores and collectible shops, including the **Antique Village** (16 shops), **Hungry Eye Gallery** (paintings, art glass, jewelry and unique antiques) and **The Millstone** (American furniture before 1840 and Canton porcelain). Copies of a brochure that lists antique shops on U.S. 301 and U.S. 1 in the Hanover Courthouse and Ashland areas are available from most of the shops.

Governor's Antiques on Meadowbridge Road near I-295 is another popular shop, best known for its collection of antique architectural materials, furniture, glass and jewelry.

Wine and Beer Shops

Many of the grocery stores in the area carry large selections of wine and beer, but if you're looking for something special, these are some of the shops that are popular among Richmonders: **The Strawberry Street Vineyard** (407 N. Strawberry Street in the Fan), **The Butler's Pantry** (River Road Shopping Center), **J. Emerson, Inc.** (414 Libbie Avenue), and **Wine & Beer** (several locations around town).

Civil War Items

OWENS BOOKS
2728 Tinsley Dr.   *272-8888*

Owens Books offers thousands of Civil War books including new, used and rare editions. You'll find books on military history, Americana, Virginiana and the South, as well as fine art prints and maps. Free catalogues are available.

RICHMOND ARSENAL

7605 Midlothian Tnpk.   272-4570

This Civil War Shop will buy, sell or trade artifacts. They carry original muskets, carbines, accoutrements, buttons, canteens, uniforms, leather goods, bullets, artillery shells, prints, relics and metal detectors.

LAGOS, INTERNATIONAL

102 W. Broad St.   648-2017

In downtown Richmond, this shop features authentic African goods including clothing, jewelry, artwork, antique masks and wooden sculptures from African countries. Dupe, a native Nigerian, opened the store in 1991.

African-American Specialty Shops

ONE FORCE BOOKS

217 E. Clay St.   644-0332

Owned by Hermion White and Lee R. Johnson, One Force Books specializes in literature about African-Americans and Africans. You'll also find cards, artwork and prints. Workshops and lectures are scheduled periodically.

AFRICAN ART AND CLOTHING

Chippenham Mall   675-0664

This new shop owned by Adebayo, a native of Nigeria, carries clothing, kente shoulder pieces, crafts, wood carvings, greeting cards, wall coverings and decorative items made in Nigeria, Ghana, Mozambique and other African countries.

Oriental Markets

ASIAN & ORIENTAL FOOD STORE

6322 Rigsby Rd.   282 6677

FARE SHARE CO-OP MARKET

2132 W. Main St.   355-5919

HANGUK ORIENTAL STORE

Branche's Shopping Center
Broad Rock Rd.   231-1312

HUNG SIK CHOE FOOD STORE

316 N. Second St.   643-7867

ORIENTAL FOOD STORE & GIFT SHOP

4803 Forest Hill Ave.   233-7443

RICHMOND ORIENTAL MARKET

431 E. Belt Blvd.   231-7624

Consignment and Vintage Clothing

CLOTHES RACK
2618 W. Cary St.   358-4693
The Clothes Rack accepts donated and consignment clothing and household items.

THE HALL TREE
12 S. Thompson St.   358-9985
At the west end of Carytown, the Hall Tree accepts consignment clothing suitable for the shopping season. Shoppers can feel confident that items sold here have passed strict quality checks and are in excellent condition.

BYGONES VINTAGE CLOTHING
2916 W. Cary St.   353-1919
Next to the Byrd Theatre in Carytown, Bygones sells vintage clothing, accessories and jewelry for men and women.

CHILDREN'S MARKET & EXCHANGE
2926 W. Cary St.   359-6950
Th Children's Market and Exchange in Carytown buys seasonal second-hand clothing and equipment. (Meaning cribs, playpens, strollers, et al. Not belts, clips, shoes, socks, etc.) You'll find a range of sizes from infant to 14, plus cotillion dresses and jackets for young girls and boys. All items are in excellent condition.

EXILE
822 W. Grace St.   358-3348
This downtown store offers clothing, jewelry and collectibles from the '40s to the '70s.

HALCYON - VINTAGE CLOTHING
117 N. Robinson St.   358-1311
A Fan District favorite, this shop features clothing, jewelry and accessories for men and women from 1890 to 1950.

Other Special Stores

Many of our popular stores are included in the descriptions of the shopping areas and malls. These are some other special places that deserve mentioning.

IGNATIUS HATS
959 Myers St.   354-0726
A graduate of Virginia Commonwealth University, Joe Ignatius Creegan moved to New York City in the late 1980s to build his career as a milliner and then moved back to Richmond in the early 1990s. He creates and constructs one-of-a-kind hats. His trademark styles include peasant hats, scholar caps, head wraps and turbans. Accents include bells, fringe and tassels. Hats in stock are about $65; custom hats cost from $135 to about $200; and men's caps are about $35.

FESTIVAL FLAGS UNLIMITED, INC.
322 W. Broad St.   780-2221
In 1971, a flag of colorful design was flown for a party, and in 1975, another flag was flown to announce the birth of a son. Since then, the two flags have flown into a thriving business and created a decorative tradition in Richmond. Known for their unique designs and quality fabrication, owner Millie Jones and the staff at Festival Flags specialize in custom work as well as national and state flags. Free brochures are available.

ALPINE OUTFITTERS
7107 W. Broad St.   672-7879
This was one of the first stores in Richmond that specialized in outdoor equipment and apparel. You'll find skiing, climbing and camping equipment, canoes

and sailboards for sale or for rent. The staff offers free advice and is very knowledgeable about outdoor adventures in the area. They also have maps of trails in the Blue Ridge Mountains. We listed the West End store. Other stores are downtown and on South Side.

C.P. DEAN
3001 Cutshaw Ave.   355-6588

This was one of Richmond's first sporting goods stores offering apparel, equipment, trophies and accessories for billiards, soccer, tennis baseball, basketball, aerobics and other sports. We listed their West End location. There are several other stores throughout the area.

CIRCUIT CITY
8401 Midlothian Tnpk.   320-8888

Headquartered in Richmond, Circuit City carries appliances, radios, televisions, audio equipment and just about everything that's electronic. They also offer car stereo installations. It's known for having a great selection and competitive prices. There are several locations around town.

FRANCO'S
1013 E. Main St.   343-0010

Franco's has offered traditional clothing for men and women for more than 20 years in the Richmond area. We listed the downtown store. Another store is on Lakeside Avenue, and there's an outlet store on Westwood Avenue.

JEFFERSON CLOTHING
1418 W. Marshall St.   358-2167

Just off Broad Street near Virginia Commonwealth University, this family-owned store is known for its service-oriented sales staff and its meticulous alterations department. The men's depart-

ments dominate the store and offer better menswear suits, tuxedos, slacks, shirts, ties and accessories at discount prices. The second floor offers casual clothing from jeans to swimwear. There's also a small but well-stocked ladies' department that specializes in suits and accessories. Separates and dresses are also carried.

OUT ON A LIMB FOR THE BIRDS
600 England St. (Rt. 54)
Ashland   798-2022

This wild bird specialty shop features nesting houses, feeders, birdbaths, bird feed and roosting boxes. It's on Route 54, one block west of U.S. 1.

PLEASANTS HARDWARE
2024 W. Broad St.   359-9381

Established in 1915, Pleasants has a reputation for providing personal service and advice. They have "most anything," including one of the best selections of brass, porcelain and iron fixtures, knobs, keys, keyholes, hinges and other furniture hardware and fixtures in the area.

SAXON SHOES
1527 Parham Rd.   285-3473

In the Ridge Shopping Center, Saxon Shoes has the largest selection of shoes in Richmond. This store is also known for having hard-to-find sizes and designer shoes. Men's, women's and children's shoes are available.

STEIN MART
7801 W. Broad St.   672-8556
9746 Midlothian Tnpk.   330-3363

This small department store sells name-brand items at low prices, including ladies', men's and children's clothing, shoes and accessories, linens and household items.

MARTIN "THE COLLECTION"

3325 W. Cary St.   *353-1400*

This shop specializes in (a unique collection of) designer accessories and custom furnishings for the home. A custom interior design studio is upstairs.

T.J. MAXX

Midlothian Market   *330-3008*
9100 W. Broad St.   *346-3113*

This department store sells name-brand items at low prices and carries primarily men's, women's and children's clothing and some household items.

Inside
Restaurants

If you like to eat out, you've come to the right place.

The Richmond area is full of great dining establishments, and local restaurant reviewers surely must be gaining weight trying to keep up with the steady flow of new ones.

One caution: Just as new restaurants open, old ones occasionally close or change hours of operation. So, before you venture forth, a call ahead might be a good idea.

This guide focuses primarily on locally owned restaurants. The chain restaurants are all here in abundant supply. But we won't waste time telling you what you already know.

The dollar sign ($) with each restaurant entry is an indication of the probable cost of dinner for two people, without figuring in the addition of alcoholic beverage and tip. Lunch at most places costs about half that of dinner. The code works this way:

Less than $20	**$**
$21 to $35	**$$**
$36 to $50	**$$$**
$51 and more	**$$$$**

What follows is not a complete list of Richmond's good restaurants, but it will get you started. To help you hone in on places that suit your mood, we have broken this chapter into descriptive groupings numbered as follows:

1. Historic Settings
2. Continental
3. Seafood and Steaks
4. Seafood Specialists
5. Steak Places
6. Vegetarian
7. 24-Hours
8. Fan District Favorites
9. British Pubs
10. Chinese
11. Egyptian
12. Ethiopian
13. French
14. Greek
15. Indian
16. Italian
17. Japanese
18. Korean
19. Mexican/Southwestern
20. Vietnamese
21. Barbecue
22. Soul
23. Family Restaurants
24. Delis
25. Fondue
26. Pizza
27. Southern
28. Lunch Places
29. Sandwiches & Beer
30. Coffee Houses and Bagel Places
31. Other Casual Places
32. Something Different
33. Street Vendors & Food Courts
34. Carryout

35. Fast Food
36. Caterers

Restaurants accept VISA and MasterCard, and in some cases American Express and other credit cards, unless otherwise noted.

1. Historic Settings

INDIAN FIELDS TAVERN

Rt. 5 at Evelynton Plantation   829-5004
$$

Indian Fields Tavern is a great place to enjoy casual elegance in the country and excellent food. The innovative fare blends both traditional and new Southern cuisine and includes entrees like fresh fish, Crab Cakes Harrison (two crab cakes on grilled Sally Lunn bread with grilled Smithfield ham and hollandaise sauce), and a mixed grill of lamb, Surry sausage and quail with hunter's sauce. Its bread pudding is probably the best you'll ever sample.

The restaurant is just a short distance from the main entrance to Evelynton Plantation on Route 5, a scenic highway that meanders through the James River plantation country. Evelynton Plantation originally was part of William Byrd's expansive Westover Plantation and has been the home of the Ruffin family since 1847. A member of the family operates the tavern. With a cozy atmosphere inside and with outdoor dining on screened porches in spring, summer and fall, Indian Fields is a popular place, so it's wise to make reservations before you go. The restaurant is open seven days a week except for Mondays in January and February. Lunch is served daily from 11 AM to 4 PM, and dinner is served daily from 5 PM to 10 PM.

COACH HOUSE TAVERN

Rt. 5 at Berkeley Plantation   829-6003
$$$

Berkeley Plantation is part of a land grant awarded by James I in the early 1600s and was visited twice by President Lincoln when it was a base for the Army of the Potomac in 1862. Here, in the Coach House Tavern, you can enjoy a meal worthy of the country's first Thanksgiving, which took place on the grounds of the plantation in 1619. Specialties in-

Shockoe Bottom dining at its best.

Credit: Metro Richmond Convention and Visitors Bureau

clude pan-roasted oysters with Surry Bacon and cream in a warm puff pastry, grilled prime rib of veal and colonial onion soup in an edible bread bowl. Reservations are required for dinner and are suggested for lunch during the spring, summer and fall and on weekends. The restaurant is open Monday through Saturday from 11 AM to 3 PM and on Sunday from 11 AM to 4 PM.

FOX HEAD INN
1840 Manakin Rd. (Rt. 621)
Goochland   784-5126
$$$$

In Goochland County's horse country, the Fox Head Inn is in an 1880s farm house filled with fox hunting motifs and surrounded by a magnificent grove of oak trees. It is within easy reach of downtown Richmond via I-64. It's wise to get directions before you venture forth. The four-course, fixed-price menu features an array of elegant selections. Specialties include homemade desserts, such as Fox Hunter pie, and Sally Lunn bread. Reservations are required, and hours of operation are 5:30 PM to 10 PM Wednesday through Sunday. Coat and tie are requested. There is no smoking in the dining rooms.

HALF-WAY HOUSE
10301 Jefferson Davis Hwy. (U.S. 1)   275-1760
$$$

Midway between Richmond and Petersburg, this is an old country tavern built in 1760. Dinner is served in the brick-floored English basement. If you like Colonial Williamsburg, you have to see this place because it's the genuine article. The menu offers a selection of filet mignon, lobster and shrimp plus daily chef's specials. Reservations are suggested. Lunch is served Monday through Friday from

11:30 AM to 2 PM, and dinner is served nightly from 5:30 PM to 10 PM.

HENRY CLAY INN
114 N. Railroad Ave.
Ashland   798-3100
$$

With a columned portico overlooking the campus of Randolph-Macon College, the Henry Clay Inn captures the comfortable elegance of a bygone era. The dining room is small and homey and specializes in Southern specialties, breads and desserts. Before or after your meal you can browse through the inn's gift shop and art gallery that features the work of local artists and artisans. The inn is next to Ashland's vintage railroad station, and if you are lucky you can enjoy the sights of passing trains. Reservations are suggested. Lunch is served Monday through Saturday from 11 AM to 2:30 PM. Dinner is served Tuesday through Saturday evenings from 6 PM to 9 PM, and "Sunday dinner" is from noon until 3 PM. Private dining is available on request.

JAMES RIVER WINE BISTRO
1520 W. Main St.   358-4562
$$

Here, in the basement of what used to be the old Stonewall Jackson School (with an adjoining 70-seat garden patio), you'll find a blend of classic and modern cuisine including pastas, seafood, smoked and mesquite-grilled meats and an eclectic salad selection. Wine is the central part of the dining experience, and the wine list includes about 130 varieties, including those from vineyards in Virginia, California, Washington, Australia and France. James River Wine Bistro was chosen as one of Richmond's top 10 restaurants in 1994 and received *Wine Spectator's* award of excellence. Hours are 11:30 AM to

12:30 AM Tuesday through Saturday, and until 10 PM Sunday. A champagne brunch is served on Sunday. The restaurant is closed Monday.

LINDEN ROW INN

100 E. Franklin St.   *783-7000*
$$$

Linden Row, which dates to the 1850s, is said to be built on the site of the "enchanted garden" where Edgar Allan Poe played as a child and to which he refers in his poem "To Helen." Its restaurant is a unique hideaway in the midst of the city — for breakfast, lunch or dinner. It also has a nifty brick-paved patio sandwiched between the inn and dependencies, where meals are served in warm weather. The menu offers seafoods, steaks and three specialty items nightly. Diners can wait for their parties in comfortable double parlors filled with period furnishings. Reservations are suggested. Hours of operation are 6:30 AM to 11 PM Monday through Friday, and until 11:30 PM on weekends.

MR. PATRICK HENRY'S INN

2300 E. Broad St.   *644-1322*
$$$

This cozy inn on historic Church Hill is one block west of St. John's Church. It offers a gourmet restaurant on the main floor, a pub in the English basement and a garden patio. The fare is imaginative and innovative and includes fresh seafood, regional cuisine, homemade breads, desserts and soups. The boneless roasted duck with molasses and fresh berries served over wild rice cakes never fails to please. It is open Monday through Saturday for lunch from 11:30 AM to 2:30 PM, and for dinner from 5:30 PM to 10:30 PM. The restaurant is closed on Sundays, except for holidays. Reservations are suggested.

P.G.T. BEAUREGARD'S

103 E. Cary St.   *644-2328*
$$

You won't find Auntie Mame, but in this restaurant in an old block of E. Cary Street you will find an English-basement cafe/bar, a shady, brick-walled patio with fountain and an upstairs dining room that's stylish without being pretentious. The bar and patio are comfortable, Old South places to enjoy light fare for lunch on Monday through Friday from 11 AM to 5 PM, and for dinner Tuesday through Saturday from 5 PM to midnight. The upstairs dining room has some of the best food and service in Richmond. Called The Thai Room, it is open for dinner Tuesday through Saturday from 5 PM to 10 PM and features Thai dishes from start to finish — fare such as green curry chicken, ginger beef, shrimp with baby corn, soups and vegetarian dishes. The Thai chef is the genuine article.

THE CLOCK TOWER

1500 E. Main St. (Main Street Station)
$$$ *643-0445*

We've included The Clock Tower (formerly known as Scarlett Shockoe Kitchen) under "Historic Settings" because it's in Main Street Station, a Richmond landmark built in 1901, and because it is situated in historic Shockoe Bottom. The station's red tile roof and clock tower are a familiar sight to travelers moving north and south on I-95. Lunch, dinner and late-night menus feature crowd-pleasers such as grilled prawns with fennel linguine, grilled Las Cruces lamb, beef and pan-fried Chesapeake crab cakes.

The service and presentation are excellent, and the food is outstanding. While the upstairs (seating 160 persons) is designed for upscale dining, the downstairs (seating 120 persons) is designed to be casual and less expensive, with jump blues, swing and rock-a-billy music at night. Entry from Main Street is up the same stone stairs trod by Richmonders in a horse-and-buggy era when the wail of a locomotive whistle signaled the start of a great adventure. Convenient parking is available in a lot across the street or at night in state parking lots around the station. Lunch is served Tuesday through Friday from 12 to 2 PM, and dinner is served Tuesday through Saturday from 6 PM to 10 PM. Late-night mini-courses from the bar are available Tuesday through Saturday until 1 AM. Reservations are suggested. The Clock Tower is available for private parties.

2. Continental

THE ASSEMBLY
9th and Bank Sts.   788-0888
$$

This elegant, award-winning restaurant is in the Commonwealth Park Suites Hotel and is adjacent to Capitol Square and to the heart of the financial district. You'll have to watch yourself to stay within the cost figure indicated above, but it can be done. Service is impeccable and specialties include seafood, prime beef, chicken, veal braised in sherry and duck. Exquisite desserts are made in house. Reservations are suggested. Hours of operation are Monday through Saturday from 5:30 PM to 10:30 PM.

THE DINING ROOM AT THE BERKELEY
12th and E. Cary Sts.   780-1300
$$$

The food is superb, the service is attentive, the atmosphere is sedate and tranquil and it's an excellent place to watch everything that's going on in the heart of

Shockoe Slip. The menu includes items such as Sesame Chicken with Three-Mustard Sauce, Bengali Grouper, Veal Belges, Seared Marinated Tuna and Sirloin of Beef with Lump Crabmeat. The restaurant has an extensive wine list from a private collection. Breakfast is served until 10:30 AM, beginning at 7 AM Monday through Friday and at 7:30 AM on weekends. Lunch (including a Sunday brunch) is served from 11:30 AM to 2 PM. Dinner service starts at 6 PM and runs until 9 PM on Sunday, until 10 PM on Monday through Saturday. Reservations are suggested.

CAFFE GALLEGO
100 S. 12th St.   775-0882
$$

In James Center II, this restaurant has some seating in the atrium, providing the atmosphere of outdoor dining. Offerings include Shrimp Scampi, steak a la Pizzaiola, shrimp and scallops in a sun-dried tomato sauce, and the chef's seasonal appetizer and entree specials. Also offered is a lunch buffet, Monday through Friday, with hot entrees, soup, 16 salads and more! Breakfast, lunch and dinner are served, and hours are from 6:30 AM to midnight Monday through Friday, 7 AM to midnight Saturday, and 7 AM to 11 PM Sunday. Reservations are suggested for lunch and dinner.

DAVIS & MAIN
2501 W. Main St.   353-6641
$

A popular place, Davis & Main offers a full dinner menu until 1 AM. Specialties include fresh grilled poultry, seafood, beef and pork, grilled garden vegetables and fruit, dinner salads, pizzas, pasta of the day and excellent sandwiches. The menu offers a suggested wine to try with

Innsbrook
Restaurants

CORNER OF WEST BROAD & COX RD.

Innsbrook
R e s t a u r a n t s

CORNER OF WEST BROAD & COX RD.

 **Boychik's Deli**

Welcome to Boychik's - "A True New York Deli"
featuring delicatessen and appetizing foods direct from
New york Often Imitated - Never Duplicated

Boychik's *Famous* Box Lunch To Go
Any Regular Sandwich, Potato Salad, Pickle, Cookie
$5.²⁵

FREE DELIVERY
$10.⁰⁰ minimum order
8 am - 3 pm
Best & Cheapest Bagels in Town
Check Our Prices 1st

Lakepointe Shopping Center
4024-B Cox Road
/4/ 1090

 **Boar's Head**

HICKORY♥HAMS
HONEY GLAZED AND SPIRAL SLICED

"Hickory Hams Cafe At Innsbrook
Has Makings For Great Sandwiches"
Richmond Times-Dispatch

Join us for a selection of:
- *Delicious Sandwiches*
- *Fresh Salads*
- *Hot Soups*
- *Gourmet Desserts*
- *Party Trays*
- *Picnic Boxes Made to Order*

**We also feature the best spiral-sliced
Hams and Turkeys in Richmond.**

Perfect for the holidays
or your in a special occasion

4040 G. Cox Road
747-4534

COOL TREATS

Dairy Queen
We Treat You Right®

- **Ice Cream • Yogurt**
- **Specialize in custom frozen cakes**

Mon.-Thur. 10am.-10 pm.
Fri.-Sat. 10am.-10 pm.
Sun. 12noon-10 pm.

4028 N. Cox Rd   270-1375

DAKOTA'S

Family dining - bring the kids.
Enjoy the finest cut beef or
pizza from our wood burning
oven - lots of choices, dine in or
on our outdoor patio.

**Saloon Country Music &
Line Dancing
Mon-Sat**
Largest dance floor in
town. Live bands
Wed-Sat and lessons
Mon & Tues nights.

4036 Cox Rd
346-2100

each of the grilled entrees. The atmosphere is casual, yet pleasantly and unpretentiously sophisticated. Don't be discouraged if there's a waiting line during the normal dinner hour; it usually moves quickly. For a late-night place where the music doesn't get turned up, this is it. The price tag on the majority of menu items will bring you in within the cost figure shown above, but there are enticing exceptions that are more costly. Hours of operation are from 4 PM to 2 AM seven days a week.

DUJOUR

5806 Grove Ave.   285-1301
$$

A hospitable and accommodating place amid the Shops on The Avenues, duJour attracts a dedicated clientele. Extra seating capacity is added with a sidewalk cafe during warm-weather months. The innovative dinner menu features seasonal offerings of fresh fish, veal, beef, pasta, lamb, pork, chicken and vegetarian items. You may have to pick menu items carefully if you want to stay within the cost figure indicated above. But you can take a guest here with confidence, and it is *the* place for Sunday brunch. Hours are from 11:30 AM to 2:30 PM Monday through Sunday, and from 5:30 PM to 10 PM Monday through Saturday. Reservations are suggested.

THE FROG AND THE REDNECK

1423 E. Cary St.   648-FROG
$$$

Jimmy Sneed ("The Redneck" and former chef of the award-winning Windows on Urbanna Creek of early 1990s fame) and Jean-Louis Palladin ("The Frog" and formerly of Washington's Jean-Louis at the Watergate Hotel) have joined in this tour de force featuring regional

dishes and classic French touches. Specialties include fresh seafood, homemade pastas, rotisserie, soups and stews. American and French wines are featured, as are American and French versions of selected dishes. Cartoons of the Frog and the Redneck festoon the walls. Hours are 5:30 PM to 10 PM Monday through Thursday and 5 PM to 10:30 PM on Friday and Saturday. The restaurant is closed Sunday. Reservations are suggested, especially on Friday and Saturday and at prime times during the week. Smoking is not permitted.

LEMAIRE RESTAURANT

Franklin and Adams Sts. 788-8000, ext. 1139
$$$$

This restaurant in the Jefferson Hotel is perhaps the most elegant dining experience in Richmond. It includes seven different dining rooms, some large and some small enough that they often are booked for private dinners. Entrees include offerings such as salmon, filet mignon, venison and pheasant. Breakfast is served daily from 6:30 AM to 11 AM. On Monday through Saturday lunch is served from noon until 2 PM, and dinner is served from 5:30 PM to 10:30 PM. Reservations are suggested.

MILLIE'S

2603 E. Main St.   643-5512
$$

When you pull up in front of Millie's you'll probably think it's time to ask for a refund on this guide book. But be not dismayed. Millie's consistently draws rave reviews for its eclectic gourmet fare described as Fusion Cuisine. The dinner menu changes monthly and focuses on good value, fresh ingredients and presentation. A great wine and dessert selection puts Millie's on a special pedestal. Its ca-

sual diner style featuring superb Wall-O-Matic jukeboxes attracts a diverse crowd, and its weekend brunches have become a Richmond tradition. No reservations are accepted, but the wait is well worth it. Midday hours are 11 AM to 2 PM Tuesday through Friday and 10 AM to 3 PM Saturday and Sunday. At night it's 5:30 PM to 10:30 PM Tuesday through Saturday, and 5:30 PM to 9:30 PM on Sunday.

THE IRONHORSE
100 S. Railroad Ave.
Ashland   752-6410
$$$

The Ironhorse in Ashland draws customers from as far afield as Fredericksburg and Williamsburg. The owners are very hands-on, and this shows in the food and service and in the warm way you will be welcomed. The menu changes monthly and has included grilled duck, fresh seafood, lamb chops and certified Angus beef. The Caesar salads are whoppers. Lunch is served from 11:30 AM to 2:30 PM Monday through Friday. Dinner is served from 5:30 PM to 9 PM Tuesday through Thursday, and until 10

PM on Friday and Saturday. Reservations are suggested for dinner and are necessary on weekends.

THE TRACK
2915 W. Cary St.   359-4781

The Track is in the Carytown area across from the Byrd Theater and offers steak, seafood and special menu items amid a casual, relaxed atmosphere built around a horse-racing motif. A dependable and consistent source of good food, The Track is among Richmond's fine small restaurants — a quiet place for a great meal. Hours are 5:30 PM to 10:30 PM Monday through Saturday. Reservations are recommended.

THYME & SAGE
606 S. Leadbetter Rd.
Ashland   550-3400
$$

For starters you might begin with fried mushrooms, lump crab meat and cheddar cheese dip or seafood bisque. Entrees include fresh seafood, a variety of poultry dishes and pasta. Cajun dishes also have been added. Desserts are extensive and include 16 different kinds of cheesecake. Thyme & Sage has made a name for itself, and reservations are suggested especially for large parties. Lunch is served from 11 AM to 2:30 PM Monday through Friday, and dinner is served from 5 PM to 9 PM Monday through Saturday. The restaurant is in the Airpark Shopping Center just off I-95 near the Atlee-Elmont exit, but call for directions if you're not familiar with the area.

ISLAND GRILL

14 N. 18th St.   *643-2222*
$$

Here you will find a contemporary American grill with innovative tropical, Caribbean and Latin accents — all coupled with the flavors of "new world" cuisine and classic culinary techniques. For more details, see the listing for this restaurant under the heading "Something Different" (Section 32).

---

3. Seafood & Steaks

BUCKHEAD'S

8510 Patterson Ave.   *750-2000*
$$$

This wood-paneled, New York-style chophouse offers generous portions and one of Richmond's most extensive wine lists with choices to complement any of their appetizers, entrees or desserts.

The staff personifies Southern hospitality and possesses an uncommon knowledge of their food and wines.

Served in a relaxed environment,

Buckhead's offerings include salmon, steaks, chops and weekly specials. Buckhead's is open Monday through Saturday from 5 to 10 PM.

BYRAM'S LOBSTER HOUSE

3215 W. Broad St.   *355-9193*
$$

Byram's has been a Richmond mainstay since the days when you could count good restaurants on one hand. It continues to have a loyal following and is a great place for live lobster, other kinds of seafood, prime steaks, Greek food and pasta. Byram's doesn't skimp on the size of its servings. The salads are masterpieces and with them comes a basket of warm Italian bread and cornbread squares. Early Bird specials are offered from 3 PM to 6:30 PM Monday through Friday. The restaurant opens at 11 AM and stays open until 10 PM Monday through Thursday, until 11 PM on Friday and Saturday and until 9 PM on Sunday. Reservations are suggested.

CHETTI'S COW AND CLAM TAVERN

21 N. 17th St.   *644-4310*
$

It's casual and offers steaks, but the emphasis is more on things like the Shockoe Bottom Clam Bake (a sampler of steamed shellfish), crabs, oysters on the half shell, Spaghetti Chetti (with mussels, scallops, shrimp and clams) and spaghetti with clam sauce. It touts itself as the "Home of The Moister Oyster Shooter." Chetti's opens at 5 PM Tues-

Insiders' Tips

Flow with the crowd in Shockoe Slip's annual Pub Crawl.

BUCKHEAD'S

This Three-and-a-half star New York Chop House offers generous portions and one of Richmond's most extensive wine lists.

Served in a relaxed environment, Buckhead's specialties include salmon, steaks, chops, and weekly specials.

**8510 Patterson 750-2000 • Open Mon-Sat 5pm-10pm
Open for lunch August 1, 11:30-2:00**

day through Saturday and then stays open on these days until 2 AM. It's closed on Sunday and Monday.

SAM MILLER'S WAREHOUSE
1210 E. Cary St.   *644-5465*
🖒🖒

Sam Miller's is one of Shockoe Slip's originals. It offers a comfortable, club-like setting, live Maine lobsters, fresh Chesapeake Bay seafood, prime rib and other popular entrees. Reservations are suggested. Lunch is served from 11 AM to 1:30 PM Monday through Saturday, and Sunday brunch is offered from 11 AM to 5 PM. Dinner hours are 5 PM to 1:30 AM.

THE TOBACCO
COMPANY RESTAURANT
1201 E. Cary St.   *782-9555*
$$$

Without question, this is The Showplace of Richmond. If you want to dazzle clients, impress your visiting relatives or just plain have dinner at a place you'll never forget, this is it. The restaurant covers three floors of an old warehouse and is filled with more than 400 19th-century

artifacts and antiques, including a brass elevator from New York's Con Edison building that carries guests through a plant-filled atrium.

The menu is extensive: steaks, prime rib, lobster, veal, shrimp, scallops, salmon, rainbow trout, chicken, crab, Virginia ham and pasta. A second serving of prime rib is on the house if you finish off the first one. Lunch is served Monday through Saturday from 11:30 AM to 2:30 PM, and dinner is served from 5:30 PM until 10:30 PM Monday through Friday, until 11 PM on Saturday and until 10 PM on Sunday. The bar is open from 11:30 AM until 2 AM daily. Reservations for dinner are accepted until 7 PM.

4. Seafood Specialists

BROOKSIDE SEAFOOD
5221 Brook Rd.   *262-5716*
$$

Brookside is one of the best seafood experiences the Richmond area has to offer. Its extensive menu includes a variety of fresh local seafood cooked to perfection. The Brookside Special is a mix of scallops and shrimp cooked in generous portions with mushrooms and onions. The restaurant is open seven days a week from 11 AM to 10 PM. Reservations are suggested.

AWFUL ARTHUR'S OYSTER BAR
101 N. 18th St.   *643-1700*
$$

Awful Arthur's has a real fish-house atmosphere complete with a roll of paper towels at each table. It's very casual and specializes in soft shells, steamed crabs, oysters, clams, shrimp and fish but also offers steak, chicken and the Awesome Burger (six ounces of ground chuck). Hours are 11:30 AM to 2 AM weekdays, noon to 2 AM on Saturday and noon to midnight on Sunday.

BLUE POINT SEAFOOD
550 E. Grace St.   *783-8138*
$$

In 6th Street Marketplace and next door to the Carpenter Center, Blue Point offers fresh fish, crab and a variety of other dishes in a comfortable, wood-paneled atmosphere. The food and service are excellent, and Blue Point will introduce you to a number of new kinds of Caesar salads. Hours are 11:30 AM until 10 PM Monday through Thursday, until 10:30 PM on Friday and Saturday, and from noon until 9 PM Sunday. Reservations are suggested.

CRAB LOUIE'S SEAFOOD TAVERN
13500 Midlothian Tnpk.   *275-2722*
$$$

A lot of people swear by this place and its fresh seafood served in an 18th-century colonial tavern setting in the Sycamore Square Shopping Center. Specialties are fresh fish and crab entrees, plus homemade relishes. Hours are 11:30 AM until 9 PM Sunday, 11:30 AM until 10

PM Monday through Saturday. Reservations are suggested.

THE CRAB HOUSE
2601 Tuckernuck Dr.   *270-3555*
$$

If you're looking for hard shell crabs in a Maryland crabhouse atmosphere, this is the place to go. Other seafood also is available. Atmosphere is casual. The restaurant used to be known as Dailey's Crabhouse. Hours are noon to 9:30 PM daily. Reservations are recommended for parties of six or more.

SHIP'S CAFE
7035 Staples Mill Rd.   *262-9048*
$$

The menu includes a full range of seafood, including crab cakes, crab imperial, stuffed flounder, oysters, scallops and shrimp. Ship's Cafe is located where Skilligalee began and where the Outer Banks restaurant used to be. The nautical atmosphere is much the same. Midday hours are from 11:30 AM to 4 PM Monday through Friday, and dinner hours Monday through Saturday are from 5 PM to 10 PM. The restaurant is closed on Sunday.

SKILLIGALEE SEAFOOD RESTAURANT
5416 Glenside Dr.   *672-6200*
$$

Skilligalee is probably Richmond's most popular seafood place. Near Reynolds Metals' headquarters and within easy reach of downtown via I-64, it has five dining rooms, three working fireplaces and a saltwater decor that includes marine artifacts, ship models and decoys. The fare offers a complete seafood menu including soft shell crabs and shad roe in-season, five to six fresh fish daily, plus steaks. Reservations are suggested for parties of five or more. Hours are 11:30 AM to 10 PM Monday through Friday, 5 PM to 11 PM on Saturday, and 5 PM to 9 PM on Sunday.

SURF RIDER GRILL

1714 E. Franklin St.	*644-8704*
13548 Genito Rd.	*744-8446*

$$

If you like straight forward food served without fancy or trendy trimmings, then you'll like Surf Rider. Hush puppies come with entrees, and crab cakes are made without fillers. Side dishes are excellent and a blackboard lists an array of daily specials. The atmosphere is very casual. Dinner hours are 4 PM to 11 PM Tuesday through Saturday. Lunch is served only at the Shockoe Bottom location where Midday hours on weekdays are 11 AM to 3 PM.

5. Steak Places

GALLEGO STEAKHOUSE AT THE OMNI

100 S. 12th St.	*344-7000*

$$$

Hefty steaks, specialty dishes and healthy fare are the stars here. The atmosphere is reminiscent of an English hunting manor, featuring rich mahoganies, brocade upholstery and elegant brass.

The Gallego Steakhouse offers custom-designed menus for special catering, group dinner meetings and special occasion events. Dinner hours are Tuesday through Saturday 5 PM to 10:30 PM.

RUTH'S CHRIS STEAK HOUSE

11500 Huguenot Rd.	*378-0600*

$$$

In the restored manor house of Bellgrade Plantation, Ruth's Chris offers a comfortable ambiance that's suitable for family or business dining. The menu includes prime steaks and chops, plus live Maine lobster and seafood. Ruth's Chris

uses U.S. Prime corn-fed beef, which is only 5 percent of available beef. Portions are large. Desserts include hot apple pie and Raspberry Ruth, an ice cream freeze of vanilla ice cream and Chambord dusted with nutmeg. Hours are 5 PM until 10 PM Monday through Thursday, until 11 PM on Friday and Saturday and until 9 PM on Sunday. The restaurant lounge opens at 4 PM. Reservations are suggested.

JW'S STEAKHOUSE

500 E. Broad St.	*643-3400*

$$

In the Marriott Richmond, this stylish restaurant showcases aged, choice beef grilled over an open flame and served with a steak herb butter. The menu also includes double-cut veal chops, pasta with seafood pesto, Southwestern chicken, a rib platter and swordfish with Parmesan cheese. Soups and desserts are delicious. JW's is open 24 hours a day.

LONE STAR
STEAKHOUSE & SALOON

8099 W. Broad St.	*747-8783*
10456 Midlothian Tnpk.	*272-0391*

$$

While this is part of a chain, Lone Star Steakhouse gets rave reviews from local restaurant critics. The walls are wooden, the floor is plank, cold longnecks fill the tables and there's country music in the air. Waitresses wear "Don't Mess with Texas" T-shirts, and the menu features eight cuts of steak, chicken, ribs and a Bubba Burger. Here you'll find great steaks, and you'll have a great time. (And you can even throw peanut shells on the floor like everybody else does.) Lunch and dinner are served daily. Hours are flexible; please call in advance.

OUTBACK STEAKHOUSE

7917 W. Broad St.   527-0583
$$

Outback Steakhouse is part of a chain, but it is an immense favorite of locals. It has a comfortable, down-home atmosphere and a menu that's filled with big juicy steaks, chicken, ribs, chops and shrimp. The 14-ounce steak is called the "Crocodile Dundee," and other lingo and decor is suitably "Down Under." Hours are from 4 PM until 10:30 PM Monday through Thursday and until 11:30 PM on Friday. Saturday hours are from 3:30 PM to 11:30 PM, and Sunday hours are 1 PM to 10:30 PM. No reservations are taken.

6. Vegetarian

Vegetarian dishes have become so popular that most Richmond restaurants today have at least one or two vegetarian entrees on the menu. But if you're really into vegetarian fare, here are several places that might be of special interest:

GRACE PLACE

826 W. Grace St.   353-3680
$

Grace Place, a pioneer in its field in Richmond, today serves what it calls an "international vegetarian cuisine." The menu offers daily specials, plus home-made desserts and breads. Hours are 11 AM until 9 PM Monday through Thursday, and until 10 PM Friday and Saturday. Grace Place is closed on Sunday. The atmosphere is casual. Smoking is not permitted.

MAIN STREET GRILL

17th and Main Sts.   644-3969
$

This neighborhood spot, even though it serves meat during the day, has a vegetarian menu at night — and it serves Stone Age sourdough hotcakes for breakfast and has vegetarian specials at lunch. Customer favorites are refried beans, humus, tabouli and wheatberry chili. Across the street from the Farmers' Market, it features whatever is in season. It is closed on Monday, but otherwise its hours are from 6 AM to 3 PM and from 6 PM to the wee hours of the morning, except on Sunday when the schedule is 9 AM to 2:30 PM.

7. 24-Hours

AUNT SARAH'S

Eight locations in Greater Richmond
$

We can't resist continuing to mention Aunt Sarah's under this heading. For years it's W. Broad Street location was a favorite all-night gathering spot. Alas, no more. The good news is that all locations still remain open at least until 3 AM on Friday and Saturday. If you're looking for pancakes, breakfast dishes and homestyle cooking, this is the place to head, no matter what the hour, from 6 AM to 10 PM Sunday through Thursday and from 6 AM to 3 AM on Friday and Saturday.

Insiders' Tips

Sample the cuisine from dozens of area restaurants at A Taste of Richmond, an annual event on Brown's Island each spring.

CASABLANCA

6 E. Grace St.	648-2020
$	

Casablanca serves late-night fare until 6 AM Wednesday through Saturday. The restaurant is described in the "Something Different" section of this chapter.

THIRD STREET DINER

Third and Main Sts.	788-4750
$	

This place is a step back into the 1950s — diner atmosphere, jukebox and all. Richmonders love it, and the restaurant serves breakfast all day and all night, plus blue plate specials, homemade desserts and a few Greek dishes such as spanikopita and grape leaves. The atmosphere is casual, and the diner is open 24 hours a day, seven days a week.

And There Are Others . . .

Other 24-hour spots are **River City Diner** at 1712 E. Main Street (closed Mondays), **JW's Steakhouse** at the downtown Marriott, the **Waffle House** (seven locations), **Denny's** (in the West End and on the Southside off I-95), the **Broad Street Diner** on W. Broad Street at Malvern Avenue and **Steak 'n' Egg Kitchen** at Patterson Avenue and Three Chopt Road. **Waters Restaurant and Lounge** at 6518 Hull Street Road offers dartboards and pool tables in addition to breakfast from midnight to 4 AM on Friday and Saturday. More and more restaurants are open until 1 AM or 2 AM, so be sure to check hours of operation listed throughout this chapter if you're in search of a late-night repast.

8. Fan District Favorites

AVALON

2619 W. Main St.   353-9709
$$

Avalon is stylish in atmosphere and comprehensive in its variety of great food and drink. Innovative cuisine is emphasized. On the menu you'll find escargo, crab cakes, filet mignon and chicken dishes, plus delicious pastas and seafood salads. It has a wide selection of microbrewery beers, and the restaurant's wine selections are excellent. Dinner hours daily are from 5 PM to 2 AM. Saturday brunch is from 11 AM to 4 PM; on Sunday from 9 AM to 4 PM.

BOGART'S

203 N. Lombardy St.   353-9280
$

Specialty sandwiches and burgers are mainstays of this cafe, known for its casual atmosphere and walls covered with Bogart movie posters. Hours are 11:30 AM to midnight Monday through Friday. The cafe is open Monday through Thursday from 11:30 AM to midnight and Friday and Saturday from 11:30 AM to 2 AM (food is served until 1 AM) Bogart's opens its popular Back Room jazz/blues club Friday and Saturday nights with dinner served from 6 PM to 11 PM and music from 9:30 PM to 1:30 AM. The club offers American grill cuisine, has a $5 minimum purchase per person and does not allow anyone younger than 21 after 9 PM. Reservations are suggested.

CAFFE DI PAGLIACCI

214 N. Lombardy St.   353-3040
$$

Caffe Di Pagliacci is a great place for great Italian food, from the traditional to the classic gourmet. For more informa-

tion, see the restaurants' listing under the head "Italian" (Section 16).

COMMERCIAL TAPHOUSE AND GRILL

111 N. Robinson St.   359-6544
$ - downstairs, $$$ - upstairs

Downstairs you'll find the focus on the restaurant's unusual selection of international beers and a spirited crowd enjoying light meals. Upstairs is a gourmet dining room with a short but eclectic menu served in an atmosphere that is reminiscent of a quiet, avant-garde New York restaurant. It does not serve lunch; hours are 4:30 PM to 1 AM daily.

HELEN'S

Robinson and Main Sts.   358-4370
$$$

Helen's is a comfortable and eclectic place with a lot of personality, even sort of a 1920s bistro feel. The food is great and includes grilled salmon, roast loin of lamb and Peking chicken. The restaurant serves dinner only and is closed Sunday and Monday. Hours vary; please call in advance.

JAMES RIVER WINE BISTRO

1520 W. Main St.   358-4562
$$

This bistro serves classic and modern cuisine including an eclectic salad selection. As the name suggests, wine is the central part of the dining experience here. See Historic Settings in this chapter for details (Section 1).

JOE'S INN

205 N. Shields   355-2282
$

Joe's is an enduring (about 40 years) Fan favorite that offers breakfast, sandwiches, Spaghetti a la Joe and a la Greek, subs and homemade dishes. The atmosphere is casual, but it gets very busy at night, so be sure to put your name on this list for a table as soon as you walk in the door. Hours are 7 AM to 2 AM seven days a week.

JOHN & NORMAN'S

2525 Hanover Ave.   358-9731
$

This restaurant is famous for its breakfasts and its homestyle lunches and dinners. Hours are 6 AM until midnight Tuesday through Saturday, and until 4 PM Sunday. It's closed on Monday.

NOT BETTY'S

2401 W. Main St.   359-4404
$

Not Betty's serves up continental, Southern and Southwestern specials along with exhibits by local artists. The atmosphere is casual. Lunch is served during the week from 11:30 AM to 2:30 PM Monday through Friday, and brunch on Sunday is at the same time. Dinner is served every day from 5 PM to midnight.

PUZZLES

301 N. Robinson St.   359-6501
$$

Here you'll find innovative cuisine in a casual atmosphere. The diversity of the menu offers a range of selections, usually including a half-dozen entrees and a daily special, plus a number of light meals. Service is attentive. Desserts are super. Puzzles is always a pleasant experience. Dinner is served from 5 PM to 11 PM Monday through Saturday. Reservations are required for parties of six or more persons.

ROBIN INN

2601 Park Ave.   353-0298
$

The service here is fast, the prices are reasonable and the restaurant has been family-operated for about 30 years. Patrons come from all over town. Specialties include spaghetti, lasagna and pizza. Robin Inn isn't fancy, but it is a place where you'll immediately feel comfortable and at home — and the food is great. Hours are 11 AM to 10 PM Tuesday through Sunday.

SIDEWALK CAFE

2101 W. Main St.   358-0645
$

Sidewalk Cafe features spaghetti, Greek fare and quick-service deli sandwiches. Daily specials include pasta dishes and subs. It's an inexpensive neighborhood place that attracts a lively crowd. We've listed it under Fan District Favorites because that's just what it is — home base for a dedicated band of regulars. It is open seven days a week from 11 AM to 2 AM.

TUNE'S

2600 W. Main St.   358-7843
$

Seafood, beef and deli items are served amid a deli/bar atmosphere. It's a well-patronized place and features a great outdoor patio and raw bar offering oysters on the half-shell, fresh crab meat and King Crab legs. Hours are 11:30 AM to 2 AM.

SOUTHERN CULTURE

2229 W. Main St.   355-6939
$$

This gastronomic experience blends Cajun, Creole, Caribbean, Mexican and pure Southern flavors with confidence and flair. Dessert portions are large enough to serve two. There's a large bar downstairs with lots of booths and an upstairs (quieter) main dining room. The atmosphere is reminiscent of New

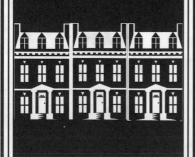

FAN
RESTAURANTS

J A M E S ● R I V E R

W i n e
B I S T R O

358-4562
1520 W. MAIN ST.

STAFFORD ST. STATION

Restaurant & Bar
2329 West Main St.
Richmond, VA 23220

359-2455

PICCOLA
● ITALY

PIZZA & SUBS
WE DELIVER

355-3111
110 W. Main Street

Avalon

2619 West Main Street
Richmond, Virginia 23220
Phone: 353-9709

Orleans with a few touches of 1950s kitsch. Hours are 5 PM to 2 AM daily.

STAFFORD STREET STATION

Stafford and W. Main Sts.   359-2455
$$

"All aboard!" The theme here is trains and anything to do with railroading. The menu is brief and focuses on regional American cuisine, like New Orleans pasta jambalaya. Sandwiches include the restaurant's signature Stafford Black and Blue, a blackened chicken breast with blue cheese on a kaiser roll. Hours are 11:30 AM to 1 AM Monday through Friday, 4 PM to 1 AM Saturday, and 10:30 AM to 2:30 PM Sunday.

STRAWBERRY STREET CAFE

421 Strawberry St.   353-6860
$

Strawberry Street Cafe is popular for its bathtub salad bar, homemade burgers, pastas, vegetarian lasagna, beef and

RichmondSpeak

If you want to understand and speak the Richmond language, you need to be familiar with these idiosyncrasies:

The River: This is the place where many Richmonders have summer homes and where they go to boat or fish. It can mean any one of the rivers flowing into the Chesapeake Bay: usually the Rappahannock, the Potomac, the York or the Piankatank, or any one of the creeks flowing into these rivers, or any bay or inlet attached thereto. It can also be used to refer to locations on the Chesapeake Bay proper. The word "river" is pronounced so that it sounds like "rivah." When Richmonders refer to rivers closer to home, such as the James and the Chickahominy, they usually refer to them by name, but not always, especially in the case of the James.

The Beach: This, for the most part, means Virginia Beach. But, in some cases, it can mean resorts on North Carolina's Outer Banks. Seaside vacations up north are at places called "The Shore" or "The Cape." In Virginia, it's "The Beach."

The Club: This usually means the prestigious Commonwealth Club, but it also can mean the Country Club of Virginia.

The Slip: This is shorthand for Shockoe Slip.

The Bottom: Likewise, shorthand for Shockoe Bottom.

Powhatan: This, among other things, is the name of a famous Indian chief and of a nearby county. It is "POW-a-tan," never "pow-HATAN."

Powhite: This one looks pretty simple. But it's not. Even many Richmonders have a problem pronouncing it properly. It should not be pronounced so that it sounds like a synonym for "white trash." You're supposed to say it — and we think we've got this right — so it comes out "POW-hite," or something reasonably close (with the emphasis on the "POW," as in Powhatan). It's worth working on, because one of the main arteries in the Richmond area is the Powhite Expressway, a route you may find yourself referring to frequently.

Henrico: This is the name of one of the counties in the Richmond area. It is pronounced "Hen-RYE-co," never "HENRY-co."

Staunton: When you pronounce the name of this community in Virginia's Shenandoah Valley, be sure you do not pay any attention to the letter "u" in the middle. It's "Stanton."

Southside/South Side: The part of the state of Virginia to the south of Richmond is the Southside (all one word), or Southside Virginia. The part of the Richmond metro area that lies south of the James River is the South Side (two words).

The Medical College: This refers to the Medical College of Virginia. This usage has slipped in recent years, and people now tend to say "MCV" instead, a term that can mean the Medical College of Virginia or the giant Medical College of Virginia Hospitals.

Vepco: Even though the name of the local electric utility is Virginia Power, lots of people still can't shake calling it "Vepco," the shorthand name used in the days when the utility was Virginia Electric & Power Company.

Nickel Bridge: This is the Boulevard Bridge. The toll to cross it used to be 5¢.

chicken. It has a casual atmosphere, a large wine selection and a children's menu. Local artists do Impressionistic chalkboard art. Burgers and quiche are half-price Monday night. Lunch is from 11:30 AM until 2:30 PM Monday through Friday. Brunch on Saturday and Sunday is served until 4:30 PM. Dinner is from 5 PM until 10:30 PM Sunday through Thursday and until midnight on Friday and Saturday. Reservations are suggested for parties of six or more.

---

9. British Pubs

FOX AND HOUNDS BRITISH PUB

10455 Midlothian Tnpk.   272-8309
$$

Steak and kidney pie, shepherd's pie, fish and chips and a lot of American options are here along with a billiard room and cozy dining in The Library. Hours are 11:30 AM to 2 AM daily.

MATT'S BRITISH PUB

109 S. 12th St.   644-0848
$$

Here you'll find things such as Scotch Pudding (beef tips, sauteed onions and English beef sausage in Burgundy sauce) and Cornish pasties (shredded beef and vegetables wrapped in a pie shell with Burgundy sauce). Hours are 11 AM to 4 PM and 5 until 10 PM Monday through Saturday, except until 11 PM Friday and Saturday.

PENNY LANE PUB

207 N. 7th St.   780-1682
$

Penny Lane has seven imported beers on tap and offers British fare, steaks, chops, lamb and seafood. The atmosphere is informal and the owner and his staff are attentive. Hours are 11 AM to 2 AM Monday through Friday and from 4 PM to 2 AM Saturday. Reservations are recommended for parties of four or more on weekends.

POTTER'S PUB
7007 Three Chopt Rd.   282-9999
$$

British pub dishes here include steak and mushroom pies, and fish and chips. Steak and seafood also are on the menu. Potter's is a popular place at night, and the crowd sings along with the band Tuesday through Saturday. Lunch is from 11:30 AM to 2:30 PM Monday through Friday. Nighttime hours are 4 PM to 2 AM Tuesday through Saturday and 4 PM to 11 PM Monday. Potter's Pub is closed Sunday. Reservations are recommended.

10. Chinese

CHINA KITCHEN
2345-B Atlee Rd.   746-9103
$

The decor is simple and unpretentious, pop Chinese tunes play in the background, and the food is excellent. The menu is extensive and offers combination meals. Many customers come in for carryout orders. Hours are from 11:30 AM until 9:30 PM Sunday through Thursday and until 11 PM on Friday. Sunday hours are 4 PM to 11 PM.

EMPIRE SZECHUAN GOURMET
4917 E. Nine Mile Rd.   226-8026
$

Empire Szechuan offers a colorful dining experience along with desserts that include fried bananas topped with orange-flavored sugar. Hours are noon to 9 PM on Sunday, 5 to 10 PM Monday through Wednesday, and 11:30 AM to 10 PM Thursday and Friday.

GOLDEN DRAGON
3028 W. Cary St.   359-4062
$$

This Chinese restaurant is a bit of an adventure with some unusual and exotic dishes on the menu that you might not expect to find. The food is well prepared, and sauces are excellent. Reservations are not required. Lunch hours are from noon until 3 PM Tuesday through Saturday and from 11:30 AM until 3 PM Sunday. Dinner is served from 5 PM to 10 PM.

JOY GARDEN
2918 W. Broad St.   358-8012
$

For many years Joy Garden was Richmond's only Chinese restaurant. Its specialties include Cantonese, Szechuan and Hunan dishes. Joy Garden opens at 11 AM Tuesday through Saturday and at noon on Sunday. Closing time is 10:45 PM. Reservations are suggested for dinner and weekends.

LITTLE SZECHUAN
4702 Forest Hill Ave.   233-7250
$$

The portions are large, and the food is definitely Szechuan, all in a neighborhood restaurant setting. Hours are 11:30 AM to 10 PM Tuesday through Thursday and on Sunday, and until 11 PM Friday and Saturday.

MANDARIN PALACE

2811 Stratford Hills Shopping Center   272-8020
$$

Don't let the shopping center address scare you off. Established by the former chef for a U.S. Ambassador, the restaurant is a longtime Richmond favorite and is located not far from the Forest Hill Avenue exit on the Powhite Expressway. Lunch and dinner are served daily and you usually do not need reservations.

PEKING PAVILION

1302 E. Cary St.   649-8888
$$

In the heart of Shockoe Slip, this restaurant offers an elegant environment and Mandarin, Szechuan and Hunan cuisine. Lunch hours are 11:30 AM to 2 PM Monday through Friday, and on Sunday. Dinner is served from 5 PM to 9:45 PM Monday through Friday, until 10:30 PM on Friday and Saturday, and until 9:30 PM Sunday. Reservations are suggested.

PEKING RESTAURANT

5710 Grove Ave.   288-8371
8904-F W. Broad St.   270-9898
$

With its attentive service and good food, Peking Restaurant has developed a loyal clientele. The menu covers a wide range from Peking specialties to Szechuan, Mandarin and Hunan dishes. Hours are from 5 PM until 9:45 PM Sunday through Thursday and until 10:45 PM Friday and Saturday. The W. Broad Street restaurant serves lunch Monday through Friday from 11:30 AM to 2:15 PM and brunch on Sunday from 11:30 AM to 2 PM

TIKI-TIKI RESTAURANT

8917 Patterson Ave.   740-7258
$$

Tiki-Tiki offers Cantonese, Szechuan, Polynesian and American dishes served in an Oriental atmosphere. Hours are 11:30 AM until 11:45 PM daily.

HUNAN EAST GOURMET

4415 W. Broad St.   353-1001
$

This restaurant serves an all-you-can-eat lunch buffet daily, as well as dinner. It is very popular with Richmonders who know good value and good food, and it features Hunan and Szechuan cuisines. Hours are 11 AM to 10 PM Monday through Friday and until 11 PM Saturday. Sunday hours are from 11:30 AM to 10 PM.

CHINA PANDA

616 N. Sheppard   359-0346
$

At the corner of Park Avenue and Sheppard, a place Richmonders will remember as the home for many years of the Rainbow Inn, the China Panda's menu selections range from pepper steak to chicken with broccoli. Seating capacity is limited, but prices are reasonable. Hours are 11 AM to 10 PM Monday through Saturday.

Pig out at the Rib Festival and the Greek Festival. Both are annual events.

YUM YUM GOOD

5612 Patterson Ave.   *673-9226*
$$

The name, you might think, is a bit silly. But the atmosphere is warm, and the food and service are critically acclaimed. The luncheon menu features a long list of specials, and the evening menus offers Hunan, Cantonese and Szechuan dishes, plus some interesting variations. Hours are 11 AM to 10 PM Monday through Thursday, until 11 PM on Friday, and from noon until 10 PM on Sunday. Reservations are not required.

CHINESE FAST FOOD

Two popular places for fast-food counter service and carryout Chinese food are **Hunan Express** at 10833-B W. Broad Street and **Ming's Dynasty** in the Hungry Brook Shopping Center at Parham Road and U.S. 1.

11. Egyptian

CLEOPATRA

7227 Jefferson Davis Hwy.   *275-6501*
$

The menu until 5 PM features such items as kofta (charbroiled ground beef with spices), falafel (a fried vegetable patty), steak in a sack, chicken in a sack and chicken shish kabob, plus traditional sandwiches, subs, hamburgers and cold plates. After 5 PM Egyptian dishes take center stage along with steaks, Virginia ham, spaghetti, chicken parmigiana and shrimp parmigiana. Hours are from 11 AM to 10 PM daily.

12. Ethiopian

YE ETHIOPIA INJERA

2923 W. Cary St.   *358-6609*
$

Injera is a crepe-like bread used in lieu of utensils to scoop up distinctive Ethiopian cuisine that includes beef, lamb, chicken, vegetables and lentils. The restaurant offers two types of injera, one made from tef, an Ethiopian flour somewhat sour in taste, the other from traditional white flour. Hours are 10 AM to 11 PM Monday through Saturday.

13. French

LA PETITE FRANCE

2912 Maywill St.   *353-8729*
$$

Marie Antoinette and Paul Elbling brought gourmet French cuisine to Richmond when they opened La Petite France a quarter of a century ago. They, and their restaurant, have become Richmond institutions. You can't go wrong here if you like great food! Hours are 11:30 AM to 2 PM and 5:30 PM to 10 PM Tuesday through Friday, and 5:30 PM to 11 PM on Saturday. The restaurant is closed Sunday and Monday. Reservations are strongly suggested.

Insiders' Tips

For a change of pace, try lunch with a Japanese flair at the Lora Robins Tea House at the Lewis Ginter Botanical Garden.

14. Greek

ATHENS TAVERN

401 N. Robinson St.   353-9119
$

The Athens Tavern was the original Greek restaurant in Richmond. Our friends who really know Greek fare say it is the best in town. If you're looking for good guvetsi, baklava, moussaka and other great food in a tavern atmosphere, why not check out the original article? Dinner is served from 5 PM to 11 PM every day. Reservations are recommended for large parties.

THE CRAZY GREEK

1903 Staples Mill Rd.   355-3786
$

This is a busy place, maybe because they serve Italian as well as Greek dishes. Portions are generous, prices are extremely reasonable, and the restaurant is ꞏꞏ ꞏꞏ ꞏꞏꞏꞏꞏ ꞏꞏ ꞏꞏꞏ ꞏꞏꞏꞏꞏꞏ ꞏꞏ ꞏꞏꞏꞏꞏ 11 PM Monday through Saturday. Reservations are recommended for parties of five or more.

DENA'S GRECIAN RESTAURANT

11314 Midlothian Tnpk.   794-9551
Sassafras Shopping Center
$$

Dena's offers Greek as well as American and Italian cuisine in a casual atmosphere. The food is top-class, and the service is excellent. The location is next to Chesterfield Mall. Hours are 11 AM to 10 PM Monday through Friday, and 3 PM to 10 PM Saturday. The restaurant is closed Sunday. Reservations are recommended for parties of five or more.

THE GREEK ISLANDS RESTAURANT

10902 Hull St.   674-9199
$

Restaurant critics rave about this place as one of the best restaurants in town. The Greek Islands is family-operated, and the bread is homemade. Specialties include chicken lemonato, stuffed grape leaves, lamb chops and Shrimp Mikonos. The restaurant opens at 5 PM daily and stays open until 10 PM except on Friday and Saturday when it doesn't lock the doors until 11 PM. Reservations are suggested.

KONSTA'S RESTAURANT & LOUNGE

2526 Floyd Ave.   359-3122
$$

Veal, Angus beef, seafood and Greek and Italian specialties are served amid casual, upscale surroundings that include stained-glass windows, cherry wood paneling, marble-top tables and brass and glass accents. Dinner is served seven days a week, and lunch is served Monday through Friday. Reservations are suggested.

STELLA'S

411 N. Harrison St.   355-3395
$$

A popular place in the VCU area, Stella's offers Greek food, seafood and pasta in a casual atmosphere. Hours for lunch and dinner are 11 AM to 10:30 PM Monday through Thursday, 11 AM to 11 PM Friday and 5 to 11 PM Saturday. Reservations are recommended for parties of five or more.

ZORBA'S

9068 W. Broad St.   270-6026
$

The fare here is not intended to be gourmet, but for those who want to savor big platters of Greek and Italian specialties. Doggie bags are so common the staff offers to box leftovers before one even digs in. Zorba's is open daily for lunch and dinner.

15. Indian

BOMBAY CURRY HOUSE
4401 W. Broad St. 359-0054
$

Bombay Curry House, even though it is one of the newer restaurants serving Indian fare, gets excellent reviews. Hours are from midday to 7 PM Monday through Thursday and 10 AM to 7 PM Friday and Saturday. It is closed on Sunday.

HOUSE OF DOSA
605 McGuire Ctr. (Southside Plaza) 233-3444
$

The House of Dosa is at the rear of the Indian Super Market in Southside Plaza and is more of a back room that serves food than a restaurant. Entry is through the store, amid the aroma of foods and spices, and you pay at the store's cash register when you leave. The menu is extensive, but it helps if you know a little bit about Indian food before you go. Personal checks are accepted, but no credit cards. Hours are from noon to 8 PM Thursday, from 10 AM to 9 PM Friday and Saturday, and from 11 AM to 7 PM Sunday.

INDIA HOUSE
2313 Westwood Ave. 355-8378
$

Entrees include Indian specialties made with chicken, lamb, vegetable, rice and seafood. The restaurant gets consistently excellent reviews and is one of the few restaurants in town to make all of the Critics' Choice lists. Lunch hours are 11:30 AM until 3 PM Monday through Friday, and dinner is served from 5:30 PM to 10 PM Monday through Saturday.

PASSAGE TO INDIA
6856 Midlothian Tnpk. 745-5291
$

At Passage to India you can specify how you want your curry: mild, medium or hot. The cuisine is excellent and the menu is wide-ranging. Restaurant critics love this place. Lunch is served from 11:30 AM until 3 PM Monday through Saturday and dinner is served from 5 PM to 10 PM every day.

FAROUK'S HOUSE OF INDIA
3033 W. Cary St. 355-0378
$

Farouk's was Richmond's first Indian restaurant and serves North Indian food in a warm, friendly atmosphere. Lunch is from 11:30 AM to 2 PM daily, and dinner is from 5 PM to 10:30 PM daily.

16. Italian

AMICI RISTORANTE
3343 W. Cary St. 353-4700
$$

Amici is truly one of the greatest restaurants in town. The service, ambiance and food are all excellent — a real dining experience. The extensive menu includes fresh homemade pasta, seafood, veal and game. Amici's classic approach to Northern Italian cooking and its attractive presentations make every meal one to remember. Reservations are a must. Dinner is served beginning at 5:30 PM until 10 PM or 11 PM every day.

DEFAZIO'S
4032-B Cox Rd. 747-5500
Innsbrook
$

Specialties include Northern Italian food, veal, local seafood, spit-roasted chicken, beef and what DeFazio's calls "the best Grand Marnier souffle in the state." The atmosphere is casual. Hours are 11:30 AM to midnight, and reservations are suggested.

CAFFE DI PAGLIACCI
214 N. Lombardy St.   353-3040
$$

This cozy, award-winning neighborhood restaurant, located in the Fan District, serves homemade Italian fare from the traditional to the gourmet. Family-owned and operated, its specialties include fresh pasta, seafood, veal and incredible desserts, plus espresso and cappuccino. Hours are 5 PM to 11 PM Monday through Saturday. Reservations are suggested.

CATALDO'S
3416 Lauderdale Dr.   360-1324
$

With an Italian trattoria atmosphere, Cataldo's is in the Shops at Wellesley shopping center in an upscale part of Henrico County. It has a large neighborhood following for its excellent ba-.... .... 11 30 AM to 10 PM.

FIGARO'S
14235 Midlothian Tnpk.   379-0910
$

This light, bright trattoria bridges two worlds in that it appeals to serious diners with excellent gourmet fare and to casual diners and take-out clientele with delicious pasta and pizza. Hours are 11 AM to 10 PM Monday through Thursday, until 2 AM on Friday and until 11 PM Saturday and Sunday. Reservations are suggested.

FRANCO'S RISTORANTE
9031-1 W. Broad St.   270-9124
$$

The Northern and Southern style Italian menu here is vast and varied. Classic parmigianas, fra diavolos and fettuccines are expertly executed by owner Paolo Randazzo. Servings are large, and the res-

taurant is a favorite of local critics (and of visiting celebrities such as Frank Sinatra). Lunch is served from 11:30 AM to 2:30 PM Monday through Friday, and dinner Monday through Friday is served from 5:30 PM to 10 PM.

ITALIAN OVEN
10921 Midlothian Tnpk.   379-1400
8982 Quioccasin Station
Shopping Center   740-1400
$

This restaurant is part of a chain, but we've included it because some of our friends consistently rave about it. The restaurant has an exhibition-style pizza-making area and two wood-fired ovens used to prepare delicious fancy and traditional pizzas, strombolis, calzones and Italian rounds of tomato, mushroom and garlic breads. There are more than 20 great pasta dishes, large salads, Italian sandwiches and an appetizer called Fryed Zucchini, named for the chain's founder, Jim Frye. The atmosphere is cheery, bright and children-friendly. Hours are 11 AM until 10 PM Sunday through Thursday and until 11 PM on Friday and Saturday.

JULIAN'S
2617 W. Broad St.   359-0605
$

Julian's opened its doors on W. Broad Street in 1947 and made possibly the first pizza in Richmond. It is family-owned, offers homemade bread and pasta and has built a stable reputation that Richmonders have come to count on. Hours are from 11 AM to 10:30 PM Sunday through Thursday, until 11:30 PM Friday, and from noon until 11:30 PM Saturday. Julian's is closed on Monday. Reservations are recommended for groups of eight or more.

HUGO'S BISTRO

6624 W. Broad St.   285-1234
at the Hyatt Richmond
$$

Here you will find a unique collection of eclectic and colorful contemporary art paired with a creative menu of Northern Italian cuisine plus steaks, lamb chops and seafood. Dinner is served 5 PM to 10 PM daily, and reservations are suggested.

L'ITALIA

10610 Patterson Ave.   740-1165
$$

This has been consistently considered one of the best Italian restaurants in Richmond for more than 20 years. Chef Vincenzo "Gino" DiLiberto, who attended the Culinary Institute of Milan, and his wife, Maria, prepare entrees from scratch every day. Hours are 5 PM to 10 PM Tuesday through Sunday.

MAMMA ZU

Pine and Spring Sts.   788-4205
$

In a former corner market in Oregon Hill, Mamma Zu opened in 1994 with rave reviews. It draws an eclectic crowd and is one of the newest see-and-be-seen spots. It offers a wide variety of inventively-prepared Italian food and has the best value in a great house wine you'll find anywhere in Richmond. The menu is posted on a blackboard, and it helps to know a little Italian when you read it. (Although the staff will do an excellent job of explaining it.) The restaurant is run by the family of the former owner of A. V. Ristorante Italiano on New York Avenue in Washington, D.C. Lunch is from 11 AM to 2:30 PM Monday through Friday. Dinner is available from 5 PM to 11 PM Monday through Saturday. Reservations are not taken.

MONTE CALVO'S

5703 Staples Mill Rd.   266-3314
$$

Monte Calvo's has good pasta, veal and seafood, and it is a place where you'll feel comfortable dressed casually or for business. Hours are from 4:30 PM until 11 PM Tuesday through Friday, and until 10 PM Sunday. Reservations are suggested.

THE OLIVE GARDEN
ITALIAN RESTAURANT

7113 W. Broad St.   672-6220
9750 Midlothian Tnpk.   330-7391
$

These restaurants, again, are part of a chain, but their fresh pasta is made daily, and their wide range of Italian cuisine and huge bowls of salad have made them popular. Hours are 11 AM until 10 PM Sunday through Thursday and until 11 PM Friday and Saturday.

SAL FREDERICO'S

1808 Staples Mill Rd.   358-9111
$$

Sal Frederico once operated Capri, which in days gone by was the Italian restaurant in Richmond, and he has developed a very strong following at his present location. Specialties are Veal alla Sal, veal chops, salmon marinara and chicken cacciatore. You'll never go wrong at Sal's. The atmosphere is friendly, and the service and food are excellent. Lunch is served Monday through Friday. Dinner is served every day except Sunday from 5:30 PM until 10:30 PM or 11 PM.

SORRENTO RESTAURANT

5602 Patterson Ave.   282-9340
$$

This restaurant has a cozy atmosphere and serves a variety of Italian dishes including homemade pastas and sauces, fresh veal hand cut in-house, homemade eggplant parmigiana, and a specialty called Espresso Pie. Sorrento has a faithful following of people who know good food and good value. Hours (dinner only) are from 5:30 PM to 10 PM Tuesday through Thursday, from 5:30 PM to 10:30 PM on Friday and Saturday, and from 5:30 PM to 9:30 PM on Sunday. Reservations are accepted.

THE SPAGHETTI WAREHOUSE
701 Bainbridge St.   *233-3083*
$

Antique signs and memorabilia (including a trolley car) decorate this Italian food emporium in South Richmond just over the Manchester Bridge from James Center. Among house specialties is a 15-layer lasagna as well as veal and chicken varieties of parmigiana and picatta. There are lots of spaghetti seasonings and sauces, all part of an extensive Italian menu. It's a great place for families, and the wait staff really caters to children. Hours are from 11 AM to 10 PM Monday through Thursday, and until 11 PM Friday. The restaurant opens at noon on weekends and stays open until 11 PM on Saturday and until 10 PM on Sunday. Even though it's a warehouse, reservations are suggested for parties of 10 or more.

LAKESIDE RESTAURANT
13550 Harbour Point Pkwy.   *739-8871*
$$

In the Brandermill Inn and Conference Center, this restaurant offers all diners a view overlooking the lake between Brandermill and Woodlake, and you also can watch your entrees being prepared in an open kitchen. The menu provides a classic variety of American, Italian and seafood dishes. Hours are 7 AM to 10 PM Monday through Friday,

8 AM to 10 PM Saturday, and from 8 AM to 9 PM on Sunday. Reservations are suggested.

THE VENICE
3556 W. Cary St.   *353-2725*
$

A mainstay of Richmond's restaurant world since 1958, The Venice has a large and loyal following. Specialties include pasta, veal, seafood and steaks. It is located at the Cary Street exit on the Powhite Expressway and can be reached from the center city via the Downtown Expressway. Lunch hours are 11:30 AM to 2:30 PM Monday through Friday. Dinner is from 5 PM to 11 PM on weekdays, and from 4 PM to 11 PM on Saturday. The Venice is closed Sunday.

THERESA'S ITALIAN VILLA
1212 N. Concord Ave.   *261-4043*
Corner of U.S. 1 and Parham Rd.
$$

Family-owned, warm and friendly, Theresa's specializes in veal, pasta, lasagna and seafood. The restaurant is open seven days a week, primarily from 11:30 AM to 2:30 PM and from 4:30 PM to 10 PM, although it stays open until 11 PM Saturday and is open all day Sunday 11:30 AM to 11 PM. Reservations are suggested.

VITELLO'S
2053 W. Broad St.   *358-0280*
$$$

Vitello's original location 10 blocks to the east looked like a 1950s diner, but inside the food was served up by a chef in a tux shirt and tie who entertained the bar crowd with dramatic flashes of flame and pan. The new location (formerly Benjamin's) is a decided improvement; otherwise the ingredients of the restaurant's solid reputation remain unchanged. Vitello's specializes in veal, seafood and haute Italian cuisine. There also are French and Cajun dishes and steaks and chops on the eclectic menu. Portions are enormous (one serving might satisfy two people). Hours are 6 PM to 1 AM Tuesday through Saturday. The restaurant gets good word-of-mouth compliments, and reservations are suggested for dinner.

---

17. Japanese

HANA ZUSHI RESTAURANT
1309 E. Cary St.   225-8801
$$

This Sushi bar offers Japanese food including traditional tempura, teriyaki, sukiyaki, cutlets, noodles, donburi and sushi. Hours are 11:30 AM to 2:30 PM Monday through Thursday, from 5:30 PM to 10 PM Monday through Thursday and Sunday, and until 11 PM Friday and Saturday.

KANPAI JAPANESE STEAKHOUSE
10438 Midlothian Tnpk.   323-4000
$$

Tables are built around gas-fired grills, and the cook's showmanship is as great as the food. Dishes include steak, chicken, shrimp, scallops and lobster. Hours are 5 PM to 10 PM Sunday through Thursday and 5 PM to 11 PM Friday and Saturday.

KABUTO JAPANESE HOUSE OF STEAK
8052 W. Broad St.   747-9573
$$

You're also in for a touch of showmanship here at Kabuto, where the chef prepares your meal "Hibachi Style" at Teppan Yaki tables. Sushi is served nightly except Monday. Lunch is served Monday through Friday from 11:30 AM to 2 PM. Dinner is served from 5:30 PM until 10 PM Monday through Thursday, until 10:30 PM on Friday and Saturday,

and from 5 PM to 9:30 PM Sunday. Reservations are suggested.

SAITO'S
611 E. Laburnum Ave.   329-9765
$$

Saito's features traditional Japanese "homestyle" cooking and has two tatami tables available for traditional seating on the floor. Saito's special is a combination of several items offering variety, especially helpful for the first-time customer. Lunch is served from 11:30 to 2 PM Tuesday through Friday, dinner from 5:30 PM to 9:30 PM Tuesday through Thursday and from 5:30 PM to 10:30 PM Friday and Saturday. Reservations are suggested.

---

18. Korean

V.I.P. RESTAURANT
7437-B Midlothian Tnpk.   675-0511
$$

While a variety of milder Chinese dishes are one the menu here, it's the gutsy Korean fare that is the main attraction. Many dishes are prepared over individual gas burners at your table, and a single serving of an entree is often large enough to serve two people. Spices and peppers are in heavy use. Side dishes are an adventure.

Hours are 11 AM to 11 PM Tuesday through Sunday and 5 PM to 11 PM Monday.

---

19. Mexican and Southwestern

CASA GRANDE
7818 W. Broad St.   755-2388
$

Casa Grande serves good Mexican food at reasonable prices. The sizzling cast-iron skillet for the fajitas creates drama as it is brought to the table. Hours are 11 AM to 2:30 PM and 5 PM to 10 PM Monday through Thursday (until 11 PM Friday), from noon until 10 PM Saturday and from noon until 9 PM Sunday.

CHI-CHI'S

9135 W. Broad St.	965-9611
8701 Midlothian Tnpk.	330-7575
2001 S. Park Blvd., Colonial Heights	526-3588

$

Mexican foods and charbroiled fare are served here in a festive, casual atmosphere. Hours are 11 AM until 10 PM Sunday through Thursday, and until midnight Friday and Saturday.

CHILI'S GRILL AND BAR

9111 Midlothian Tnpk.	320-6132

$

While Southwest Texas and Mexican food are the specialties here, you'll also find delicious hamburgers. Living up to its name, Chili's is a popular place for the grill and bar crowd. Hours are 11 AM to 11 PM Monday through Thursday, 11 AM to midnight Friday and Saturday, and from noon until 10 PM Sunday.

COYOTES

1323 W. Main St.	353-2555

$

Tequila-lime chicken, the Cowboy Burger, pasta, black-bean cakes, chilis and cheese-stuffed jalapeños are all part of the fare and western motif. Lunch is served from 11:30 AM to 2:30 PM Monday through Friday, and dinner is from 5 to 10 PM Tuesday through Thursday and until midnight Friday and Saturday. Sunday deck hours are 4:30 to 10 PM.

DAKOTA'S

4036-C Cox Rd.	346-2100

$$

A country-western restaurant and entertainment center, Dakota's offers some of the most distinctive and varied Southwestern dishes in Richmond. It is known for its vibrant atmosphere, pleasant service and big servings of good food. Hours for lunch are 11 AM to Monday through Friday. Dinner is served from 5 PM to 10 PM Monday through Thursday and from 5 PM to 11 PM Friday and Saturday.

EL TORO MEXICAN CAFE

4013 W. Broad St.	354-8902
301 S. Center St., Ashland	752-8384

$

In addition to superb food, atmosphere and service, El Toro offers a selection of vegetarian dishes, and there is a children's menu. Both locations are open for lunch from 11 AM to 2 PM Monday through Saturday. Dinner is served from 5 PM to 9 PM Monday through Thursday, and until 10 PM Friday and Saturday. If you are looking for good Mexican food, El Toro is hard to beat.

MEXICO RESTAURANT

6406 Horsepen Rd.	282-7359
5313 Williamsburg Rd.	226-2388

$

This bright, colorful restaurant offers distinctive Mexican food that goes beyond standard fare. For example, if you thought Mexican dishes were all ground beef, beans, lettuce and taco sauce, try this restaurant's Mole Poblano made with chicken. Hours are from 11 AM to 2:30 PM and 5 PM to 10 PM Monday through Friday, and from noon to 9 PM on Saturday and Sunday.

MOONDANCE SALOON

9 N. 17th St.	788-6666

$

Black bean cakes, Texas wedges, fajitas, corn chowder, gazpacho, barbecue, beef and chicken-fried steak are all part of the fare at this place where everybody has a good time. A mounted buffalo head and stuffed coyote add to the frontier atmosphere. Prices are moderate and people go here not only to eat but to watch other people. Hours are 11 AM to 2 AM Tuesday through Friday and from 5 PM to 2 AM on Saturday. The restaurant is closed Sunday and Monday.

CACTUS CAFE

935 W. Grace St.   359-7271
5713 Hopkins Rd.   275-9030
$

"Beef Lovers, Chicken Lovers, Vegetarians, All Well-Rounded and Uncertain Individuals, Choose Your Own Combinations," proclaims the menu. Everything Mexican is here, including eight "especialidades." Formerly called Speedy Gonzales, the Cactus Cafe uses cholesterol-free canola oil, no MSG and no lard. Hours are 10:30 AM until 9 PM Monday through Thursday and until 10 PM Friday and Saturday.

TEX-MEX CAFE

3511 Courthouse Rd.   745-6440
$

If you're looking for Mexican food in South Richmond, this is the place — housed in an authentic dining car. Hours are 11 AM to 9 PM Tuesday through Thursday, and until 10 PM Friday. Only dinner is served on weekends, from 5 to 10 PM on Saturday, and until 9 PM Sunday. The restaurant is closed on Monday. Reservations are suggested for six or more persons.

EL MATADOR

6925 Hull St.   276-3512
Horsepen at Betty Ln.   285-3813
$

You can bring your whole group here and eat a whole lot of very good Mexican food, then get a bill low enough to make you want to do the Mexican hat dance (but don't try it because you'll be too full). Both locations serve lunch and dinner seven days a week; please call about hours.

EL PASO

11521 Midlothian Tnpk.   794-7238
$

Stuccoed walls, bright blankets and oversized sombreros are part of the cheerful atmosphere here. The menu ranges from the standards to a long list of house specialties. Lunch and dinner are served daily. Call about hours.

EL RIO GRANDE

1324 W. Cary St.   278-9244
$

The restaurant is long and narrow like a cantina, has slow-turning ceiling fans and a photo of Pancho Villa. Local restaurant critics can't seem to say enough good things about this restaurant and its food. Lunch and dinner hours Monday through Friday are 11 AM to 2:30 PM and 4:30 PM to 10 PM. Only dinner is served on weekends, from 3 PM to 11 PM Saturday, and from 4 PM to 9 PM Sunday.

20. Vietnamese

CHOPSTIX

3129 W. Cary St.   358-7027
$

This small restaurant seats only 36 people, but it has been tastefully redecorated. Here you can try things such as shrimp on sugar cane, marinated and grilled beef, exotic stews, a vegetarian plate, fried spring rolls filled with meat and vegetables, delicious soups and stir-fry dishes. There also are roll-your-own dishes with paper-thin crepes and vegetable accompaniments. Hours are Tuesday through Saturday from 11:30 AM to 10 PM.

SAIGON GOURMET
11033 Hull Street Rd.   *745-0199*
$

Favorites here are crispy spring rolls, steamy noodle soup and grilled items that come with salad, rice noodles and rice paper for wrapping. The atmosphere is stark but sparkling clean, bright and airy. Weekday hours are 10 AM to 10 PM. Saigon Goumet opens at 11 AM on weekends and serves until 11 PM on Saturday and until 10 PM on Sunday.

SAIGON RESTAURANT
903 W. Grace St.   *355-6633*
$

The setting is simple, and there's a no-fuss ambiance about this place, but the food is good and is moderately priced. You'll find that the fare stacks up against similar dishes that are more expensive at other places. The literati from around town are faithful supporters. Hours are 11 AM to 2 PM, 5 PM to 10 PM Monday through Friday and noon to 10 PM Saturday. It's closed on Sunday.

TU-DO
6004 W. Broad St.   *282-9011*
$

Tu-Do offers one of the widest selections of Vietnamese food in Richmond. Dishes are fixed with duck, quail, pork, shrimp, eel, squid and frog legs. Hours are 10:30 AM to 10 PM Monday through Thursday and 10:30 AM to 1 AM Friday and Saturday. Tu-Do is closed on Sunday.

VIETNAM GARDEN
3991 Glenside Dr.   *262-6114*
$

From spring rolls to Vietnamese ravioli, this restaurant offers a full array of Vietnamese cuisine. The restaurant, which opened in 1992, quickly captured the tastebuds of local restaurant critics. Hours are Sunday through Thursday from 11 AM to 10 PM, and Friday and Saturday from 11 AM to 11 PM. It is closed Monday.

21. Barbecue

ALLMAN'S BARBECUE
9130 Jefferson Davis Hwy.   *271-9710*
$

Allman's specialties include a pork plate and ribs plus homemade apple pie and peach cobbler. It's got hush puppies, black-eyed peas, greens and cole slaw, and they'll arrange a take-out Pig-Out Party for you on two day's notice. Allman's opens at 11 AM and stays open until 8 PM Monday through Thursday and until 9 PM Friday and Saturday.

ANDY'S BARBECUE
Spring Hill Shopping Center   *740-4075*
Mechanicsville
$

This 55-seat saloon is outfitted like an old western bar. Patrons enter through swinging doors. This watering hole is geared toward the professional crowd that likes to have a drink and something to eat after work. It serves lunch and dinner and is open until 9 PM.

BILL'S BARBECUE
Ten locations in the Richmond area   *353-2757*
$

Established in 1930, Bill's over the years has been synonymous in Richmond with the word "barbecue." It's a popular place, and it specializes in Virginia-style barbecue, freshly squeezed limeades and lemonades, family-made pies (including regional sweet potato pies, lemon chess pies and cream-topped icebox fruit pies) and special breakfast items. Service is quick, and the restaurants are well-run. Hours are seven days a week from 7 AM to 10 PM. Credit cards are not accepted.

CAROLINA BAR-B-QUE

3015 Nine Mile Rd.   649-3424
$

If you like your barbecue Carolina-style, this is the place. Also you'll find deviled crab, shrimp, fish and bologna burgers. Hours are 11 AM to midnight Monday through Thursday and Sunday, and on Friday and Saturday the place stays open until 3 AM. Credit cards are not accepted.

EXTRA BILLY'S STEAK & BAR-B-QUE

5205 W. Broad St.   282-3949
$

"Where there's smoke there's barbecue," the saying goes, and it is usually hard to miss the aroma as you approach Extra Billy's. It has a large seating capacity and is near The Shops at Willow Lawn. Specialties are a barbecue sandwich and plate, baby back ribs, a brisket plate and prime rib. Hours are from 11:30 AM until 10 PM Monday through Thursday, and until 10:30 PM Friday. Saturday hours are 5 PM to 10:30 PM.

HOUNDSTOOTH CAFE

U.S. 301 and Rt. 54   537-5404
Hanover Courthouse
$$

The walls are decorated with hunt prints and brass horns, there are formal curtains at the windows and Coalport china graces the shelves. A stuffed fox dressed in a red jacket smiles from a corner. Not your usual kind of barbecue place. But that's what this restaurant is famous for, as well as for fresh seafood and other dishes; all are well prepared. The dining rooms are relaxed, and the bourbon-laced derby pie is decadent. The restaurant is in the small, historic village of Hanover Courthouse. Hours are 11 AM until 8 PM Tuesday through Thursday, and until 9 PM Friday and Saturday. The restaurant is closed Sunday and Monday.

PIERCE'S PITT BAR-B-QUE

10825 Hull Street Rd.   674-4049
1116 E. Main St.   643-0427
Regency Square Mall   741-4043
$

Bon Appetit magazine says "this is as good as it gets." You'll agree if you like hickory-smoked pulled pork barbecue. The setup is serve-yourself. The Hull Street location has picnic tables for outside dining and a country store that sells knickknacks. Hull Street hours are 11 AM to 9 PM Sunday through Thursday and 11 AM to 10 PM Friday and Saturday. The Main Street location is open only on weekdays from 10 AM to 6 PM. The Regency Square schedule corresponds with opening and closing hours for the mall.

SMOKEY PIG RESTAURANT

212 S. Washington Hwy. (U.S. 1)   798-4590
Ashland
$$

The Smokey motto is "I Dig the Pig," and there are pig pictures and pig ornaments galore. Specialties, in addition to ones you might expect, such as baby back ribs, hush puppies and homemade desserts, include crab cakes. It is family-operated, and it's a popular place for locals and for travelers. Hours are 11 AM to 9 PM Tuesday through Saturday and noon to 9 PM on Sunday. The restaurant is closed on Monday.

THE FARM HOUSE
7519 Jefferson Davis Hwy.   *271-6472*
$$

This place is nationally known for its barbecue sauce and ribs. The red carpet starts on the floor and runs right up the wall. Hours are 11 AM until 10 PM Tuesday through Thursday, until 10:30 PM Friday, and from 5 PM until 10:30 PM Saturday. Reservations are recommended for parties of eight or more.

22. Soul

SECOND AND MARSHALL ST.
318 N. Second St.   *643-6516*
$

You'll be greeted warmly and will feel at home at Second and Marshall Street. The breakfast menu includes egg sandwiches and homemade biscuits. For lunch and dinner you'll find perennial downhome favorites — broiled or blackened lake trout, fried seafood, ribs, cole slaw, greens, gumbo, lemon chess pie, sweet potato pie and more. Dishes are named for famous African-Americans such as Maggie Walker, Giles Jackson, Arthur Ashe Jr., Frederick Douglas and L. Douglas Wilder. Cool jazz plays on the sound system. Lunch hours are 11 AM to 3 PM Monday through Friday. Dinner is from 5 PM to 9 PM on weekdays and from 7 PM to 11 PM on Saturday.

SUGAR & SPICE
2116 E. Main St.   *788-4566*
$

Workers in Shockoe Bottom make a beeline for Sugar & Spice during noontime rush so, if you're heading there at midday, time your visit before noon or after 1:30 PM. One side of the menu is devoted to breakfasts (including biscuits and gravy), the other side lists lunch items (including bologna burgers and soups and homemade pies, cakes and cobblers). Dinner is served only on Friday and includes pork chops, barbecue and Martha's special fried chicken. Hours are 8 AM to 1 PM Monday through Thursday and from 8 AM to 9 PM Friday. The restaurant is closed Saturday and Sunday. Credit cards are not accepted, but payment may be made in cash or by personal check.

WOODY'S INN
2128 W. Cary St.   *359-2535*
$

The fare is similar to Sugar & Spice. The chicken wings are special. Be aware that Woody's has real soul atmosphere in that it is a hot spot for jazz lovers, so if you want a quiet meal, go early. On the other hand, if jazz is your kind of music, plan to stick around and enjoy it. Woody's opens at 6 PM and stays open until midnight Monday through Thursday, until 2 AM Saturday, and until 1:30 AM Sunday.

23. Family Restaurants

FUDDRUCKERS
8317 W. Broad St.   *747-4779*
$

This place is popular in part for its easygoing atmosphere and for its delicious burgers. Fuddruckers grinds its own beef daily and makes its own buns, so you can imagine how tasty the end result is. Children, and those not having to watch a waistline, also love Fuddruckers' shakes and malts, handmade with whole milk and hand-dipped ice cream. The little ones also enjoy Monday nights when they are entertained by costumed characters, leaving Mom and Dad more time to savor their meals. There's also live music on Tuesday nights. Hours are 11 AM to 10 PM Sunday through Thursday, and 11 AM to 11 PM Friday and Saturday. In summer, the restaurant stays open until 11 PM seven days a week.

DABNEY'S RESTAURANT
1501 Robin Hood Rd.   *359-8126*
$

The buffet and menu here include a lot of good old solid food: things like meat loaf, baked and fried chicken, crab cakes, beef Stroganoff, buttery spoon bread and warm rolls. Hours are 7 AM to 10 PM daily.

OLD COUNTRY BUFFET
7801 W. Broad St.   *672-1183*
$

At this buffet you pay before you pick up your food, instead of afterward as in most cafeterias. For a fixed price you get as much or as little as you want from a half-dozen buffet islands, each with its own supply of plates, flatware and napkins. Islands include salads, fresh fruits, breads and biscuits, vegetables and entrees, and desserts and beverages. The atmosphere is comfortable; booths line the walls; and there are plenty of small tables. The food is good, and there are usually lots of children. Special prices for senior citizens and children are available. Weekday hours are 11 AM to 8:30 PM Monday through Thursday, and until 9:30 PM Friday. Expanded hours on weekends are from 8 AM to 9:30 PM Saturday, and until 8:30 PM Sunday.

SHONEY'S
177 E. Belt Blvd.
12531 Jefferson Davis Hwy., Chester
4935 Nine Mile Rd.
11500 Midlothian Tnpk.
9963 Hull St.
3555 W. Cary St.
7009 W. Broad St.

8415 W. Broad St.
7101 Staples Mill Rd.
103 Washington Hwy., Ashland
$

This is family eating that is affordable, enjoyable and truly tasty. The six city locations of this chain are popular with tourists and visitors alike. The gigantic All-U-Can-Eat Breakfast Bar attracts a lot of loyal followers and not only offers traditional breakfast foods but also low-fat and low-cholesterol selections (plenty of fresh fruit, low-fat English muffins, low-fat milk and cholesterol-free Bundt cake) for the health conscious along with cereals for the younger crowd like Captain Crunch and Trix. The menus for breakfast, lunch and dinner are extensive. Shoney's offers 50¢-off Senior Meals, regular specials such as Family Night, when children 12 and younger eat free, and a $2.99 Breakfast Bar from 6 AM to 8 AM on Friday. Hours on most days are from 6 AM to 11 PM, but the restaurants stay open until 3 AM on Friday and Saturday when they offer a Midnight Breakfast Bar.

24. Delis

BOULEVARD RESTAURANT & DELI
5218 W. Broad St.   *282-9333*
$

The Boulevard Restaurant & Deli is a popular spot not far from the Shoppes at Willow Lawn, and it serves a breakfast menu all day. It specializes in quality Kosher meats, homemade soups, salads and desserts. It also carries Virginia wines. Hours are 10 AM to 3 PM Sunday through Saturday.

BOYCHIK'S DELI
4024-B Cox Rd.   *747-1030*
$

Boychik's gets its bagels from New

York, and they are available fresh each day in a wide variety of choices. In addition to bagels and fish platters, potato knishes and matzoh ball soup, Boychik's has cheeseburgers, western omelettes, steak dinners and Italian entrees. Hours are 7 AM to 9 PM Monday through Saturday and 9 AM to 4 PM on Sunday.

COPPOLA'S

2900 W. Cary St.   *359-6969*
$

This is the headquarters for Italian meats and for Heros, meatball sandwiches and vegetarian subs. It is open for lunch and dinner Monday through Saturday.

THE 42ND STREET CAFE

1223 Bellevue Ave.   *262-6206*
$

The 42nd Street Cafe is within the Northside's famous Belle Bakery, does a big carryout business and has full bar, booth and table capacity for 20 or so patrons. It offers distinctive breads, pastries and desserts made on the premises, an extensive wine selection, and it serves up delicious specialty coffees, espresso and cappuccino. Italian and deli specialty items include Chicken Marsala, New York-style Reubens and vegetarian pizzas (among seven varieties). Desserts include a "dry" sundae made of chocolate cake topped with whipped cream, chocolate glaze and a cherry. Hours are 7:30 AM to 9 PM Wednesday through Sunday and 7 AM to 7 PM Monday and Tuesday.

GLEN ALLEN DELI

9129 Staples Mill Rd.   *672-6013*
$

Great fresh bread and great meats (thinly sliced) are essential to a great sandwich, and the Glen Allen Deli has both. The deli case overflows with cheeses,

meats and freshly made salads and desserts. This is a small place, but you won't be disappointed. Hours are 11 AM to 8 PM Monday through Friday, and from noon until 8 PM Saturday. Credit cards are not accepted, but personal checks are.

HICKORY HAMS CAFE & DELI

4040 G. Cox Rd., Glen Allen   *747-4534*
$

Hickory Hams, in the Innsbrook Shoppes, serves a variety of sandwiches, soups and salads. This Atlanta-based company also offers spiral-sliced hams and turkeys. Hours are 10 AM to 6 PM Monday through Friday, 11 AM to 3 PM on Saturdays.

MANHATTAN DELI

9550 Midlothian Tnpk.   *330-3845*
$

It's in a Midlothian Turnpike shopping center and it may be far too clean and courteous to be a true New York delicatessen, but local restaurant critics say it does an excellent job of capturing the spirit. The shelves are filled with an array of beer, display cases show off cheesecakes, and there are first-rate Reubens, sailors, subs, four varieties of franks, soups and bagels. A chalkboard lists daily specials. Hours are 11 AM to 9 PM Monday through Saturday.

PADOW'S HAM & DELI

1601 Willow Lawn	*354-1993*
1110 E. Main St.	*354-1931*
1920 Midlothian Tnpk.	*354-1996*
9720 Midlothian Tnpk.	*285-4283*

$

If you mention Padow's to Richmonders it means "ham." For more than 50 years Padow's has been the local king of Smithfield ham, country ham, honey glazed ham and slab bacon. You can buy the whole ham at Padow's or

you can get them to put together sandwiches and platters. They also carry Virginia peanuts and other delicacies.

NEW YORK DELICATESSEN

2920 W. Cary St.   355-6056
$

Specialties here include New York-
style deli sandwiches, clubs and subs,
salad bowls and platters, omelettes,
smoked fish, Nova and whitefish. Deli
meats and fish come from New York, and
the bagels are fresh. The New York Delicatessen has been in business for more
than 50 years. Hours are 8 AM to 8:30
PM weekdays and 9 AM to 8:30 PM on
weekends.

SUE'S COUNTRY KITCHEN

1213 Summit Ave.   353-5408
$

To be sure, Sue's carries the hot lunch
specials with meat, vegetables and rolls
you'd expect from a country kitchen. But
the deli fare here is the real standout —
hot pastrami and Swiss on rye, sailors,
creamy potato salad, soups and rich desserts. Hours are 6 AM to 3 PM Monday
through Friday. Credit cards are not accepted.

25. Fondue

THE MELTING POT

Gayton Crossing Shopping Center   741-3120
$$

The Melting Pot has tables with built-
in burners to heat fondue pots filled with

peanut oil or spice bouillon. Every-
thing from appetizers to dessert is a
do-it-yourself cooking experience.
Hours are 5 PM to 11 PM Sunday
through Thursday, and until midnight
Friday and Saturday.

26. Pizza

BOTTOMS UP PIZZA

1700 Dock St.   644-4400
$

Bottoms Up, at 17th and Dock streets,
is one of the really "in" places in Rich-
mond. One draw is its interesting loca-
tion, not only in an old building in
Shockoe Bottom, but along part of the
old canal and practically under three rail-
road trestles that pass overhead. But the
big draw is its variety of exceptional top-
pings that include seafood, fruit, unusual
vegetables and even alligator — all used
to produce a truly gourmet pizza. Bot-
toms Up opens at 11:30 AM every day
and stay open until 11 PM Monday
through Wednesday, until midnight
Thursday, until 2 AM Friday and Satur-
day and until midnight Sunday. Reser-
vations are not accepted.

PICCOLA ITALY PIZZA & SUBS

1100 W. Main St.   355-3111
$

Piccola Italy, in the VCU area, has
some of the best pizza in town. The place
stays open until midnight weekdays and
until 2 AM on weekends.

STEVE'S PIZZA
1299 W. Broad Street Rd., Oilville 784-0166
$

Steve's is strictly a take-out place, but we list it here because the specialty is pizza, maybe some of the best in the area. The establishment is in a red barn on the portion of Broad Street Road that runs through Oilville, reasonably close at hand if you live in the far West End or if you work in Innsbrook. Quantity and quality are both excellent. (His medium deluxe would qualify as a large at most pizza places in town.) You also can get a half-pound hamburger and a one-pound lettuce salad with all of the fixings. Count on about 15 to 20 minutes for your pizza with homemade crust to be prepared. Or, call in your order in advance as most people do. Steve's is closed on Monday but otherwise open from 11:30 AM to 2 PM and from 4 PM to 9 PM.

27. Southern

BLACK-EYED PEA
10201 Midlothian Tnpk.   560 3168
9498 W. Broad St.   762-4821
$$

Juicy pot roast, Mom's Meat Loaf and roasted chicken, plus charbroiled T-bone steak, are all part of the homestyle menu here.

Hours are 11 AM to 10 PM Sunday through Thursday and 11 AM to 11 PM Friday and Saturday.

BRENDA'S
Rt. 623 at Rockville-Manakin   784-4323
Exit 173 S. from I-64 (old Exit 33)
$

Winner for three years of *Style Weekly's* Best Southern Cooking accolade, Brenda's serves homestyle fare with dinner specials every day. The restaurant has everything from sandwiches to full-course steak and seafood dinners. Hours are 7 AM to 8 PM Tuesday through Thursday and Sunday, and 7 AM to 9 PM Friday and Saturday. It's tucked back in the woods, so keep a sharp eye out for the entrance. Reservations are recommended for parties of eight or more on weekends. Payment may be made only with cash or by check.

FRECKLE'S RESTAURANT
5724 Patterson Ave.   288-3354
$

If you're a good ol' boy you'll love Freckle's. The amazing thing is that a lot of its clientele includes Main Street bankers and West End country club members. The owner holds court at a center table, and the cooking is real down-home, with great breakfasts. Regular dinner specials include fried catfish (Wednesdays), fresh-cut New York strip (Thursdays) and homemade backfin crab cakes (Fridays). Just about everybody thinks the crab cakes are the best in town. Hours are 7 AM to 9 PM Monday through Friday, 7:30 AM to 9 PM Saturday, and 8 AM to 6 PM Sunday. Sunday breakfast is served until 2 PM. The restaurant has an outdoor patio and grill. Only cash and checks are accepted.

MAGNOLIA
3207 N. Boulevard   359-9441
$$

This restaurant, in the Holiday Inn near The Diamond, is one of the best in Richmond. The focus is on Southern food, including Virginia-cured ham, Virginia seafoods, fried chicken and country biscuits topped with gravy. But Magnolia also offers delicious steaks cooked to order and Escargot di Napoli and Fettucini Caprice. A soup and salad bar are included in the price of all entrees. Presentation and service are first class. Hours are 11 AM to 2 PM and from 5 to 10 PM daily.

McLeans Restaurant

4001 W. Broad St.   358-0369
$

Salt herring, country ham, buckwheat cakes, roe and eggs, and free grits with gigantic breakfasts are the staple at McLeans. Specializing in county-style cooking, McLeans is home of "The Biggest Breakfast in Town." For lunch and dinner you'll find hamburgers and sandwiches and things like bean soup and meatloaf smothered in gravy. Hours are 6:30 AM to 3 PM Monday through Friday and 11 AM to 3 PM Friday through Sunday. Carryout is available.

28. Lunch Places

Back to Roots

321 N. Second St.   No Phone
$

This is an all-natural vegetarian cafe with an African-American flavor. It offers a daily soup and salad special for takeout or eat-in.

Becky's

100 E. Cary St.   643-9736
$

Becky's has a following of regulars that makes it almost club-like. Lunch is from 11 AM to 3 PM Monday through Friday, and you'll find breaded veal cutlet, slabs of roast beef with gravy and slow-cooked green beans. The restaurant also serves breakfast beginning at 7 AM. At night for dinner from 5 PM to 10 PM Monday through Friday the place undergoes a metamorphosis. The atmosphere remains unpretentious, but the menu shifts into culinary high gear with dishes such as

fresh fettuccine with lump crabmeat in a garlic Chardonnay cream sauce.

Cafe Ole

2 N. Sixth St.   225-8226
$

If your mood is Mexican and you're looking for a downtown lunch spot, then Cafe Ole's the place. Step up to the kitchen counter, place your order, and in a few minutes the cook will call your number. Most tables are designed for parties of two, but there are some larger tables for groups as well as an eating bar with stools along the wall.

Chesapeake Bagel Bakery

10839 W. Broad St.   346-3400
(across from Innsbrook)
Shops at Willow Lawn   285-5000
$

Fourteen varieties of fresh-baked bagels, nine flavors of cream cheese, sandwiches, salads, homemade soups, desserts, party platters and a large variety of beverages — everything is here for eat-in or carryout feasts built around bagels or croissants. For breakfast or lunch, Chesapeake Bagel is open seven days a week.

Chez Foushee

203 N. Foushee   648-3225
$

Chez Foushee has an interesting roundup of sandwiches including grilled London broil, turkey and smoked Gouda, house pimento cheese, Foushee garden pocket and albacore tuna salad. Everything is upscale including the decor and the magazines in the reading rack. And everything is homemade, including soups, fresh pasta salads, sandwiches, hot entrees and desserts (with offerings such as key lime pie, white chocolate cheesecake and lemon butter cake). Chez Foushee offers full catering service and

will deliver box lunches or prepare them for pickup. Only cash or checks are accepted.

CHIOCCA'S PARK AVENUE INN

2001 Park Ave.   355-9219
$

There are not very many tables here, but it's a longtime favorite gathering place for regulars who know the sandwiches are great. It is not open on Monday.

FABULOUS FOODS

2029 Huguenot Rd.   320-0615
$

The atmosphere is relaxing and tea-room-like. Fruit salads, nut-studded chicken salads, rich casseroles, pot pies, hot and cold soups and assorted sand-wiches are the typical fare. For dessert you'll find lemon chess pie and bread pudding. Fabulous Foods is in the Hu-guenot Village Shopping Center and is open from 10 AM to 3 PM Monday through Saturday. MasterCard is accepted.

FANTASTE

1201 W. Main St.   355-1642
$

Fantaste has only 16 seats, so you need to arrive early if you want to get one at lunchtime. Specialties include homemade daily specials, muffins, Teriyaki chicken, classic Greek and Caesar salads and fresh desserts. Hours are 11 AM to 3 PM Monday through Friday. Only cash or checks are accepted.

THE DAIRY BAR

1602 Roseneath Rd.   355-1937
$

For nearly 50 years this has been a popular place for breakfast and lunch.

Breakfast specialties include herring roe and eggs and salt herring. Lunch specialties include club sandwiches, probably the best milk shakes in town and ice cream. Hours are 7 AM to 3:30 PM Monday through Friday and 7 AM to 3 PM Saturday.

HOMEMADES BY SUZANNE
10 S. Sixth St. (in the Atrium)   775-2116
$

This is a bright, clean place with excellent food, and it's convenient to just about everything downtown. There are homemade soups, a famous shrimp salad, chicken salad, potato salad, made-from-scratch brownies, pastries and pies, and cream puffs filled with custard and whipped cream. You can eat here or get boxed lunches to carry out. Hours are 9:30 AM to 3 PM Monday through Friday. Smoking is not permitted.

JOHNSON'S GRILL & RESTAURANT
1802 E. Franklin St.   648-9788
$

In addition to lunch, breakfast is served here Monday through Saturday beginning at 6 AM. The lunch menu includes home-cooked items, fresh vegetables, homemade bread and desserts. Johnson's is a longtime favorite for downhome food and serves lunch Monday through Friday until 1 PM. Takeout orders are a specialty.

JOSIE'S CAFE & GALLERY
3449 W. Cary St.   358-6890
$

Josie's Cafe & Gallery offers a casual atmosphere, food that is regional American with a twist of California, and a very good wine list. One of the new owners was the executive chef at The Butlery before it closed in 1992. Lunch is from 11 AM to 3 PM Tuesday through Saturday.

Dinner also is served on these days from 5 PM to 10 PM, and Sunday brunch is from 9 AM to 3 PM. Josie's is closed Monday.

APPLEBEE'S NEIGHBORHOOD GRILL & BAR
South of the James:
900 Moorefield Dr.
10823 Hull Street Rd.
2611 Old Hundred Rd.
North of the James:
5400 W. Broad St.
9601 W. Broad St.
And in Regency Square Mall   330-3954
$

Applebee's offers sandwiches and burgers in a casual atmosphere and an all-you-can-eat rib special Sunday, Monday and Tuesday. But its also offers a Lightning Lunch from Monday to Saturday, a lunch it promises within 14 minutes or you get it free. It's part of a chain, but it is so popular that it deserves mention here. Hours are from 11 AM until 1:30 AM Monday through Saturday and until 11 PM on Sunday.

HOBO'S GRILL
5805 Patterson Ave.   285-3512
$

Club sandwiches are among the treats here. Box lunches are available. Hours are 9 AM to 4 PM Monday through Friday, and until 2 PM on Saturday.

MANHATTAN BAGEL
4028 Cox Rd.   346-4889
Pocno Green Shopping Center   560-9448

You'll find 18 varieties of bagels baked fresh daily. The full-service grill is open for breakfast and lunch and serves sandwiches and six kinds of cream cheese

PERLY'S
111 E. Grace St.   649-2779
$

Perly's Delicatessen is club-like and

has a loyal following. The menu ranges from deli sandwiches and soups to gazpacho and vegetarian fare. The place is casual and friendly. It also serves great breakfasts.

RIDGE DINER
Ridge and Three Chopt rds.   282-4107
$

Owner Jack Georges formerly ran the snack bar at the Westwood Pharmacy. There are daily lunch specials, and the diner also serves breakfast as well as a light dinner menu that features spaghetti, hamburgers and chicken pot pies. Hours are 6:30 AM to 3 PM Monday through Sunday.

SHOCKOE BELLE
1417 E. Cary St.   648-3764
$

Opened by Jimmy Sneed of the Frog and the Redneck, Shockoe Belle features gourmet pizza, salads, grilled fish and meat. Lunch is from 11:30 AM to 2:30 PM Monday through Friday. Sunday brunch is from 11 AM to 3 PM.

STEVE'S RESTAURANT
110 N. Fifth St.   649-3460
$

The friendly atmosphere and fast service here is coupled with basic food and homestyle cooking. Hours are 7 AM to 3 PM Monday through Friday.

29. Sandwiches and Beer

BAMBOO CAFE
1 S. Mulberry St.   No phone
$

The Bamboo offers homemade soups and desserts, sandwiches, steaks, seafood and chicken in a casual atmosphere. Hours are 11 AM to 2 AM daily.

BUDDY'S
325 N. Robinson St.   355-3701
$

Home cooking, along with sandwiches and burgers, is served here. The atmosphere is very casual. Hours are 11 AM to 1 AM Sunday through Thursday and until 2 AM Friday and Saturday. Sunday breakfast starts at 10 AM.

GOODFELLA'S
1722 E. Main St.   643-5022
$

If you're headed for "The Bottom" and want bar fare and progressive rock, then Goodfella's may just be made to order. It serves dinner only and is not open Sunday or Monday.

HILL CAFE
2800 E. Broad St.   648-0360
$

A popular spot on Church Hill, Hill Cafe offers an innovative nouvelle cuisine menu. Desserts are made fresh daily by a nearby bakery. It has a casual, neighborhood atmosphere, and children are welcome. Hours are 11:30 AM until midnight Sunday through Wednesday, and until 2 AM Thursday through Saturday.

PHILIP'S CONTINENTAL LOUNGE
5704 Grove Ave.   288-8687
$

Known simply as "Phil's," this has been the "in" place in the West End since before World War II. The menu includes club and sailor sandwiches, meat loaf, burgers and baked chicken. Hours are 9 AM to midnight daily, except Sunday when they are noon to 8 PM.

WINESHOP BISTRO
4922 E. Millridge Pkwy.   744-8888
$

In Market Square at Brandermill, the

Wineshop Bistro is a retail wine store with a restaurant attached. The atmosphere is casual, and the fare is basically French. If you want, you can browse through the shop, select a bottle of wine, then have it served with your lunch for a small corkage charge. Wineshop Bistro also serves dinner (including a Wednesday night Wine Tasters Special), but the cost will be double the price range indicated above. Hours for lunch are 11 AM to 2 PM Tuesday through Thursday. Dinner is served from 5 PM until 9 PM Tuesday through Thursday, and from 5 PM to 10 PM Friday and Saturday. The restaurant is closed Sunday and Monday. Reservations are suggested Tuesday through Thursday and are required on Friday and Saturday.

30. Coffee Houses and Bagel Places

THE BIDDER'S SUITE
917 W. Grace St.   355-5707
$

This is a true underground coffee house in the style of the '60s where people gather for good coffee, cuisine and conversation. Coffee includes espresso and cappuccino, and the cuisine includes abundant salads, sandwiches and light fare and delicious desserts. The theme is "Alice in Wonderland," and each visit is like a "Through the Looking Glass" adventure. Bidder's Suite opens at 8 AM on weekdays and at 11 AM Saturday and Sunday, and stays open until 2 AM.

COFFEE & CO.
2928 W. Cary St.   355-2040
$

A gourmet coffee house and bakery, Coffee & Co. is open seven days a week. It's a pleasant place to relax with great coffees, espresso drinks or a house-blend cappuccino. Sample their croissants, bagels, muffins, cookies, brownies, cakes, fresh-baked bread and other works of the baker's art. On week nights there are Word Parties: monologues, poetry and book readings, plays and folk singers. Coffee & Co. opens at 8 AM daily and closes at 5 PM, except on Saturday when hours are extended to 7 PM.

VIRGINIA COFFEE & TEA COMPANY
1211 W. Main St.   355-2739
$

This cafe in the trendy area of W. Main seems to be a favorite among Fan District residents and VCU students. Not only is there a large variety of coffee and tea, but it also offers pastries, boxed and light fare lunches, a variety of teapots and other fine bakery items. Local artwork hangs on the walls, and a jazz pianist plays an upright piano at lunch Tuesday and Thursday (except in the summer months). Here you'll find all of the coffees and pastries you'll need for a delightful break in the day. Hours are 7 AM to 5:30 PM Monday through Friday and 9 AM to 5 PM Saturday.

WORLD CUP
204 N. Robinson St.   359-5282
Cox Rd. in Innsbrook   346-9287
$

Classic music plays, the shelves are lined with travel books and current magazines, and there are plenty of things to nibble on. Come here for civilized beginnings to the day, for lunch, or to unwind after a hectic day. Hours are 7 AM to midnight Monday through Thursday, 7 AM to 2 AM Friday, 8 AM to 2 AM Saturday and 9 AM to 11 PM Sunday. Credit cards are not accepted.

Coffee houses are growing in number in Richmond. Other coffee houses and places with a coffee house atmosphere and/or fare include:

Belle Kuisine, Stony Point Shopping Center, 272-2811;

The French Quarter Coffee and Creamy, 10837 Hull Street Road, 675-0154;

Chesapeake Bagel, 10839 W. Broad Street, 346-3300 ; The Shops at Willow Lawn, 285-5000;

Christie's Cafe & Bakery, 3109 W. Cary Street, 353-9782;

Grove Avenue Coffee & Tea Co., 5802 Grove Avenue, 288-6211;

The Lazy Bagel, 12th and E. Main, and at 3156 W. Cary Street, 355-7035;

Manhattan Bagel, 4028 Cox. Rd., 346-4889; 9550 Midlothian Turnpike, 560-9448;

None Such Place, 1717 E. Franklin Street, 644-0832 (open until midnight Monday through Thursday, until 2 AM Friday and Saturday, and until 10 PM Sunday).

Shockoe Espresso and Roastery, 104 Shockoe Slip, 648-3734

---

31. Other Casual Places

ALYSON'S
404 Westover Hills Blvd.   *230-1800*
$$

Alyson's specializes in seafood and ribs. Weekday opening hour is 11 AM; on weekends it's 8 AM. Closing is at 1 AM Tuesday through Thursday and on Sunday, 3 AM on Friday and Saturday. Alyson's is not open on Monday.

ANTHONY & GEORGE'S RESTAURANT
7505 Staples Mill Rd.   *266-4182*
$$

The pasta, steaks and prime rib are great, and the service is excellent. Here you'll find a broad menu and a comfortable atmosphere. Hours are 11 AM to 9 PM Sunday through Thursday, 11 AM to 10 PM Friday, and 4 PM to 10 PM Saturday.

BISTRO R
10190 W. Broad St.   *747-9484*
$$

This American bistro has a California feel about it and is a favorite West End place to see and be seen. Chef Robert Ramsey is a gold medal winner, and the menu features Mediterranean-style fish, pasta and grilled items. Vegetable dishes are exquisite. On Monday through Saturday lunch hours are 11:30 AM to 3 PM, and dinner hours Tuesday through Saturday are 5:30 PM to 9:30 PM. Bistro R is closed Sunday. Candlelight at dinner provides an elegant atmosphere, yet it's casual enough for an impromptu dinner with friends. Reservations are suggested.

BUBBA'S
4000 Williamsburg Rd.   *236-3262*
$

Bubba's is everything the name implies, including pool table, pinball machines, country music on the jukebox, gun-rack-equipped pickups in the parking lot and guns mounted on the wall. The menu also is what you might expect and includes bologna burgers, fried chicken sandwich, pizza and Bubba's popular 21-piece shrimp dinner with cole slaw and fries. Hours are 9 AM to 2 AM seven days a week.

BUCKHEAD'S
8510 Patterson Ave.   *750-2000*
$$$

Buckhead's serves prime rib, veal, lamb chops and seafood. See the listing under Steaks and Seafood (Section 3) for more information.

THE BUS STOP
1210 E. Cary St.   788-9933
$$

The offerings here include a variety of cold sandwiches, quiche, burgers, a salad bar at lunch, and prime rib, shrimp, chicken and veal for dinner. Hours are 11:30 AM to 2 AM Monday through Saturday. The restaurant is closed Sunday.

CARY STREET CAFE
2631 W. Cary St.   353-7445
$$

Fresh seafood, steaks, chicken, sandwiches, salads, pizza and homemade soups are the fare. Hours are 4 PM to 2 AM Monday through Saturday.

CHARLEY'S STONY POINT CAFE
3088 Stony Point Rd.   323-3984
$$

Signature dishes, steaks, seafood and sandwiches are served in this popular place. Hours are 11 AM to 10 PM Monday through Thursday, 11:30 AM to 11 PM Friday, noon to 11 PM Saturday, and 11 AM to 10 PM Sunday.

CHRISTIE'S CAFE & BAKERY
3109 W. Cary St.   353-9782
$

Christie's is a good destination for a light meal with a variety of possibilities. A wood-fired oven, one of the few in town, is used to turn out individually-made pizzas and calzone. In addition, there are great sandwiches, salads, platters and specials, plus an extensive array of coffees and baked goods to savor with coffee. The emphasis on a wholesome vegetarian-style menu is so successful you'll never miss the beef. Hours are 8 AM to 10 PM Monday through Friday,

and until 11 PM on weekends. Credit cards are not accepted.

CHUGGER'S
OLD TOWN PUB & EATERY
900 W. Franklin St.   353-8191
$

The cozy pub-like atmosphere here provides a setting for some of the best and most reasonably-price food in town, including a roast beef sandwich on a Kaiser roll drenched in natural juices that is unquestionably the most delicious you will find anyplace. The sweet Bermuda onion deep-fried in cayenne-enriched butter is a must as an appetizer. Draft beer comes in small, medium and large glasses, the latter being really pitcher-size. It's all a far cry from the old Chesterfield Tea Room that occupied this site for many, many years. Hours are 11 AM to 2 AM Monday through Sunday.

CHIOCCA'S
425 N. Belmont Ave.   355-9992
$

A snug, homey neighborhood place, Chiocca's has been a longtime favorite where many customers are regulars — well-known to the staff and to others. Food is basic but good. Hours are 11:30 AM to midnight Wednesday through Monday. It is closed Tuesday. Check are accepted, but credit cards are not accepted.

DELANEY'S CAFE & GRILL
10622 Patterson Ave.   740-1921
$$

Delaney's is casual and has the feel of a neighborhood place. It offers good food and reasonable prices including a children's menu with all items at $2. The menu provides a good selection of seasonal specialties, good soups, fresh salads and enticing desserts. Delaney's opens at 11:30 AM during the week and stays open until 10 PM Tuesday through Thursday and until 11 PM Friday and Saturday. Hours on Sunday are from 11 AM to 9 PM including brunch hours from 11 AM to 3 PM. Reservations are suggested for large parties.

DOT'S BACK INN

4030 MacArthur Ave.   *266-3167*
$

Here you'll find standard lunch fare such as Rosie the Riveter's Lunch Pail (a grilled cheese sandwich and a bowl of homemade soup). It's an old-fashioned neighborhood hangout with old-fashioned prices and World War II headlines on the wall. Hours are 9 AM to midnight Monday through Saturday.

GATSBY'S

1212 E. Cary St.   *782-2341*
$$$

It's here that one of Richmond's famous chefs prepares veal, lamb chops, prime rib and daily specials that match the availability of fresh ingredients. The restaurant is open for dinner only: 6 PM to 11 PM Tuesday through Thursday, and until midnight Friday and Saturday. Gatsby's is in Shockoe Slip.

JAN'S

9501 Woodman Rd.   *266-5303*
$

This is a pleasant, comfortable spot on the North Side that's easy on the wallet and that offers an appealing family-style menu. Hours are 11 AM Monday through Thursday and 11 AM to midnight Friday and Saturday.

MELITO'S

8815 Three Chopt Rd.   *285-1899*
$

In addition to world-famous hotdogs, Melito's serves American-style food that includes daily specials. It's varied menu and location makes Melito's a super-popular West End gathering spot. Hours are 11 AM until midnight Monday through Thursday, and until 1 AM Friday and Saturday. Reservations are suggested on weekends.

NICKEL BRIDGE RAW BAR & GRILL

5011 Forest Hill Ave.   *233-6948*
$$

The Boulevard Bridge is affectionately known to many Richmonders as Nickel Bridge, hence the name of the restaurant (which is near the southern end of the bridge). The food is excellent, and you can count on getting more than your five cents' worth of seafood, pasta and steaks, plus homemade sauces, breads and special desserts. Hours are 11 AM to 1:30 AM Monday through Friday, 4 PM to 1:30 AM Saturday, and 10 AM to 3 PM Sunday.

NONE SUCH PLACE

1721 E. Franklin St.   *644-0832*
$

Situated on the corner of 18th and E. Franklin Street in Richmond's oldest commercial building in Shockoe Bottom, None Such Place features two floors of casual, fine dining specializing in contemporary Virginia cuisine exquisitely prepared by executive chef Michael Hall. All desserts are prepared fresh on premises. The restaurant and bar offers a great atmosphere — old brick, wood beams, flickering candlelight and a blazing fireplace in winter — for after work, dinner or a late-night rendezvous. Lunch is from 11:30 AM to 2:30 PM Monday through Friday, and brunch on Sunday is from 11 AM to 2 PM. Dinner is from 5:30 PM to 10 PM Sunday through Thursday and from 5:30 PM to 2 AM

Friday and Saturday. Reservations are recommended.

PARAGON

1718 E. Main St.   *788-1101*
$$$

Paragon, situated on a busy block in Shockoe Bottom, specializes in Italian and American fare. Hours are 6 AM to 2 AM on weekdays, and 8 PM to 2 AM on Saturday. Paragon is closed Sunday and Monday.

SHACKLEFORD'S

10496 Ridgefield Pkwy.   *741-9900*
$$

Hidden in the corner of the Gleneagles Shopping Center on Ridgefield just west of Pump Road, Shackleford's offers a mixed American grill cuisine. Innovative dishes and a comfortable, informal atmosphere make it a popular place. Hours are 11 AM to midnight daily.

THE SLIP AT SHOCKOE

11 S. 12th St.   *643-3313*
$

The fare here includes chicken, meatballs, shrimp and sandwiches, and there's dancing after 10 PM Friday through Sunday on a lighted dance floor. Hours are 7 AM to 4 PM Monday and Tuesday, until 9 PM Wednesday and Thursday, and until 4 AM Friday. Saturday hours are 9 PM to 4 AM and Sunday hours are 6 PM to 1 AM.

TACO BOTTOM AT
CASTLE THUNDER CAFE

1726 E. Main St.   *648-3038*

$

The basics of Mexican fare are the staple here — burritos, tacos, tortillas, guacamole and the like. There's a side-walk deck for outside dining. Hours are 4:30 PM to 2 AM Monday through Friday and 2:30 PM to 2 AM Saturday.

T.C. WEST
NEIGHBORHOOD STEAK HOUSE

7502 W. Broad St.   *755-6869*
$$

The imaginative menu here offers some of the widest variety in town. It is operated by the same people who brought Richmond The Tobacco Company. This, however, is a casual place with a simple and inexpensive wine list. Lunch is served from 11:30 AM to 2:30 PM every day except Sunday. Dinner hours are 5 PM to 10 PM Monday through Thursday and until 11 PM Friday and Saturday.

T.J.'s GRILL AND BAR

Franklin and Adams Sts. 788-8000, ext. 1134
(in The Jefferson Hotel)
$$

Sandwiches — including maybe the best burger in town — seafood, steaks and pasta are served here in a comfortable setting that almost has the feel of a private club. Service begins in late morning and runs until midnight daily. T.J.'s has a free buffet that caters to the after-work crowd in the early evening.

THE TAVERN AT TRIANGLE PARK

7110-F Patterson Ave.   *282-8620*
$$

Crab cakes, grilled chicken salad, pasta and fresh fish are among the specialties. The enclosed deck is heated in the winter and open in the summer. The Tavern at Triangle Park has a mix of casual ambiance and good food that makes it one of the West End's most popular watering holes. Come here early for dinner because the place fills up fast. Hours are 11 AM to midnight daily.

VILLAGE CAFE

939 W. Grace St.   *353-8204*
$

The Village Cafe is on the edge of the VCU campus. It's an interesting place to go if you have plenty of time and want to catch up on some of the latest trends in counterculture fashions or if you just want to gaze out of the big windows at the passing scene on Grace Street. If the Village Cafe takes its name from Greenwich Village, then it's apt. The menu is varied, but the food here takes second place to other attractions. The cafe opens at 8:30 AM Monday through Friday, at 9 AM Saturday and Sunday, and it remains open every day until 2 AM.

32. Something Different

ANNABEL LEE

4400 E. Main St.   *222-5700*
$$$

This riverboat cruises the James and passengers can enjoy a buffet lunch, brunch or dinner. Served from the ship's complete on-board galley, the menu includes traditional Virginia favorites and Chesapeake Bay specialties. Old Virginia Lunch Cruises are from noon to 2 PM Wednesday through Friday and from 11 AM to 1 PM on Saturday. The Champagne Brunch Cruise on Sunday is from 1 PM to 3 PM. A special Plantation Brunch trip downriver to Westover, Evelynton and Berkeley plantations is provided Tuesday from 10 AM to 5:30 PM. Dinner cruises depart at 7 PM Wednesday through Saturday and at 6 PM on Sunday. Boarding starts a half-hour before departure. Reservations are recommended. Smoking is permitted on the outer decks only.

CARRIAGE COURT
CAFE AT MAYMONT

1700 Hampton St.   *358-7166*
$

The Cafe is in the cobblestone courtyard of the Carriage House at the 100-acre Maymont park and museum. Lunchtime fare of gourmet-style sandwiches and salads is offered. Catering is by A Movable Feast. There's ample free parking. Hours are 11:30 AM to 2 PM Wednesday through Friday from April through early October.

CASABLANCA

6 E. Grace St.   *648-2040*
$

The food here is superior, and the decor does a pretty good job of making you feel like you are in Rick's American Cafe on the set of the famous 1940s movie. The menu of main courses and sandwiches is creative, and dishes are named for Peter Lorre, Sydney Greenstreet and others associated with the film. Specials of the day are always outstanding, and the place shows promise of becoming a Richmond classic. Lunch is served on weekdays from 11:30 AM to 3 PM. Dinner and late-night fare is served on Wednesday through Saturday from 5 PM to 6 AM (that's right, 6 AM) — a real boon for the wee-hours crowd. It is closed Sunday.

DAVID'S WHITE HOUSE RESTAURANT

Rt. 155 (just off U.S. 60)   *966-9700*
Providence Forge
$$$$

The menu is broad-ranging, with dishes like the Plantation Platter, Oysters Weyanoke and other specialties. In a restored turn-of-the-century farmhouse in Providence Forge (midway between Richmond and Williamsburg via U.S. 60), the restaurant is operated by David Napier, one of the original owners of Indian Fields Tavern. Napier's culinary capabilities are well-known by Richmonders who are devoted to fine food. The restaurant is open Tuesday through Sunday for breakfast from 6:30 AM to 11 AM, for lunch until 4 PM, and for dinner from 5 PM to 10 PM. Reservations are recommended.

THE GARDEN AT LINDEN ROW INN
100 E. Franklin St.   783-7000
$

This is a great place for a pleasant outdoor lunch on a nice day. Information on Linden Row Inn is included in the preceeding "Historic Settings" section (Section 1).

LEWIS GINTER BOTANICAL GARDEN
1800 Lakeside Ave.   262-9887
$

Lunch at the Lewis Ginter Botanical Garden at Bloemendaal is served in the Lora and Claiborne Robins Tea House Monday through Saturday from 11:30 AM to 2 PM. Sunday lunch also is served during April and May from noon until 3 PM. Fresh menu selections are provided by Suzanne.

NORTH POLE
Crozier   784-4222
$$

This place is in the horse country of Goochland County, and its food and ambiance are comfortable and unassuming. Hours are 5 PM to 10 PM Wednesday through Sunday.

O'TOOLE'S GAY NINETIES
4800 Forest Hill Ave.   233-1781
$

Seafood, beef and ribs are served here, and if you time it right you can participate in a sing-along. Hours are 11 AM to 2 AM daily.

RACK-N-ROLL CAFE
1713 E. Main St.   644-1204
$

Equipped with nine-foot pool tables and offering good food, Rack-N-Roll is a great place to unwind with your friends. The atmosphere is comfortable, the sound system and TV are state of the art, and there are Game Day Specials on Sunday and Monday. Doors open at 11:30 AM Monday through Friday and at 4 PM Saturday and Sunday, and they stay open seven days a week until 2 AM.

TEXAS-WISCONSIN BORDER CAFE
1501 W. Main St.   355-2907
$

From bratwurst and potato pancakes to chili and enchiladas, the menu is what the restaurant's name implies. There's never a dull moment here. Hours are 11 AM to 2 AM daily.

THE GARDEN
AT THE VALENTINE MUSEUM
Valentine Museum Garden (seasonal) 355-1642
$

From April through October you can slip in the back entrance to the magnificent walled garden at the Valentine Museum and enjoy a tranquil lunch prepared before your eyes. Offerings include stir-fry, custom omelettes, fresh pasta, meats grilled to order, deli sandwiches, salads and desserts. Hours are 11 AM to 2 PM Monday through Friday. Only cash and checks are accepted.

HAVANA '59
16 N. 17th St.   649-CUBA
$$

The owners have gone to great lengths to create an authentic atmosphere of Havana in the days when it was a city of pleasure with a balmy sensuality that affected visitors and natives alike. Fresh fruit

Good Food
Good Friend
and
Glorious
Weather!

Havana '59

16 NORTH 17TH STREET RICHMOND VA 23219
804-649-CUBA

drinks and Cuban and American Diner fare are part of the scene, harking back to the glory days of Sloppy Joe's and Floridita. This place is designed for good friends, good food, good fun and a good cigar. Havana '59 opens at 5 PM Monday through Friday and at 9 PM on weekend nights. It stays open until 2 AM.

ISLAND GRILL
14 N. 18th St.   643-2222
$$

Classic culinary techniques are the foundation, and flavors of "new world" cuisine are the inspiration for this contemporary American grill with innovative tropical, Caribbean and Latin accents. The Island Grill's food, service and sleek city bistro elegance have met with rave critical acclaim. A fresh mixed grill entree with unique tropical sauces is offered daily, along with corn-fed steakhouse-size steaks (real whoppers), seafood and other house specialties. This is a great place if you are in search of a change of pace or just a really good meal. Cocktails and dinner are served from 5:30 PM until closing Monday through Saturday. A late night menu is available. Reservations are suggested.

LIBERTY VALANCE
7017 Forest Hill Ave.   320-4276
$

The jukebox plays country tunes, and the spirits of the Old West and of John Wayne are alive and well here in the decor and theme, as well as in drinks called Miss Kitty and Calamity Jane. Entree portions are for big appetites and feature beef, ribs and great desserts. You can even get a root beer float served in a glass cowboy boot. Liberty Valance opens at 11 AM Tuesday through Friday and at 8 AM Sat-

urday. It closes at 9 PM Tuesday through Thursday and on Sunday, and at 10 PM Friday and Saturday.

MICHEL'S RESTAURANT
421 E. Franklin St.   643-1268
$$$

In the New Orleans-style building at the corner of Fifth and East Franklin in downtown Richmond, Michel's is operated by the chef and partner in the former West End Grill. The emphasis remains much the same as it was at the Grill: fine dining featuring European classics, especially those of French and German origin. Lunch is from 11:30 AM to 2 PM Monday through Friday. Dinner begins at 5:30 PM and is served until 10 PM Monday through Wednesday, and until 11 PM Thursday and Friday. Sunday brunch is served from 10:30 AM to 2:30 PM.

MEMPHIS BAR AND GRILL
119 N. 18th St.   783-2608
$$

Memphis specializes in what it calls "international redneck" fare. This includes Southern pork chops and mashed potatoes, but most of the menu is sophisticated with items like those with origins in places like India, Indonesia and California. Seafoods are fresh and lively, and the salads are great, as are the sandwiches (including roast beef with Memphis Mayonnaise) and "the greatest root beer float you'll ever have." This is a big hangout for expatriate Yankees, maybe because the hosts include a graduate of the Hard Rock Cafe in New York. Hours are noon to 2 AM Monday through Friday, and 5 PM to 2 AM Saturday (with some of the area's hottest bands). The restaurant is closed on Sunday.

OSCAR'S CLUBHOUSE

14311 Brandermill Woods Tr.   744-4118
$$

The location, in the middle of the Brandermill Woods retirement community, might make you hesitate. But if you are looking for pleasant clubhouse ambiance and good food, this is a great place to go, especially if you are searching for a restaurant in the Brandermill area. The entrees are nicely balanced among chicken, beef and seafood choices, and there are a number of lighter selections. Hours are 11:30 AM to 2 AM Monday through Friday, and 4:30 PM to 9 PM Saturday and Sunday.

OUT OF BOUNDS

2701 W. Broad St.   355-7390
$

Televised sports and a long bar flanked by pool tables hold center stage at this casual spot on W. Broad near Boulevard. Don't look for anything fancy on the menu, but there's plenty of variety ranging from reasonably-priced pasta dishes and pizza to chicken and 16-ounce T-bone steaks. Hours are 11 AM to 2 AM daily.

POE'S PANTRY AND PUB

2706 E. Main St.   648-2120
$$

At the end of E. Main Street across from Tobacco Row, Poe's offers friendly service and a casual atmosphere. Its large glassed-in eating area is a nice place to relax and imagine what this neighborhood might have looked like in the days when Poe edited the *Southern Literary Messenger* about a dozen blocks up the street, or when the Confederate Navy Yard was just down the hill. Menu items, while basic, are tagged with names such as Tell Tale Hearts of Artichoke and Raven Chili. Lunch is from 11 AM to 4 PM daily, and dinner is from 5 PM to 10 PM daily. Light fare is available until 2 AM daily.

RED OAK CAFE

Rt. 623 at U.S. 250, Manakin-Sabot   784-2330
$$

If you're looking for great food at an unexpected location in the country, this Goochland County restaurant offers a delightful and casual atmosphere and diverse dishes from applewood-smoked rainbow trout to grilled salmon, plus great desserts. Only dinner is served on Monday through Saturday, and this is from 5 PM to 10 PM Monday through Thursday and from 5 PM to 11 PM Friday and Saturday. Only brunch is served on Sunday, and this is from 11 AM to 2:30 PM.

RENDEZVOUS CAFE

6034 Stonewall Pkwy.   730-7237
$

This cafe is tucked away in the Cold Harbor Shopping Center, but it's a cozy neighborhood place that attracts a friendly group of regulars. If you're in the Mechanicsville area and are looking for good food prepared by a great cook, venture no farther. Hours are 11:30 AM to 2 PM and from 5 PM to 10:30 PM Monday through Saturday.

RICHBRAU BREWERY
AND QUEENS ARMS PUB

1214 E. Cary St.   644-3018
$$

The big draw of this microbrewery is the beer and ale produced on premises. But the club-like atmosphere provides an interesting background for lunch or dinner, and the food is good. Hours are 11:30 AM to 2 PM and 5 PM to 10 PM Monday through Saturday. It is closed Sunday.

Other "craft brewery" bars in town include **Legend Brewing Company** (321 W. Seventh Street, on the South Side), **Commercial Taphouse & Grill** (111 N. Robinson Street; see "Fan District Favorites" section of this chapter) and **Cobblestone Brewery & Pub** (110 N. Eighth Street).

SIMON'S CAFE
3325 W. Cary St.   *359-3366*
$$

Simon's is in the gallery of a church that has been remodeled into a mini-mall. In the winter the tables are arranged inside around a fountain. In the summer they are placed on a large portico overlooking W. Cary Street. It's an unusual location for a restaurant, but where else can you window shop while you have lunch or dinner? Lunch is served from 11 AM to 4 PM Monday through Saturday and dinner from 5 PM to 10 PM Wednesday through Saturday.

TEA OR BRUNCH AT THE JEFFERSON
W. Jefferson at Franklin St.   *(Tea) 788-8000*
$

The Palm Court at The Jefferson Hotel is a great place for afternoon tea, which is served daily. Sunday brunch, from 10:30 AM to 2 PM, is served in the lower lobby with the grand stairway as a backdrop. It's a great place to give visitors a taste of the quintessential South.

WINNIE'S CARIBBEAN CAFE
Second and E. Main Sts.   *649-4974*
$$

Winnie's began serving up Caribbean cuisine long before it became a trend. Spanish, Portuguese, Dutch, African and East Indian influences blend in the menu. Recorded reggae music and Caribbean colors and decor add to the atmosphere. Lunch hours are 11 AM to 3 PM Monday through Friday and dinner hours are from 6 PM to 10 PM Monday through Saturday (including an all-you-can-eat buffet from 6 PM to 10 PM on Friday). Winnie's is closed on Sunday.

ZEUS GALLERY
201 N. Belmont Ave.   *359-3219*
$$

Local art exhibits are featured here. The menu changes frequently but usually includes beef, chicken, seafood, pasta and vegetarian dishes. Midday hours are 11 AM to 2 PM Friday and Saturday and from 10 AM to 3 PM for Sunday brunch. Dinner is served beginning at 5 PM Tuesday through Sunday.

33. Street Vendors & Food Courts

Street vendors with their food carts are seemingly everywhere downtown and in other parts of the city at midday, and they offer fare that ranges from the basic to the gourmet. Lots of people like to pick up their lunches from these sources, then find a sunny spot in the plazas of the James Center, in the MCV area around 12th and Marshall or elsewhere to enjoy a picnic break with a few friends. On 10th Street just south of Cary Street you'll find carts operated by some of Richmond's finest restaurants: **Simons Cafe**, **La Siesta** and **Pierce's Pitt Bar-B-Que**. Food carts usually are set up about 11 AM on weekdays and stay on site until about 3 PM.

Food courts in shopping centers also are favorites for eat-in or to-go fare. Shopping centers with major food courts (including on-site tables and seating) are 6th Street Marketplace, Cloverleaf Mall, Virginia Center Commons, Regency Square, The Shops at Willow Lawn and Chesterfield Towne Center. Most have about a dozen food vendors. All are open during regular mall hours, are wheelchair accessible and offer designated nonsmoking sections.

34. Carryout

Almost any restaurant will be happy to fix carryout meals if you call in advance. Some, such as Bottoms Up Pizza, will even deliver within specified geographical bounds and within certain periods of the day.

For starters, here is a list of some local favorites in the carryout business:

BELLE KUISINE
3044 Stony Point Shopping Center 272-2811
$

Belle Kuisine's peanut butter cookies and Heath bar cookies are out of this world. But the main events are the lunch and dinner entrees (including pastas), the salads and the locally produced specialty foods.

THE CALL GIRL
6359 Jahnke Rd. 320-4753
$

This drive-through has meat loaf, fried chicken, fried shrimp, marinated beef short ribs, even fried chicken gizzards. The varied menu also includes good sandwiches, veggie fries and lots of other selections. The milk shakes are some of the best in town.

CHESAPEAKE BAGEL BAKERY
10839 W. Broad St. 346-3400
Across from Innsbrook
$

Fourteen varieties of fresh-baked bagels, nine flavors of cream cheese, sandwiches, salads, homemade soups, desserts, party platters and a large variety of beverages — everything is here for eat-in or carryout feasts built around bagels or croissants. For breakfast or lunch, Chesapeake Bagel is open seven days a week.

CHICKEN BOX
3000 Third Ave. 228-2442
$

Carryout fast food here includes fried chicken the way it used to be made.

DAIRY QUEEN
4028 N. Cox Rd. 270-1375

This ice cream store only is open late to satisfy your sweet tooth. Dairy Queen serves frozen yogurt as well as soft ice cream and specializes in custom ice cream cakes. This is the home of the Blizzard, a frozen thicker-than-a-shake concoction of soft ice cream blended with fruits, candies or cookies. Dairy Queen is open Monday through Thursday from 10 AM to 10 PM, Friday and Saturday from 10 AM until 11 PM and Sunday from noon until 10 PM.

FANTASTE
1201 W. Main St. 355 1642
$

Fantaste's offerings are covered in the preceeding "Lunch Places" section. Pick up and delivery times are available seven days a week.

GOURMET DELIGHTS
3158-B W. Cary St. 358-7713
$

Gourmet Delights serves up daily a wide assortment of fresh sandwiches, croissants, quiches, salads, breads, muffins, soups and desserts. It also offers espresso and cappuccino. Patio seating is available. Hours are 9 AM to 6 PM Monday through Friday; 9 AM to 5 PM Saturday; and 10 AM to 4 PM Sunday.

HOMEMADES BY SUZANNE

10 S. Sixth St.   775-2116
102 N. Railroad St., Ashland   798-8331
$

Homemades by Suzanne's specialties also are covered previously in "Lunch Places" (Section 28).

INCREDIBLE EDIBLES

1 N. Belmont Ave.   353-3356
$

In keeping with its name, Incredible Edibles offers temptations that range from tarragon chicken and chicken and artichoke pasta salad to some of the most fantastic baked goods and desserts you find anywhere. There are a few tables for those who want to dine in.

THE LAZY BAGEL

3156 W. Cary St.   355-7035
$

This eatery serves nothing but bagels, more than a half-dozen varieties, as well as toppings ranging from hummus to olive pimento cream cheese. Also offered are a meal-size Caesar salad and desserts that include a Toll House Cookie Pie.

A MOVEABLE FEAST

1318 E. Cary St.   644-3663
$

The carryout fare here is truly international. A Moveable Feast is the caterer for the Carriage Court Cafe at Maymont.

MAINLY PASTA

2227 W. Main St.   359-9304
$

If it's pasta, it has to be here!

MEDITERRANEAN BAKERY & DELI

6516 Horsepen Rd.   285-1488
$

This bakery and deli welcomes visitors in at least a half-dozen scripts and languages outside the door. When you leave you'll carry home goodies that easily could have been picked up from a street vendor in Beirut.

NICK'S PRODUCE & INTERNATIONAL FOOD

400 W. Broad St.   644-0683
$

If burgers and fries never quite fill you up, you owe it to yourself to try one of Nick's deli sandwiches.

SALLY BELL'S KITCHEN

708 W. Grace St.   644-2838
$

Sally Bell's is a genuine Richmond institution. It has a secret recipe for making deviled eggs. Its box lunches are popular, so be sure to call ahead.

STONEWALL MARKET

4917 Grove Ave.   358-3821
$

Stonewall Market, in a fashionable section of the West End, is much more than your average run-of-the mill grocery store and will prepare box lunches and deli trays to go. Call in advance.

TAKEOUT TAXI

$ 282-8294

Takeout Taxi offers delivery to your home or office from great restaurants in the Richmond area. Corporate accounts are welcome, or payment may be made by cash or credit card. Minimum order is $10, and there is a modest delivery charge. Service is available from 5 PM to 9:30 PM Sunday through Thursday, and until 10:30 PM Friday and Saturday.

TOKYO TERIYAKI

918 W. Grace St.   355-7517
$

Teriyaki and tempura are the specialties here along with dishes such as chicken

Street vendors do a bustling business downtown at midday.

katsu, fish katsu and miso soup. Call-in orders are prepared to go. Tokyo Teriyaki is a good place to sample Japanese food. White it specializes in take-out orders, there are a few tables, and servers are helpful and knowledgeable.

UKROP'S CARRYOUT CAFE

9645 W. Broad St.	965-0573
5700 Brook Rd.	264-1595
Heritage Building	
10th and Main sts.	648-5633
1611 Bell Creek Rd.	746-4441
13700 Hull Street Rd.	739-8886
8028 W. Broad St.	270-9621
253 N. Washington Hwy.	798-1305
6401 Centralia Rd.	796-1120
3000 Stony Point Rd.	323-0306
1008 Sycamore Sq.	794-7074
Village Shopping Center	288-5263
4717 Walmsley Blvd.	275-7861
9600 Patterson Ave.	740-7030
Gayton Crossing	740-9167
$ (All locations)	

Operated by the famous Richmond grocery chain, the Ukrop's carryout cafes are hard to beat when it comes to freshness and quality. They have a detailed one-page menu, and you can watch food being prepared on the spot, or you can fix your own. For breakfast, lunch or dinner, hours are from 8 AM to 10 PM Monday through Saturday. The Ukrop's Cafe in the Heritage Building (Fresh Express) is open from 7 AM to 6 PM Monday through Friday. The Cafe location in the Village Shopping Center is the talk of the town and is one of the best of the lot.

VIE DE FRANCE

1501 E. Cary St.	780-0748
$	

In the atrium of James Center II, Vie de France offers an extensive array of croissants, muffins and Danishes, and a menu with a decided country French flair.

• **155**

Specials are posted daily. Party trays and catering are a specialty.

WINGS

1127 W. Main St.   354-9997
$

Wings, in the VCU area, specializes in a variety of rapidly prepared, low-cost foods such as burgers, Buffalo wings, steak sandwiches, chicken filet sandwiches, barbecue and salads. It serves lunch and dinner. There are tables and chairs for those who want to eat in. You can get carryout orders or call for delivery.

---

island
GRILL
• 14 N. 18TH ST. •

"...a fresh culinary breeze on the Richmond restaurant scene. Added to that short list of the truly spectacular."
Style Weekly

"...a lot of good vibes in this place."
Washington Post Magazine

"excellent...imaginative dishes with attention-grabbing presentation."
Richmond Times-Dispatch

American • tropics grill
• steaks • seafood
• specialties
(804)643-2222

---

35. Fast Food

For fast food the way it used to be served, and for fast-food architecture that looks like something out of the '50s try:

Bullets, with locations at 7712 W. Broad Street, 1501 E. Ridge Road, 2224 Chamberlayne Avenue, 10100 Midlothian Turnpike, and 400 E. Belt Boulevard;

Checkers, with locations at 1157 Azalea Avenue, 4510 W. Broad Street and 7900 W. Broad Street;

Rally's Hamburgers at 4802 W. Broad Street;

Sonic Drive-In at 2067 Huguenot Road at Robious Road, and at 13923 Hull Street Road.

The burgers and fries are great at all of these places (and sell for 99¢ at Checkers), and Sonic features roller-skating waitresses and thick ice cream floats.

36. Caterers

The Richmond area has a lot of excellent caterers. Here are the names and phone numbers of a few:

Cateraide	355-1642, (800) 355-1642
Catering by Jill	741-0183
duJour	288-8119
Fancy Settings	643-1621
Homemades by Suzanne	798-8331
I Cater	266-3992
Konsta's	359-3122
Mr. Patrick Henry's	644-1322
Thyme & Sage	550-3400

The Bell Atlantic Yellow Pages' listing of caterers covers five pages. This list includes the names of many local restaurants.

Inside
Nightlife

Shockoe Bottom is *the* place to go for nightlife. Richmond's newest clubs, restaurants and bars continue to pop up in old warehouses and office buildings throughout this abandoned industrial area near downtown. The "Bottom" also features The Flood Zone, a popular local concert hall.

In historic Shockoe Slip, an established nightlife area up the hill from the Bottom, you can dance, listen to live music and go bar-hopping at numerous restaurants and clubs in restored tobacco warehouses and historic buildings all within a few city blocks. You can also sample Richmond's own special brew made on premise at the Richbrau Brewery, as well as products made by other guest breweries.

When all the clubs close up, you can have a late-night (or early morning) breakfast at the River City Diner, a '50s-style restaurant with booths and juke boxes that's open all night on the weekend.

In the Fan District, you'll enjoy live music, dancing and a friendly, neighborhood atmosphere at the many pubs, restaurants and bars along Main Street and throughout this historic community near downtown. Other popular night spots are at Innsbrook and at area hotels. Richmond also has many unique neighborhood bars and pubs where you can meet and chat with friends over a cold one while you watch an interesting parade of local characters.

Interest in country music has been growing for several years and helped launch Dakota's, Richmond's largest country music club. Many country music clubs offer two-step and line dancing lessons, and a number of shops and boutiques specialize in weekend cowboy attire — western clothing, hats and boots.

Throughout the area, nightclubs offer a wide range of local and regional bands, and you can hear live music and go dancing every night of the week. Occasionally you can hear nationally known bands or past acts in a small club setting or at the Mosque or the Coliseum. If you like being the center of attention, you'll find Karaoke at a number of clubs.

With so many colleges and universities here, there's a good supply of talented local musicians. Clubs also book groups from Virginia Beach, North Carolina and other nearby areas. To find out who's playing where, check the listings in the *Richmond Times-Dispatch*, *Style Weekly* or *Night Moves*; listen to your favorite radio station, or call Rock Line at 353-7625, the WRXL Concert Line, 345-1020, or WVGO Concert Information, 345-0106.

For something different, Matt's Comedy Club is a popular choice, and billiards has become a fashionable alternative at upscale pool clubs. If you really want to break tradition, try a rock 'n' roll evening at Skate America.

For those who have a taste for the arts, there's the Richmond Symphony plus a wide range of musicals, plays, dinner theaters and dance performances. Fans of the silver screen will find a good selection of new as well as classic films, and there are special events and concerts at the Richmond Coliseum, the Classic Amphitheatre at Strawberry Hill, the Mosque, the Carpenter Center, 6th Street Marketplace, Innsbrook, Dogwood Dell, The Boulders and Paramount's Kings Dominion.

If you like spectator sports, you'll find plenty of college action all year, as well as professional baseball, hockey and auto racing.

In this section, we've listed some of the most popular nightspots in the following categories: Top 40/Beach & Dance, Rock/Progressive, Blues/Jazz/Piano, Acoustic/Folk, Country/Bluegrass, Karaoke, Comedy, Pool & Billiards and Other Popular Bars and Nightspots by area of town. A list of movie theaters by section of town is also provided. Although clubs are listed by the kind of entertainment they usually offer, don't lock them into any one kind of music or crowd. A club can be progressive one night and jazzy the next. Crowds vary too. Please be aware that some of the clubs are also great restaurants and vice versa. For information about sports, special events or the arts, please see those chapters of this book.

As we go to press, some of the nightclubs and restaurants will undoubtedly be coming under new management or changing their hours and entertainment schedule, so be sure to call ahead before you go. Virginia ABC laws prohibit the sale or consumption of alcohol after 2 AM, so most clubs have "last call" around 1:30 AM and close at 2 AM on Friday and Saturday. They all accept major credit cards unless otherwise noted.

Top 40, Beach and Dance Music

THE BUS STOP

1210½ E. Cary St.   788-9933
Open until 2 AM
Cover charge: varies

If you're 18 or older, you can dance through smoke, lights and bubbles to a variety of Top 40 DJ music upstairs.

GLENN'S RESTAURANT

1509 Chamberlayne Ave.   321-3444
Open until 2AM Mon. - Sat.
Closes at 12 PM on Sunday
Cover charge: varies

Glenn's is a popular family-owned restaurant and nightclub that opened in 1937. Rock 'n' roll is featured in the disco Wednesday through Saturday and attracts the 30s crowd. Oldies are played on Friday from 5 PM to 9 PM, followed by progressive music until 1:30 AM. Live music on Sundays begins at 9 PM and features jazz musicians. Lunch, dinner and appetizers are available. The dress is casual.

LIGHTFOOT'S

W. Broad St. and I-64
Hyatt Richmond   285-1234
Open until 2 AM

Tuesday is ladies' night, the most popular event at this club in the Hyatt Hotel, with music by local radio DJs and special giveaways. Wednesday nights feature local radio DJs and giveaways. Local and regional bands play Top 40 dance music on Fridays and Saturdays. There's a good mix of professionals and the 25 to 35 crowd. There is a dress code, and it is enforced. Most people wear business attire or nice casual clothes. The decor features a dance floor surrounded on two sides by raised seating areas, high back cushioned chairs and a marble bar. A full-service bar and appetizers such as quesadillas, buffalo wings and chicken fingers are available. It's best known for its after-work drink specials and complimentary buffets.

PEPPERMINT LOUNGE

Holiday Inn
Rt. 10 and I-95 Chester   748-6321
Open until 2 AM Mon. - Sat.
Closes at 12 PM Sun.

You'll feel like you've entered a time machine at this lounge where they play only music from the '50s, '60s and '70s. Red and white candy stripes dominate the decor. Hula hoops hang from the ceiling, and old hubcaps and guitars cover the walls. There's a small dance floor. A full-service bar and food are available.

RAZZLE'S

9848 Midlothian Tnpk.   330-0007
Open until 2 AM Wed. - Sat.
Closes at 12 PM on Tues.

Dance the night away to a variety of music. DJs play Top 40 on Friday and Saturday but mix it up on other nights. On Tuesday, it's beach music; Wednesday features a radio DJ with giveaways, and Thursday is country night.

In the Best Western Hotel, Razzle's is usually packed on the weekends with about 600 people between 21 and 30. Beach music tends to draw on older crowd.

A full-service bar, buffet dinner and snacks are available.

THE TOBACCO COMPANY

1201 E. Cary St.   782-9431
Cover charge: usually $3

The Tobacco Company offers live music on the first floor and dancing in the Tobacco Club in the basement of this renovated old tobacco warehouse in Shockoe Slip. Known for its three-story atrium and antique furnishings The Tobacco Company features a working exposed-cab elevator brought from the Consolidated Edison building in New York.

On the first floor cocktail level of the restaurant, you'll enjoy pop rock, blues and acoustic groups Tuesday through Saturday. The atmosphere is upscale and comfortable. You can sit at the bar, at a table or in an intimate grouping of chairs and couches.

Downstairs, the Tobacco Company Club has one of the most popular sunken dance floors in Richmond. Live bands and DJs play a variety of danceable Top 40 music. There are two full bars, and sandwiches and appetizers are available. Business travellers and people of all ages come here. The conservative crowd is mostly 21 to 35 and single. The dress code is flexible but enforced. Most of the crowd here wear nice casual or business attire. Khakis and button-downs prevail. The club is open from 8 PM until 2 AM from Thursday through Saturday. The club starts getting full around 10 PM.

VISION'S BEACH CLUB

Holiday Inn Executive Conference Center
Koger Center Blvd.   379-3800
Open until 2 AM Fri. - Sat.
Closes at 11 PM on Sun.
Call for other hours.

You can dance the shag, the bop or line dances at this West End club where beach music, Top 40 and oldies are ever popular. DJs offer a variety of music Wednesday through Saturday. You'll find beach music fans of all ages, from 21 to older than 70, dressed up or down depending on the occasion. The club offers a huge dance floor with lots of brass and bricks and an outdoor deck that's open year round. Liquor, beer, wine and appetizers are offered. The atmosphere is friendly, and the service is good.

Rock/Progressive

HAVANA '59

16 N. 17th St.   649-2822
Open until 2 AM Thurs. - Sat.
Call for other hours.

One of the hottest new clubs in the Bottom, Havana '59 serves up a stylish Cuban atmosphere with potted plants, ceiling fans, imported cigars and a themed menu that features items such as spicy black bean soup. After dinner on the weekends, DJs play a variety of music from an old Jeep suspended from a wall near the ceiling. There is a small dance floor downstairs. A large dance floor is

expected to open soon on the second floor. Located across from the historic Farmer's Market, Havana '59 looks like an old garage from the '50s with large roll-up garage doors at the entrance. The club plans to raise these during warm weather to create an open front and even more of a balmy Cuban atmosphere. Havana '59 attracts a varied clientele, and the dress is casual but somewhat sophisticated. This club is so popular, there is almost always a crowd waiting to get in on the weekend. To avoid the wait, try making reservations for a late dinner.

MEMPHIS BAR & GRILL

119 N. 18th St.   783-2608
Open until 2 AM Tues. - Sat.

Jazz, rock-a-billy, soul, alternative rock and a variety of other musicians play at this New York-style bar Wednesday through Saturday. Tuesday night features an acoustic act. Full-bar service is available, and beer drinkers will delight in the large selection of micro-brewery beers and monthly beer-tastings. Crab dip, quesadillas and spicy Bajou wings are

Credit: Virginia Division of Tourism

The Richmond Coliseum attracts national headliner musical groups.

favorite accompaniments. The restaurant has an artsy look with creative tiling, balcony seating, a sunken dining area, church pews, exposed bricks and high ceilings. Patio dining is also available. While many of the places in the Bottom appeal to a young crowd, Memphis attracts a blend of all ages. Dress is casual. The cover fee ranges from $2 to $8.

MOON DANCE SALOON

9 N. 17th St.   *788-6666*
Open until 2 AM Tues. - Sat.

Acoustic musicians perform at this Southwestern-style restaurant on Wednesday and Thursday nights, and rock-a-billy, blues and rock 'n' roll bands play every Friday and Saturday. Mounted buffalo and coyote wall hangings, Ansell Adams prints and Peruvian and Brazilian accents create a unique atmosphere. A full-service bar is available. The crowd is slightly older, about 25 to 40. Dress is casual. The dinner menu features Mexican, Cuban and South American cuisine. Reservations are recommended before 8 PM. The cover charge ranges from $3 to $6 on weekends.

MULLIGAN'S SPORTS GRILLE

4024-A Cox Rd.   *346-8686*
Open until 2 AM Mon. - Sat.
Closes at 10 PM on Sun.

This popular West End sports bar at Innsbrook offers live modern rock bands on Friday and Saturday and DJ music on Wednesdays and Thursdays. Mulligan's also sponsors chartered trips to sporting events and big holiday parties with giveaways, bands and contests. Mulligan's St. Patrick's Day party draws more than 6,000 people. The club also sponsors "Fridays at Five" with live music in the courtyard.

Decorated with sports memorabilia, Mulligan's has two bars, a dining area, a large dance floor and band room. You can play pool, basketball, pinball, foozball and darts, and you can watch thousands of satellite channels on seven big screens and over 30 TVs. There's also a relaxing outdoor patio overlooking the brook that runs through the Innsbrook complex.

After work, you'll find a lot of business people enjoying the club's happy-hour specials, and at night there's a good mix of people mostly from the West End in their mid-20s to 40s. Families with children are welcome. Mulligan's specializes in steaks, seafood and chicken that you can grill yourself on the area's largest indoor charcoal pit. Dining room reservations are recommended.

Mulligan's also has a restaurant at the 6th Street Marketplace in downtown. Live music is offered there on Fridays and before and after certain events at the Richmond Coliseum.

THE CLOCK TOWER RESTAURANT & CLUB

1500 E. Main St.   *643-0445*
Open until 2 AM Thurs. - Sat.
Call for other hours
Cover charge: varies

In the historic Main Street Station, The Clock Tower Restaurant & Club offers a sophisticated setting in a big space with a casual attitude. You'll see everything from blue jeans to black tie. The huge dance floor downstairs features some of the most danceable, upbeat DJ music in town.

Appetizers such as vegetable tarts, spicy chicken tenders and jumbo lump crab dishes are available downstairs. The full menu is served in the upstairs dining area which is occasionally converted into a concert area for special shows.

Formerly the home of Scarlett's, the decor features marble floors, 25-foot-high ceilings, Corinthian columns and wall murals depicting trains coming into Main Street Station.

THE FLOOD ZONE

11 S. 18th St.   643-6006, (800) 594-TIXX
Ticket prices vary

The Flood Zone is a large concert hall in a renovated old tobacco warehouse in Shockoe Bottom that accommodates about 1,000 people. The club books a variety of groups that play college alternative, blues, reggae, punk, blue grass, rock, African and other popular music that appeals to a wide range of concert fans from college students to couples in their 40s. Even the Richmond Symphony plays here occasionally. Shows are offered four to six nights a week. Regional groups play on Thursdays. Large shows with national groups are booked for other nights.

"Weekend Loft Parties" on Fridays and Saturdays are dance nights with DJs.

The club includes two levels, a large cushioned dance floor in front of the stage, three bars, and one of the best sound systems in the region. Some seating is available, but people usually stand or dance. A balcony overlooks the first level, and a small venue and casual restaurant recently opened on the third level to showcase new and local talent.

Bottled and draft beer is available. Tickets may be purchased in advance at Digits and Plan 9 Records. Shows featuring nationally known groups usually sell-out, so it's a good idea to buy tickets in advance. Dress is very casual.

BOTTOM'S UP PIZZA

1700 Dock St.   644-4400
Open until 2 AM Fri. - Sat.
Call for other hours

Owners Dirk Graham and Coalter Turpin serve arguably the best pizza in town at this popular "see and be seen" hangout in the Bottom under the Triple-Pass of railroad tracks. Live music is offered throughout the week. Call first to find out if a band is playing the night you plan to go. In warm weather, bands play on the outside deck. People who come here tend to be well-mannered, and there's a good mix of couples and singles 25 and older. The dress is mostly casual, but you see everything from jeans to tuxedos. The decor is typical of the area with exposed bricks, ceiling beams, neon accent lights and black-and-white floor tiles. As you might expect, it's always crowded here.

Blues/Jazz/Piano

BOGART'S BACKROOM

203 N. Lombardy St.   353-9280
Open until 2 AM Fri. - Sat.

The Joe Scott Quartet plays jazz and rhythm and blues every Friday from 9:30 PM to 1:30 AM at this small intimate club in the back room of Bogart's cafe-style restaurant in the Fan. Saturday night features the Jazzmaniacs with Steve Kessler and Glenn Wilson. The atmosphere is laid back and appeals mostly to couples. You see everything from suits to jeans, and a lot of people in their late 20s to 40s. The decor is dark and woody with exposed bricks. High-backed booths provide a sense of privacy, and advertisements from the 1940s and '50s add to the nostalgic charm. A full-service bar, Mediterranean-style cuisine and appetizers are available. Open since the 1970s, Bogart's is one of the oldest clubs in the city area. Dinner reservations are accepted.

PARK PLACE WEST

217 W. Clay St.   *783-1711*
Open until 2 AM Sun. - Fri.
Open until 4 AM on Sat.
Cover charge: $3 for live entertainment

Live bands and/or DJs play jazz and Top 40 music Wednesday through Saturday starting at 9 PM. There's an open mike on Thursday and lipsynching on Saturday. Opened by Glenn Brown in 1988, Park Place West offers two floors, an outside deck and two full bars. The dance floor is upstairs, and you can eat and drink on both levels. Dinner, appetizers, liquor, beer and wine are served. Regulars enjoy the chicken wings, seafood and Park Place Punch. Breakfast is served from 1 AM to 4 AM on Saturday.

The majority of customers here are 30-ish, successful black professionals who dress the part. This is the kind of place where the mayor, city council members and professional sports players come to unwind. Tablecloths, mirrors, plants and ceiling fans contribute to the upscale, friendly atmosphere.

Acoustic/Folk

CASTLE THUNDER CAFE & TACO BOTTOM

1724-26 E. Main St.   *648-3038*
Open until 2 AM every night

Recently voted the "most likely to get rowdy on a weekend," this corner cafe with a coffeehouse atmosphere usually books solo performers or small groups Tuesday through Thursday nights. The decor features lots of mahogany and French doors that open onto a sidewalk patio. It's a small place, and it gets crowded quickly. A lot of people like to meet here and enjoy West Coast-style Mexican food. Special drink prices are offered after work during happy hours.

MAIN STREET GRILL

1700 E. Main St.   *644-3969*
Open until 1 AM Fri. - Sat.
Open until 12 PM Tues. - Thurs.
No credit cards

This is a small, folksy, low-key place, in an old, grill-style restaurant. You'll find a wide variety of entertainment here and people who don't like to watch television. On Thursday nights you can enjoy Old-time Jam, featuring Appalachian-style mountain music, and on Fridays and Saturdays the grill offers a variety of live music, cabaret-style acts and even poetry readings. The third Friday of every month is Irish Music Jam.

Musicians have an open invitation to participate in the Old-time Jam and the Irish Music Jam. There is a regular core of musicians that usually appears, and as many as 15 musicians have been known to bring their fiddles, banjos, mandolins, harmonicas and dulcimers. They all play for free, so be prepared when they pass the hat.

Tuesday is slide night. Bring your favorite slides and watch the show.

Established in 1953 by former owner Wally Bless, the grill is the oldest restaurant in Shockoe Bottom. Known as the "Home of the Paco," the restaurant serves a popular pita sandwich filled with unusual ingredients. It features vegetarian food, beer, wine and herbal teas. Like most of the places in the Bottom, it's not unusual to see people waiting outside to get a seat on weekends. They don't take reservations.

SAM MILLER'S WAREHOUSE - CAPTAIN MORGAN'S ROOM

1210 E. Cary St.   *644-5465*
Open until 1:30 AM.

Well established, Sam Miller's was one of the original restaurants in Shockoe Slip. Acoustic acts play here on Fridays and Saturdays. The restaurant specializes in Chesapeake seafood and offers a full-service bar, soup, sandwiches and late-night munchies. The club features a sit-down bar and lounge-style seating. You'll find a good mix of people in their 20s, 30s and 40s here. The atmosphere is casual, and the decor features antiques.

POE'S PANTRY AND PUB

2706 E. Main St.   *648-2120*
Open until 2 AM every night.

This cozy, neighborhood bar, decorated with a raven, photographs of Poe and old Richmond, offers live acoustic music every Friday and Saturday night and an open mike for acoustic musicians on Sundays beginning at 4 PM. In a renovated gas station at the top of the Bottom, the pub is right across the street from the Lucky Strike smokestack. Be sure to try the ribs. A full-service bar is available.

RICHBRAU BREWERY

1214 E. Cary St.   *644-3018*
Open until 2 AM Wed. - Sat.
Closes at 12 PM Mon. -Tues.
and at 9 PM on Sun.

Acoustic musicians play here Tuesday through Thursday. Rock 'n' roll and rhythm and blues bands play here on weekends. Billiards, foozball and darts are available. Several beers are brewed on the premises. A full-service bar and restaurant is available. (See the related sidebar.)

Country/Bluegrass

DAKOTA'S SALOON

Innsbrook   *346-2100*
Open until 1:30 AM Mon. - Sat.
Open Sunday for dinner only
Cover: $3 - $4

Country music and southern rock groups perform in this huge Western-style saloon every Wednesday through Saturday night. Big name national acts are booked occasionally. The saloon can accommodate several hundred people with cocktail seating or about 400 people for concerts. The dance floor is one of the largest in Richmond and features special lighting and TV monitors so you can see yourself dance. Dance lessons are available on several weeknights.

Exposed beams, wooden floors, longhorns, Indian headdresses and mounted stuffed animals add to the Western mood. A long, long bar runs the length of the saloon, and bar stool seating overlooks the dance floor. Patio and deck seating is available in warm weather.

The snack menu features Western-style appetizers and pizza baked in a wood oven.

LONGHORN SALOON & GRILL

6922 Staples Mill Rd.   *262-9292*
Open until 2 AM Wed. - Sat.
Cover Charge: $2 to $3

DJ or live country music is offered Wednesday through Saturday at this *Gunsmoke*-style saloon and eatery. Known as a place to go for a good time, Longhorn's offers dance lessons for beginners and advanced dancers, singles and

Richbrau . . .
A Brew of Our Own

After many years, Richmond has a beer of its own once again.

In Shockoe Slip, at 13th and Cary streets, two local beer drinkers, David Magill and Graham Ramsay, opened the Richbrau Brewery several years ago and brought back the name if not the flavor of Richbrau beer.

Magill and Ramsay purchased the name of Richbrau from the Home Brewing Company, which made Richbrau beer until it went out of business in 1969. Although some Richmonders liked the beer, others had a less than kind opinion of it. Magill and Ramsay are using different recipes. A native of England, Ramsey is the pub's brewer and holds a doctorate in chemistry.

Inside, the atmosphere is friendly, and the decor is similar to an old English pub with a restaurant. An eight-table, Victorian-style billiards lounge is upstairs. Behind the scenes are a lot of stainless steel barrel fermenters and cool storage tanks connected with a complex array of pipes and valves.

The pub regularly brews and serves Golden Griffin, a light ale; Old Nick, a pale ale; and Big Nasty, a porter. Seasonal beer and guest beers from other brew pubs are also offered, and a full-service bar is available.

Beer also makes its way into the beer and onion soup and beer battered onion rings. The moderately priced menu includes a variety of items such as crawfish etouffe, fried calamari and shrimp primavera along with more traditional items such as steaks, hamburgers, sandwiches and, of course, nachos and chicken wings.

Pool tables, darts and foozball are available. The billiards lounge upstairs may be rented for private parties.

couples. The crowd is mixed and mostly single. You'll see a lot of cowboy hats, boots and casual country attire. A full-service restaurant and bar overlooks the dance floor from the "Cat House" upstairs.

MIDWAY LOUNGE

Lee Davis Rd.   746-8630
Open until 1:30 AM Wed. - Sat.
Closes at 9 PM Sun. - Tues.
Minimum Cover Charge: $1 on Fri. and Sat.

The Midway Lounge in Mechanicsville is one of the oldest and one of the most popular country music dance spots in the area. DJs play a mix of music Wednesday through Saturday. Recently, they expanded their format to include Top 40, Classic Rock and rock 'n' roll music along with country. Two-step and line dance lessons are available. Dress is neat but casual — a lot of jeans and nice slacks. Food, liquor, beer and wine are available.

Karaoke

Several clubs regularly offer karaoke. Schedules vary, so be sure to call first to find out when it's offered.

CADDY'S
13312 Midlothian Tnpk.   794-3007

MAXWELL'S
Sheraton Airport Inn
4700 S. Laburnum Ave.   226-6508

SHU'S LOUNGE
Holiday Inn - Downtown
301 W. Franklin St.   644-9871

Other Popular Bars and Nightspots

Some of these are described in more detail in the Restaurants chapter.

Shockoe Bottom

AWFUL ARTHUR'S OYSTER BAR
101 N. 18th St.   643-1700

GOODFELLAS RESTAURANT
1722 E. Main St.   643-5022

PARAGON
1718-20 E. Main St.   788-1101

RIVER CITY DINER
1712 E. Main St.   644-9418

ROCKBOTTOM CAFE
13 N. 17th St.   225-1382

THE FROG AND THE REDNECK
1417 E. Cary St.   643-FROG

THE ISLAND GRILL
14 N. 18th St.   643-2222

Church Hill

THE HILL CAFE
2800 E. Broad St.   648-0360

The Fan

COYOTE'S
1323 W. Main St.   353-0525

JOE'S INN
205 N. Shields Ave.   355-2282

CARY STREET CAFE
2631 W. Cary St.   353-7445

NOT BETTY'S
2401 W. Main St.   359-4404

SANTA FE
2232 W. Main St.   359-8252

SOBLES
2600 W. Main St.   358-7843

BUDDY'S PLACE
Robinson St. and Stuart Ave.   355-3701

THE TROLLEY
1627 W. Main St.   353-4060

RICK'S CAFE
1847 W. Broad St.   359-1224

DAVIS & MAIN
2501 W. Main St.   353-6641

TEXAS-WISCONSIN BORDER CAFE
1501 W. Main St.   355-2907

West End

HOOTER'S
7912 W. Broad St.   270-9464

POTTER'S PUB
Village Shopping Center   282-9999

South Side

O'TOOLES GAY NINETIES
4800 Forest Hill Ave.   233-1781

CADDY'S
13312 Midlothian Tnpk.   794-3007

SUNDAY'S
4602 Millridge Pkwy.   744-2545

Comedy

COMEDY CLUB AT
MATT'S BRITISH PUB
109 S. 12th St.   643-JOKE, 644-0848
Admission: $8 per person

In Shockoe Slip, the Comedy Club at Matt's British Pub features two live performances by professional comedians every Friday at 8 PM and 10:30 PM, and Saturday at 8 PM and 11 PM. Shows are about an hour and 40 minutes and include three entertainers. Drinks, sandwiches and snacks are served during the shows in a nightclub atmosphere downstairs from Matt's restaurant.

After five years in Richmond, the club has booked performers such as Ricky Kalmon, Klaus Meyers, Jay Leno, Andrew Dice-Clay, Warren Hutcherson and Richmond's own Brett Leake, who made his television debut on "The Tonight Show."

The decor is rustic, and the crowd dresses comfortably. The intimate atmosphere makes the Comedy Club a favorite of comedians all over the country. It seats about 125 people and has been compared to comedy rooms in New York. Owner Anita Fletcher has two other clubs: The Comedy Club in Williamsburg and the Comedy Club at the Carolinian in Nags Head, North Carolina.

Matt's serves British food and offers a full-service bar. If you want to eat dinner at Matt's, make dinner reservations for about 2 hours before the show. The shows usually sell out by Friday, so make your reservations early.

Pool and Billiards

BREAKERS
4032-A Cox Rd.   747-7665
Open until 2 AM every night

Sipping cocktails and playing pool has become very fashionable at this Innsbrook club next to DeFazio's. You can also play darts. There is a sit-down bar and seating near the pool tables and a patio and bar overlooking the brook and waterfall. The decor features lots of brass. You'll find a good mix of people here from professionals to couples. Nice casual attire is preferred. A full-service bar and a full menu with food by DeFazio's is available. Nine-ball and eight-ball tournaments are held here every week, and the club sponsors a Monday night league.

RACK 'N ROLL
1713 E. Main St.   644-1204
Open until 2 AM every night
Cover: $1 - $2

Live bands play rock and progressive music on Friday and Saturday night while you play pool and watch satellite sports shows on strategically placed TVs. The club has seven pool tables and sponsors leagues and tournaments. A full-service bar is available. The menu offers just about everything from filet mignons and burgers to salads, sandwiches and quesadillas. You'll see mostly couples here in their 20s and early 30s. The dress is casual.

SIDE POCKET
2012 Staples Mill Rd.   *353-7921*
Open until 2 AM every night

You can play billiards, pool, video games, chess, checkers, backgammon or watch TV while you enjoy your favorite brew at this West End hangout in the Crossroads Shopping Center. Sandwiches, shrimp, chicken wings and other snacks are available as well as daily meal specials. This is a very casual place with reasonable prices and a good mix of people. There are tables and seats near the pool tables, or you can sit at the bar or at a table in the snack room. Nine-ball tournaments are held here monthly.

Movie Theaters

Here's a list of movie theaters by area. To find out what's playing, just check the "green section" or the entertainment section of the daily newspaper. Many offer gift certificate books and have special children's matinee series.

BYRD MOVIE THEATRE
2908 W. Cary St.   *353-9911*

Richmond's oldest movie palace, the Byrd Theatre, was built for $900,000 and opened on Christmas Eve, 1928. It became a Virginia historic landmark in 1977 and is the only old-style movie palace left in Richmond. Eddie Weaver and other local organists still play the theater's Wurlitzer organ — the largest in the area. The Byrd offers 99¢ movies and other entertainment.

Chesterfield

WESTOVER 99 CENT THEATRE
4712 Forest Hill Ave.   *233-2106*

MIDLOTHIAN 6 CINEMAS
7901 Midlothian Tnpk.   *272-9300*

GENITO FOREST CINEMA 9
11000 Hull St.   *276-8100*

UNITED ARTISTS THEATRES
Chesterfield Towne Center   *379-7800*

CLOVERLEAF MALL CINEMA 8
7201 Midlothian Tnpk.   *276-6600*

CHESTER CINEMAS
13025 Jefferson Davis Hwy.
Chester   *796-5911*

SOUTHPARK MALL CINEMAS
374 Southpark Mall
Colonial Heights   *751-0060*

SOUTHGATE CINEMAS
5955 Midlothian Tnpk.   *233-2777*

West End

CINEMA & DRAFT HOUSE
8099 W. Broad St.   *747-6300*

BYRD THEATRE
2908 W. Cary St.   *353-9911*

RIDGE CINEMA 7
1510 E. Ridge Rd.   *285-1567*

WEST TOWER CINEMAS
Westend Dr. and W. Broad St.   *270-7111*

WESTHAMPTON CINEMA 1 & 2
5706 Grove Ave.   *288-9007*

WILLOWLAWN CINEMAS 4
Willow Lawn Mall
Highland Springs   282-7323

HENRICO THEATRE
305 E. Nine Mile Rd.   737-7661

Ashland

ASHLAND THEATRE
203 England St.   798-3990

Hanover

VIRGINIA CENTER 14
10091 Jeb Stuart Pkwy.   261-5411

Credit: Virginia Division of Tourism

The stately Jefferson Hotel offers some of the most luxurious accommodations in Richmond.

Inside
Accommodations

There was a period of time in the late 1980s when a new hotel opened in Richmond at the rate of one every other month.

As a result, guest rooms in the area's 150 hotels and motels now exceed 11,000. This means you'll probably be able to find just about anything you want in terms of accommodations with up-to-date amenities.

The following guide is not a complete listing of hotels, motels, inns and bed and breakfasts, but the list includes some of our favorites and will get you started. Most places have nonsmoking rooms available.

The dollar sign ($) code with each entry indicates what it will cost for one night's lodging during the week for a room with two people. It works as follows:

$20 to $30	$
$31 to $50	$$
$51 to $75	$$$
$76 and up	$$$$

Keep in mind, since this is a guide, that rates are subject to change and that weekend rates often are substantially less.

All hotels and motels described in this chapter accept VISA and MasterCard, and many also accept other major credit cards. It's always wise to call ahead and make reservations because when a major convention hits town, rooms can be difficult to find at the last minute.

For your convenience, hotel accommodations are listed geographically: downtown, east, north, south and west.

Downtown

BERKELEY HOTEL
12th and Cary Sts.   780-1300
$$$$

This is an AAA four-diamond, European-style hotel centrally located in historic Shockoe Slip, two blocks from the State Capitol. It has 55 rooms, an excellent restaurant, valet parking for room and dinner guests, and a complimentary health club. The largest of its three meeting rooms will accommodate 150 persons, the smallest, 12. Its Governor's Suite has a 25-foot vaulted ceiling, two baths (one with a Jacuzzi) and three terraces with a skyline view of the city. The hotel is handicapped accessible.

COMMONWEALTH
PARK SUITES HOTEL
Ninth and Bank Sts.   343-7300
$$$$

At the edge of Capitol Square, this prestigious AAA four-diamond hostelry is the home of The Assembly Restaurant and Maxine's for informal dining. Its 59 rooms are all suites. There are three meeting rooms. The hotel is accessible to the handicapped, and pets are allowed.

HOLIDAY INN HISTORIC DISTRICT
301 W. Franklin St.   *644-9871*
$$$

This is the home of Virginia legislators when the state's General Assembly is in session, and it's a popular overnight place for bus tours. It has 216 rooms, three suites and four meeting rooms. There is a restaurant with a second-floor view of historic Franklin Street as well as a first-floor lounge off of the lobby. It is handicapped accessible, and pets are allowed.

JEFFERSON HOTEL
Franklin and Adams Sts.   *788-8000*
$$$$

The Jefferson has no peer in Richmond. It has earned a coveted AAA five-diamond rating and a four-star rating in the Mobil Travel Guide. Built in 1895 and totally renovated in the 1980s, it has everything you would expect of a legendary grand hotel. Upper and lower lobby areas are connected by a magnificent stairway that easily could have been a model for the one in *Gone With The Wind*. There are 274 guest suites and rooms. Its 23,000 square feet of meeting space includes 12 versatile rooms plus a Grand Ballroom resplendent in gold detail. A state-of-the-art fitness center is available to guests. The hotel is the home of a gourmet restaurant, Lemaire, and of T.J.'s Bar & Grill.

LINDEN ROW INN
100 E. Franklin St.   *783-7000*
$$$$

Linden Row is a modern restoration of seven antebellum townhouses, three Garden Quarter buildings and a carriage house (now the dining room for Inn guests). Its 70 guest rooms, including seven parlor suites, are appointed with Empire furnishing and modern amenities. Guests may use fitness facilities of the YMCA one block away. There's one meeting room that will accommodate up to 32 persons theater-style, and suites also can be used for meetings. If you like history, you'll love Linden Row and its central location. It is handicapped accessible and has received an AAA four-diamond rating.

MARRIOTT RICHMOND
500 E. Broad St.   *643-3400*
$$$$

The Marriott, with 30,000 square feet of meeting space and a direct connection to the Richmond Centre, is action central. It has 401 guest rooms including two presidential suites, four hospitality suites and four executive suites. Three restaurants offer guests dining possibilities ranging from JW's Steakhouse to a lobby lounge/buffet. The hotel has an indoor pool, hydrotherapy whirlpool, saunas, weight room, tanning salon and aerobics instruction. Complimentary guest parking is available in an adjacent 1,015-space lot. The AAA four-diamond hotel is handicapped accessible and has an in-house audio visual company.

OMNI RICHMOND
100 S. 12th St.   *344-7000*
$$$$

The ultramodern Omni enjoys a strategic location in the James Center adjacent to Shockoe Slip and Richmond's financial district, and it is just a few blocks from the State Capitol. The Omni's 363 first-class guest rooms feature in-room movies, executive desk with phone, and a mini-bar. There are 10 parlor suites and two hospitality suites, each with an area for entertaining. There are 42 Omni Club rooms on two floors with private lounge and a concierge. About 14,000 square feet of meeting space is available in 13 rooms, and the hotel has an indoor pool and free

LINDEN ROW INN

Enjoy the unique and Greek Revival Architecture of this historic Inn located within walking distance of museums, entertainment shops and other attraction. This AAA four diamond Inn offers a full continental breakfast and an evening wine and cheese reception. For reservation, please call 804-783-7000.

100 E. Franklin St.

underground parking. The Omni is handicapped accessible and is the home of Caffe Gallego and of Gallego Restaurant & Wine Bar. It has received an AAA four-diamond rating.

RADISSON HOTEL RICHMOND

555 E. Canal St.   788-0900
$$$$

The Radisson Hotel Richmond is a 296-room, full-service hotel with a spectacular view of the James River. It has an indoor swimming pool and health facilities complete with Jacuzzi, sauna and exercise equipment. The Radisson offers handicapped access and more than 8,000 square feet of meeting space in nine rooms which, along with its restaurants, are on its second floor and easily reached from the hotel's parking deck.

East

BEST WESTERN AIRPORT

5700 Williamsburg Rd
Sandston   222-2780
$$

This airport hotel has 122 guest rooms, four suites and more than 1,100 square feet of meeting space in four rooms. There's an outdoor pool plus a restaurant on premises. The hotel is handicapped accessible.

DAYS INN AIRPORT

5500 Williamsburg Rd.
Sandston   222-2041
$$

Days Inn Airport has 100 guest rooms, an outdoor pool, one meeting room that will accommodate up to 35 persons theater-style and a restaurant. The hotel is handicapped accessible. Pets are allowed.

ECONO LODGE AIRPORT
5408 Williamsburg Rd.
Sandston   222-1020
$$

Econo Lodge Airport has 53 rooms, but no meeting facilities. Pets are allowed.

HAMPTON INN AIRPORT
5300 Airport Square Ln.
Sandston   222-8200
$$$

With an outdoor swimming pool, 125 guest rooms (including "no smoking" rooms), a hospitality suite and a free deluxe continental breakfast, this Hampton Inn provides comfortable accommodations at the airport. It has two small meeting rooms. Pets are allowed, and there is handicapped access.

RICHMOND AIRPORT HILTON
5501 Eubank Rd.
Sandston   226-6400
$$$$

This new Hilton has 158 guest rooms, a restaurant (called Wings), a heated outdoor pool, an exercise room, and it is handicapped accessible. Its seven meeting rooms cover 4,500 square feet, are flexible and are capable of handling up to 400 persons theater-style. Guest suites are ideal for small meetings of up to 12 people.

HOLIDAY INN AIRPORT
5203 Williamsburg Rd.
Sandston   222-6450
$$$

This is the largest airport hotel, with 230 guest rooms. It has seven meeting rooms covering almost 7,000 square feet, which together are capable of handling theater-style seating for up to 600 persons. There is a restaurant on premises; the hotel is handicapped accessible; and pets are allowed.

LEGACY INN/AIRPORT
5252 Airport Square Ln.
Sandston   226-4519
$$

All accommodations here are handicapped-accessible ground-floor rooms; pets are welcome; there's an outdoor pool; and nonsmoking rooms are available. Eleven of the 123 rooms have kitchenettes.

MOTEL 6
5704 Williamsburg Rd.
Sandston   222-7600
$$

Motel 6 at the airport has 121 guest rooms. It has handicapped access and an outdoor swimming pool. Pets are allowed.

SHERATON AIRPORT INN
4700 S. Laburnum   226-4300
$$$$

The Sheraton Airport's ground-floor atrium complex consists of an indoor heated pool, whirlpool, exercise gym, saunas, hair care center, gift shop and meeting and banquet rooms. A buffet breakfast is served daily in the atrium, and the hotel's Maxwell's Restaurant and Pub offers casual dining. There are 151 guest rooms and suites and 11 meeting rooms. The hotel is handicapped accessible, and pets are allowed.

SUPER 8 MOTEL
5110 Williamsburg Rd.   222-8008
$$

This airport motel has 51 rooms and is handicapped accessible.

North

BEST WESTERN HANOVER HOUSE
I-95 at Atlee-Elmont Exit
Ashland   550-2805
$$$

The restaurant here is a popular gathering place for people who work nearby. Hanover House has 93 guest rooms and six meeting rooms. Ramps provide access for the handicapped, and there's an outdoor swimming pool.

BEST WESTERN KINGS QUARTERS
I-95 and Rt. 30
Doswell   876-3321
$$

Near King's Dominion, this Best Western has 248 rooms and one suite. There is a restaurant on premises and an outdoor pool. Pets are allowed, and it is handicapped accessible.

COMFORT INN ASHLAND
101 Cottage Green Dr.
Ashland   752-7777
$$

Free continental breakfast is offered here, nonsmoking rooms are available, and there's an outdoor pool, a health center and handicap access. Accommodations include 126 rooms and two suites.

ECONO LODGE NORTH
5221 Brook Rd.   266-7603
$$

This Econo Lodge has 187 guest rooms and three meeting rooms. There's a restaurant on premises and an outdoor swimming pool. Pets are allowed.

HOJO INN BY HOWARD JOHNSON
I-95 and Rt. 54
Ashland   798-9291
$$

With 98 rooms, this HoJo Inn in Ashland offers a restaurant on premises, nonsmoking rooms, an outdoor pool, and handicapped access.

Spend summer nights listening to music at Dogwood Dell.

Insiders' Tips

HOLIDAY INN ASHLAND
I-95 and Rt. 54
Ashland   798-4231
$$$

Holiday Inn Ashland has 165 guest rooms and one suite. There are three meeting rooms. It has access for the handicapped, an outdoor swimming pool and a restaurant on premises.

HOJO INN BY HOWARD JOHNSON
801 Parham Rd.   266-8753
$$$

This West End HoJo Inn offers 82 guest rooms, a restaurant, an outdoor swimming pool and handicapped access.

RAMADA INN NORTH
5701 Chamberlayne Rd.   266-7616
$$

This Ramada Inn has 104 rooms, handicapped access, a restaurant and an outdoor swimming pool. Its six meeting rooms cover 4,500 square feet.

QUALITY INN NORTH
9002 Brook Rd.   266-2444
$$$

This Quality Inn has 63 rooms, one suite, a restaurant and an outdoor swimming pool.

SUPER 8 MOTEL
5615 Chamberlayne Ave.   262-8880
$$

With a convenient Northside location, this Super 8 offers 61 guest rooms and is handicapped accessible.

South

BRANDERMILL INN
13550 Harbour Pointe Pkwy.
Midlothian   739-8871
$$$$

The 59 guest rooms here are all two-level suites. The inn offers a boardroom and a conference room for meetings, and it has an outdoor swimming pool and an indoor Jacuzzi and health spa. Its Lakeside Restaurant specializes in American-Italian cuisine and seafood, and it has a nightclub lounge. The inn is handicapped accessible.

BEST WESTERN GOVERNOR'S INN
9848 Midlothian Tnpk.   323-0007
$$

The Governor's Inn offers 49 guest rooms, two suites, six meeting rooms, an outdoor swimming pool and hot tub, a restaurant on premises and is handicapped accessible. Small pets are allowed, but a deposit is required for dogs.

COMFORT INN
2100 W. Hundred Rd.
Chester   751-0000
$$$

Ten suites and 123 guest room are available in this Comfort Inn. There are three meeting rooms. Handicapped access is provided, and there is a restaurant and an outdoor swimming pool. Pets are allowed.

COMFORT INN CORPORATE GATEWAY
8710 Midlothian Tnpk.   320-8900
$$$

Here you will find a restaurant, outdoor pool and four meeting rooms, all backed up by 156 guest rooms and five suites. Guest accommodations include large rooms with a seating area for entertaining, refrigerators, cable television, microwaves on request, complimentary continental breakfast and a newspaper. The inn is handicapped accessible.

DAYS INN CHESTER
I-95 and Rt. 10
Chester   748-5871
$$

This Days Inn has 120 guest rooms

12th & Cary Streets
P.O. Box 1259
Richmond, VA 23210
(804) 780-1300

Management by N.R. & Associates

*Exceptional service,
Classic cuisine, Tranquil
ambience. Created to be an
establishment dedicated to
preserving innkeeping as
an art, The Berkeley
Hotel's charm and gracious
attention to guest needs
recreates the era when
service was paramount.*

and 52 suites. It is handicapped accessible and has a restaurant and an outdoor swimming pool. Pets are allowed.

DAYS INN CHESTERFIELD
1901 Huguenot Rd
Midlothian 794-9999
$$$

Days Inn Chesterfield has 120 guest rooms and four meeting rooms. It is handicapped accessible.

DAYS INN MIDLOTHIAN
6346 Midlothian Tnpk. 276-6450
$$

This motel has the largest meeting room capacity of any of the Days Inns in Chesterfield County. Its three meeting rooms cover more than 5,000 square feet and will accommodate up to 400 persons theater-style. There are 170 guest rooms and three suites. A restaurant is on the premises, and handicapped access is available.

ECONO LODGE SOUTH KINGSLAND
2125 Willis Rd. 271-6031
$$

This new Econo Lodge on Richmond's south side has 48 guest rooms. Pets are allowed.

ECONO LODGE WEST
6523 Midlothian Tnpk. 276-8241
$$

This motel on Chesterfield County's Midlothian corridor has 72 economy-priced guest rooms. There is handicapped access, and pets are allowed.

ECONOMY HOUSE MOTEL
2302 Willis Rd. 275-1412
$$

There's a restaurant on premises, 70 guest rooms and two meeting rooms at this motel. It has an outdoor swimming pool, and pets are allowed.

HOLIDAY INN
EXECUTIVE CONFERENCE CENTER
1021 Koger Blvd. 379-3800
$$$$

Part of the Koger Center off Midlothian Turnpike, this Holiday Inn has extensive meeting facilities. Its 11 meeting rooms will handle 900 persons in theater-style seating. There are 200 guest rooms and two suites. A fitness center next door offers indoor/outdoor tennis, racquetball, a soccer field, a baseball diamond and basketball courts. The inn has a restaurant, an outdoor swimming pool and is accessible for the handicapped.

HOLIDAY INN CHESTER

2401 W. Hundred Rd.
Chester   748-6321
$$$

An outdoor swimming pool, a restaurant, 167 guest rooms and two meeting rooms are part of the facilities at this Holiday Inn on Richmond's far south side. It is handicapped accessible.

HOLIDAY INN SOUTHEAST

I-95 and Bells Rd.   275-7891
$$$

This Holiday Inn offers 173 guest rooms and three meeting rooms. Amenities include a restaurant and lounge, an outdoor swimming pool and handicapped access. Pets are allowed.

INDIAN HILLS INTERSTATE INN

2201 Indian Hills Rd.   526-4772
$$

The lounge here has live country music nightly. The inn offers 102 rooms, a restaurant on premises, an outdoor pool, nonsmoking rooms and handicapped access. It permits pets.

LA QUINTA MOTOR INN

6910 Midlothian Tnpk.   745-7100
$$$

Here you'll find 130 guest rooms, two small meeting rooms, an outdoor swimming pool and a restaurant. There is handicapped access, and pets are allowed.

RAMADA INN SOUTH

2126 Willis Rd.   271-1281
$$$

There's a restaurant on premises, an outdoor pool, handicapped access, and

nonsmoking rooms are available. Accommodations include two suites and 98 rooms.

RED ROOF INN CHIPPENHAM

Chippenham Pkwy. and Midlothian Tnpk.
$$ 745-0600

This Red Roof Inn offers 81 guest rooms, has handicapped access and allows pets.

RED ROOF INN SOUTH

I-95 and Bells Rd.   271-7240
$$

This Red Roof Inn on I-95 south of the city has 109 guest rooms, is handicapped accessible and allows pets.

SHERATON PARK SOUTH

9901 Midlothian Tnpk.   323-1144
$$$

One of the classier hotels in this part of Richmond, the Sheraton Park South has 200 guest rooms, four suites, 10 meeting rooms and a popular restaurant. For conventions and banquets, the facility can accommodate groups ranging from 10 to 400 persons. Amenities include an indoor-outdoor swimming pool, sauna, Jacuzzi and health club. Jogging trails wind around adjacent lakes. The hotel is handicapped accessible, and pets are allowed.

SUPER 8 MOTEL

8260 Midlothian Tnpk.   320-2823
$$

This Super 8 has 80 guest rooms, one suite and one small meeting room. It is handicapped accessible, and pets are allowed.

SUPER 8 MOTEL

2421 Southland Dr.
Chester   748-0050
$$

Juts off I-95 at Route 10 and U.S. 301, this motel offers waterbeds, four specially-

designed handicapped rooms, 45 rooms and two suites. Pets are allowed with permission, there's an adjacent restaurant, and nonsmoking rooms are available.

West

AMERISUITES
4100 Cox Rd.
Glen Allen   747-9644
$$$

Part of the sprawling Innsbrook Corporate Center, Amerisuites has an outdoor swimming pool, 126 guest suites and three meeting rooms. It is handicapped accessible.

COMFORT INN EXECUTIVE CENTER
7201 W. Broad St.   672-1108
$$$

This Comfort Inn, just off the Broad Street exit on I-64, has 122 guest rooms,

one suite, a small meeting room and an outdoor swimming pool. It is handicapped accessible.

COMFORT INN MIDTOWN
3200 W. Broad St.   359-4061
$$$

Meeting facilities here include six rooms with a capacity of 550 person theater-style. There are 196 guest rooms and eight suites. Access for handicapped individuals is available at the front door and from the parking deck. There's an outdoor pool, and pets are allowed.

COURTYARD BY MARRIOTT
6400 W. Broad St.   282-1881
$$$

Across Broad Street from Reynolds Metals Company's corporate headquarters, the Courtyard by Marriott has 145 guest rooms, 13 suites, an outdoor swimming pool and two small meeting rooms. It is handicapped accessible.

FAIRFIELD INN

7300 W. Broad St.   672-8621
$$

A total of 124 guest rooms are available in this Fairfield Inn. It has an outdoor swimming pool and is handicapped accessible. Fairfield Inn is the economy chain of Marriott International.

DAYS INN

1600 Robin Hood Rd.   353-1287
$$

Near The Diamond and just off I-95 at the Boulevard Exit, this Days Inn has a restaurant, an outdoor pool, handicapped access and 99 rooms. Pets are allowed.

DAYS INN WEST BROAD

2100 Dickens Rd.   282-3300
$$

Just off the I-64/Broad Street Exit, this motel has 182 guest rooms, one small meeting room, and an outdoor swimming pool. It is handicapped accessible, and pets are allowed.

BEST WESTERN JAMES RIVER INN

8008 W. Broad St.   346-0000
$$$

This 177-room Best Western has three meeting rooms that can accommodate up to 100 persons in theater-style seating. It has an outdoor swimming pool and handicapped access, and it offers free van service to the airport and Amtrak station.

EMBASSY SUITES HOTEL

2925 Emerywood Pkwy.   672-8585
$$$$

With an indoor swimming pool, full-service fitness facilities, 226 suites and eight meeting rooms that can handle up to 450 persons theater-style, this hotel is

just off W. Broad Street near the I-64 interchange. It has a restaurant and is handicapped accessible.

HAMPTON INN

10800 W. Broad St.   747-7777
$$$

This Hampton Inn offers 136 guest rooms, two meeting rooms with audio/visual equipment, an outdoor swimming pool and a free continental breakfast. This hotel is handicapped accessible.

HOLIDAY INN CROSSROADS

2000 Staples Mill Rd.   359-6061
$$$

The Holiday Inn Crossroads is the only scheduled in-town pickup point for the Washington-Richmond airport ground shuttle. It has 144 guest rooms, seven suites, an outdoor pool, a restaurant and three meetings rooms with a capacity of 225 persons theater-style. There is handicapped access, and pets are allowed.

HOLIDAY INN I-64 WEST BROAD

6531 W. Broad St.   285-9951
$$$$

The lounge here has nightly entertainment and is one of Richmond's popular nightspots. It also has a quieter place to unwind that's called The Club. There are 280 guest rooms, 10 suites and nine meeting rooms capable of handling up to 575 persons theater-style. The catering department can prepare anything from a coffee break to a full dinner. The Holiday Inn has a fitness club and an indoor swimming pool. It is handicapped accessible.

HOLIDAY INN CENTRAL

3207 N. Boulevard   359-9441
$$$

At the Boulevard exit from I-95, the

Holiday Inn Central is a place where you will find flowers everywhere, even in its Magnolia Restaurant. It has an outdoor swimming pool, 183 guest rooms, one suite, and five meeting rooms capable of handling up to 550 persons theater-style. It is handicapped accessible.

HOWARD JOHNSON-DIAMOND STADIUM
1501 Robin Hood Rd.   *353-0116*
$$$

This Howard Johnson near The Diamond offers 115 rooms, 20 two-room suites, nonsmoking rooms, a restaurant, an outdoor pool and handicapped access.

HYATT RICHMOND
6624 W. Broad St.   *285-1234*
$$$$

The West End's prestige hotel, the Hyatt has 372 guest rooms and suites surrounding a 9,000-square-foot indoor-outdoor pool and garden courtyard. It is the home of two popular restaurants: Hugo's (an Italian bistro) and the plant-filled Greenhouse. Here also you will find Lightfoot's lounge, a longtime favorite. Recreational facilities, in addition to the swimming pool, include a health club,

lighted tennis courts and a jogging course with exercise stations. Topping it all off are 24 meeting rooms encompassing 28,000 square feet, with the largest room capable of accommodating almost 7,000 people theater-style. The hotel is handicapped accessible.

MARRIOTT RESIDENCE INN
2121 Dickens Rd.   *285-8200*
$$$$

If you like lots of elbow room, one of the 80 suites here should do the job. It's just off of W. Broad Street near I-64. Nonsmoking suites are available; pets are allowed; there's an outdoor pool and handicapped access. Extended-stay executive accommodations can be arranged.

RAMADA INN WEST
Parham and Quioccasin Rds.   *285-9061*
$$$

Near Regency Square shopping center, Ramada Inn West has 105 guest rooms, 16 suites, three meeting rooms capable of handling up to 225 persons theater-style, a restaurant for breakfast and an outdoor swimming pool. It is handicapped accessible.

RED CARPET INN EXECUTIVE CENTER

5215 W. Broad St.   288-4011
$$

Here you'll find Red Carpet ameni-
ties including a full-service restaurant,
exercise and laundry facilities, banquet
rooms, an outdoor swimming pool and
monthly and weekly rates. The inn is near
The Shops At Willow Lawn.

SHONEY'S INN OF RICHMOND

7007 W. Broad St.   672-7007
$$$

Shoney's Inn is near the Broad Street
Exit on I-64 and offers 120 guest rooms,
three suites, a small meeting room, a restaurant and an outdoor swimming pool.
Pets are allowed, and it is handicapped
accessible.

SUPER 8 MOTEL

7200 W. Broad St.   672-8128
$$

One of the smaller lodging facilities
in the Richmond area, this Super 8 has
49 guest rooms and three small meeting
rooms. It is handicapped accessible.

Bed and Breakfasts

It is necessary to make advance reser-
vations at all Richmond bed and break-
fasts. Some have private baths, some
don't, and most do not permit smoking.
So be sure you inquire about these things
if they are important to you.

A reservation service for bed and
breakfasts in the Richmond area and in
Williamsburg is operated in Richmond
by Bensonhouse at 353-6900.

Ashland

THE HENRY CLAY INN

114 Railroad Ave.   798-3100
$$$$

This magnificent inn probably

shouldn't be listed under Bed & Break-
fasts because it has 14 rooms, one suite,
private baths, Jacuzzis, fireplaces, grand
porches with rocking chairs, a highly-ac-
claimed restaurant serving home-style
food and an art and gift gallery. Adjacent
to Randolph-Macon College, it has a
cozy, small-town, bygone-era feel about
it, although it was rebuilt from the ground
up in 1992. Reception rooms are avail-
able for social events.

Charles City County

Along historic Route 5 and within
about a 25-minute drive from downtown
Richmond are:

EDGEWOOD PLANTATION

4800 John Tyler Memorial Hwy. (Rt. 5)
$$$$ 829-2962

This Victorian mansion drips with
history, charm and romance. It has six
bedrooms, 10 fireplaces, period canopy
beds, vintage clothing, museum antiques,
candlelight breakfasts, a pool and hot tub.

NORTH BEND PLANTATION

12200 Weyanoke Rd.   829-5176
$$$$

Built in 1819 for Sarah Harrison, sis-
ter of U.S. President William Henry
Harrison, this manor home is surrounded
by 250 acres of land and served as Gen.
Sheridan's headquarters during the Civil
War. Furnishings include antiques and
rare books. The plantation desk used by
Gen. Sheridan still has labels affixed in
1864. The five guest rooms all have pri-
vate baths. Comfort and hospitality are
hallmarks. A billiard room is available
to guests, and a swimming pool and
horse shoe, croquet and volleyball fa-
cilities are on-site. A full country break-
fast is served.

PINEY GROVE
AT SOUTHALL'S PLANTATION
16920 Southall Plantation Rd.   *829-2480*
$$$$

On the National Register of Historic Places, this secluded country retreat in Virginia's James River Plantation Country offers spacious rooms with private baths and fireplaces. Mint juleps or Hot Toddies (depending on the season), Virginia wines and plantation breakfasts are served.

Fan District

ABBIE HILL GUEST LODGING
2206 Monument Ave.
$$$$ *353-5855*

This elegantly-restored federal townhouse is in the heart of one of Richmond's most prestigious historic districts. It's within walking distance of mu
... . In addition to spacious rooms, family antiques and fireplaces, Abbie Hill offers afternoon tea and full breakfasts.

BE MY GUEST BED AND BREAKFAST
2926 Kensington Ave.   *358-9901*
$$$$

This elegant, colorful 1918 home is near the Virginia Museum of Fine Arts, the Virginia Historical Society and Carytown's shops. It offers comfortable accommodations and full breakfasts.

EMMANUEL HUTZLER HOUSE
2236 Monument Ave.   *353-6900*
$$$$

This enormous 8,000-square-foot Italian Renaissance mansion features mahogany paneling, leaded-glass windows and a fireplace in the guests' living room. It has four spacious queen and twin rooms, each with a private bath, some with Jacuzzis. A full breakfast is served.

Church Hill

Near historic St. John's Church are:

MR. PATRICK HENRY'S INN
2300 E. Broad St.   *644-1322*
$$$$

The inn has a gourmet restaurant, an English-basement pub and a garden patio. Guest suites have fireplaces, private baths and kitchenettes, and some have private balconies.

THE WILLIAM CATLIN HOUSE
2304 E. Broad St.   *780-3746*
$$$$

Tastefully restored, the William Catlin House is a Richmond classic. Its five rooms and two suites offer a variety of comforts.

Corporate Apartments

Corporate executives in the process of moving to Richmond can arrange temporary housing in a variety of ways. Two of the places that specialize in short-term apartment needs are:

THE BERKSHIRE
300 W. Franklin St.   *644-7861*

This modern high-rise in the Franklin Street historic area offers one- and two-bedroom apartments on a daily or monthly basis. The Berkshire has a 24-hour reception desk and garage parking.

MARRIOTT RESIDENCE INN
2121 Dickens Rd.   *285-8200*

In the West End near the Broad Street exit from I-64, the Residence Inn has one- and two-bedroom suites with fireplaces, kitchens and maid service.

Inside
Campgrounds

If you like hunting, fishing, bird watching, hiking, or just being outdoors, you'll find some of the most beautiful scenery, native wildlife, and well-managed state and national park campgrounds within an hour or two of Richmond. To the west, you can camp high atop the majestic Blue Ridge Mountains, in secluded valleys and meadows, or beside lakes and rivers. To the east, you can camp under pine trees or beside the ocean dunes, so close to the seashore that you can hear the waves.

From backpacking and wilderness camping to deluxe resort areas, there are more than 400 private and government-owned campgrounds in Virginia. Some have drive-in sites; others can be reached only by boat or by foot.

If you want to camp close to Richmond, the nearest state park that offers camping facilities is the Pocahontas State Park in Chesterfield County, just 20 minutes from downtown. This is the only campground in the metropolitan area that offers a complete outdoors experience.

There are also a few private campgrounds in the area that cater to people who are just looking for a place to stay. If you're from out of town and you plan to visit Paramount's Kings Dominion amusement park, or if you need a campground near the Richmond area, Paramount's Kings Dominion Campground and the Americamp Richmond-North are both popular.

Camping seasons and fees are subject to change, so we suggest that you call ahead to verify the following information.

Campgrounds

POCAHONTAS STATE PARK
Manager: Ed Swope
Park Office   *796-4255*
Reservations   *(800) 933-7275*
Camp Sites: $10.50 per night plus tax
Water and electrical hookups are not available.
A dump station is provided.

One of the original six state parks built by the Civilian Conservation Corps, the Pocahontas State Park opened in 1936. The park includes more than 7,600 acres of forest land surrounding Swift Creek Lake and Beaver Lake in Chesterfield County, just 20 minutes from downtown Richmond.

Area residents come here to enjoy the outdoors in a full-service park environment that's close to home. An Olympic-size pool, trails, biking, fresh water fishing and canoeing, as well as wildlife and history programs are available. Be sure to visit the wildlife exhibits at the Visitors Center and find out more about what the park has to offer. If you want some help deciding what activities would be the most enjoyable for you, talk to the park staff.

They will be happy to help you plan your visit. The park is also within easy travel distance to historic attractions in Richmond and Petersburg. Wooded sites are available for tents or recreational vehicles. Group camping and a few primitive cabins for groups are also available. The sites include a tent pad and picnic table. Additional facilities include modern bath houses, hot water showers, concessions, row boats, canoes and paddle boats.

Holidays and weekends are very busy, and reservations are recommended. (During the week, you probably won't need one.) Reservations may be made by phone or in person at the campground or at any state park during the camping season. Walk-in reservations are also handled at the State Parks Office in downtown Richmond, 203 Governor Street, Suite 306. Group camping reservations are handled only through the park office. MasterCard and Visa are accepted. A maximum of six people is allowed at each site.

The park grounds are open year round, and camping is available mid-March through November. Special activities are seasonal.

Take Exit 6 off I-95, then go west on Route 10 to Route 655, Beach Road; or take Exit 7, go north on Route 150 to Route 10, and go east to Beach Road.

AMERICAMPS RICHMOND-NORTH

396 Air Park Rd.   798-5298
Camp sites: Pull through with full hookups $21.25 per night; $17.25 tents; water and electric $19.25, plus tax

Sites are available for tents and recreational vehicles at this partly wooded campground conveniently located just off I-95, about 15 minutes north of Richmond. Take the Lewistown Road Exit and follow the signs. Facilities include laundry, a game room, playground and pool. It's open all year.

KINGS DOMINION CAMPGROUND

I-95 and Rt. 30
Doswell   876-5355
Manager: Michael Dorton
Camp sites: $18 per night; with water and electricity $22; with sewer hookup $24.50

This shady campground offers comfortable tent and recreational vehicle sites in a woodsy area adjacent to the amusement park. Sites with modern hookups are available. If you plan to enter the park in the late afternoon, be sure to ask about discounts on admission for campers. Free shuttle service is available to and from the park, or you may walk; it's less than ¼ mile to the park.

The campground facilities include a large swimming pool, playground, game room and complete camp store. A 7-Eleven and several fast-food restaurants are also just a few minutes away on Route 30. Hot showers and bath houses are provided. If you want a campfire, bring your own grill. . . . It's against county law to have uncontained ground fires.

Reservations are recommended. Call about one month in advance to reserve a site for holidays. Call two weeks in advance for other times. The campground is open from March to mid-October. Fees are based on five people per site. Off-season rates are available during March, April, May, September and October.

To get here, from I-95 take the Doswell Exit and go east about ¼ mile on Route 30. The campground is on the right after you pass Paramount's Kings Dominion.

Information Sources

You'll get a good idea of how many parks and campgrounds are near the

Richmond area if you look at the state map published by the Virginia Division of Tourism. Some information about the campground facilities and phone numbers are included. If you would like more information, we suggest that you contact the following organizations:

TOURISM
DEVELOPMENT GROUP, VIRGINIA
1021 E. Cary St.   *786-4484*

This state office will send you information about state and national parks and campgrounds in Virginia.

VIRGINIA DIVISION OF STATE PARKS
203 Governor St., Ste. 306   *786-1712*

This state office will send you information about state parks and cabin facilities and a directory of state and private campgrounds that are members of the Virginia Campground Association.

VIRGINIA
CAMPGROUND ASSOCIATION
2101 Libbie Ave.   *288-3065*

This association will provide you with information about private campgrounds in Virginia.

Inside
Parks and Recreation

The Richmond area offers more than 60 parks and more than 5,000 acres of park land. Some are historical, others offer play equipment, hiking, nature trails, fishing, boating and picnicking. There are festivals, charity runs, pet walks and educational programs.

There's also plenty of participant sports action for youth, adults, seniors and people with disabilities. You'll find organized soccer, baseball, softball, basketball, volleyball, tennis and swimming. You'll also find bicycling, canoeing, kayaking, sailing, windsurfing, rock climbing, ice skating, roller skating, spelunking and more.

Whatever you like to do, you're sure to find a park or a recreational sport to match your interests.

In this chapter, we've organized information about parks and recreational activities by jurisdictional areas. The City of Richmond and each surrounding county has a Department of Recreation and Parks that is responsible for park facilities and sponsors or cosponsors organized sports, community events and senior programs. If you would like more information, maps or brochures, contact the Department of Recreation and Parks in Richmond, 780-5944, Henrico, 672-5100, Hanover, 798-8062, or Chesterfield, 748-1623.

Credit: Metro Richmond Convention and Visitors Bureau

The James River provides a wide range of recreational activities such as canoeing.

General information about soccer, swimming, bicycling, canoeing and other sports that are not necessarily organized by jurisdictional area is included after the city and county information. Golfing is so popular, we cover it in a special chapter.

City of Richmond

Parks

The city's Department of Recreation and Parks maintains and operates the city parks including the James River Park System, historic city cemeteries and community centers. The city also coordinates and sponsors organized sports programs and maintains dozens of ball fields and sports facilities that are available for residents and league play. A variety of classes, programs and events for youth and adults including arts and crafts, sports, music, games, dance and nature programs are also offered daily at community centers and other park facilities.

If you have questions about activities and facilities, contact your neighborhood recreation center or call the Citizens Assistance Coordinator at 780-5712. If you want to reserve a shelter or community center for a group or special event, call 780-5935.

BATTERY PARK

At Hawthorne Avenue and Overbrook Road, this park features tennis courts, a playground, a community center and a swimming pool. It was the site of gun batteries during the Civil War.

BROWN'S ISLAND PARK

At the bottom of S. Seventh Street, you'll find Brown's Island Park at the end of Canal Walk. Benches overlooking the river provide scenic resting spots. This is the site of the World Rib Championship, A Taste of Richmond and the annual rubber duckies race to benefit the Big Brothers. A variety of weekend events is also held here.

BRYAN PARK

At Bellevue Avenue and Hermitage Road, Bryan Park is famous for its Azalea Gardens. There are tennis courts, three picnic shelters, a fishing lake, and wooded and open spaces.

BYRD PARK

At Boulevard and Idlewood Avenue, Byrd Park offers three lakes, paddleboat rentals (summer only), two picnic shelters, ballfields, tennis courts, the Carillon (a World War I memorial), and Dogwood Dell, an outdoor amphitheater where the Festival of Arts is held each summer. Tennis is especially popular here. It's also the site of the annual Run for the Arts. For information call 780-8137.

CHIMBORAZO PARK

At E. Broad Street near 32nd Street, this park has an exercise cluster with equipment for people with disabilities. The park was the site of the Chimborazo Field Hospital — the largest in the world during the Civil War. The park now serves as the headquarters of the National Battlefield Park System.

CITY GOLF RANGE

On N. School Street, this new golf range features all-weather tees and natural turf tees, target greens, a practice bunker and a pro shop. Open from mid-February to mid-November, the range is lighted and handicapped accessible. Buckets of balls are available for a fee.

FESTIVAL PARK

This park is downtown at 6th Street Marketplace between the Coliseum and the Crystal Palace. You can enjoy concerts and other special events here such as Friday Cheers and a New Year's Eve Party. For information about upcoming events see the newspaper or call Downtown Presents. . . at 643-2826.

FOREST HILL PARK

On 41st Street, this park used to be the site of the Forest Hill Amusement Park and was the end point of the Forest Hill streetcar. The park offers a picnic area, lake, walkways, two shelters, tennis courts, a meeting house and a small azalea garden.

KANAWHA PLAZA

At Clay and Eighth streets, this landscaped plaza features a fountain with a pool. It's a popular lunch spot for downtown workers and the site of numerous events.

JAMES RIVER PARK

At 22nd Street and Riverside Drive, this is Richmond's Urban Wilderness Park. You'll enjoy walking along trails here with great views of the river. There's also a visitors center and fishing. Educational programs are offered on weekends or by appointment for groups. The park has five sections — Main, Pony Pasture, Huguenot Woods, North Bank and Belle Isle.

The main section of the park is on the south side of the river between the Boulevard and Lee bridges. Flatwater and whitewater canoe trips are available here. Information, maps, trail guides, interpretive tours and rest rooms are at the visitors center, which is accessible by foot from the parking lots at 42nd and 22nd streets.

Pony Pasture is on the south bank of the river, 2 miles downstream from the Huguenot Bridge on Riverside Drive. Fishing and birdwatching are excellent here. An easy whitewater canoe run begins here and ends at the visitors center.

Huguenot Woods is also on the south bank, directly under the Huguenot Bridge. This is a good place to begin a flatwater canoe trip.

The North Bank section is on the north side of the river at the end of Texas Avenue. A pedestrian bridge crosses railroad tracks and the canal down to the edge of the river. Fishing is good here too.

Belle Isle is directly under the Lee Bridge and may be reached by a pedestrian bridge from the Tredegar Street side or by foot from the 22nd Street parking lot across the river bed when water levels are below five feet. A wheelchair route is also available. The island is the site of the notorious Civil War prison, and the remains of the historic iron foundry can still be seen. Walking trails feature interpretive signs, and the whitewater rapids offer excellent kayak and canoe runs for highly skilled boaters. The fishing is good here, and it's free, but you must comply with state licensing regulations. A floating fishing pier was recently constructed at the old granite quarry pit. Call 780-5311 for more information on fishing. Swimming is not recommended because of fast-moving water, rocks, rapids and dangerous undertows.

JEFFERSON HILL PARK

At 21st and E. Marshall streets, this park features a bandstand, tot lot, exercise trail and a beautiful view of the south side of the city. A steam train is buried under the hill from an October 2, 1925, cave-in. A commemorative plaque is at the sealed entrance to the tunnel off 18th Street.

LIBBY HILL PARK

At the intersection of 28th and E. Franklin streets, Libby Hill Park is one of the original three parks in the city's parks system. It features the Confederate Soldiers and Sailors Monument, a small park house and a great view of the south side of the city. The walkways, seating and antique lighting have been renovated.

MAYMONT PARK

At 1700 Hampton Street, this beautiful, 100-acre Victorian estate is operated by the Maymont Foundation with assistance from the Richmond Department of Recreation and Parks. For more information about the park see the Attractions chapter or call the Maymont Foundation, 358-7166.

MONROE PARK

At Belvidere and W. Franklin streets near Virginia Commonwealth University and the Mosque, Monroe Park was the site of the first Virginia State Fair in 1854. The park offers walking paths, benches, a park house and a decorative fountain.

OREGON HILL LINEAR PARK

This new park parallels Belvidere and covers about a five block area from Idlewood Avenue to Riverside Park. Features include a jogging trail and natural amphitheater.

POWHATAN HILL PARK

At Williamsburg Road and Northampton Street, this park offers tennis courts, a playground, a comfort station and a community center. The name of the park comes from the legend that

Chief Powhatan used the area for a tribal campground in Colonial times.

TRAVELLAND

Full-size exhibits of a train, a jet plane and other modes of transportation are here at the Tourist Information Center at Robin Hood and Hermitage roads. This is a great place to let the kids climb and explore. For tourist information call 358-5511.

Sports

If you would like more information about opportunities to participate in sports in Richmond call 780-6091. For seniors information call 780-6093, or contact a community center near you.

Youth Sports

LITTLE LEAGUE BASEBALL

There are five leagues for children from about ages 6 to 15. The youngest children play T-Ball to learn the fundamentals of the game. Fields are provided by the city. Teams are open to girls and boys.

FOOTBALL

Most of the community centers sponsor football teams in the fall, beginning in September. Participation is free. City Championships are in November at Hovey Field.

CHEERLEADING

Cheerleading squads for girls age 16 and younger are formed at all recreation centers that offer football. The squads are trained by volunteers and cheer at Saturday games. During the first week of November, the squads compete to see who will cheer at the City Championships during halftimes. Participation is free. Cheerleading squads are also formed for football and soccer teams. A cheerleading jamboree is held each fall at the Arthur Ashe Center.

BASKETBALL

Most of the community centers sponsor teams beginning in early January. Participation is free. City Championships are held in late March. Teams are also organized by the Boys Club and the Jewish Community Center.

TENNIS

In cooperation with area tennis associations, the city offers more than 140 tennis courts throughout the city for individual or group play. Competitive and instructional tennis programs are available for youths age 6 to 16.

VOLLEYBALL

Children's coed volleyball programs are available at some community centers. Call for more information.

SOCCER

The Richmond Department of Recreation and Parks coordinates soccer teams through community centers to provide opportunities for boys and girls ages 5 to 16 to learn the fundamentals of the game. Teams compete on a regular schedule from mid-September through mid-November. Teams are offered for different age levels, and coaches are trained volunteers. Practices are after school hours, and games are usually held on Saturdays. Playoffs are at the end of the season for the City Soccer Championships. The city also sponsors a traveling team. More information about soccer is included at the end of this chapter.

Fitness Trails

Self-guided fitness trails with written instructions and equipment for exercising are at Byrd Park, Pine Camp Arts Center, Reid Community Center, Chimborazo Park and Canoe Run Park. The Chimborazo Park offers an exercise cluster with equipment for people with disabilities.

Ice Skating

During freezing winter weather, ice skating is permitted on the boat and fountain lake in Byrd Park. If the ice is thick enough for safe skating, announcements are made through the local news media. Barrels and wood are provided along the edge of the lake to provide warmth for skaters.

Sledding

Sledding is permitted at all Richmond parks after it snows in the winter. Barrels and wood are provided at Bryan Park, Forest Hill Park and Powhatan Park. For more information, call parks operations, 780-5393.

Gymnasiums

Several gymnasiums at city schools are available for residents to use. For more information call 780-6091.

Adult Sports and Activities

SOFTBALL

The city provides facilities for adult softball in cooperation with the Amateur Softball Association. Men's, women's and coed teams are formed according to ability levels.

BASKETBALL

There are several adult leagues including the Industrial League, composed of teams formed by employers, the Open League and the Church League.

VOLLEYBALL

The Richmond Volleyball Club sponsors leagues and outdoor tournaments played on grass, sand and asphalt courts. Men's, women's and coed teams are formed according to ability levels.

OTHER

The city's community centers offer a variety of classes and activities for adults including fencing, boxing, aerobics, yoga, walking clubs, weight training, tennis, volleyball, basketball, martial arts, self defense and swimming. They also offer arts and crafts, dance, chess, bingo, safety classes, trips and more.

Senior Citizen Activities

In cooperation with the Council of Senior Citizens Organizations (COSCO), the Affiliated Senior Citizens of Metropolitan Richmond, the Capital Area Agency on Aging and the Richmond City Commission on the Elderly, the city offers a wide variety of activities, programs, trips, clubs and events for seniors. Programs and services are based on geo-

graphical service areas. For more information call 780-8015.

Therapeutic Recreation Program

All Richmond area residents who have a disability may participate in the Therapeutic Recreation Program. Activities include swimming lessons, bicycling, tennis, basketball, wheelchair basketball, bowling, walking, soccer, arts and crafts and after-school clubs. Each spring, the city also sponsors the Rainbow Games, an athletic competition for children and young adults between 7 and 21 who are blind or who have another disability. Events include track and field and swimming. Offices are at Pine Camp Therapeutic Programs Cottage, 4901 Old Brook Road, 266-2246. The TDD phone number is 780-8087.

Chesterfield County

Parks

Chesterfield offers about 20 parks including Henricus Historical Park, at the site of the second major English settlement in Virginia; Point of Rocks Park overlooking the Appomattox River; Rockwood Park with its popular nature center; and Pocahontas State Park, the nearest state park to the metropolitan area.

Residents may also participate in varied sports and recreation programs in-

Insiders' Tips

Through the center of Richmond you'll find the Falls of the James, the only urban whitewater run in the country.

cluding major sports leagues, fencing, karate, gymnastics and lacrosse. The county also offers classes and programs in rock climbing, spelunking, gem hunting, nature programs, dance, self defense for women, herb gardening and arts and crafts. Boating, canoeing/kayaking, ocean fishing, scuba diving, sailing, bateau rides and group skiing trips are also offered as well as special events such as Rainbow of Arts, an arts and crafts festival in the fall, Kite Day and a series of free summertime outdoor concerts with the Richmond Symphony.

The department also sponsors summer camps, a lecture series, activities and programs for seniors and people with disabilities.

For more information about Chesterfield parks, recreation and sports call 748-1623.

HENRICUS HISTORICAL PARK

On the banks of the James River on the site of the second major English settlement in Virginia, this park features a walking trail with views of the river. It's accessible from Dutch Gap Boat Ramp and the Henricus Park Boat Landing. Additional information is included in the chapter on Attractions under Citie of Henricus.

BENSLEY PARK

At 2900 Drewrey's Bluff Road, this park opened in 1988 and features a picnic area, play equipment, softball and baseball fields, a football field, tennis courts, a concession area and a community center.

FORT STEVENS HISTORICAL PARK

At Pams Avenue and Norcliff Road, this two-acre park opened in 1988 and features trails around Civil War embankments and a picnic area.

POINT OF ROCKS PARK

This 190-acre site is in a remote area at Enon Church and Ruffin Mill roads. Visitors walk on trails and boardwalks through a marsh teeming with plants and wildlife to an observation deck overlooking the Appomattox River.

IRON BRIDGE PARK

On Va. 10 across from Chesterfield Airport, this 367-acre park features four softball fields, a baseball field, four tennis courts including two with artificial clay surfaces, two outdoor handball/racquetball courts, a volleyball area and a handicapped-accessible basketball court. There are also 3 miles of nature trails, a 5-mile mountain bike trail and a boardwalk crossing Reedy Creek Marsh. Concession stands are available.

ROCKWOOD PARK

This is the oldest and most popular park in Chesterfield. It includes the Rockwood Nature Center which is housed in a recently constructed log cabin. The center features hands-on exhibits, wildlife and environmental displays related to the area. It also offers an archery range, garden plots, 3.5 miles of nature trails, picnic shelters, play equipment, ballfields, tennis courts and restrooms.

HUGUENOT PARK

This 57-acre park on Robious Road is heavily wooded and features azalea gardens, playgrounds, athletic fields, tennis and basketball courts and a fitness trail. Wheelchair tennis is available here.

POCAHONTAS STATE PARK

This full-service state park is described in detail in the Campgrounds chapter. Call 796-4255 for more information.

ETTRICK RIVERSIDE PARK

On the Appomattox River at 21601 Chesterfield Avenue across from Virginia State University, this park features walking trails, a bridge to an island, picnic areas and the remains of a 19th-century mill. A community building is expected to open in 1995.

GOYNE PARK

At 5300 Ecoff Avenue, this park offers playing fields, tennis courts, a picnic shelter and play equipment. An undeveloped area has woods, fields and a small stream.

HARROWGATE PARK

At 4200 Dean Drive, this neighborhood park has tennis courts, playing fields, picnic and playground areas and a fitness trail.

MATOACA PARK

At 1900 Halloway Avenue, this park features tennis courts, playing fields, a lighted basketball court, picnic shelter and play equipment.

Sports

Contact the Chesterfield Department of Parks and Recreation, 748-1623, or watch the local newspapers for information about how to register for the following Chesterfield sports.

Youth Sports

LITTLE LEAGUE BASEBALL

There are three youth baseball leagues in Chesterfield. Children register directly with the Huguenot and Chesterfield leagues, or they may join the Chesterfield Baseball Club through their neighborhood athletic association. This is the largest club and includes about 30 athletic associations. Several thousand children play baseball each year, from T-Ball (age 5 and older) to teams for youths age 18 and younger. Most of the fields are provided and maintained by the county. Girls and boys may join. The season begins in March and ends in July. There are several post-season tournaments.

SOFTBALL

The Chesterfield Girls Softball League offers slow pitch softball to girls and boys ages 6 to 18. The season is from March to July. The Chesterfield United Girls' Softball League includes mostly fast-pitch teams at the high school level. Participation is open to girls age 10 and older, and the season begins in May.

BASKETBALL

There are five basketball leagues for children — Chesterfield, Ettrick-Matoaca, Bon Air/Southampton, Chester Jaycees and Chesterfield Girls. Girls teams are available in all of the leagues. The season is from November to mid-March. Registration begins as early as August. Teams are open to youths age 6 and older. Skill development and sportsmanship are stressed with the youngest players, and competition is low-key. The focus becomes more competitive with children age 8 and older.

FOOTBALL

The Chesterfield Quarterback League plays from August to November and includes teams from about 30 Athletic Associations in the county. Flag football teams are available for children around age 6, and older groups play tackle football. Teams are formed according to age. Championships are held at the end of the season. The county provides and maintains the fields.

CHEERLEADING

Hundreds of cheerleading teams are formed through the neighborhood athletic associations for football and basketball teams according to age levels. Championships are held at the end of the seasons.

TENNIS

Tennis lessons are available for youths age 10 and older. Classes are taught at Iron Bridge Park and the Byrd Athletic Complex. Fees vary.

LACROSSE

The Chesterfield Lacrosse Club plays in the Midlothian area each spring. Boys and girls in high school and middle school are eligible to participate. Call the De-

partment of Parks and Recreation at 748-1623 for more information.

Fencing

Boys, girls and adults may participate in fencing throughout the year with the Chester Knights Fencing Club. Since leadership for the club changes regularly, it is best to call the Department of Parks and Recreation at 748-1623 for more information.

Challenge Course

This is a rope course designed to promote initiative and confidence and strengthen group dynamics, communication and teamwork. Life-altering experiences are common among participants. Request a copy of the course brochure for more information. This is ideal for groups,

Credit: Richmond Newspapers

Soccer is a popular sport played year round in Richmond.

classes and scout troops. High- and low-course options are available. Instructors are extensively trained and certified.

Therapeutic Sports

Specially designed programs for people who have a mental or physical handicap include adaptive swimming, wheelchair tennis, basketball, bowling, miniature golf, hiking, softball and Little League Baseball. The department also sponsors social activities and the annual Rainbow Games for youths and young adults age 7 to 21 who have disabilities. The events include track and field, swimming and instructional clinics.

Adult Sports

Basketball, softball, football and volleyball leagues are available for adults age 18 and older. Contact the county for details.

Coaches Certification Clinics

The Chesterfield Chapter of the National Youth Sports Coaches Association conducts clinics for the spring and summer seasons. Classes are usually held in February.

Gymnasiums

Various school gymnasiums are open for the public periodically. Contact the county for scheduling information. There is no fee to use the facilities.

Senior Citizen Programs

Special programs and activities for seniors include walking programs, trips, tennis, volleyball, exercise classes, softball and the Golden Olympics.

Henrico County

Parks

Henrico County operates about 25 park facilities. We've included a sampling of them here. For more information or for group reservations at certain parks call 672-5100.

DOREY PARK

At 7200 Dorey Park Road, off Darbytown Road, Dorey is one of Henrico's largest parks. The 400-acre park features seven picnic areas, tennis courts, ballfields, an equestrian ring, exercise and hiking trails and a small fishing pond. A new recreation center in a renovated dairy barn recently opened here and includes three classrooms, two conference rooms, a multipurpose room, an arts and crafts room, an activity room and a kitchen. Call 795-2334 for rental information. In the fall, this is the site of Christmas in September, an annual arts and crafts show with more than 140 exhibitors.

SHORT PUMP PARK

At 3401 Pump Road, this is a neighborhood park with playing fields, a picnic shelter and softball, soccer and football fields.

THREE LAKES PARK

Three Lakes Nature Center features a 50,000-gallon outdoor aquarium, the largest in Central Virginia, a Nature Center and a 90-acre park where plant, fish, bird and animal life abound.

Surrounded by a lush forest, the Nature Center is on the edge of one of the park's three spring-fed lakes. You can stroll around the deck and view the aquarium from above, or you can go below for an underwater view of the same kinds of fish that live in the park's lakes. You'll come face-to-face with largemouth bass, bluegill, redear sunfish and black crappie.

The upper level of the Nature Center is filled with special exhibits focusing on the aquarium, lakes, wetlands, animal life and the forest. Visitors learn about the environment and the plants and animals that live here as well as how to maintain and preserve them. Classes, workshops and special programs are also available.

In addition to the Nature Center, this 90-acre park offers fishing, hiking, two picnic shelters, play equipment, an exercise trail and an observation deck.

Three Lakes Park is off Wilkinson Road at Sausiluta Drive. Call 262-4822 for more information or to schedule group tours.

DEEP RUN PARK

This 167-acre park at 9900 Ridgefield Parkway, offers five picnic shelters, two ponds, soccer and football fields, basketball courts, play areas, an exercise trail and a multiuse outdoor area. A pedestrian/bike trail connects the recreational areas.

CRUMP MEMORIAL PARK

In Glen Allen, this park features the 150-acre Meadow Farm, a restored pre-Civil War middle-class farm. It's used as a living history museum interpreting rural life in the 1850s. The park also offers picnic shelters, nature trails, play equipment and horseshoes. Civil War reenactments, encampments and holiday events are scheduled throughout the year. For more information, see the Attractions chapter or call 672-5100 or 672-1367.

DEEP BOTTOM PARK

Picnicking and pier fishing are available at this public boat landing in Varina at 9525 Deep Bottom Road. Boaters have access to the James River. The county is planning a 58-acre park next to the landing. There is a canoe launch here with direct access to the scenic Four Mile Creek.

LAUREL SKATE PARK

At 10301 Hungary Spring Road in the Laurel Recreation Area, this $3/4$-acre facility includes a street skate area with a variety of ramps and obstacles, a freestyle skate area and a 6½-foot-deep combination bowl. The park is open daily, weather permitting, for skateboarding and in-line skating. The recreation area also includes athletic fields, play equipment and concessions. For information and a schedule, call 67-BOARD or 672-5100.

GLEN ALLEN SOFTBALL COMPLEX

Formerly known as North Run, this 12-acre facility at 2175 Mountain Road includes four lighted baseball fields.

VAWTER STREET PARK/ GLEN LEA RECREATION AREA

At 4501 Vawter Avenue, this 352-acre park offers a scenic nature trail, picnic facilities, play equipment and soccer, softball and football fields.

HIDDEN CREEK

This $7^1/3$-acre playground at 2415 Brockway Lane features a memorial for the Shuttle Challenger crew.

OSBORNE BOAT LANDING

This was the site of several recent Bass Masters Classics. The boat landing is on the James River at Osborne Turnpike and Kingsland Road.

Sports

Henrico County offers a diversified schedule of sports and special programs for youth and adults including sailing, kayaking, canoeing, rock climbing, skiing, spelunking and hunting. Other activities and programs include martial arts, arts and crafts, trips, dancing, after-school and summer playground programs, preschool activities, gardening and lots more.

The county also offers special programs for people with mental or physical disabilities and a very active seniors program.

For information about county-sponsored activities or to find out how to contact other sport associations in the area, call the Department of Recreation and Parks at 672-5100.

Youth Sports

LITTLE LEAGUE BASEBALL

Area leagues include Bethlehem, Chamberlayne, Glen Allen, Glen Lea, Highland Springs, Lakeside, Sandston, Tuckahoe, Varina and Virginia Randolph. Girls and boys from age 6 to 17 are invited to participate.

GIRLS SOFTBALL

Girls age 6 to 17 may participate in area softball leagues including the Bethlehem Girls, Western Girls and Old Dominion Girls.

BASKETBALL

Registration is usually held the third Saturday in November at Byrd Middle School on Quioccasin Road. Youths age 8 to 17 may participate. Teams are formed according to age levels. Games are usually played on Saturdays in western Henrico gymnasiums, but standings are not kept. The emphasis is on instruction. About 650 kids are involved in the program each year.

FOOTBALL

Information about football programs is available from the county. There are numerous leagues that play in the Metro Youth Football Association including Bethlehem, Chamberlayne, Glen Lea, Highland Springs, Kanawha, Laurel, Sandston, Tuckahoe, Varina and Virginia Randolph. Leagues play teams from throughout the metropolitan area.

Adult Sports

VOLLEYBALL

Coed volleyball is offered in the fall, winter and spring. Games are usually played at the Brookland Middle School.

BASKETBALL

Basketball teams play at the Tuckahoe Middle School in the winter from November through March and in the summer from June through August.

BASEBALL

There is also an Over-Thirty Baseball League that plays in the spring and summer. Contact Andy Crane, 672-5156, for further information.

Insiders' Tips

The late Col. Charles H. Reed of Richmond played a key role in the rescue of the Royal Lipizzan stallions in Czechoslovakia during World War II.

Credit: Richmond Newspapers

*Skateboard enthusiasts enjoy Laurel Skateboard Park
in Henrico County.*

GOLF

The county sponsors two adult golf tournaments each year. The Best Ball Tournament is held in June. Participants play at three area courses. The Two-Man Scramble is held in October at the Belmont Golf Course.

OTHER SPORTS

Rugby and lacrosse are two of the newest sports offered to adults. Call for more information.

Gymnasiums

About 15 school gymnasiums are open for basketball and other activities. Call the county for a list of schools and a schedule.

Special Programs

A variety of activities for people who have mental or physical disabilities are offered through the county including dances, picnics, crafts, workshops, martial arts, bumper bowling, basketball, softball, swimming and training for the Special Olympics.

Coaching Clinics

Henrico County offers coaching clinics for adults who coach youth sports. For information contact the county.

Senior Citizen Programs

People age 55 and older can participate in a variety of activities including the Golden Olympics, trips, special programs, billiards, bowling, golf, softball, tennis, volleyball, water aerobics and walking clubs.

Hanover County

Parks

Hanover County has five parks and offers elementary school playgrounds for public use in the summer. The county also maintains a boat launch area on the Pamunkey River off U.S. 301, a mile north of Hanover Courthouse, and a boat launch area on the South Anna River on Va. 54, a mile west of Patrick Henry High School. To reserve a park facility call the Hanover County Parks and Recreation Department, 798-8062.

A variety of recreational programs are offered including summer camps, nature and wilderness camps, sports clinics and classes on archaeology, boating skills, dance, horseback riding, fine arts, computer skills, languages, photography, cake decorating, music and more.

HANOVER WAYSIDE

On U.S. 301, 5 miles south of Hanover Courthouse, Hanover Wayside is a 32-acre park with a picnic shelter and tables, a ballfield and a pond. It is maintained by the Atlee Ruritan Club as a community project.

POOR FARM PARK

Near Patrick Henry High and Liberty Middle schools, Poor Farm Park is about 3 miles west of Ashland on Va. 54. Its 270 acres include an outdoor amphitheater, nine new soccer fields, a new archery range, nature trails, a picnic shelter, grills and a toddler play area. Volleyball, horseshoes and 5 miles of mountain bike trails are also available. The Hanover Humane Society's Pet Walk and the county's annual Spring Fest are held here.

NORTH ANNA BATTLEFIELD PARK

Developed and owned by General Crushed Stone Quarry, this 75-acre park is managed by Hanover County Parks Department. It contains trench works with rifle pits from the Battle of North Anna that are considered to be some of the most pristine examples of Civil War earthworks in existence. Explore the park and learn its history through an interpretive trail system. The park is open by appointment only. Call the department for reservations.

COURTHOUSE PARK

On U.S. 301 south of Hanover Courthouse, this new park will offer six soccer fields, a pond, jogging trail, shelter and tot lot when construction is complete. About 50 acres of the 363-acre site will be developed during the next several years.

COLD HARBOR BATTLEFIELD PARK

About 50 acres surrounding the historic Garthright House, once used as a field hospital during the Civil War, have been developed as one of Hanover's newest parks. In Cold Harbor, on Va. 156, the park, known by locals as Garthright Park, includes a 2-mile trail system with interpretive signage that leads visitors through Civil War trench works and rifle pits.

Sports

Hanover County cosponsors youth and adult sports leagues. The county also offers adult classes in a variety of subjects including kayaking and jazzercise. For registration and schedule information, watch the local newspapers. A complete list of activities, sports leagues and programs is published periodically in the *Herald Progress* newspaper. For more information about recreation, programs and

sports, call the Hanover County Parks and Recreation Department, 798-8062.

Youth Sports

Hanover County sponsors or cosponsors basketball, volleyball, baseball and softball, football, soccer and wrestling leagues. A children's gymnastics program is also available.

FOOTBALL

Teams are formed in the fall based on age and weight. There are three football leagues in Hanover County — Ashland, Blue Star and Mechanicsville. All the leagues play in the Metropolitan Youth Football Association and compete with teams throughout the Richmond area. The season is generally from August through November.

BASKETBALL

Basketball leagues in Hanover County include the Ashland Youth Recreation Association and the Hanover Youth Recreational Association. Teams compete within their league from November through March. Teams are formed by age levels for kids 6 to 18.

SOFTBALL

Leagues in Ashland, Mechanicsville, Atlee and Rockville form teams for youth 6 to 18. Girls fast-pitch teams are now available. Teams play within their leagues from March through July.

LITTLE LEAGUE BASEBALL

Youths age 6 to 18 may participate in baseball leagues from T-Ball to the Big Leagues. Fundamentals are stressed in T-Ball. Older children play competitively and try out for teams. In Hanover, leagues operate in Atlee, Ashland, Mechanicsville and Rockville. The season is usually March through July. There are championship playoffs at the end of the season, and All-Star teams are selected to represent the area in post-season competition.

Senior Citizen Programs

The county offers dances with live bands, trips, bowling leagues, softball, aerobics, a newsletter and other activities for seniors including an annual picnic at Wayside Park and a luncheon each year in Mechanicsville.

Adult Sports

There are numerous men's, women's and coed softball leagues. For information about adult basketball, volleyball, softball or bowling leagues call 798-8062.

Other Sports

BICYCLING

Tour the Richmond area by bicycle, and get a closer look at parks, monuments and intriguing architecture. There are several bicycle tours on state-maintained roads in the area, and mountain bikes are permitted at Pocahontas State Park. Maps and information on bike tours in the metropolitan area, Washington, D.C. and the Blue Ridge Mountains are available from **Two Wheel Travel**, 2934 W. Cary Street; or **Rowlett's** at Broad Street and Staples

Mill Road. Group rides around the area are regularly sponsored by the Richmond Area Bicycling Association (RABA), 266-7562. *Rides Around Richmond*, published by RABA, includes information on about 50 tours in the area. Bike rentals are available only from Two Wheel Travel. Rates start at $15.

Here's a sampling of a few popular and relatively easy rides:

The 30-minute Windsor Farms Tour will take you through this residential neighborhood beginning at Locke Lane and ending at Cary Street Road. You'll ride by Agecroft Hall and the Virginia House — you may want to allow time to visit these historic attractions.

The Battlefield Park Tour will take you on suburban and rural routes that pass by a Civil War fort, a marina and farmland. This route begins and ends at Fort Harrison off Va. 5 (New Market Road) in eastern Henrico County.

The Bellona Arsenal Tour starts at Huguenot and Buford roads and travels through suburban and scenic rural areas of Chesterfield County. Steep hills on this tour will give you a good work out.

There are also several racing teams in the area. Participation on most of the teams is by invitation only, however, Team Richmond, sponsored by Retreat Hospital, is open for all levels by application. Any U.S. Cycling Federation member may participate.

Insiders' Tips

Jog on Monument Avenue's median strip.

TENNIS AND RACQUET SPORTS

Tennis instruction and leagues for youth and adults are offered by a number of private clubs and through county and city departments of parks and recreation. There are also several tournaments open to amateurs and professionals. Information on the tournaments is available from tennis shops, clubs and tournament locations as well as the local news media. Entry fees vary.

The City Tennis Championships, sponsored by NationsBank, are played annually in May at Byrd Park. The competition is open to amateurs and professionals who live in the Richmond area. Matches are held over a four-week period. Tournaments include the Rated Championships (based on ability level), the Family Tournament, Seniors (age levels from 35 and older), Juniors (age levels from 12 and younger to 18) and the Adult Open (no age restriction).

The State Championships are held in August at Raintree Swim and Racquet Club. This tournament is open to men and women, professionals and amateurs. Participants must be Virginia residents. Prize money is awarded.

The City Clay Court Championships are held in July at the Jefferson-Lakeside Country Club. This tournament is for men only and precedes the State Men's Clay Court Championships at Riverside Wellness and Fitness Center in July.

Racquetball courts are available in 13 clubs, and 11 facilities offer indoor tennis. Eight clubs offer both. Most of the courts are in private clubs available to members and guests only. Major clubs include:

American Family Health and Racquet Club, 9101 Midlothian Turnpike, 330-3400, and 5750 Brook Road, 261-1000. Facilities at each location include four racquetball courts.

Burkwood Recreation Association, Studley Road, 730-1066. Facilities include eight outdoor hard tennis courts with lights and four hard indoor tennis courts. Racquetball courts are under development.

Capital Club, 1051 E. Cary Street, Suites 300 to 400, 788-1524. Facilities include two racquetball courts and two squash courts.

Clubfit, 6593 Mechanicsville Turnpike, 730-3390. Facilities include three racquetball courts.

Country Club of Virginia, 6031 St. Andrews Lane, 288-2891. Facilities include six indoor tennis courts, 18 outdoor courts (12 clay, six hard), three platform tennis courts, two racquetball courts and two squash courts.

Courtside Racquet and Fitness Center, 13620 Genito Road, 744-4263. Facilities include two racquetball and three indoor tennis courts. This was called Courtside at Brandermill.

Courtside West, 1145 Gaskins Road, 740-4263. Facilities include three racquetball and three indoor tennis courts.

Ironbridge Indoor Tennis and Fitness Club, 7211 Iron Bridge Road, 271-4500. Facilities include four indoor tennis courts.

Raintree Swim and Racquet Club, 1703 Raintree Drive, 740-0026. Facilities include two racquetball, four indoor tennis courts and 10 outdoor tennis courts. (Two are covered; eight are lighted.)

Richmond Athletic Club, 4700 Thalbro Street, 355-4311. Facilities include eight racquetball courts and three outdoor (clay) tennis courts.

Riverside Wellness and Fitness

Center - Briarwood, 11621 Robious Road, Midlothian, 794-8454. Facilities include four racquetball courts and four indoor and 13 outdoor tennis courts (10 clay and three hard with lights).

Robious Sports and Fitness Center, 10800 Centerview Road, Midlothian, 330-2222. Facilities include two indoor and four outdoor tennis courts, plus six racquetball courts.

Salisbury Country Club, 13620 Salisbury Road, Midlothian, 794-8188. Facilities include four racquetball courts, three indoor and 12 outdoor courts (10 clay, two hard).

Westwood Racquet Club, 6200 W. Club Lane, 282-3829. Facilities include four indoor clay courts, 13 outdoor courts (11 clay, two hard), two racquetball courts and two squash courts.

Willow Oaks Country Club, 6228 Forest Hill Avenue, 320-3244. Facilities include four indoor and eight outdoor tennis courts (six clay and two hard courts with lights).

BOWLING

AMF Hanover Lanes, expected to open by 1996, will be the largest bowling center in Virginia. The 59,000-square-foot facility will feature 56 lanes and showcase the latest bowling equipment manufactured by AMF. The center will also include bumper lanes, a large game room, billiards room, pro shop and a spacious concourse area.

Duckpin bowling is available only at **Plaza Bowl**, 523 South Side Plaza, 233-8799, and tenpin bowling is available at nine alleys in the area.

Instruction and leagues for seniors are offered by some of the county and city departments of parks and recreation and at area bowling alleys. You'll also find numerous employer and church leagues throughout the area. Bumper bowling for kids is available at some of the alleys.

CANOEING AND KAYAKING

The James River and other nearby rivers offer a variety of flatwater and whitewater trips. See the description of the James River Park in this chapter for more information.

Instruction and trips are offered through local departments of parks and recreation and by private organizations including **James River Runners**, 286-2338, and the **Richmond Raft Company**, 222-7238. *Virginia Whitewater*, a book by Richard Corbett, provides detailed descriptions of canoe and kayak trips in the state. You can get a copy from **Alpine Outfitters** or **Blue Ridge Mountain Sports**. Canoes and camping equipment can also be rented from Alpine Outfitters, 794-4172 or 672-7879.

WINDSURFING

The Swift Creek Reservoir at Brandermill is a great place for windsurfing. There are several public access points. Windsurfing equipment can be rented from Alpine Outfitters, 794-4172.

GYMNASTICS

Some of the Parks and Recreation Departments offer instructional gymnastics for youth age 5 to 18 at area schools. There are also several private gymnastics schools including Richmond Olympiad, 794-2813; Hanover Olympiad, 550-3319; Life Gymnastics, 346-3535; and Virginia International Gymnastics Schools, Inc., 276-7039.

Rock Climbing

The old Manchester Bridge ruins on the south side of the James River under the new bridge is a very popular site for rock-climbing enthusiasts. Take the pedestrian bridge to Belle Isle, in the James River Park, and you'll see where people have climbed on the rocks and ruins. Courses in rock climbing are offered by some of the local departments of parks and recreation.

Wrestling

There are several wrestling associations in the area for children from age 5 to 13 including the Metropolitan Youth Wrestling League, the Hanover Youth Wrestling League and the Chesterfield Youth Wrestling League. Children compete within their leagues according to weight and age. The emphasis is primarily on fundamentals and developing self-esteem. The season is usually December through February.

Fishing and Hunting

Fishing

The James River is one of the best smallmouth bass streams in the nation, and it's also a good place for catfish, bream, muskie and largemouth bass.

From its headwaters near Covington to the fall line at Richmond, the upper James River is ideal for smallmouth fishing. The lower James River from below Richmond to the Chesapeake Bay is warmer and has more salinity, which makes it a great place for largemouth and striped bass. Catfish, bream and other panfish are found in both sections of the river.

You can find good fishing spots at several places in the James River Park, and the Virginia Department of Game

and Inland Fisheries maintains 14 boating access points. There are also several private marinas, launch sites and canoe and boat liveries that offer rentals.

For a list of public fishing waters in Virginia, plus license requirements and angling tips, contact the Virginia Department of Game and Inland Fisheries, 4010 W. Broad Street, Richmond 23230.

If you are interested in fishing in the Chesapeake Bay, the ocean or other tidal rivers that flow into the Bay, you can get a copy of a *Guide to Virginia Saltwater Fishing*, published by the Virginia Saltwater Fishing Tournament, 968 S. Oriole Drive, Suite 102, Hauser Building, Virginia Beach 23451, or call 491-5160. We also recommend a book by Bob Gooch, *Virginia Fishing Guide*, University Press of Virginia.

Hunting

Hunting seasons in Virginia begin with dove hunting in September. The major seasons for deer, turkey, small game and black bear open in November and remain open for 60 to 90 days. For information about licensing, where to go, public hunting lands, methods of hunting and harvest figures by county, contact the Virginia Department of Game and Inland Fisheries, 4010 W. Broad Street, Richmond 23230. We also recommend a book by Bob Gooch, *Virginia Hunting Guide*, University Press of Virginia.

Swimming

There are about 100 public and private outdoor swimming pools in the Richmond area serving almost every neighborhood. There are also several indoor pools for winter swimmers who don't have access to a college or university facility.

Indoor swimming and lessons offered through the Richmond Department of Recreation and Parks are available at the Calhoun Community Swimming Pool, 436 Calhoun Street, 780-4751, and at the Swansboro Swimming Pool, 3160 Midlothian Turnpike, 780-5088.

YWCA

Chickahominy
5401 Whiteside Dr., Sandston   737-9622

Downtown
2 W. Franklin St.   644-9622

Tuckahoe
9211 Patterson Ave.   740-9622

Chester
3011 W. Hundred Rd.   748-9622

North Richmond
4207 Old Brook Rd.   329-9622

South Richmond
7540 Hull St. Rd.   276-9622

PRIVATE CLUBS
Riverside Wellness and Fitness Center -
Briarwood   794-6880

Burkwood Recreation Association
Studley Rd.   730-2472

Raintree Swim and Racquet Club
1703 Raintree Dr.   740-1035

Jewish Community Center
5403 Monument Ave.   288-6091

COMPETITIVE SWIMMING
Competitive swimming is open to children as soon as they can swim through age 18. In recent years, some of the swimmers in Richmond have qualified for Olympic trials.

There are four summer swimming leagues in the area — Greater Richmond Aquatic League, James River Aquatic League, Richmond Metropolitan Aquatic League and Chesterfield Aquatic Club. The leagues are composed mostly of private clubs and compete within themselves. All leagues have championships at the end of the summer season. About 5,000 kids participate.

There are also several year-round state teams in Richmond — Team Richmond Aquatic League (Burkwood Recreation Center), Poseidon (Riverside Wellness and Fitness Center), the Dolphin Club (Jewish Community Center) and The Richmond Racers (Calhoun and Swansboro Pools). About 500 kids swim on the state teams and compete against swimmers from around the commonwealth. They progress to regional and national competitions depending on their ability. Noncompetitive coaching is also available for year-round swimmers. The state teams usually offer 12-month or eight-month programs.

Horseback Riding

Richmond's proximity to many parks and rural areas offers numerous opportunities for horseback riding, a very popular sport in the area. There are many local horse shows and several state horse shows at the State Fairgrounds. There is also an equestrian ring at Dorey Park in Henrico County. One academy in the area, Magnolia Centre for Special Equestrians, 273-0183, offers riding programs for people with disabilities.

Information about trails in the area is available from the following organizations:

VIRGINIA COMMISSION OF
GAME AND INLAND FISHERIES
P.O. Box 11104
Richmond 23230   367-1000

VIRGINIA DIVISION OF FORESTRY
P.O. Box 3758
Charlottesville 22903   977-6555

VIRGINIA DIVISION OF STATE PARKS
203 Governor St., Ste. 306
Richmond   786-1712

Walking,
Jogging and Running

There are a number of fitness and nature trails in area parks, but you'll see most people out walking, jogging and running in their neighborhoods or down Monument Avenue. Shopping malls are also popular for indoor walkers and walking clubs. If you are interested in a walking club, contact the YMCA, the YWCA or your local department of parks and recreation for more information.

The Richmond Newspapers Marathon is a sanctioned event and attracts hundreds of local runners each year. (See the chapter on Sports for more information about the marathon.) There are also numerous running events and walkathons to benefit local charities or nonprofit organizations. Two of the larger charity events are Run for the Arts and the March of Dimes Walkathon. Details and schedules are published through the local news media and posters around town.

Some popular trails for walking or jogging are in Maymont Park, James River Park, Powhite Park, Byrd Park, Petronius Jones Park, Pine Camp Park, Battlefield Park, Rockwood Park, Point of Rocks Park, Henricus Historical Park, Iron Bridge Park, Huguenot Park, Pocahontas State Park, Cheswick Park and Dorey Park.

Soccer

Soccer is a well-established year-round sport in the Richmond area for children and adults. Recreational and competitive teams are formed for many different age groups and skill levels, and a new program called Soccer Start was recently formed for disadvantaged children, mostly from the inner city. (See Youth Soccer below for more information.)

For children as young as those in kindergarten, there are house leagues that are formed mainly along geographical lines. These emphasize the fun and fundamentals of the game. Tryouts are not required, and league standings are not usually kept.

Travel or select teams are for more skilled players from age 9 through 18. These teams compete against other teams in the same age group, and standings are kept. They may play in tournaments and compete for the annual Virginia State Cup. Tryouts are usually required.

In addition to clubs and travel teams, the city and county departments of recreation and parks also offer recreational soccer programs.

YOUTH SOCCER
Skitch Hogan, volunteer   285-8067

Teams for boys and girls age 5 and older are sponsored by about a dozen community, recreation and sports organizations in the area. Games are played at schools, churches, parks and athletic fields. Players do not have to play on the team closest to them geographically, but they may not play for more than one team. Registration dates are usually publicized

Geese congregate at Byrd Park throughout the year.

in local newspapers about two months before the season begins.

The main organizations are:

Atlee Youth Sports (Mechanicsville and northeastern Hanover County), Chester Enon Youth Soccer Association (southeastern Chesterfield County), Chickahominy Youth Soccer League (northern Henrico County, south-central Hanover County), Dale Youth Soccer Club (southern Chesterfield County), Eastern Football Club United (Varina, Sandston, Highland Springs and eastern Henrico), F.C. Richmond (northern Chesterfield, Bon Air, South Richmond), Midlothian Youth Soccer League (western, southwestern and northwestern Chesterfield), Pocoshock Valley Youth Soccer League (northeastern Chesterfield), Powhatan Soccer Association (Powhatan County), Reams Road Athletic Association (central Chesterfield), Richmond Neighborhood Soccer Association (Richmond north of the river), Richmond Strikers Soccer Club (western Richmond, western and northwestern Henrico).

The Metropolitan Youth Soccer League is the local organization that supervises competitive play for Richmond and Tri-Cities area travel teams and for those from Charlottesville, Spotsylvania, Culpeper and Orange.

Soccer Start is a local program that uses instructors from the Richmond Kickers and volunteers to provide instruction and summer soccer camps for disadvantaged youth. For more information contact Bill Flowers, 747-8100.

GIRLS SOCCER

Travel Teams: Steve Row	*320-4619*
House Leagues: Joe Porter	*672-1112*

Girls-only soccer is gaining popularity, and local organizers expect even more participation during the next few years. The Central Virginia Girls Soccer League (CVGSL) promotes both recreational house leagues and competitive travel teams. Teams play in the spring and fall.

Girls age 9 or 10 through the 8th grade play a recreational inter-club schedule within their age groups and travel to fields throughout the Richmond area.

Under the supervision of CVGSL,

travel teams compete with teams in the same age group within the Richmond area and against other travel teams from Tidewater, Fredericksburg, Charlottesville and Roanoke.

ADULT SOCCER

Chesterfield Adult Soccer Association   779-4123

There are two divisions — men up to age 40 and those age 40 and older.

Central Virginia Soccer Association 744-2872

This association has a competitive program for men in the fall and spring. They also have a seven-a-side competitive program for men during the summer.

Richmond Strikers Club   288-GOAL

This club usually offers a competitive summer program for men age 30 and older.

Chesterfield Women's
Соссы Лосыlation   330-2929

This league is divided into two divisions — women younger than 30 and those 30 and older.

Chesterfield Coed Soccer League   748-1128

This is a summer recreational program for men and women age 21 and older.

Fitness Centers

There are numerous fitness centers throughout the area. Here's a sampling of some of the popular ones. You may also want to refer to this chapter's listings under Tennis and Racquetball.

American Family Health & Racquet Club, three locations: 9101 Midlothian Turnpike at the Arboretum, 330-3400; 3421 Cox Road at Tower Plaza, 346-9600; and 5750 Brook Road, 261-1000. This club offers free weights, cardiovascular programs, pools with retractable roofs, aerobics, basketball, racquetball, whirl-

pool and sauna, martial arts, aerobics and exercise classes.

Clubfit, 6593 Mechanicsville Turnpike, Mechanicsville, 730-3390. This club offers Nautilus, racquetball, free weights, exercise equipment, aerobics, personal training, handicapped classes and saunas.

Courtside at Brandermill, 13620 Genito Road, 744-4263. This club offers aerobics, Nautilus, tennis, racquetball, karate, nutrition and diet programs and special children's programs.

Jewish Community Center of Richmond, 5403 Monument Avenue, 288-6091. The JCC offers indoor swimming, racquetball, tennis, basketball, soccer, volleyball, aerobics, exercise machines, free weights, saunas, steam rooms, whirlpools and exercise programs for all ages.

Main Street Nautilus, 1509 W. Main Street, 353-0057. This club offers Nautilus and cardiovascular equipment including Lifecycles, Stairmasters and rowing machine. Aerobics and supervised workouts are available.

Mike's Olympic Gym, 1161 Old Hickory Drive, 746-5022. This gymnasium offers free-weights, cardiovascular and selectorized equipment, aerobics, athletic training, tanning beds, whirlpools and nutritional guidance.

Richmond Athletic Club, 4700 Thalbro Street, 355-4311. This club offers tennis, racquetball, aerobics, Nautilus, free weights, basketball, karate, steam room and sauna, whirlpool and child care.

Robious Sports and Fitness Center, 10800 Centerview Drive, 330-2222. This club offers indoor swimming, gymnasium, outdoor track, racquetball, tennis, whirlpool, outdoor running and fitness testing.

Work Out Wonder Gym & Fitness Center, Inc. (WOW Gym), 443 England

Street, Henry Clay Shopping Center, Ashland, 798-1392. This club offers free weights, Nautilus, Lifecycles, boxing and aerobics.

YMCA, seven locations: 2 W. Franklin Street, 644-9622; 3011 W. Hundred Road, Chester, 748 -9622; 5401 Whiteside Road, Sandston, 737-9622; 4207 Old Brook Road, 329-9622; 7540 Hull Street Road, 276-9622; 9211 Patterson Avenue, 740-9622 and 300 England Street, Ashland, 798-0057. The Y offers gymnasiums, swimming pools, individual and group exercise programs, running tracks and specialized exercise machines. YMCA programs are open to men, women and children.

YWCA, 6 N. Fifth Street, 643-6761. The YWCA offers a gymnasium, indoor track, weight room, steam room, sauna, indoor pool, aquatics programs and individual and group exercise programs. YWCA programs are offered to men, women and children.

Inside
Golf

From scenic riverside fairways to historic 1920s-style courses, there are more than 20 golf courses in the Richmond area. About half are open to the public, and the others are private clubs open to members and guests.

If you can escape for a weekend, you'll also find excellent golfing at well-known Virginia resorts such as Wintergreen, The Homestead, Kingsmill and Tides Inn.

Unlike some northern states where the climate is too cold for winter golf, Richmond golf addicts never have to suffer from withdrawal. Although fewer people play from December to mid-March, golfing is a year-round sport in Virginia.

The best public courses are usually very crowded during midsummer and on the weekends. You'll have better luck getting a tee-time and avoiding the crowds if you try to play them in the fall when it's a little bit cold or it looks like rain.

If you're thinking of joining a private club, many of them have waiting lists. However, you might be able to join some of the newer clubs such as The Dominion Club at Wyndham or The Foundry in Powhatan.

Public Courses

Here are some of the most interesting and a few of the most reasonably priced public courses:

RIVER'S BEND COUNTRY CLUB
11700 Hogan's Alley   530-1000
6,671 yards/par 71/slope rating: 132
Fees: $35.50 weekdays; $40.50 weekends (cart included)
Seasonal specials available.
Reservations may be made up to a week in advance.

Open since 1992, this well-conditioned, semiprivate club was originally designed as a private club. It features ravines, bluffs and the river. The finishing holes are unique and challenging. It's kind of expensive and among the priciest of the public clubs. This one is definitely for target golfers.

MILL QUARTER PLANTATION
Rt 620
Powhatan   598-4221
6,994 yards/par 72/slope rating: 118
Fees: weekdays $19 walking, $31 with cart; weekends $25 walking, $37 with cart; special rates for 9-holes, weekday foursomes and seniors.
Reservations are suggested for weekends or holidays. Call the preceding Monday.

You'll find that this Chesterfield County course is similar to a private club and is one of the better public courses in the area. It's a long course with large greens that are usually in pretty good shape. Sneak out on a weekday if you want to avoid the weekend crowds. Located off Route 60, it's popular with Midlothian and Chesterfield area residents.

BELMONT PARK RECREATION CENTER

1600 Hilliard Rd.   266-4929
6,418 yards/par 71/slope rating: 122
Fees: $17 weekdays, $20 weekends, carts $30
Special rates are available for seniors, juniors
and Henrico County residents.
Reservations are suggested for weekends and
holidays. Tee-times are required daily.

Belmont is a public course that used to be the old Hermitage Country Club before it was purchased by Henrico County. It's an old-style, World War I-era course that has benefited from numerous improvements. Fees are reasonable, but it's very crowded and difficult to get in a quick round. Play this one in the late fall to avoid the crowds.

BIRKDALE

8511 Royal Birkdale Dr.
Chesterfield   739-8800
6,014 yards/par 71/slope rating: 118
Fees: $35 weekdays, $42 weekends (cart
included)
Seasonal fees and special rates for seniors
Reservations are required. Call 5 days in advance.

This is an upscale neighborhood course in Chesterfield, near Clover Hill High School. The course is short, and a lot of fairways are tight. It's a real sluggers' course, similar to the Crossings.

SYCAMORE CREEK

1991 Manakin Rd.
Manakin-Sabot   784-3544
6300 yards/par 70/slope rating: 124
Fees: $29 weekdays, $36 weekends and
holidays, carts included.
Special fees for seniors and juniors.
Reservations required. Call on Wednesday.

This Scottish-inspired course opened in 1992 and is a close and convenient al-ternative for West End golfers. Tuckahoe Creek winds through this course that features a tremendous amount of grass pot bunkers, rolling hills and mounds. Even the best shot-maker will be challenged by the 15 water holes. Although this is a public course, you'll feel like you're playing at a private country club.

GLENWOOD GOLF CLUB

3100 Creighton Rd.   226-1793
6,464 yards/par 71/slope rating: 114
Fees: $15 weekdays, $25 weekends, carts $30
Special weekday rates for women, juniors and
seniors.
Reservations are required for weekends and
holidays. Call the preceding Saturday.

Like Belmont, this is another good bargain course, situated just 5 minutes from downtown. Built in the 1920s, Glenwood is the oldest continuously operated course in Richmond. It's very popular, and fees are low. If you hit the ball a long distance, you'll love the low scores you can get on this tricky, rolling, short course.

THE CROSSINGS

800 Virginia Center Pkwy.
Glen Allen   266-2254
6,619 yards/par 72/slope rating: 126
Fees: $37 weekdays, $42 weekends (includes
cart)
Special rates are available for nine-holes, ladies,
juniors and seniors. Special winter rates are
offered December through March.
Pull carts and coolers are not allowed.
Walking is permitted before 9 AM or after 2 PM
on weekdays and on weekends after 2 PM.
Reservations are required. Call one week in
advance.

Insiders' Tips

Go to the Hyatt Richmond Hotel for Sunday brunch.

The Signet Open held at Willow Oaks Country Club brings golfers from all over the state to Richmond.

This is one of the most popular sites in the city for corporate outings and is often closed to the public. It used to be the old Ethelwood Golf Course, a private course owned by Hermitage Country Club. Almost every golfer in the area has played here several times. It's well-conditioned and has some unusual holes. It's difficult to get a tee-time on weekends, but you might get a chance to play during the week.

THE HOLLOWS GOLF COURSE
Rt. 2
Montpelier 883-5381
6,505 yards/par 72/slope rating 118
Fees: $14 weekdays, $20 weekends. Special rates available for nine-holes and twilight hours after 4:30 PM.
Carts are $7 for nine-holes, $10 for 18-holes. Walking and pull carts are permitted.
Call after 12 PM on Wednesdays for weekend reservations.

This semiprivate club features an easygoing, country atmosphere. Located west of Richmond in Montpelier, the course is open on the front nine and wooded on the back nine. A putting green and driving range are available. To get here, take Rt. 110, 33 East off I 295.

Private Courses

These are a few of the best private clubs in the area. You must be a member or a member's guest to play them. If you get an invitation to play at any of these, don't turn it down.

FOUNDRY GOLF CLUB
3225 Lees Landing Rd.
Powhatan 598-9898
6,750 yards/par 72/slope rating: 128

Some say this is one of the most challenging and exclusive courses in the area. There are a lot of dog legs and fast, undulating greens. A scenic creek with small waterfalls runs through the middle of the heavily wooded terrain. Open since 1992, the course is the center point of a residential development now under construction. Membership is by invitation only.

DOMINION CLUB AT WYNDHAM

6000 Dominion Club Dr.
Glen Allen   *360-1200*
7,089 yards/par 72/slope rating: 129

This million-dollar course is the center point of the Wyndham residential community and is one of the newest courses in the area. Designed by Curtis Strange, the course is playable by all levels of golfers from beginners to professionals. The terrain includes a mixture of pines and hardwoods, lakes and the Chickahominy River. Nine holes involve water. The **Nike Dominion Open** has been held here each year since 1993.

JEFFERSON-LAKESIDE COUNTRY CLUB

1700 Lakeside Ave.   *266-2382*
6,106 yards/par 71/slope rating: 113
Guest fees: $20 weekdays, $35 weekends and holidays.
Carts: $20 for 18-holes, $11 for 9-holes (for two golfers)
Walking and pull carts are permitted.
Reservations for members are suggested for weekends and holidays.

Preserved from the 1920s, the course was designed by Donald Roth and is the centerpiece of a neighborhood. The first four holes are the toughest. The course is relatively short with tight fairways and plenty of trees. It's definitely a "placement" golf course. The club has a truly open admissions policy and a good interracial mix of members. Former Virginia Governor Doug Wilder is a member here.

HERMITAGE COUNTRY CLUB

Rt. 676
Manakin-Sabot   *784-3811*
Guest Fees: $40 weekdays, $45 weekends and holidays
Carts: $24 for 18-holes, $12 for 9-holes
Manakin Course: 6,691 yards/par 72/slope rating: 115
Sabot Course: 6,947 yards/par 72/slope rating: 127

Reservations for members are suggested for weekends and holidays.
Call after 8:00 AM on Friday.

In Goochland, Hermitage Country Club offers two courses: the Manakin and the Sabot. The PGA Seniors Tour was held here when Richmond was included on the tour. The new nine holes on the backside of the Sabot course were designed by Arthur Hills and feature water hazards on every hole. Most area golfers have played here. The club has a large membership, and it does allow some corporate outings. Initiation fees are high, and there is usually about a two-year waiting list for new members.

WILLOW OAKS COUNTRY CLUB

6228 Forest Hill Ave.   *272-1455*
6,684 yards/par 72/slope rating: 120
Guest Fees: $30 weekdays, $35 weekends and holidays
Carts: $21 for 18-holes, $13 for 9-holes
Reservations are suggested every day. (Closed on Mondays.)

With the James River as its neighbor, this course features hills, bluffs and beautiful scenic holes overlooking the water. Considered to be one of the top five courses in Virginia, Willow Oaks is the site of the **AMF/Signet Open State Championship**. Built in the 1950s, the course is very compact and easy to walk. The small greens make this a real shotmakers' course.

COUNTRY CLUB OF VIRGINIA

Westhampton Course
6031 St. Andrews Ln.   *288-2891*
James River and Tuckahoe Creek Courses
709 S. Gaskins Rd.   *288-2891*
Westhampton: 5,703 yards/par 69/slope rating: 110
James River: 7,022 yards/par 72/slope rating: 33
Tuckahoe Creek: 6,933 yards/par 72/slope rating: 128

This is an ultra-exclusive club with three courses and one of the highest initiation fees in the area. Membership is by invitation only. The James River Course was recently redesigned by Rees Jones. Originally designed by William Flynn, it has been rated as one of the top five courses in the state by *Golf Digest*. Several U.S. Amateur Championships have also been held here. The Westhampton Course was designed by Donald Roth, and Joe Lee contrived the layout for the Tuckahoe Creek Course. If you play here, you're well-connected.

Golf Shops

MULLIGAN'S
9127 W. Broad St.
T.J. Maxx Shopping Center   *747-7277*

If you're looking for something special or need quick repairs on your equipment, Mulligan's, in the West End, has a good reputation for providing fast service and custom equipment.

RICHMOND GOLF CENTER
5918 W. Broad St.   *288-4653*
1105 Alverse Dr.
(Off Midlothian Tnpk.)   *379-8333*

This is Richmond's discount golf supermarket. They offer quality pro-line equipment, repairs, club fitting and try-out ranges. You can find their stores in the West End and in Southside.

Thousands of runners compete in the annual Richmond Newspapers Marathon.

Inside
Sports

From hard-driving auto races and professional baseball, to slam-dunkin' basketball and rock-em, sock-em action on the ice, Richmond has plenty of year-round excitement for sports enthusiasts.

Leading the list is the Richmond International Raceway, the Richmond Braves — top farm team for Major League Baseball's Atlanta franchise — and the Renegades hockey team. Plus, with four colleges and universities in the area, there's enough basketball to keep even the most avid hoop fan happy, especially when you consider that two of the universities play at the Division I level and frequently appear in the NCAA Tournament.

Richmond is also gaining national attention as an NCAA basketball town. In 1990 the NCAA Southeast Region Tournament was held at the Richmond Coliseum, and in 1994 the NCAA returned to the Coliseum for the Women's Final Four. The city is also a site for world-class bicycle racing in the annual Tour DuPont.

There's plenty of sports action throughout the year. You can see college football, tennis, marathons, soccer, lacrosse, field hockey, professional wrestling and tractor pulls.

Since many people who work in the Richmond area graduated from Virginia schools, sports provide lots of ammunition for friendly office rivalries. Pick a local team to root for, follow news about sports at the University of Virginia and Virginia Tech, and you'll have plenty to talk about.

Tickets are usually available at the gate for most sporting events in the area, with the exception of Winston Cup races and some games between local rivals such as the University of Richmond and Virginia Commonwealth University, Virginia Union and Virginia State, and Randolph Macon and Longwood.

The purpose of this chapter is to acquaint you with the major spectator sports in the area. If you're interested in participant sports, you'll find that information in the chapter on Parks and Recreation.

Baseball

RICHMOND BRAVES

Peanuts, Cracker Jacks, talented baseball players and old fashioned family fun. Take me out to the Diamond, home of the Richmond Braves, the top minor league team in the Atlanta Braves farm system.

Just one step away from the "big leagues," the Richmond Braves compete at the elite Triple-A level. During the last few years, more than 50 former R-Braves have played in the majors, including Dale Murphy, Brett Butler, Steve Avery and

Dave Justice. In fact, 19 members of the 1991 National League Champion Atlanta Braves played for Richmond.

The Braves have been a Richmond tradition since 1966, when the National League Milwaukee Braves moved to Atlanta following the 1965 baseball season. The move forced Milwaukee's previous Triple-A franchise, the Atlanta Crackers, to find a new home. No team played in Richmond in 1965 after the New York Yankees moved their farm team, then known as the Richmond Virginians, to Toledo in 1964.

With features such as sky boxes and a restaurant behind first base where you can watch the games while you dine, the Diamond is considered one of the finest ball parks in the minor leagues. Several million fans have passed through its gates since it was built in 1985 with contributions from local governments, businesses and individuals.

Part of the atmosphere at the Diamond is created by the sculpture of a giant Indian brave named Connecticut who is seen peering over the top of a wall. On loan to the Diamond for several years by artist Paul DiPasquale, the sculpture was almost purchased by an outside interest and removed from the stadium. It's now a permanent part of the ballpark thanks to a fundraising campaign headed by Signet Bank.

If you get to the games early, you might get a hug from the Diamond Duck, and kids love to get the free hats, gloves, candy bars and other promotional merchandise given to the first fans who arrive.

The home schedule usually runs from April through August. Located on the Boulevard, the Diamond is easy to get to from I-95 or I-64. For game and ticket information, call the Braves office at 359-4444.

Auto Racing

RICHMOND INTERNATIONAL RACEWAY

Richmond International Raceway (RIR) at the Virginia State Fairgrounds in Henrico County, put Richmond on the map as a major NASCAR city and a place to see hard-driving, rock 'n' roll-style auto racing. The thoroughly modern track has more than 60,000 reserved seats and draws the largest crowd of any sports event in Virginia.

Each year, the raceway hosts two Grand National Series races and two Winston Cup Series races — "The Pontiac Excitement 400" in March and "The Miller Genuine Draft 400" in September. NASCAR's Modified Tour Division and the NASCAR's Late Model Stock Cars also appear at the raceway in the spring for a duel Saturday afternoon event called the Winston NASCAR Twins.

RIR has existed since the mid-'50s but was completely remodeled in 1988. The 3/4-mile track, the only one of its kind on the NASCAR circuit, is banked at 14 degrees in the turns. The 60-foot-wide track was expanded from its previous half-mile length to give the drivers more room to maneuver.

If you plan to go, be warned . . . all roads leading to the raceway are clogged with fans coming and going. In fact, a section of Laburnum Avenue is converted into a one-way street on race days. If you want to avoid heavy traffic, plan to arrive 2 or 3 hours before the race starts. Suggested traffic routes are usually published in the newspaper. Parking is free. Shuttle bus service is also provided from several locations around town.

Seats sellout fast, so buy your tickets early. Raceway ticket and information offices are open all year. Call 345-RACE (345-7223). Camper parking spots with hookups are available. For information call 228-3200.

SOUTHSIDE SPEEDWAY

Every Friday night, April through September, auto racing fans can watch NASCAR/Winston Series races at the Southside Speedway. Each week more than 70 competitors circle the 1/3-mile asphalt oval known as the "Toughest Short Track in the South." NASCAR Modifieds are an added feature on selected nights. Free parking, full concessions and novelty items are available. For more information call (804) 744-1275.

RICHMOND DRAGWAY

The dragway opens the first Sunday in March each year and offers sanctioned drag racing programs each weekend through November. For more information call 737-1193.

Ice Hockey

RICHMOND RENEGADES

The Renegades provide ice hockey fans with slam-bang, rock 'n' roll action up and down the rink. More than 5,000 loud, boisterous, fight-loving fans add to the excitement. Formed in 1990, the Renegades play in the East Coast Hockey League at the Coliseum in downtown Richmond. For ticket information call 643-7825.

Cycling

TOUR DUPONT

Every May, more than 30,000 Richmonders line the streets to watch world class bicyclists sprint through the city in the Tour DuPont, one of the top three bicycle races in the world. The lineup includes world-reknown riders such as Raul Alcala, Lance Armstrong, Greg LeMond, Malcolm Elliott and Viatcheslav Ekimov.

Spectators will also be able to watch the Tour DuPont Women's Challenge race just before the Tour DuPont riders enter Richmond. Top women riders in the United States are invited to participate in a criterion race around several blocks downtown.

A proliferation of news teams covering the race brings international media exposure for Richmond since the race is telecast throughout the world. For some people, watching the news teams and support activity surrounding the race is as interesting as the race itself.

The race usually begins in Wilmington, Delaware, where DuPont is headquartered and winds through several East Coast states. The overall Tour DuPont winner has the lowest cumulative time for the entire 10-day race that covers about 1,200 miles. There are also daily winners for point-to-point races from one city to another or for circuit races such as the one held in Richmond around several city blocks.

A good place to watch the race is from historic Shockoe Slip, the downtown financial district or on the 23rd Street hill. Special activities, music, giveaways, food booths and souvenirs near the start/finish line at 10th and Cary add to the carnival-like atmosphere.

DuPont began sponsoring the event in 1991. DuPont has made contributions to cycling technology and advanced aerodynamics through the manufacture of light weight materials used in riders' clothing and equipment. For more information call Medalist Sports, Inc., 354-9934.

Soccer

RICHMOND KICKERS

Owned by Bobby Lennon and coached by John Kerr, the Richmond Kickers soccer team joined the United States Interregional Soccer League (USISL) in 1993.

All of the Kickers are Virginia-based players who are former collegiate standouts, current college players and professional players.

The USISL is comprised of teams from eight regions throughout the country. The Kickers compete in the Eastern Division.

Fan support is excellent. Richmond has one of the highest attendance records in the entire league. More than 2,500 fans attend games at the University of Richmond Soccer Complex on campus. For schedules and more information call 644-5425. Tickets are available at the gate.

Marathon Running

RICHMOND NEWSPAPERS MARATHON

The Richmond Newspapers Marathon is the area's biggest participant sporting event with about 3,000 runners, joggers and wheelchair racers lining up for the start. Sponsored each year in October by Richmond Newspapers, Inc., the marathon is sanctioned by the Athletic Congress and is a qualifier for all other marathons. The event includes a full 26.2 mile marathon, a 13.1 mile half-marathon and a 5-mile race.

Although some world class runners participate, most of the racers are the same people you see jogging around town every day. Thousands of spectators turn out to cheer for friends, relatives and neighbors. It's a great excuse for a party or a curbside picnic. A variety of special activities downtown near the start and finish at Sixth and Broad add to the festivities.

If you're interested in participating, entry forms are available at Richmond Newspapers several months before the race. For more information call 649-6325.

Tennis

The annual men's and women's state tennis championships are usually held the first week in August at the Raintree Swim and Racquet Club, 1703 Raintree Drive. As many as 64 men and 32 women compete on eight hard courts. Players must be Virginia residents. Prize money is awarded. Many of the winners have achieved high rankings in the men's and women's professional circuit. The championships are open to the public. Admission is free. Food and beverages are available. For more information call 740-0026.

Colleges and Universities

Virginia Commonwealth University

Virginia's largest urban university, Virginia Commonwealth University sprawls in and around the downtown area and includes the Medical College of Virginia. Best known in sports for its men's basketball program, VCU also offers women's basketball and men's baseball. It does not have a football team. The Rams are members of the Colonial Athletic Association, NCAA Division I, which includes the University of Richmond,

Arthur Ashe Jr.

For Emily Clore, a 48-year-old former cafeteria worker, "he wasn't Martin Luther King Jr., and he wasn't Malcolm X. But when you saw him, he stood for something. He wasn't always talking, but he always had something to say."

For the Rev. Jesse Jackson, president of the Rainbow Coalition, "he turned anger into energy, and stumbling blocks into steppingstones."

Arthur Ashe Jr.

They both were talking about Arthur Ashe Jr., who once told an interviewer his life was built "on the values I learned in Richmond. It comes from those role models I came in contact with as a kid." As a tennis legend and as a human rights crusader, Arthur Ashe Jr. was the kind of person all of us would like to be.

He gained fame winning Wimbledon and the U.S. Open, being ranked No. 1 in the world twice, playing and captaining the U.S. Davis Cup team and, as Secretary of Commerce Ron Brown noted, "playing and integrating an utterly white game—and winning." But he gained even greater accolades for his off-court accomplishments and the manner in which he went about them. He raised public consciousness about AIDS, the plight of African-Americans, Haitians and South Africans, and he helped launch an operation called Virginia Heroes in his hometown to try to provide the kind of role models that were so important to him in his formative years.

"The situation concerning African-American males . . . is bleaker than people would imagine," he said. "When I was growing up it was the middle-class Negro community that set the culture. Now it's set by the lower economic level, by the rap music, the way they wear their hats."

Born in Richmond on July 10, 1943, Ashe was four years old when his family moved out of an uncle's home on Brook Road and into a small, one-story house at 1610 Sledd Street on the Brookfield Playground where his father had just been named supervisor. The 18-acre city recreational park was located between Chamberlayne Avenue and Brook Road one block from Virginia Union University, which in those days was Richmond's largest recreational facility for African-American residents.

"Although Arthur came of age in a segregated society, he had access to something most youngsters, white or black, didn't have: tennis courts right outside his door," says Dr. Francis M. Foster, a retired dentist and one of

Richmond's foremost authorities on the history of the city's African-American community.

As an elementary schoolboy, Ashe already was showing great promise as a tennis player. He was enrolled in a junior-development program sponsored by the American Tennis Association, a tennis organization for African Americans, and at age 10 he was fortunate enough to be taken under the wing of Dr. Robert W. "Whirlwind" Johnson, a Lynchburg dentist who spent his own money coaching and developing Ashe's abilities.

One little-known fact about Ashe is that he also was an outstanding baseball player. "He was a superior ballplayer," Dr. Foster says. "He had the speed of a gazelle and a sharp batting eye."

At Maggie Walker High School Ashe was "the perfect student, quiet and studious," recalls Roy A. West, former Richmond mayor and at that time a substitute teacher at Maggie Walker. "He paid attention in class. He didn't chitchat with other students. In fact, he didn't say much at all. But when Arthur did speak, you knew this was an intelligent young man."

After his junior year at Maggie Walker he left his family behind and moved to St. Louis, a tennis hotbed in those days, where he completed high school and pushed ahead with his tennis. He received a scholarship to the University of California, Los Angeles, which then had the dominant collegiate tennis program in the country. He became UCLA's No. 1 player and the first African-American ever chosen for the U.S. Davis Cup team.

The years that followed are the story everyone knows: the mercurial rise in the tennis world, the bypass heart surgery and his retirement from tennis in the late 1970s, his induction into the International Tennis Hall of Fame in 1985, and his disclosure he was suffering from AIDS as the result of a tainted blood transfusion during surgery.

The Brookfield Playground and the house on Sledd Street are gone now — the site today of Richmond's main post office. More than 6,000 mourners crowded the nearby Arthur Ashe Jr. Center for his funeral, on February 10, 1993, before he was buried in Woodland Cemetery in Richmond's East End.

At the funeral New York Mayor David Dinkins said what was on every mind: "Arthur Ashe was just plain better than most of us."

American University, East Carolina, George Mason, James Madison, William and Mary, UNC at Wilmington and Old Dominion. For tickets and information, call the sports information office at 828-1RAM.

BASKETBALL

Coached by Sonny Smith, VCU has one of the strongest, most exciting, basketball programs in the state. In the 1980's, the Rams appeared in five NCAA tournaments and advanced to the quarterfinal of the NIT. Before moving to the Metro Conference in 1991, the Rams won four regular-season championships in the Sun Belt Conference and three Sun Belt Tournaments, more than any other team in the league. In 1993, they participated in the NIT, only to lose in the first round to Old Dominion University.

Credit: Metro Richmond Convention and Visitors Bureau

The Diamond is home to the Richmond Braves.

The 1984-85 team was probably the best VCU team in history. At the end of the season, the Rams were ranked 11th by Associated Press and UPI polls

Since 1974, 15 VCU players have been drafted into the NBA, including Gerald Henderson, Calvin Duncan, Rolando Lamb and Mike Schlegel.

Known by many fans as the "cardiac" Rams, the team has earned a reputation for playing fast-paced, exciting games that are frequently decided at the final buzzer.

An average of 7,000 fans attend games at the Richmond Coliseum, the largest basketball facility in the state with a seating capacity of 10,716.

If you can't make it to the Coliseum, you might be able to watch the Rams on television. VCU has been on television more than any other team in the state.

VCU's women's basketball team has also grown in popularity over the years and attracts 300 to 500 fans at each game played in the Franklin Street Gym on campus. In 1994, VCU was host to the Final Four in women's basketball.

BASEBALL

VCU's men's baseball team has been ranked as one of the top 25 Division I teams in the country. Several hundred fans attend games at the Diamond on the Boulevard near I-64 and I-95.

University of Richmond

Basketball and football are the main sports played at the University of Richmond in the West End. The football team plays in the Yankee Conference, NCAA Division I-AA. All other teams are in the Colonial Athletic Association, NCAA Division I. Other CAA teams include Virginia Commonwealth University, American University, East Carolina, George Mason, James Madison, William and Mary, UNC at Wilmington and Old Dominion.

With the exception of football, which is played at the UR Stadium near downtown Richmond, all sports are played on campus.

To get to the campus from South Side, cross the Huguenot Bridge, turn left onto River Road, then turn right onto College Road.

From other locations, take the Glenside Road S. Exit off I-64 to Three Chopt Road. Go east about a half-mile and turn right on Boatwright Drive.

For tickets and information, call the ticket office at 289-8388 or the athletics office at 289-8363.

BASKETBALL

On any given night, the Richmond Spiders can defeat any team in the country. They have a record of significant wins over nationally ranked teams, including a victory over Syracuse in the 1991 NCAA Tournament. One of the biggest upsets in college basketball, it was the first time a #15 seeded team defeated a #2 seeded team.

The Spiders are coached by Bill Dooley, who was named Coach of the Year in 1994. Dooley replaced the highly respected Dick Tarrant who retired in 1993.

Since 1981, the Spiders have participated in at least five NCAA Tournaments, and they reached the "Sweet 16" in 1988. They've also had a number of trips to the NIT. UR players who've joined the National Basketball Association include Curtis Blair, John Schweitz and John Newman.

Home games are played on campus at the Robins Center which has a seating capacity of about 9,000. Depending on the game, 8,000 or more fans may attend. Games with other Virginia teams and nationally ranked teams have been known to sell out.

The women's basketball team faces several Top-20 teams and has had a string of undefeated seasons in recent years. Games are well-attended by 700 to 1,000 fans.

FOOTBALL

UR football games are close-scoring and fun to attend, especially if you arrive early enough for a pregame tailgate party. The most popular games are with William & Mary, VMI and James Madison.

In the '80s, the Spiders reached the NCAA I-AA playoffs twice and they had a first-round NFL draft choice — Barry Redden. Redden played with the Los Angeles Rams, the Cleveland Browns and the San Diego Chargers. Another former UR player, Brian Jordan, 1985-1988, played with the Atlanta Falcons.

Coached by Jim Marshall, widely respected for his offensive mind, the Spiders play in the Yankee Conference, one of the strongest and most respected Division I-AA conferences in the country. The conference includes Connecticut, Massachusetts, Maine, New Hampshire, Richmond, Rhode Island, Boston, Villanova, Delaware, James Madison, Northeastern and William & Mary.

Home games are played at the UR Stadium on McCloy Street between

Insiders' Tips

NASCAR events at the Richmond International Raceway draw the largest crowds of any sports event in Virginia. The track has more than 60,000 reserved seats.

Credit: Richmond Newspapers

Earnhardt overtakes Rudd at the Richmond International Raceway.

downtown Richmond and the university campus. The stadium is the second-largest facility in the Yankee Conference and seats 22,611. Restrooms, concessions and souvenir stands are conveniently placed throughout the stadium. You can buy tickets at the gate or in advance. Plenty of parking is available.

OTHER SPORTS

Men's soccer games usually draw about 2,000 spectators at the UR Soccer Complex on campus. The Spider's baseball games are played on campus at Pitt Field.

Virginia Union University

At Lombardy Avenue and Brook Road, close to downtown Richmond, Virginia Union University is a member of the Central Intercollegiate Athletic Association (CIAA), which consists of 14 historically African-American institutions: Bowie, Elizabeth City, Fayetteville, Hampton, Johnson C. Smith, Livingston, Norfolk State, North Carolina Central, Saint Augustine's, Saint Paul's, Shaw, Virginia State, Virginia Union and Winston Salem.

Virginia Union is primarily known for its basketball and football programs. For information or tickets call the sports information office at 257-5840.

BASKETBALL

Virginia Union has always had one of the best basketball teams in the state. Coached by Dave Robbins, the Panthers are frequently ranked No. 1 in the CIAA and in the Top 10 teams of NCAA Division II.

Panthers who made it to the professional ranks include Charles Oakley, Terry Davis, A.J. English and Tim Price (Harlem Globe Trotters).

Men's and women's basketball games are played off campus at the Arthur Ashe Center at the corner of Boulevard and Robin Hood Road near the Diamond.

FOOTBALL

Virginia Union holds the NCAA Division II record for the most consecutive winning seasons. One of the best games of the year is the Gold Bowl Classic, an annual rivalry between the Panthers and Norfolk State. All games are played at Hovey Field on campus.

Randolph Macon College

Winning is a tradition at Randolph Macon College in Ashland, a small school best known for its basketball and football teams. Macon also offers men's and women's soccer, baseball, lacrosse, women's basketball and field hockey. All teams play in the Old Dominion Athletic Conference which includes 13 NCAA Division III schools in Virginia and Guilford College in North Carolina.

All sports are played on campus. To get to Randolph Macon, take Route 54 W. exit off I-95 in Ashland. For tickets and information call 752-7223.

BASKETBALL

Coached by Hal Nunnally, the men's basketball team is a top-ranked NCAA Division III team. The team has won several Old Dominion Athletic Conference Championships and made it to the Final 16 in the NCAA Division III Tournament in 1991.

Randolph Macon joined the ODAC league in 1989, when it switched to the Division III level. All games are played at Crenshaw Gymnasium. About 600 fans usually attend.

FOOTBALL

To say football is a big deal here would be an understatement. Randolph Macon's football team has won more ODAC championships than any other team in the conference. Coached by Joe Riccio, football games usually draw about 2,000 to 2,500 fans, except at the homecoming game and the annual game with Hampton Sydney College when it's not unusual for 5,000 to 6,000 fans to pack the stands.

Historically, Randolph Macon was one of the first schools in the nation to field a competitive football team in 1881. Only 17 schools in the United States had football teams before Randolph Macon. Fans may remember running back Remon Smith (1984-1987), who holds the record as the leading rusher in Virginia collegiate history (4,276 yards).

Home games are played on Day Field.

OTHER SPORTS

Other popular sports at Randolph Macon include men's and women's soccer, baseball, lacrosse and women's field hockey. Admission to these games is free.

Inside
Medical Care

The American Medical Association has designated Richmond as a Prime Medical Center and *Health* magazine has named the city as No. 1 in the nation based on opportunities for a combination of a healthy lifestyle and first-class medical care.

The Greater Richmond Yellow Pages carry about 75 pages of listings of physicians, almost twice as many pages as it devotes to local lawyers.

Because of the size of Richmond's medical community and because of the wide range of specialties it encompasses, it is impossible to begin to do it justice in these few pages. But here are some names and numbers that will help out in emergency medical situations and that will help you locate a physician, dentist or other medical professional.

Emergency 911 Number

Dialing 911 will put you in touch with an enhanced emergency communications network that serves Richmond and the counties of Chesterfield, Goochland, Hanover, Henrico and Powhatan. The system can identify the address from which you are calling and is designed to take care of emergency, fire, police and rescue calls. If you need emergency medical transportation you also can call 911, but you should call a rescue squad or am-

bulance services' business telephone number if your need is simply for routine transportation to or from a hospital. If you call 911 in a non-emergency you are subject to a fine.

Rescue Squads

A number of excellent rescue squads and ambulance services serve the Richmond area. Those listed here provide services free of charge, except for Richmond Ambulance Services, Inc., which charges for its services.

City of Richmond

FOREST VIEW
VOLUNTEER RESCUE SQUAD
5327 Forest Hill Ave.   *232-8971*

Forest View Volunteer Rescue Squad serves areas south of the James River, north of Midlothian Turnpike and west of Cowardin Avenue. It also responds to calls in parts of Chesterfield County.

RICHMOND AMBULANCE AUTHORITY
Non-emergencies   *254-1111*

Richmond Ambulance Authority (RAA) is city-wide in scope, but it responds to calls from areas served by volunteer rescue squads only if needed. RAA has established 23 geographic posts around the city. When the dispatcher receives a call, the ambulance at the closest post responds. Ambulance crews are shifted from post to post as calls are answered in an effort to keep all posts covered at all times. RAA operates as an advanced life support system. Each ambulance is staffed with one paramedic or cardiac technician and one emergency medical technician. A paramedic dispatcher is on duty 24 hours a day to provide instructions over the phone until an ambulance arrives. An annual membership for unlimited emergency and non-emergency service can be purchased for $49. Nonmembers pay $388 for each emergency trip and $258 for each non-emergency trip.

WEST END
VOLUNTEER RESCUE SQUAD
1802 Chantilly   359-3590
The West End Rescue Squad responds to calls west of the Boulevard in the city and to calls in a portion of Henrico County connected to Richmond's West End.

Chesterfield County

BENSLEY-BERMUDA
VOLUNTEER RESCUE SQUAD
2500 Rio Vista St.
Chester   748-6122
This rescue squad serves southern Chesterfield County in the area stretching from Colonial Heights to the Richmond city limits and from Hopewell to Chesterfield Courthouse.

ETTRICK-MATOACA RESCUE SQUAD
5711 River Rd.
Matoaca   590-2104
As its name implies, this rescue squad serves the southeastern part of Chesterfield County.

FOREST VIEW VOLUNTEER SQUAD
8008 Midlothian Tnpk.
901 Grove Rd.   232-8971
In addition to its Forest Hill Avenue base, this rescue squad has substations on Midlothian Turnpike and Grove Road to serve the Chesterfield County area south of U.S. 360 to the James River.

MANCHESTER
VOLUNTEER RESCUE SQUAD
3500 Courthouse Rd.   276-4344
The Manchester squad responds to calls in western Chesterfield county.

Hanover County

ASHCAKE
VOLUNTEER RESCUE SQUAD
2501 Ashcake Rd.
Mechanicsville   746-2397
Ashcake serves the U.S. 301 area halfway to Mechanicsville and halfway to Ashland.

ASHLAND
VOLUNTEER RESCUE SQUAD
203 Duncan St.
Ashland   798-8000
The Ashland Volunteer Rescue Squad responds to calls in central Hanover County.

EAST HANOVER
VOLUNTEER RESCUE SQUAD
9375 Walnut Grove Ave.
Mechanicsville   746-5883

WEST HANOVER
VOLUNTEER RESCUE SQUAD
Va. 715
Montpelier   883-6336
These volunteer rescue squads serve the eastern and western parts of the county, as their names indicate.

Henrico County

HENRICO
VOLUNTEER RESCUE SQUAD
5301 Huntsman Rd.
Sandston   226-1669
In Sandston, the Henrico Volunteer Rescue Squad serves the eastern part of the county.

LAKESIDE
VOLUNTEER RESCUE SQUAD
2007 Timberlake Ave.   266-7498
This volunteer rescue squad serves the central and northern parts of Henrico County.

TUCKAHOE
VOLUNTEER RESCUE SQUAD
1101 Horsepen Rd.   288-6686
Tuckahoe Volunteer Rescue Squad responds to calls in the western part of the county. It has a substation at 2324 Pump Road.

Public and Nonprofit Health Services

There are many health organizations, clinics and services that are publicly funded or are supported by private contributions. Many charge patients on a sliding scale based on their ability to pay. Some of these organizations and services include:

Fan Free Clinic, 1721 Hanover Avenue, 358-8538, 358-6140

McGuire Veterans Administration Medical Center Outpatient Clinic (for veterans only), 1201 Broad Rock Boulevard, 230-0001

Memorial Guidance Clinic, 2319 E. Broad Street, 649-1605

Richmond Area High Blood Pressure Center, 1200 W. Cary Street, 359-9375

Richmond AIDS Information Network, 1721 Hanover Avenue, 358-6343

Richmond Medical Center for Women, 118 N. Boulevard, 359-5066

VCU/MCV A. D. Williams Clinic, 1200 E. Marshall Street, 828-3780

Salvation Army Boys and Girls Club and Neighborhood Center, 3701 R Street (for club members) 222-3122

VCU Psychology Services Center, 806 W. Franklin Street, 367-8069

Virginia League for Planned Parenthood, 517 W. Grace Street, 788-6725

The City of Richmond Department of Health operates the Southside Plaza Clinic at 4730 Southside Plaza, 780-5300; the Calhoun Health Center at 436 Calhoun Street 780-4513, for family planning, pediatrics and maternity; the Civic Clinic at 500 N. 10th Street in Room 114, 780-6855, for chest diseases, communicable diseases and immunization for foreign travel and in Room 109, 780-6850, for maternal and child care. The Vernon Harris Clinic at 719 N. 25th Street, 780-1021, offers prenatal and pediatric care for women, infants and young children and also houses the Community Health Center, 782-9514, to help people learn how to stay healthy and prevent illness.

The Richmond Department of Mental Health and Mental Retardation is a source for general information on mental health and substance abuse, 780-4536, and on mental retardation services, 780-6896. The Richmond Community Mental Health Center is at 501 N. Ninth Street, 780-6900, and has a 24-hour emergency service that can be reached by dialing 780-8003.

The Henrico County Health Department's main offices are at Parham and Hungry Spring Road, 672-4651. The department operates the East Henrico County Clinic No. 2 at 3810 Nine Mile Road, 236-3190, and the Henrico Mental Health Center at 10299 Woodman Road, 261-8500 or 261-8484 (24-hour number).

The Chesterfield County Health Department can be reached at 748-1691, and the phone number for its Mental Health Center is 748-1227.

The phone number for the Hanover County Health Department is 752-7802; its Mental Health Center can be reached at 798-3279.

Finding A Physician or Dentist

Physicians

If you don't have friends, relatives or business associates who can recommend a physician, there are a number of services and organizations in town ready to help you. These include the Richmond Academy of Medicine, 643-6631, which offers a referral service that involves more than 1,000 physicians and specialists. Based on your description of your needs, the service will provide the names of three physicians. Another professional organization, the Virginia Academy of Family Physicians, 358-1721, will provide a list of member physicians.

Hospital Corporation of America, which has three area hospital affiliates: Chippenham Medical Center, Johnston-Willis and Henrico Doctors Hospital provides the Greater Richmond Physician Referral Service, 330-4000 or (800) 888-DOCS, that offers information on physicians affiliated with HCA hospitals.

Medical College of Virginia Hospitals has an in-house physician referral service, (800) 762-6161, and many services provided by MCV Hospitals are accessible through this number. More than 750 physicians in Central Virginia are listed with the Virginia Referral Service at 270-DRDR or (800) 468-0199, a service of St. Mary's Hospital.

Hospital-operated physician referral services include:

Charter-Westbrook Hospital	261-7121
Chippenham Medical Center	320-3627
Henrico Doctors Hospital	323-1HDH
HealthSouth Medical Center	747-5757
Johnston-Willis Hospital	330-4007
Psychiatric Institute of Richmond	784-2220
Retreat Hospital	254-5156
Richmond Community Hospital	225-1707
Richmond Eye and Ear Hospital	775-4500
Richmond Memorial Hospital	358-7911
Stuart Circle Hospital	359-WELL

Dentists

The American Dental Association's local chapter, the Richmond Dental Society, 379-2534, has a member referral service, and dentists are referred to patients according to location by the Dentist Information Service, 649-0283. Multi-dentist "team" practices include:

ANDERSON & STONER

4922-B W. Broad St.	282-4279
4859 Finlay St.	222-0609

SHERRY DODSON-GORDON, D.D.S.
10322 Iron Bridge Rd.   748-6677

W. BAXTER PERKINSON JR.,
D.D.S. & ASSOCIATES, LTD.
1600 Huguenot Rd.   794-9789
6441 Iron Bridge Rd.   743-8166
2200 Pump Rd.   740-0511
6605 Mechanicsville Tnpk.   730-3400
10138 Hull St. Rd.   276-8539

FRIENDLY GENTLE DENTISTRY
CHARLES W. MARTIN, D.D.S.
MICHAEL D. PFAB, D.D.S.
11201 Huguenot Rd.   320-6800

Chiropractors

Almost 260 chiropractic doctors are listed with the Virginia Chiropractic Association, 353-8699, or with the Chiropractic Referral Service, Inc., 644-HELP.

Walk-In Medical Centers

Like metropolitan areas across the nation, Richmond has a number of walk-in family medical centers. Most are open every day for extended hours, and no appointment is necessary. These centers include:

MEDCARE
12900 Jefferson Davis Hwy.
Chester   796-2373

PATIENT FIRST
2205 N. Parham Rd.   270-0237
2300 E. Parham Rd.   264-8025
11020 Hull Street Rd.   744-8515
8110 Midlothian Tnpk.   320-8504

URGENT CARE
Glenside Dr. at Staples Mill Rd.   262-4763

McGUIRE MEDICAL GROUP

(Call first for appointment; physician on call 24 hours, 346-1500).

7702 Parham Rd.	346-1500
10431 Patterson Ave.	741-6200
9325 Midlothian Tnpk.	323-0800
1117 Hanover Green Dr., Mechanicsville	730-1111

Eye Care

RICHMOND OPTICAL

2821 Parham Rd.	747-6662
6512-P Mechanicsville Tnpk.	730-2020

VIRGINIA EYE INSTITUTE

400 Westhampton Station
General information: 287-4216
Satellite locations:
St. Mary's Hospital
Johnston-Willis Medical Building
Richmond Medical Port
Mechanicsville Medical Center
Centre Court Building, Chesterfield

This outpatient facility is staffed by some of the most well known and respected eye-care physicians in Richmond. Located at the north end of the Huguenot Bridge, VEI provides a full range of eye care ranging from pediatrics to geriatric ophthalmology. Full-service care is also provided at the listed satellite locations.

Orthopedics

Orthopedic specialists serving the Richmond area include:

HENRICO ORTHOPAEDIC ASSOCIATES, LTD.

7660 Parham Rd., Ste. 102
(HealthSouth Medical Center) 747-1111

RICHMOND ORTHOPAEDIC CLINIC, LTD.

1400 Westwood Ave. 355-7411
(Office also at 9220 Forest Hill Ave.)

TUCKAHOE ORTHOPAEDIC ASSOCIATES, LTD.

8919 Three Chopt Rd. 288-4033
(Office also at 4405 Cox Rd. in Innsbrook)

Sports Medicine

Sports medicine centers are geared to caring for weekend athletes as well as team members. They offer clinics, workshops and seminars on how to prevent injuries. And, of course, they treat and help rehabilitate injuries once they occur. Theirs is a specialized field of medicine that keeps them on call 24 hours a day. Local sports medicine centers include:

CHIPPENHAM MEDICAL CENTER SPORTS MEDICAL CENTER

Chippenham Pkwy. and Jahnke Rd. 320-7272

STUART CIRCLE SPORTS

Mechanicsville Medical Center
811 Cold Harbor Rd. 730-1003

VCU SPORTS MEDICINE CENTER

104 N. Belvidere St. 786-0713

Inside
Hospitals

Richmond is a pace-setting medical center and has the fourth largest university-affiliated teaching hospital in the nation. Its medical researchers are the lead players in a national study of childhood cancer, it is a focal point of genetic research, and it is the national headquarters of the United Network of Organ Sharing that links transplant centers, organ procurement organizations and laboratories across the United States.

The city is emerging as a hub of biomedical firms and is the home of the Center for Innovative Technology's Biotechnology Institute where work is underway on everything from sleep disorders to clinical trials of a vaccine to prevent tooth decay. A new 20-acre, $180 million, 1.5-million-square-foot Virginia Biotechnology Research Park in downtown Richmond, when complete, could employ as many as 3,000 scientific and support personnel. The park is adjacent to Virginia Commonwealth University's Medical College of Virginia, one of the top-ranking medical schools in sponsored biomed research. Already more than 50 biotech companies have been attracted to the Richmond area and a Virginia Biotechnology Association has been formed.

Richmond surgeons pioneered heart and kidney transplants, and many of the transplantation procedures used today were perfected at the Medical College of

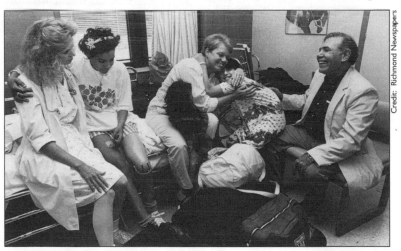

The Children's Hospital offers special care for children and young adults.

Virginia many years ago. Gerontology professionals seek the latest information on aging through the Medical College of Virginia's Geriatric Education Center, which produces live, interactive teleconferences throughout the world.

Among the medical resources available to Richmond area residents are 12 acute care and eight specialty hospitals.

MEDICAL COLLEGE OF VIRGINIA HOSPITALS
401 N. 12th St.   *786-9000*

Nationally renowned for its emergency medical facilities and Level I trauma center, Medical College of Virginia Hospitals is the only local hospital listed in the book *The Best Hospitals in America*. Its heart transplant program was one of the first two in the nation to be certified by Medicare. Surgeons at the hospitals today also perform liver, kidney, heart-lung, pancreas, bone marrow, corneal, bone and tissue transplants. Its Massey Cancer Center is in the vanguard of cancer research, exploring tumor immunology, anticancer drug therapy and childhood cancer. Neonatal intensive care and research into infant health problems are among specialized programs at the Children's Medical Center. The first civilian burn unit in the country was opened here, and the hospitals are the site of one of a handful of federally funded geriatric education and psychiatric centers in the country. With 902 beds and 92 outpatient clinics, Medical College of Virginia Hospitals is a formidable asset for the city.

HUNTER HOLMES McGUIRE VETERANS AFFAIRS MEDICAL CENTER
1201 Broad Rock Rd.   *230-0001*

This is the second largest health care facility in the Richmond area. Named af-

ter the local physician who originated the concept of free care for veterans after the Civil War, the hospital has been serving veterans since 1946. The original facility was replaced about a decade ago by a new $116 million, 814-bed hospital that features a wide range of services. Strongly affiliated with Medical College of Virginia Hospitals, it houses one of the largest transplant centers in the nation. Its 120-bed spinal cord injury center has received widespread acclaim. The hospital's other special units include a hospice and a nursing home. There are also units for surgical and intensive care, coronary care and drug and alcohol dependency treatment.

CHARTER WESTBROOK BEHAVIORAL HEALTH SYSTEMS
1500 Westbrook Ave.   *266-9671*

This private psychiatric and addictive disease treatment facility for children, adolescents and adults is affiliated with Charter Medical Corporation and is Virginia's largest private psychiatric hospital. The 210-bed facility provides free 24-hour assessments, referring patients to an appropriate program and physician. It also operates a counseling center in Fredericksburg.

CHILDREN'S HOSPITAL
2924 Brook Rd.   *321-7474*

Children's Hospital offers specialized inpatient and outpatient services for children and young adults, from birth to age 21. Medical-surgical specialties include developmental pediatrics, allergy, anesthesiology, cardiology, dentistry, endocrinology, gastroenterology, neurology, neurosurgery, physical medicine and rehabilitation, ophthalmology, oral surgery, orthopedic surgery, otolaryngology, plastic surgery, radiology, rheumatology and urology. In addition, the hospital offers special therapy and support services including career development, child-adolescent psychology, education, child-life activities, nutrition counseling, occupational and physical therapies, social services and speech pathology audiology. The Motion Analysis Laboratory at Children's Hospital is one of only a few of such facilities on the East Coast and is designed to provide help for individuals with functional problems.

CHIPPENHAM MEDICAL CENTER
7101 Jahnke Rd.   *320-3911*

South of the James River with 470 beds, Chippenham Medical Center is Central Virginia's largest private comprehensive health care facility. Special units include the Virginia Heart Center, the Chest Pain and Emergency Room, Women's Medical Center, Central Virginia Laser Center, Sleep Disorders Center, Sports Medicine and Occupational Health Center, and the Diabetes Treatment Center. Its Fast Track Emergency Room is designed to separate those with minor medical needs from acutely ill patients. Chippenham also is the home of a 113-bed psychiatric facility, the Tucker Pavilion, 323-8695, which includes a geriatric unit. The hospital is owned by Columbia/HCA Healthcare Corp.

HENRICO DOCTORS' HOSPITAL
1602 Skipwith Rd.   *289-4500*

This popular 340-bed West End hospital is a comprehensive facility and has been recognized as one of America's Best Heart Hospitals by a book of the same name. Its Women's Pavilion offers obstetrics, infertility treatment, newborn and pediatric intensive care and pediatrics. Its Virginia Transplant Center handles heart, liver and kidney transplants. The hospital's Virginia Laser Center was the first hospital in the state to perform innovative laser surgeries, including laproscopic vagotomy, a laser treatment of stomach ulcers. The mid-1990s saw the addition of an expanded Pediatrics Center (with a pediatrics emergency room), a Joint Replacement Center, a Chest Pain Center and an Orthopedic/Neurological Unit.

HEALTHSOUTH MEDICAL CENTER
7700 Parham Rd.   *747-5600*

HealthSouth, once known to Richmonders as St. Luke's, is a 200-bed hospital in the West End. The medical center offers excellent acute care services in most medical and surgical areas and specializes in oncology, orthopedic and sports medicine. In addition, it also houses both inpatient and outpatient physical rehabilitation facilities and the Virginia Center for Pain Management. The medical center's free Dial-a-Nurse service enables people to call 747-5757 and to speak with a nurse who will answer questions, send information or make a referral to a doctor.

JOHNSTON-WILLIS HOSPITAL
1401 Johnston-Willis Dr.   *330-2000*

Chesterfield County's only hospital, this 330-bed acute-care facility is Richmond's newest and has the latest in laser and diagnostic technology. Its reputation has attracted top specialists, and it has 11 service centers that work together to promote faster and safer recovery. These include the Center for Outpatient Surgery, Physical Rehabilitation Services, the Center for Work Re-Entry, Home Therapies, the Healthy Weigh Weight Loss Program, Physician and Fertility Referral, Pediatrics and the hospital's own Sports and Fitness Center. The hospital also has a 24-hour full-service emergency center as well as cancer, heart, diabetic and women's health centers. A new wing provides private, homelike Family Centered Single Room Maternity Care that allows husband/family overnight stays. The hospital is owned by Columbia/HCA Healthcare Corp.

METROPOLITAN HOSPITAL
701 W. Grace St.   *775-4100*

This hospital has 180 beds, all in private rooms at semiprivate rates. It is the only general medical-surgical hospital in the Richmond area where you will find this kind of a deal. The hospital is located in the VCU area and has a 24-hour emergency room. In addition to medical and surgical services, intensive care and outpatient surgery, Metropolitan Hospital specializes in occupational medicine, the only hyperbaric medicine between Washington, D.C. and Duke University (Durham, North Carolina), and psychiatric and neurological care. In cooperation with VCU's Medical College of Virginia, it operates a sports medicine center nearby.

PSYCHIATRIC INSTITUTE OF RICHMOND
12800 West Creek Pkwy.   *784-2200*

Psychiatric Institute of Richmond (PIR) has a new 84-bed facility in the West Creek section of western Henrico County. The full-service facility offers outpatient, day treatment and brief-stay acute services for adults and adolescents. It also offers 24-hour assessment and referral services to anyone in need. PIR's innovative psychiatric and substance-abuse treatment alternatives are designed to meet the challenges of today's lifestyles.

REHABILITATION HOSPITAL OF VIRGINIA
5700 Fitzhugh Ave.   *288-5700*

A specialized, multi-disciplinary team here provides inpatient care, day treatment and outpatient services and hydrotherapy. It is "Dedicated To Rebuilding Lives, One At A Time."

RETREAT HOSPITAL
2621 Grove Ave.   *254-5100*

In the Fan District and near the Virginia Museum, Retreat traces its roots to the days when it was the first hospital in Richmond. Always known for a high level of personal care, the 230-bed hospital has made substantial investments in recent years in new technology and facilities. It has a 24-hour emergency center and offers a full range of inpatient and outpatient medical and surgical services. The hospital specializes in cardiology with open heart facilities, orthopedics, endoscopy, pulmonary medicine, neurology, oncology and senior services. It serves Hanover County with an outpatient surgical center in Mechanicsville at 6606 Lee Park Road, 730-9000.

RICHMOND COMMUNITY HOSPITAL
1500 N. 28th St.   *225-1700*

This is the only acute care hospital on the city's east side. Besides general medical-surgical patients and an expanding

You found them the right school and the right neighborhood. What about the right hospital?

Welcome to Richmond. We think you'll find it's a great place to live and raise a family. It's also a great place to be when you need state-of-the-art medical care, because Bon Secours Health System offers you the choice of two outstanding medical facilities.

St. Mary's Hospital, 5801 Bremo Road, 285-2011, is a full-service hospital that offers these speciality tailored services for a growing family:

- Pediatric Emergency Center
- Family Life Education programs
- Complete labor-delivery-recovery suites
- St. Mary's physician referral line, 270-DRDR

Bon Secours-Stuart Circle Hospital, located on Monument Avenue at Stuart Circle, 358-7051, is a general medical/surgical service hospital offering customized programs to meet specific needs:

- Call For Health 359-WELL (physician referral/health information)
- Chemical Dependency Unit
- Chest Pain Center (part of our 24 hour emergency services)

Bon Secours Health System, we care for our community.

ST. MARY'S HOSPITAL®
BON SECOURS-STUART CIRCLE HOSPITAL
Bon Secours Health System

outpatient ambulatory service, the 60-bed hospital treats heart conditions and other serious medical or surgical complications. Its psychiatric unit specializes in treatment of adult patients with chronic or acute mental disorders.

RICHMOND EYE AND EAR HOSPITAL
1011 E. Marshall St.   *775-4500*

As Richmond's only specialty care surgical hospital, Richmond Eye and Ear Hospital is the leading provider of microsurgery of the eye, ear, nose and throat as well as of oral, plastic and reconstructive surgery. The hospital's Virginia Center for Cosmetic and Reconstructive Surgery offers free educational consultations. The Specialist Connection, the hospital's physician referral program, can be reached at 775-4527. Free educational pamphlets are available on numerous specialty care topics. Richmond Eye and Ear Hospital has the most complete inventory of state-of-the-art ophthalmology equipment and services in the region.

RICHMOND MEMORIAL HOSPITAL
1300 Westwood Ave.   *254-6000*

Richmond Memorial Hospital, the newest medical discovery, is a full-service, 419-bed acute-care facility offering the latest in technology combined with personalized service.

Its cardiology service line is extensive and provides a "seamless continuum of care" offering a full range of both invasive and non-invasive diagnostic and treatment procedures. The Heart Alliance is a partnership that combines MCV's highly skilled cardiac surgeons with Richmond Memorial Hospital's highly trained and qualified cardiologists and state-of-the-art technology.

The BirthPlace is a sophisticated full service maternity department that combines the creature comforts with the latest technology to monitor mothers and babies, before, during and after birth. A neonatal nursery, equipped with some of the most sophisticated equipment, offers the best of care available.

A full range of other offered services include a 24-hour emergency room, an advanced laser surgery program, and psychiatric care that includes complete medical supervision, as well as ambulatory surgery.

Hanover Medical Park, sister facility to Richmond Memorial Hospital, opened in January of 1993 in Hanover County. Outpatient services include a Diagnostic and Treatment Center (owned and operated by Richmond Memorial Hospital), a physical rehabilitation center (owned and operated by Sheltering Arms Physical Rehabilitation Hospital), Medical College of Virginia's Cancer Treatment Center, a urology center (operated by the Urology Center) and a cardiac rehabilitation program. These centers are anchored by a medical office building and mall that offers physicians offices, The Community Center for Health Education, a pharmacy and a variety of retail medical outlets. In addition, Memorial Regional Medical Center, Hanover's first full-service acute care hospital, is slated to open on the Hanover Medical Park campus in 1997.

ST. MARY'S HOSPITAL
5801 Bremo Rd.   *285-2011*

In the West End, St. Mary's is housed in impressive facilities at Monument Avenue and Bremo Road. It has 391 beds and an active emergency room (including a Children's Emergency Center), and it provides an broad array of services. These include coronary, intensive and medical-surgical care, a comprehensive

THE RETREAT HOSPITAL

EST. 1877

THE RETREAT HOSPITAL

2621 GROVE AVENUE
RICHMOND, VA
23220

(804) 254-5100

RETREAT REGIONAL MEDICAL CENTER

7016 LEE PARK ROAD
MECHANICSVILLE, VA
23111

(804) 730-9000

The Retreat Hospital is proud to be Richmond's First Hospital. Located in the historic Fan District, we have a long tradition of providing quality health care to the Richmond community. We are a general acute-care facility. Our cardiac care program includes angioplasty, cardiac catheterization, stress testing and other diagnostic and therapeutic procedures. Our outpatient surgery center in Mechanicsville offers a broad range of services. Call us for information on our speakers' bureau, seniors' program, and other services.

cancer program, hospice, total joint replacement, psychiatric care, sleep disorders and women's services. Its nursery and maternity New Life Center is a popular place, and the hospital has a neonatal and pediatric intensive care unit. St. Mary's is the home of the Virginia Kidney Stone Center. It offers home health care and ambulatory surgery, and it has introduced a new bedside registration program.

SHELTERING ARMS
PHYSICAL REHABILITATION HOSPITAL
1311 Palmyra St.   *342-4100*

Sheltering Arms, a nonprofit institution, provides the state's most comprehensive physical rehabilitation services. With the area's only therapeutic heated swimming pool, Sheltering Arms offers pool memberships to anyone with a disability. Inpatient and outpatient programs are offered to individuals with brain injury, stroke, spinal cord injury, arthritis, amputation, neuromuscular disorders such as MS, Post-Polio Syndrome and Parkinson's. Specialty outpatient clinics are provided for treatment of sports and orthopedic injuries. Day Rehabilitation and Vocational Industrial Services are offered at Sheltering Arms at Stony Point Medical Park (9200 Forest Hill Avenue, 320-7711), and another satellite location is in Hanover Medical Park (6110 Meadowbridge Road in Mechanicsville, 730-0196).

STUART CIRCLE HOSPITAL
413 Stuart Cir.   *358-7051*

In the Fan District at the intersection of Monument Avenue and Lombardy Street, this 153-bed general medical/surgical hospital offers a full range of advanced services. Special services include chemical dependency, intensive care,

coronary care, cardiac services, women's unit, accredited mammography services, occupational medicine, orthopedics including sports medicine, home health, and surgical services including laparoscopy and laser surgery. Stuart Circle was the first hospital in Virginia to open a chest pain center as part of its 24-hour emergency room.

If you are looking for a doctor or if you have medical questions, you can dial its Call For Health line, 259-WELL, and get answers from registered nurses.

VIRGINIA TREATMENT
CENTER FOR CHILDREN
515 N. 10th St.   *786-3129*

Formerly affiliated with the state mental health department, this public psychiatric hospital for adolescents and children is now part of Medical College of Virginia Hospitals. With a wide range of services, the center provides inpatient hospitalization as well as partial hospitalization programs. It is unusual in that it reaches out to serve Virginia's mental health system with training opportunities, public education, technical assistance and consultation rooted in 30 years of experience with young Virginians and their families. In 1990 it was the only psychiatric hospital in Virginia rated among the top 10 percent nationally and in 1992 won a national award from the American Psychiatric Association.

VIRGINIA HEART INSTITUTE
205 N. Hamilton St.   *359-9265*

The Virginia Heart Institute was established in 1972 as the first outpatient cardiac hospital in the United States to provide ambulatory cardiac catheterization. The early identification of coronary disease led to the development of a cardiac rehabilitation program in 1976 for patients with prior coronary angiography. In order to treat heart disease in its early stages, the Virginia Heart Institute recommends a complete heart screening with its state-of-the-art equipment and techniques for individuals 35 years of age and older. Once a patient is diagnosed with heart disease, the Virginia Heart Institute offers a treatment and monitoring program with the patient resuming a normal, healthier lifestyle. Common treatment includes drug therapy which may eliminate the need for cardiac surgery.

NOVACARE
REHABILITATION HOSPITAL OF VIRGINIA
5700 Fitzhugh Ave. 288-5700

This 40-bed facility offers comprehensive rehabilitation services on an inpatient and outpatient basis. Specialty programs are designed for individuals dealing with situations like the aftermath of brain injury, stroke and joint replacement.

Credit: St. John's Church

St. John's Church, where Patrick Henry delivered his "give me liberty or give me death" speech.

Inside
Worship

Considered by many to be the single most important piece of legislation ever passed, the Virginia Statute for Religious Freedom was the first in the world to protect free expression of individual religious beliefs. Largely the work of Thomas Jefferson and James Madison, it became law on January 16, 1786, in the old Statehouse at the northeast corner of 14th and East Cary streets. Subsequently it was the basis for the first article of the First Amendment to the Constitution, the Bill of Rights.

With this heritage, it should not be surprising then that Greater Richmond is populated today by about 800 places of worship.

While the city's early roots were in the Baptist, Presbyterian and Anglican churches, the area today consists of a wide variety of religious traditions. The city's first Jewish congregation was organized in 1789 and was one of the first in the country. The metropolitan area is now the home of three sitting Christian bishops, five Islamic mosques, a Hindu temple and a Buddhist monastery. And the Richmond area is now seeing the establishment and growth of ethnic Christian congregations including those consisting of Vietnamese Catholics, Spanish Seventh-day Adventists, Chinese Baptists and Korean Presbyterians.

Most Richmonders of African lineage are Baptists. In the rich fabric of African-American Baptist history there probably has been no more colorful figure than the Rev. John Jasper who founded the Sixth Mount Zion Baptist Church on Duval Street. In his famous sermon, "De Sun Do Move," which is still reenacted during Black History Month, he quoted verses from Genesis, Exodus and Revelation to prove the sun rotated around the earth. His theme came from Joshua's battle when he asked the sun to stand still. If someone in the Bible asked the sun to stand still, it had to be moving, right? By the time he died in 1901 at age 89, Mr. Jasper had delivered the message 250 times across the South, including once before the General Assembly of Virginia.

Local places of worship include:

Baptist
(African-American Heritage)

FIFTH BAPTIST CHURCH
1415 W. Cary St.   *355-1044*

Fifth Baptist is a very old church that has been on West Cary Street for many years. It now is housed in a magnificent new building across the street from the location of its previous home.

FIFTH STREET BAPTIST CHURCH
2800 Third Ave.   *321-5115*

With about 900 members, Fifth Street Baptist was a gathering place for early civil rights meetings. Its members include prominent local leaders.

FIRST AFRICAN BAPTIST CHURCH
2700 Hanes Ave.   *329-7279*

This church has roots that led *Harper's Weekly* in 1874 to describe it as "the oldest colored church in America, if not the world." Originally, in the late 1700s, blacks and whites worshipped together in what then was called the First Baptist Church. Later, when white members increased in wealth and numbers, they moved a couple of blocks uptown and built a new First Baptist Church, leaving the old building to the black members. The remaining congregation then adopted the name First African (Baptist) Church. With more than 1,000 members, First African Baptist today draws families from all over town.

FIRST BAPTIST
CHURCH OF SOUTH RICHMOND
1501 Decatur St.   *233-7679*

A major congregation in South Richmond, this church's former pastor reputedly was an important figure in community action.

SECOND BAPTIST CHURCH
1400 Idlewild Ave.   *353-7682*

Organized in 1846, the church's membership today includes a number of important figures in Richmond's African-American establishment. A major annual event is its Easter Pageant.

THIRTY FIRST STREET BAPTIST CHURCH
823 N. 31st St.   *226-0150*

Although this is a relatively newer church (1915), it is progressive and growing. Membership now totals about 1,600 persons.

TRINITY BAPTIST CHURCH
2811 Fendall Ave.   *321-2427*

This is another progressive and growing church, with membership numbering about 4,000. It has ministries that are telecast Sunday evening and again at midnight Sunday on cable television.

Baptist (Southern Baptist Convention)

FIRST BAPTIST CHURCH
2709 Monument Ave.   *355-8637*

With more than 3,700 members, the church occupies an entire block at the corner of Monument Avenue and Boulevard. The congregation traces its lineage back to 1780 when organizers first met in a small house on Church Hill (at that time called Union Hill) and then built the first Baptist Meeting House in the 1790s. Christmas and Easter services are telecast live, and regular 11 AM Sunday services are videotaped, edited for time length and telecast the following week.

GROVE AVENUE BAPTIST CHURCH
8701 Ridge Rd.   *740-8888*

With more than 2,000 members, this is probably the largest fundamentalist Southern Baptist congregation in town. Organized in 1868, the church was relocated to its present site in 1977. The 11 AM Sunday service is telecast live and then rebroadcasted the following Saturday night on cable television.

SECOND BAPTIST CHURCH
Gaskins and River Rds.   *740-7101*

Organized in 1820, the church relocated to its present West End location in 1967. It now occupies an imposing structure that has been added to over the years. Membership numbers more than 1,300 persons.

Episcopal

GRACE & HOLY TRINITY EPISCOPAL CHURCH
8 N. Laurel St.   *359-5628*

Located in the Virginia Commonwealth University area and facing Monroe Park, the church is a combination of Grace Church, organized in 1858, and of the Church of the Holy Trinity, formed in 1874. The present Gothic church building dates to 1924 and has been added to in recent years. Membership totals about 1,000 communicants and members come from all over town.

ST. JAMES'S EPISCOPAL CHURCH
1205 W. Franklin St.   *355-1779*

With more than 1,600 members, St. James's traces its roots to 1835 when it was farther downtown. The present building was erected in 1912, and its spire is a dominating landmark when you are traveling east on Monument Avenue. Membership from all over the city includes congregants who maintain family ties originally established by their parents and grandparents. The church's 11 AM Sunday service is broadcast on radio.

ST. PAUL'S EPISCOPAL CHURCH
700 E. Franklin St.   *643-3589*

Established in 1845, this historic church is on the edge of Capitol Square. Among the famous who have worshipped here are Robert E. Lee, Jefferson Davis and England's King Edward VII when he was the Prince of Wales. As might be expected with a downtown church, the congregation's 1,100 communicants come from all parts of the city.

ST. STEPHEN'S EPISCOPAL CHURCH
6004 Three Chopt Rd.   *288-2867*

With 2,600 communicants, St. Stephen's is the largest Episcopal Church in Richmond. Its origins date back to 1911. It is in the West End and draws its membership primarily from this part of town. The church has close ties to St. Christopher's and to St. Catherine's, two nearby parochial schools.

Greek Orthodox

STS. CONSTANTINE & HELEN GREEK ORTHODOX CATHEDRAL
30 Malvern Ave.   *358-5996*

This is the largest Greek Orthodox cathedral between Atlanta and Washington, D.C. It was designated a cathedral in the early 1970s and coordinates Greek Orthodox churches in Virginia. Membership numbers about 2,500 communicants. The church sponsors an annual Greek Festival, the largest of its kind in the country, which draws 35,000 people over a four-day period.

Jewish

BETH AHABAH CONGREGATION
1111 W. Franklin St.   *358-6757*

Richmond's Beth Shalome congregation, organized in 1789, was the sixth oldest Jewish congregation in the United States. Beth Shalome was absorbed into Beth Ahabah congregation in 1898. Beth Ahabah today is the largest reformed Jewish congregation in Richmond, and its members include many prominent families.

CONGREGATION OR ATID
501 Parham Rd.   *740-4747*

Congregation Or Atid is the youngest conservative Jewish congregation in the city, and it is in a part of town that has seen rapid growth in recent years.

KENESETH BETH ISRAEL
6300 Patterson Ave.   *288-7953*

This is the major orthodox synagogue in Richmond. Another large orthodox congregation is Young Israel of Richmond at 4811 Patterson Avenue.

TEMPLE BETH-EL
3330 Grove Ave.   *355-3564*

Temple Beth-El, with more than 900 families, is the oldest and largest conservative Jewish congregation in Richmond.

Church of Jesus Christ of Latter-day Saints

The Church of Jesus Christ of Latter-day Saints' beginnings in Richmond and the Tri-Cities saw a handful of people meeting in homes and under shade trees in the 1870s. Today membership has grown to nearly 7,000, with 20 individual congregations meeting throughout metropolitan Richmond, the Tri-Cities and surrounding counties. Information on the location of local meeting houses and other church information can be obtained by calling Mrs. Sandi Poulsen at 751-0935.

Lutheran

BETHLEHEM LUTHERAN CHURCH
1100 W. Grace St.   *353-4413*

With a history going back to 1852, Bethlehem Lutheran is affiliated with the Missouri Synod. Membership is drawn from all over the city. The church established Richmond's first Christian day school in 1856, an educational institution today known as Luther Memorial School. The church in 1983 installed a new Taylor & Boody organ de-

signed after those of 17th century North Germany.

FIRST ENGLISH LUTHERAN CHURCH
1603 Monument Ave.   *355-9185*

First English Lutheran traces its roots back to St. Mark's Church, formed in 1869, and to First English Lutheran, formed in 1876. It is affiliated with the Evangelical Lutheran Church in America. Membership comes from all over the city.

Moravian

REDEEMER MORAVIAN CHURCH
10201 Robious Rd.   *323-3864*

Redeemer Moravian, founded in 1987, is one of the city's newest churches, but it is part of the oldest Protestant denomination that traces its origins to 1457. The congregation numbers about 120 people.

Presbyterian

SECOND PRESBYTERIAN CHURCH
5 N. Fifth St.   *649-9148*

With a very committed presence in the center city, Second Presbyterian has about 850 members who live in various parts of Richmond. The history of the church goes back to 1845, and it is the place where Stonewall Jackson once worshipped. The church operates a nationally recognized child-care center on weekdays.

GRACE COVENANT PRESBYTERIAN CHURCH
1627 Monument Ave.   *359-2463*

Grace Street Presbyterian Church, organized by John Blair, the city's first resident Presbyterian minister, and the Church of the Covenant were united in 1915 to form Grace Covenant. The present church building was erected in 1923, and the congregation's 800 members come from The Fan, the Northside and the West End.

FIRST PRESBYTERIAN CHURCH
4602 Cary Street Rd.   *358-2383*

First Presbyterian has a large membership that is based primarily in the West End. It was originally downtown and has a history that goes back to 1812. Known first as "The Presbyterian Church in the City of Richmond," its name was changed to First Presbyterian in 1816.

FIRST UNITED PRESBYTERIAN CHURCH
3401 North Ave.   *321-5374*

This church, with a strong African-American heritage, for many years retained its affiliation with the northern branch of the Presbyterian Church.

WESTMINSTER PRESBYTERIAN CHURCH
4103 Monument Ave.   *355-6885*

In its theological orientation, this congregation, in the words of its brochure, "is moderate and median and conscientiously reformed. Strong identification is made with the traditional beliefs of the Presbyterian heritage."

Roman Catholic

CATHEDRAL OF THE SACRED HEART
823 Cathedral Pl.   *359-5651*

In an imposing setting facing Monroe Park near Virginia Commonwealth University, The Cathedral serves a membership representing about 900 households throughout the city. The Cathedral's magnificent edifice was completed in 1906.

ST. EDWARD'S CHURCH
2700 Dolfield Rd.   *272-2948*

South of the James River, St. Edward's, formed in 1959, serves more than 2,000 households in that part of the city and in Chesterfield County. Also south of the James is the **Church of the Epiphany**, 11000 Smoketree Drive, which was established in 1979 and today serves more than 1,900 households.

ST. BRIDGET'S CHURCH
6006 Three Chopt Rd.   *282-9511*

In the West End, St. Bridget's serves nearly 2,000 households that include many prominent Richmonders. The church was built in 1949.

ST. MARY'S CHURCH
9505 Gayton Rd.   *740-4044*

In the far West End, the parish of St. Mary's, formed in 1962, has grown to where it now serves upward of 2,000 households.

ST. PATRICK'S CHURCH
213 N. 25th St.   *648-0504*

On Church Hill, St. Patrick's is small in membership (139 households) but large in history (1859).

Stroll along Monument Avenue in the annual Easter Parade.

Insiders' Tips

HOLY ROSARY
1209 N. 33rd St.   *222-1105*

Also on Church Hill, Holy Rosary, formed in 1953, serves 240 households predominantly of African-American heritage.

Unitarian

THE FIRST UNITARIAN CHURCH
1000 Blanton Ave.   *355-0777*

Located on the edge of Byrd Park, First Unitarian is the city's only Unitarian congregation.

United Methodist

CENTENARY UNITED METHODIST CHURCH
411 E. Grace St.   *648-8319*

With a history that goes back to 1810, Centenary has become synonymous with downtown Richmond, but its members come from all over the city.

REVEILLE UNITED METHODIST CHURCH
4200 W. Cary St.   *359-6041*

Reveille United Methodist Church has more than 1,200 members and is across West Cary Street from Windsor Farms. The present church, built in 1951, takes its name from Reveille House (c. 1720) which is on the site. A frequent visitor at the house was John James Audubon, the great American naturalist.

TRINITY UNITED METHODIST CHURCH
903 Forest Ave.   *288-6056*

The founders of this church first held meetings in the old Henrico County Courthouse in the late 1700s and then built what was then known as First Church in 1800. The name Trinity was adopted in 1828. The church moved to its present location in 1945, and membership now totals more than 3,000.

Assemblies of God

WEST END ASSEMBLY OF GOD
401 Parham Rd.   *740-7042*

The West End Assembly is a family- and missions-oriented congregation numbering about 1,350 persons. Formed in 1969, it has a Christian music and fine arts program that includes presentation of *The Master's Plan* every Easter at The Carpenter Center, as well as special Christmas and Fourth of July programs.

Buddhist

DHAMMACAKKARAMA BUDDHIST MONASTERY AND TEMPLE
6016A Windsor Dr.
Mechanicsville   *730-3946*

The Venerable Bhante Kim Cang, a Buddhist monk who left Cambodia on foot in the mid-1980s, operates the monastery and temple in his home. He sees to the needs of several hundred Buddhists in the area who either visit him in the temple or receive him and a fellow monk during larger functions in the area.

Hindu

HINDU CENTER OF VIRGINIA
6051 Springfield Rd.   *346-9954*

The 6,000-square-foot center serves about 400 Hindu families in the Richmond area and is the only Hindu temple between Washington, D.C. and North Carolina. The center conducts daily rituals and is the home of Hindu spiritual and cultural events.

A Gateway to Growth

Deer, Skyline Drive, Va. Division of Tourism

Just minutes from the heart of Richmond's business district lies a 236-acre corporate community, beautifully integrated into its natural setting... Atlee Station.

Strategically situated in Hanover County, in the quiet Virginia countryside, Atlee Station offers access to the expanding markets of the Eastern Seaboard and to a wide network of interstate, air, rail and water networks. This affiliated development of Richmond-based Media ▓▓▓▓▓▓▓▓▓▓ ideal for the development of corporate headquarters, research and development firms, operations centers and professional offices.

Nestled in a park like setting, which will include lakes, woodlands and scenic walking trails, Atlee Station offers a location committed to a progressive, diversified corporate development and a flourishing natural environment.

For additional information contact William R. Elliott, Jr. at (804) 649-6623.

ATLEE STATION

'Short Of The Moon, We Can Get You There.

Richmond International Airport

Box A-3, Richmond, Virginia 23231-5999
804-226-3000 • Fax 804-222-6224

Islam

ISLAMIC CENTER OF VIRGINIA
1241 Buford Rd.   320-7333

The center is south of the James River. Its members are mostly Middle Eastern natives.

MASJID BILAL
400 Chimborazo Blvd.   222-9825

Masjid Bilal owns its own mosque and school. Its roots go back to the days when Elijah Muhammad was seen as a modern prophet who would lead the nation's Black Muslims into their own land.

MASJIDULLAH
2211 North Ave.   321-5988

This is the Richmond area's newest Islamic congregation. It is an indication of the growing number of conversions, especially among African-Americans, to Islam.

Other Religious Traditions

Here are telephone contacts for information about other places of worship not covered in the preceding thumbnails.

Anglican Catholic Church	358-5231
African Methodist Episcopal	643-8157
African Methodist Episcopal Zion	644-7586
Apostolic	780-0841
Armenian Apostolic	282-3818
Baha'i Faith	262-8070
Brethren	288-6439
Christian (Disciples of Christ)	359-3509
Christian and Missionary Alliance	270-0440
Christian Methodist Episcopal	232-5680
Christian Science	353-1065
Church of Christ	264-8040
Congregational Christian	276-5338
Eastern Orthodox	266-3364
Faith Landmark Ministries	262-7104
Friends Meeting of Richmond	358-6185
Freewill Baptist	270-9463
Holiness	230-6133
Jehovah's Witnesses	794-8009
Marionite	270-7234
First Mennonite	359-1340
Nazarene	746-0335
Reformed Presbyterian Church in America	272-8111
Seventh-Day Adventist	353-2331
United Church of Christ	358-9291
United Pentecostal	276-1105

Wrought-iron fences, brick sidewalks and cobblestone streets are all part of the
historic flavor of Church Hill.

Inside
Real Estate

A national study of 70 metropolitan areas by Ernst & Young ranks Greater Richmond among the more affordable housing markets in the nation. The median price of a new three-bedroom home in the Richmond region is $135,585, and apartment rents range from $385 to $850 per month depending on size and location. *Kiplinger's Personal Finance* magazine ranks Richmond from the financial standpoint as the most promising place in the nation to buy a home.

All of this means you can live comfortably in Richmond without spending an arm and a leg. And the lifestyle options are wide-ranging. Whether its in-town and urban or suburban or rural, the chances are very good that you'll be able to find a neighborhood and an architectural style that meets your desires and needs. Downtown living is on the upswing, so if you like this way of life you should check out the possibilities.

Annual events such as the HomeSights home show, the Parade of Homes and the Homearama are good ways to get a sampling of what's going on.

To make the search for your home or apartment a little easier, metropolitan Richmond is divided into numbered real estate areas. The numerical designations of these areas are used by the Multiple Listing Service and in most real estate advertising.

The simplest way to understand how this numbering system works is to remember that Area 10 covers the center city, including the downtown business district, The Fan and Church Hill. From here, everything spreads out in quadrants. Zones in the 20s (such as areas 20, 22 and 24) are to the west, zones in the 30s are to the north, zones in the 40s are to the east, and zones in the 50s and 60s are across the James River to the south.

This chapter includes some names, addresses and phone numbers of people who can help you get settled in, whether you want to rent or buy. Space does not permit a complete listing of real estate brokers, builders and firms in other categories, so you may want to talk things over with friends or coworkers before picking up the phone.

Relocation Services

Relocation specialists can do a lot to smooth your move to or around the Richmond area, especially if yours is a two wage-earner or single-parent household where time is at a premium. Local specialists in relocation include:

BOWERS, NELMS & FONVILLE, INC.
Relocation Service Center
4435 Waterfront Dr., Innsbrook   346-4411
The Relocation Division of Bowers,

Nelms & Fonville offers a full range of services tailored to meet the individual needs and interests of people considering a move to the Richmond area. It even provides clients with a toll-free telephone number so that they can conveniently get answers to questions or make requests for information. Information obtained in pre-move consultation is used by a relocation specialist to prepare a personalized welcome kit and to plan an individualized tour of the metropolitan area and its neighborhoods. The tour may include lunch at one of Richmond's restaurants. The relocation team assists with temporary housing and with hotel, restaurant and car rental reservations. The team also searches out an agent with interests similar to the clients for the home-finding process.

NAPIER-OLD COLONY RELOCATION CENTER
Relocation Center
2009 Huguenot Village
Shopping Center   272-7653

With 35 years of experience in real estate, Napier-Old Colony Realtors is well aware of the special needs of newcomers to the Richmond area. Its Relocation Center works diligently to tailor services to each individual family so that moves will be as worry-free as possible. Working with corporate clients of transferees referred through the PHH Homequity Relocation Network, Napier-Old Colony's Relocation Center provides pre-move counseling and hotel reservations in addition to area and neighborhood tours. Information on schools, mortgages, neighborhoods, taxes, cost of living and special interests are provided to all clients. Through the *Places Rated Almanac* computer program, transferees may compare Richmond with their present location. The Relocation Center's goal is to make a new town feel like home.

RICHMOND RELOCATION SERVICES, INC.
412 Libbie Ave.   282-7200

Richmond Relocation Services and its residential real estate division, Virginia Properties, provides destination and residential real estate services to incoming transferees. It provides full-day tours of city and county neighborhoods, career counseling for spouses, schooling information for children, tax planning, community networking and legal assistance. As an independent resource, it works to address individual needs in a way that enhances employer-employee relationships. Through Virginia Properties it helps transferees purchase a home, find a rental home or arrange a temporary living situation.

VIRGINIA LANDMARK RELOCATION SERVICES
1807 Libbie Ave.   285-3935

Richmond has been Virginia Landmark's home town for more than 30 years, and its relocation services staff works with both individuals and corporations. It offers a highly individualized approach as it works to help newcomers get plugged in to the community based on their special interests. Virginia Landmark begins with advance personal contact to discuss plans for the initial visit. Individualized information packages are prepared and a specialized orientation tour is arranged that can encompasses everything from the arts to community organizations. It helps with the housing search, appointments with mortgage lenders and with recommendations on professionals whose services may be needed in connection with the move.

Lunch is delivered on moving day, and Virginia Landmark hosts informal gatherings for newcomers to enhance their knowledge of the city after the move. It does not charge for its relocation services.

VIRGINIA RELOCATION
6726 Patterson Ave.   282-4031

Virginia Relocation provides complete residential relocation services to the individual and corporate transferee, be it in connection with a permanent home, rental property or temporary housing. Its standard relocation services include spousal career assistance, public and private school information, home buying counsel, personalized tours of the Richmond area, car rental and moving company discounts and buyer representation, all free of charge. Virginia Relocation's affiliate Realtors are experienced and accommodating, and the service is a member of the Employer Relocation Council and the Virginia Economic Developers Association. Its toll-free number is (800) 633-6643.

Temporary Housing

Some temporary housing options are described in the Corporate Apartments section of the Accommodations chapter of this guide and also under the Apartment Property Managers section below. But here are some people who can take care of all of the details for you.

QUALITY GUEST SUITES
2251 Dabney Rd.   359-8534

Quality Guest Suites, a division of Wynne Guild, is a specialist in corporate relocation and temporary housing. Its accommodations provide furniture and accessories (such as television, pots and pans, towels and sheets) and it will take care of services such as utilities, telephone, cable television, and even maid service if you want it. Cost is less than that of an average hotel room. Time limitations may apply to certain apartments. The firm's toll-free phone number is (800) 338-8534.

KING PROPERTIES, INC.
4825 Radford Ave.   788-4588

King Properties has three locations with one-, two- and three-bedroom furnished suites with phone, cable television, pool, tennis and more. Minimum stay is seven days. King Properties can be reached nationwide by calling (800) 457-1007.

SUMMIT PROPERTIES
3012 Stony Lake Dr.   272-6155

Fully furnished apartments complete with housewares, utilities, cable, maid service, social activites, pools and fitness centers are offered at four locations by Summit. Its toll-free number is (800) 784-8348.

Renting a Home or an Apartment

A wide variety of home and apartment rental options is available in the Richmond area, and you should have no problem finding a place that suits your lifestyle. As you look around, be sure to get answers to these questions:

1. Does the rental rate include utilities, especially those needed for heat and electricity? Some landlords include utilities such as gas for cooking and heating as part of the rent package; others do not. It can make a big difference.

2. How large a deposit is required? Usually this is a month's rent, but it can be as low as $200.

3. Are there any fees or charges for various expenses that are not refundable?

4. If you have a pet, will the landlord permit the kind of pet you have and, if so, is any extra fee or deposit required?

5. If you should need to move out early because of a job offer in another city or as a result of a change in marital status, can you sublease or transfer the lease to another tenant?

The landlord determines how long the lease will run. Usually it is for one year, but some offer six-month and even month-to-month leases. Most leases require you to notify the landlord 30 to 90 days in advance if you want to terminate; otherwise, most leases automatically renew for another term. Read your lease carefully before you sign it. This is the time to resolve questions and, if mutually agreeable, to modify or add clauses to the lease. Remember that the lease is a legal document, so treat it accordingly. A properly executed lease is for your protection as well as the landlord's.

With these guideline in mind, here are some places to begin your search:

AROUND THE JAMES
2611 Parham Rd.   *346-4911*

This is a free apartment-finding service representing more than 40 apartment communities in the metropolitan area. Fees are paid by apartment owners. If you tell them what you are looking for, they will help you find it. They also will help you locate furnished corporate apartments, even on short notice. The firm's toll-free number is (800) 899-1285.

APARTMENT FINDER
9738 Gayton Rd.   *272-7368*

This locator service publishes a free pocketbook-size guide full of colorful ads, checklists, maps and helpful information. The guide contains a mail-in card that can be used to obtain more information

on specific apartment communities or services. The guide is published quarterly and is available at locations throughout the metropolitan area and by mail. Apartment Finder maintains a Resource Center at its Gayton Road address, (800) 999-4720, which offers up-to-the-minute information on prices and availability and features short- and long-term leases.

APARTMENT GUIDE
8002 Discovery Dr., Ste. 311   *288-9238*

This is a handy pocket-size guide that can be picked up free of charge at 7-Eleven stores and a wide variety of other locations. It is divided by geographical parts of the city. One nice thing about this guide is that it provides rental rates in most cases.

APARTMENT INFORMATION CENTER
5703 Pony Farm Dr.   *329-6666*

GSC's Apartment Information Center can be reached at the above telephone number or toll-free within Virginia at (800) 542-3276 or toll-free nationwide at (800) 368-7669.

Newspaper Classified Ads

The classified advertising columns of area newspapers are good places to find that one-of-a-kind rental. Apartment and home rental ads appear daily in the *Richmond Times-Dispatch*, and the newspaper carries apartment ads in great abundance on Sunday. *Style Weekly*, available free in many locations, is often the best place to look for the really nifty locations. It's published every Tuesday, and copies go fast. If you're looking for a rental in Ashland or in one of the counties, you also should keep an eye on weekly newspapers serving these areas.

Some of the best rentals are never advertised. These are the apartments and homes that have so much appeal that they are literally passed from friend to friend. The best way to find places like this is through networking with business associates and friends.

Apartment Property Managers

Some of the larger apartment communities in the metropolitan area are managed by these firms:

AVALON PROPERTIES

4405 Cox Rd.   270-9884

Apartment communities managed by Avalon are new and upscale and include Champions Club and Hampton Glen in the Innsbrook area and Chase Gayton on Gayton Road near Quioccassin Road.

COLONY MANAGEMENT CORPORATION

8814 Fargo Rd.   282-2900

Colony offers townhouse-style apartments in the Far West End, on the Northside and south of the James. Many offer tennis courts, clubhouses, swimming pools and fitness facilities. Apartment sizes range from efficiencies to three bedrooms. Corporate and short-term leases are available.

EWN PROPERTIES, INC.

530 Southlake Blvd.   794-3967

Apartments and apartment homes managed by EWN Properties are new and state-of-the-art with a wide variety of amenities. They come in sizes ranging from one to three bedrooms and are designed for upscale living. Locations are on the Northside near Virginia Center Commons, in the West End and in Chesterfield. EWN's properties include communities such as The Meadows (West End), Cross Creek (Chesterfield) and The Timbers (Bon Air). The firm's toll-free number is (800) 926-5563.

F&W MANAGEMENT CORP.

1812 E. Blackburn Rd.   266-6597

Laurel Pines, managed by F&W and located near the airport, offers new one-, two- and three-bedroom apartments, a health club, pool and tennis courts.

FOGELMAN MANAGEMENT

2344 Hickory Creek Dr.   346-4580
4200 Harwin Pl.
Glen Allen   747-0729

Fogelman manages the Hickory Creek apartments near I-64 and Parham and the Champions Club apartments in the Glen Allen area. Both are new and upscale and offer things like fireplaces, gourmet kitchens, swimming pools and fitness facilities. One-bedroom/one-bath and two-bedroom/two-bath floor plans are available.

GENERAL SERVICES CORP. (GSC)

5703 Pony Farm Dr.   329-6666

GSC, "The Apartment People," manages 15 apartment communities that offer a wide choice of locations in the West End, Chesterfield County and on the Northside. Most have swimming pools and athletic and fitness facilities. One has a nine-hole putting green and six lighted tennis courts. Many have social programs. Gas utilities are included for heat, hot water and cooking. GSC publishes a Richmond-area Apartment Locator which can be picked up free of charge at many locations. The Apartment Locator contains descriptions and a map of GSC apartment locations.

INSIGNIA MANAGEMENT GROUP

9711 Marble Hill   741-2303

Insignia's properties include Marble Hill in the West End and Sunrise in Chesterfield County. Both have pools and recreational facilities and are available in one-, two- and three-bedroom floor plans.

KING PROPERTIES, INC.

4825 Radford Ave.   353-1122

Representing eight apartment communities, King Properties offers more than 50 floor plans ranging from one-bedroom and one-bedroom/loft arrangements to three-bedroom layouts. Apartment locations are in the West End and south of the James. Short-term corporate and guest apartment leases are available at three locations.

LAWSON REALTY

3900 Arcadia Ln.   346-8724

Lawson's Braeton Bay complex of new one- and two-bedroom apartments is off Three Chopt Road in the West End and offers a fitness center and other recreational amenities. Apartments with fireplaces are available.

McCORMACK BARON MANAGEMENT SERVICES, INC.

2 S. 25th St.   649-1850

These are the people who handle the leasing of Tobacco Row. In the Shockoe Bottom area and just to the east of the city's financial district, Tobacco Row covers 15 blocks of old tobacco factories along the James River and is the largest historic renovation project in the nation. Apartments include many amenities. Some have fireplaces, and there is a swimming pool.

MORTON G. THALHIMER, INC.

1313 E. Main St.   648-5881

One of Richmond's major real estate sales and management firms, Morton G. Thalhimer offers apartments ranging from The Berkshire, a downtown luxury highrise, to those in the West End.

MANAGEMENT SERVICES CORP.

2337 Harbor Village Ct.   747-6968

Harbor Village, managed by MSC, offers two-bedroom/two-bath apartments and is located in the far West End. But its big draw includes its lush landscaping, lighted tennis courts, sand volleyball court and other amenities.

MARK MERHIGE REAL ESTATE, BROKERAGE & DEVELOPMENT, INC.

114 Virginia St. 780-3140

Mark Merhige has specialized in the development and rehabilitation of historic properties since 1986 including two Shockoe Slip/Shockoe Bottom apartment properties: Shockoe Hearth at 1417 E. Cary Street and the Wm. Hill Building at 114 Virginia Street.

SENTINEL

9507 Spendthrift Cir. 527-1496

Sentinel's two West End apartment communities are new and offer one- and two-bedroom units. There are two-tier swimming pools at both locations as well as a wide range of athletic and fitness amenities. Some units have vaulted ceilings, fireplaces and/or balconies.

SOUTHERN MANAGEMENT GROUP

7633 Hull Street Rd. 746-8866

Mill Trace Village in the Mechanicsville area is managed by Southern Management Group. The apartment community offers a lakeside pool, waterfront tennis and other amenities needed for active lifestyles.

SUMMIT PROPERTIES

3012 Stony Lake Dr. 272-6155

Summit offers a number of apartment communities, one in the West End and the others in Bon Air and Midlothian. They have active social programs and offer a range of athletic and fitness amenities. Its Old Buckingham Station community in Chesterfield is situated on 50 acres and has one-bedroom/one-bath and two-bedroom/two-bath units as well as penthouses.

UNITED DOMINION REALTY TRUST

10 S. Sixth St. 780-2691

United Dominion manages a variety of affordably priced apartments and apartment townhouses in the West End and on the Northside and Southside. Amenities vary from location to location but include swimming pools, play areas for children and fully furnished guest apartments for friends and family.

WILTON COMPANIES

9101 Patterson Ave. 740-7192

Homestyle living at affordable prices is offered by the Wilton Companies in its 17 different apartment communities in the West End Apartments. Apartment townhouses range in size from one bedroom to three bedrooms. Amenities includes swimming pools and play areas for children.

Buying a Home in Richmond

There are about eight basic steps to buying a house in Richmond. If all goes well, this is how it works:

1. With the help of an agent, the buyer signs a sales contract that is submitted to the seller with a good faith deposit. The deposit is usually held by the selling broker until closing, when it is credited to the sales price of the house. In Richmond, the usual contingencies in a contract include inspections of the property, the ability to secure financing and the sale of the buyer's present home. In 1993 it became law that the seller must provide the buyer at the time of contract signing either a disclosure statement regarding the seller's knowledge of existing problems with the property, or a disclaimer statement signed by both parties that the property is being sold "as is."

2. The sales contract is accepted and signed by the buyer. From this point on, the average closing time is 60 to 90 days.

3. The buyer submits a mortgage application that includes a detailed financial statement. The lender orders an appraisal of the property, a credit report and verifications of employment and of the source of funds for the down payment. The lender asks for a check at this time to cover costs of the credit report and the appraisal.

4. The lender receives the credit report and appraisal; the mortgage application is approved; a loan commitment is issued to the purchaser; and the closing package usually is sent to the buyer's attorney who will handle the closing.

5. The buyer's attorney orders a title examination and survey, title insurance and usually the homeowners insurance policy.

6. About a week before closing, the buyer and seller notify utility companies of change of ownership.

7. Closing is usually held at the office of the buyer's attorney. The closing represents the transfer of title. The buyer checks with the attorney's office several days before closing to find out the amount of the cashiers check needed at closing to cover the balance of the down payment, closing costs and escrow items.

8. Immediately after closing, the attorney records the transaction at the appropriate courthouse, and the buyer receives the keys. The buyer takes possession.

Publications you may find helpful in your search for a new home include:

METRO REAL ESTATE

333 E. Grace St.   *649-6478*

Published by Richmond Newspapers, Inc., this magazine-format publication is issued twice monthly and is available free of charge at locations throughout the metro area. It contains photographs of homes for sale and stories about residential communities and real estate professionals.

HARMON HOMES

(Richmond Edition)   *(800) 955-5516*

This publication, available free at many locations, contains residential listing offered by real estate firms on the area.

Realtors

There are about 4,000 licensed real estate agents in the Richmond Multiple Listing Service directory. A number have earned the status of Realtor through extensive professional training and adherence to a strict code of ethics. These professionals can be identified by the gold "R" lapel pin and by the symbol when it is used on business cards and stationery.

One of the most far-reaching changes in services provided by Richmond real estate firms in recent years has been the introduction of the "buyer's agent." Traditionally, a real estate agent has fiduciary responsibility to the seller. Now more and more firms have agents who can be engaged to look out for the interests of the buyer and to negotiate on the

Insiders' Tips

Richmonders enjoy saving and restoring historic buildings.

buyer's behalf. If this kind of service is of value to you, be sure to ask about it.

The real estate firms selected for this guide are recognized as some of the best. There are others in town who are excellent, but space does not permit a complete listing. The Yellow Pages are a good reference for all of the firms in town, and a complete listing is available from the Richmond Association of Realtors at 5002 Monument Avenue, 358-5358.

BOWERS, NELMS & FONVILLE, INC.

9510 Ironbidge Rd., Chesterfield	748-4440
5702 Grove Ave. (West End)	288-8888
4660 S. Laburnum Ave. (East End)	236-0300
7331 Old Cavalry Dr., Mechanicsville	746-1850
13626 Hull St. Rd., Harbour Pointe	744-1073
4435 Waterfront Dr., Innsbrook	346-4411
8411 Patterson Ave. (West End)	740-7206
3307 Church Rd. (West End)	270 9083
11600 Busy St., Midlothian	794-9650

This is the largest residential real estate firm in town. With more than 400 associates and 12 strategically located offices, it covers the whole metropolitan area and offers a complete range of services. It is a member of RealAssist, the Mortgage Network, Genesis and Realty Network, Inc. If you want a new home you can customize to your own tastes, its offices on Waterfront Drive have specialists in this kind of property. It also has an office in Kilmarnock that specializes in river property in the Northern Neck area.

CENTURY 21
OLD RICHMOND REALTY LTD.

910 Parham Rd.	741-4090
6512 Mechanicsville Pike	746-4868
9820 Midlothian Tnpk.	320-7337

This firm is one of the largest Century 21 franchises in the area and is hooked into Century 21's nationwide referral network. It is involved in in-town and suburban residential sales throughout the metropolitan area, from starter homes to more expensive property. It also handles sales of new modular homes that are available in many attractive styles and that can cut construction time in half.

CENTURY 21 SIGNATURE REALTY

2800 Buford Rd.   330-4222

This firm, in the heart of Bon Air, provides full-service residential real estate services. Its sales associates are experienced in residential resale, new construction, financing and relocation.

COLDWELL BANKER
HALL & BUCKINGHAM

2820 Waterford Lake Dr.   744-1494

This firm specializes in residential property south of the James River, although its listings include attractive city and country property throughout the metropolitan area. It also offers high-quality new homes beginning in the $80s and running up to those of more than 4,000 square feet. In addition to residential sales and new home construction, the firm offers commercial services.

COLDWELL BANKER
VAUGHAN AND COMPANY, INC.

9701 Gayton Rd.   740-6683

Vaughan and Company specializes in the West End, although you will find property in Chesterfield, Powhatan and Hanover counties and on Richmond's Northside among its listings. It also works with builders of new homes and a large part of its business is in this kind of property.

THE COVINGTON COMPANY

5809 York Rd.   288-8317

The Covington Company has residential specialists ready to provide service for people relocating within the Richmond area as well as those coming to Richmond from other places. Experience, sensitivity to personal needs, and knowledge of the local residential market give Covington the ability to serve needs of both buyers and sellers.

EAST WEST REALTY

14700 Village Square Pl.
Midlothian   *739-3800*

A full-service firm, East West Realty specializes in residential real estate in Chesterfield County. East West Realty is an affiliate of East West Partners of Virginia. The developer of the nationally recognized lakefront communities of Woodlake and Brandermill, East West Realty represents homes and homesites in the award-winning planned communities of Foxcroft, Woodlake and Brandermill. Homes in these communities range in price form the $90s to $500,000, offering a great selection of new and resale homes in styles that range from traditional to contemporary.

ERA
WOODY HOGG & ASSOCIATES

7284 Hanover Green Rd.   *222-4644*
1360 Parham Rd.   *262-7371*

This is another large ERA firm. With two offices north of the James River, one in Mechanicsville and the other in the West End, it is a full-service residential real estate firm.

HIGHLANDS REALTY

8400 Highland Glen Dr.   *748-7361*

Highlands Realty is the place to call for information about The Highlands, a planned, 1,000-family community near Chesterfield Courthouse with large lots, a lake and a golf course. Homes range from $150,000 to $400,000.

METROPOLITAN REAL ESTATE, INC.

12089 Gayton Rd.   *741-4108*

In the West End of Richmond, Metropolitan Real Estate, Inc. specializes in new home real estate. Metropolitan represents the communities of FoxHall and Riverlake Colony with properties from $220,000.

THE PRUDENTIAL
JAMES RIVER, INC.

8900 Three Chopt Rd.   *288-8351*
1700 Huguenot Rd.   *378-0100*

This is a large firm that is involved in residential and commercial sales and also offers property management and relocation services. It has offices in the West End and in Chesterfield County and, in addition to sales of existing property, represents builders of new homes.

NAPIER-OLD COLONY REALTORS

2009 Huguenot Village
Shopping Center   *272-7653*
11000-G Three Chopt Rd.   *747-7653*
1574 East Parham Rd.   *262-7653*
13356 Midlothian Tpk.   *794-4531*

One of the area's largest real estate firms, Napier-Old Colony has served the needs of the Richmond community for about 40 years. Its original offices were in Northern Chesterfield County. There are now offices conveniently north and south of the James River to better serve the entire metropolitan area.

Napier-Old Colony offers homes in a wide variety of styles and price ranges. In addition to traditional brokerage services, Napier has buyer brokerage services available. Specializing in relocation services, Napier works with many local corporations and is the exclusive representative of PHH Homequity, the nation's oldest and largest relocation company. Additional services include in-house mortgage origination through PHH US Mortgage and custom home design and construction through Napier Signature Homes.

NEVILLE C. JOHNSON, INC.

4905 Radford Ave.   355-7981

Neville C. Johnson in the late 1950s pioneered the designation "The Fan" for the neighborhood stretching from Harrison Street to the Boulevard. Before that, property in the area was advertised simply as townhouses. The firm, with offices in the West End, today specializes in residential properties ranging in value from $150,000 to $1 million and in property management. It has expanded beyond its original Fan District base and now also is active in the Near West End, the Far West End and south of the James. It also handles some country property. It has a referral setup.

RE/MAX COMMONWEALTH

7201 Glen Forest Dr.   288-5000
3436 Lauderdale Dr.   360-5200

This RE/MAX firm was formerly known to Richmonders as Brooks & Innes. Located in the West End, RE/MAX specializes in residential property, farms and property management.

RE/MAX EXECUTIVES

1520 Huguenot Rd.   794-2150

This firm specializes in residential properties south of the James River. It offers a complete range of real estate services.

THE PRUDENTIAL
SAVAGE & COMPANY

9321 Midlothian Tnpk.   560-ROCK

The Prudential Savage & Company has been a major factor in the residential real estate market south of the James River for many years.

SIMMONS-BAKER REALTY

605 Research Rd.   794-9488

Simmons-Baker represents more than a dozen subdivisions in Chesterfield, the West End and Hanover County. Homes in these communities are of colonial design and are known for their excellent construction and competitive pricing within the $80,000 to $120,000 range. The firm offers a total range of real estate services including property sales, property development and property management. It is the exclusive listing agent for Emerald Homes.

SLATER REALTORS

2737 McRae Rd.   320-1391
5905 W. Broad St.   288-1978
Woodlake Office   739-5253

Slater serves all parts of the metropolitan area, has phone lines that are open 24 hours a day and offers relocation assistance. It represents a number of builders in Chesterfield and its Brandermill Realty, 744-1000, represents new and resale homes in Brandermill, named the best planned community in America by *House & Garden* magazine.

C. PORTER VAUGHAN, INC.

7801 Pleasant Pond Ln.   271-5500
9201 Forest Hill Ave.   320-9661

This sizable firm has offices on both sides of the river and is a member of the All Points Relocation Service. Its total range of real estate services includes residential property, property development and property management. It is the developer of the prestigious Salisbury subdivision.

PROCTOR REALTY COMPANY

6726 Patterson Ave.   282-3136

Founded in 1949, Proctor Realty has an excellent reputation. With 18 sales associates, the firm has been recognized as one of Richmond's most productive real estate companies on a per-agent basis. Its seasoned personnel are knowledgeable about the whole Richmond area. In addition to residential, farm and land sales, Proctor Realty has a commercial division and an affiliate relocation company, Virginia Relocation. Proctor Realty is a member of MLS, ICS Property Information Service, the Certified Residential Specialist Group and of national, state and local boards of Realtors.

VIRGINIA LANDMARK CORPORATION
1807 Libbie Ave.   285-3935

Virginia Landmark has been an important player in the Richmond real estate market since the early 1960s. Its residential arm handles sales throughout the city, and the firm has been involved in the development of single family subdivisions as well as condominium construction and conversion. It assists corporations in selling houses of employees transferred out of the Richmond area.

VIRGINIA PROPERTIES
412 Libbie Ave.   282-7300

The exclusive Richmond-area affiliate of Southebys International Realty, Virginia Properties is a division of Richmond Relocation Services. It also is a charter member of the National Trust Historic Real Estate Program. It handles properties through the metropolitan area.

YOUNGBLOOD, INC. REALTORS
2520 Professional Rd.   272-4663

With offices south of the James River, this firm specializes in residential sales. It has a referral service.

Builders

It was a challenge to come up with the following list of Richmond homebuilders. We basically used top-ranking firms in terms of sales volume, but we also have included builders se-

lected for other reasons. Some of the builders listed here work primarily on their own projects. Others will follow you wherever you want to go.

AUSTIN-DAVIDSON, INC.
3919 Deep Rock Rd.   346-9444

Custom homes in the $200,000 to $400,000 range are the specialty of Austin-Davidson, which builds primarily in Wyndham, Wellesley and Church Run. It has also built homes in Goochland and in other parts of the metro area. The firm's solid reputation is founded on a track record of more than 15 years. It builds to its own plans or from the plans of a client. Austin-Davidson homes have been featured in the Parade of Homes and Homearama.

BYRD CONSTRUCTION CO., INC.
400-K Southlake Blvd.   378-0531

Established in 1988, Byrd Construction Co. currently builds new homes throughout the metropolitan Richmond area. In 1989 Byrd closed on one house — in 1994 Byrd closed on 64 houses at an average sale price of $170,000. These houses were built in Hanover, Chesterfield, Powhatan, Henrico and New Kent counties. Byrd's five furnished model homes range in price from $89,950 to $213,000 and feature products such as gas fireplaces, skylights, Florida rooms, and luxury cabinets and baths. Byrd currently builds in Kings Charter, Arbor Landing, North Oaks, Pine Creek Bluffs, Shadow Creek, Amstel Bluffs, Huguenot Farms and other subdivisions.

COLONIAL HOMECRAFTERS, LTD.
3717 Sovereign Ln.   360-4188

Colonial Homecrafters each year builds 20 to 25 transitional and colonial-design homes in the $250,000 to $500,000 range. The family-run business places great emphasis on quality and customer satisfaction. Most of Colonial Homecrafters' custom homes are in western Henrico County along the Pemberton, Gayton and River Road corridors. In addition, the company today is building from its plans or from customer plans in Riverlake Colony, FoxHall, Royal Oaks and The Colonies.

EAGLE CONSTRUCTION
OF VIRGINIA, INC.
9701 Gayton Rd.   *741-4663*

Eagle Construction ranks as one of the biggest builders in the Richmond area in terms of volume. It builds in western Henrico subdivisions such as Wyndham, Wellesley, Gayton Ridge, Barclay and Eagle's Ridge. Its houses range in price from $80,000 to $300,000.

MIKE DUMONT
CONSTRUCTION COMPANY, INC.
11508 Allecingie Pkwy.   *379-9141*

Mike Dumont has been well known for 20 years for exceptional transitional, contemporary and traditional custom homes ranging in price from $130,000 to $1 million in Richmond's most sought-after neighborhoods. His firm has received Best In Show, Best Landscaping and Best Interior and Exterior Design awards from the Richmond Home Builders Association. All of his homes carry a 10-year home owner's warranty.

EMERALD HOMES
P.O. Box 13711, 23225   *674-5551*

Established in 1984, Emerald builds traditional starter homes, typically in the 1,300- to 2,000-square-foot size. It ranks among the top 10 builders in the Richmond area in terms of sales volume. The firm is now building in 10 subdivisions in Chesterfield, Hanover and Henrico counties and is represented by Simmons Baker Realty at 794-9488.

LIFESTYLE BUILDERS & DEVELOPERS
9512 Iron Bridge Rd.   *768-0702*

Lifestyle is a builder of semi-custom new homes, mainly in Chesterfield County, but also in subdivisions in Hanover and Powhatan counties. The style is transitional, with plenty of windows. Normally extra amenities are included as standard features. Prices range from $90,000 to $300,000. Lifestyle made a clean sweep of all of the Best Furnished Model awards in the 1993 Richmond Home Builders competition and won eight top awards in the 1993 Parade of Homes — more than any other builder in Parade of Homes history. Fully decorated models are open daily from 1 PM to 5 PM in most subdivisions in which Lifestyle builds. Lifestyle currently is building in Foxcroft, Amstel Bluff, Walthall Creek, Providence Creek, Windsor, Sherwood, Michaux Creek, Birkdale, Stonebridge, Jordon on the James and in Stoney Glen West.

THE MCGURN COMPANY
4062 Crockett St.   *264-1977*

McGurn Construction has built more than 700 single-family homes in the Richmond area since 1981. It handles everything from 1,400- to 1,600-square-foot starter homes to 5,500-square-foot Georgian design/build projects. It currently builds in Chesterfield, Hanover and Henrico counties.

NAPIER SIGNATURE HOMES
2009 Huguenot Rd.   *323-1900*

Napier Signature Homes designs and builds homes in the price range from the $180s and up. It gives great attention to detail, quality materials, craftsmanship and personal supervision. Napier Signature Homes are designed to meet a variety of individual lifestyles and tastes and include innovative concepts and up-to-date features.

REGENCY HOMES

1209 E. Cary St.   *643-0296*

Award-winning Regency Homes brings 20 years of experience to each home it builds. Using state-of-the-art technology, Regency has built throughout Maryland and, most recently, in Northern Virginia and Richmond. Regency Homes' "Home to Home Commitment" is designed to meet homebuyers' specific needs. Regency's dedication to quality, valua and service has made this builder one of the most reputable and stable in the region.

RYAN HOMES

9030 Stony Point Pkwy.   *272-7835*

Ryan is among the top 10 homebuilders in the Richmond area in terms of sales volume. A part of the Richmond residential scene since 1970, it builds 1,500- to 2,800-square-foot, single-family homes in the $76,000 to $180,000 range. Ryan has won numerous Richmond Home Builders Association awards. Ryan developments range from transitional townhomes to single-family houses, and the company builds in Craig's Mills, Doubletree, Huntwood, Wedgewood Manor, Olde Colony Estates, Kennedy Station, Arbor Meadows, Oakway Manor, North Run Ridge, Laurel Lakes and Gayton Glen, all in Henrico County.

STERN HOMES

Innsbrook Corporate Center   *747-8040*

Sidney Stern and Dave Dickerson founded Stern Homes on the ideals of customer service and satisfaction. Now, with the help of architects from Boca Raton, Atlanta and Washington, D.C., Stern Homes has broadened its scope to include superior design. Stern melds traditional and contemporary design elements including "celebrated entries," naturally lit interiors with two-story spaces and vaulted ceilings, and colonial details such as chair rails, crown molding, raised panel kitchen cabinets and period stairways. Stern Homes builds in several West End communities including Foxhall and Wyndham. Prices start at $190,000 ($270,000 in Foxhall and Wyndham).

SUNSHINE BUILDERS, INC.

P.O. Box 161
Mechanicsville 23111   *730-9746*

Sunshine Builders has developed a reputation of trust and integrity over the years. Phil DuHamel, its president, believes in quality workmanship and has been involved in the construction of new homes totaling more than $50 million, primarily in Hanover County. From design through construction, Sunshine Builders emphasizes energy-saving technologies. It will build on any site, and its commitment to customer satisfaction is backed by a 10-year homeowners warranty.

TEAL BUILDING CORPORATION

8602 Staples Mill Rd.   *266-2600*

Teal is involved in 16 different subdivisions and is currently focusing on homes in the $80,000 to $200,000 price range. Since 1970 it has built more than 3,000 homes. Teal relies on real estate professionals to sell more than 80 percent of its homes. This relationship with the real estate community, plus value provided the home buyer, has been responsible for a great deal of the company's success. It is one of the Richmond area's top-ranking builders in terms of sales volume.

TOMAC CORP.

13301-C Midlothian Tnpk.   *794-4534*

Tomac Corp. was formed in 1974 and has gained a reputation over the years as a builder of well-constructed, low-utility-cost homes. The firm has ranked No. 1 or No. 2 in new-home sales volume in the Richmond area since 1984. It offers traditional and transitional style homes with excellent energy-saving features and maximum usable living space. Tomac builds in Chesterfield, Hanover and Henrico counties in the $100,000 to $250,000 price range.

J. R. WALKER & CO., INC.

3022 Bretton Ln., Glen Allen   *672-0857*

J. R. Walker and Co. is committed to customer involvment within each facet the construction process; each home is approached as a team effort between customer and builder. The prospective homeowner may choose from a variety of home options, including colonial, transitional and contemporary designs of lasting quality and value. J. R. Walker and Co.'s attention to detail and finish is evident in each design. This company builds homes in a range of prices and in a variety of locations in the Richmond metropolitan area.

WILL & COSBY & ASSOCIATES, INC.

2611 N. Parham Rd.   *346-9922*

Will & Cosby builds custom homes to suit clients rather than making them work with particular models and stock plans. The firm is very flexible in how the contract is structured and encourages owners to do some of the work themselves

(i.e. sweat equity). It will work with plans drawn up by the owner's architect or with plans drawn up by the firm's in-house designer and draftsman. Its offices at Parham Road and I-64 feature product displays, and it has model homes available to help clients visualize ideas and design concepts. Will & Cosby is a fourth-generation Richmond firm.

OTHER BUILDERS

Other builders who have been recommended by our friends include:

Bishop Custom Homes
2607 Annakay Crossings
Midlothian   *379-4985*

R. A. Lowry
4011 Traylor Dr.   *272-8387*

Parker Lancaster Corp.
711 Moorefield Park Dr.   *231-3100*

R. M. Pierce, Inc.
9001 Three Chopt Rd.   *285-1141*

Millwork

If you need custom millwork, here are the names of three excellent sources, one in the city, one in Chesterfield and the third in eastern Henrico County. In addition to supplying finished material delivered to the job site, they have the lumber and advice needed by do-it-yourselfers.

Siewers Lumber & Millwork
1901 Ellen Rd. (near The Diamond)   *358-2103*

James River Building Supply
100 Lumber Dr.
Sandston   *788-0756*

Woodworkers Supply
430 Southlake Blvd.   *794-0883*

Landscape Services

Visiting the Maymont Flower and Garden Show in February at the Richmond Centre will fill your mind with all kinds of landscaping ideas. Whether its a new shrub here, a little replanting there or a complete redo, here are some people who can help:

BROOKMEADE SOD FARM, INC.
Rt. 1, Box 547
Doswell 23047   883-6338

These people have been growing quality sod for the best lawns in Virginia since 1968.

COMMONWEALTH NURSERY & MULCH CENTER
Rt. 617 and U.S. 250
Oilville   784-4805

Commonwealth offers complete landscape design and installation services. Speak with Margaret Hartz.

DOVER NURSERIES, INC.
111 Deer Keep   784-4456

Dover Nurseries has provided Richmond with personal landscaping services for more than 20 years. It works with clients on a one-on-one basis to develop a plan that is tailored to the home and yard and to individual needs and tastes.

HUDGINS LANDSCAPING
16831 Hull Street Rd.   739-5100

Hudgins offers full-service landscaping and specializes in new home plans and upgrading of existing landscaping. Family-owned and operated, its Farm and Garden Center in Chesterfield County offers five greenhouses and three acres of shrubs, trees, annuals, perennials and topiaries.

ILLUMINATIONS
5218 Eastbranch Dr.
Glen Allen   360-4060

As the name suggests, this firm specializes in the design and installation of landscape lighting. The man to speak with is Charles Powell, president.

JAMES RIVER NURSERIES, INC.
Rt. 1, Box 1601
Ashland 23005   798-2020

James River Nurseries has been shaping the local landscape with trees, shrubs, flowers and greenery since 1983. It offers landscaping consultation, design and installation, and it has a division that installs irrigation systems.

J&S LANDSCAPING
West End   740-0998
South Side   231-6286

J&S specializes in retaining walls of railroad ties and timberwork. It also does backhoe and bulldozer work, drainage work, lawn renovation, patios and sidewalks.

SNEED'S NURSERY
8756 W. Huguenot Rd.   320-7798

Maybe you just want to do a little landscape renovation. Or, maybe you're looking for someone who can handle a major design and installation job. In either case, Sneed's is a good place to call.

SOUTHERN STATES LANDSCAPE SERVICE
8718 W. Broad St.   747-9315
1200 Alverser Dr., Midlothian 379-8111

Some people might not think of Southern States as a landscape service, but it has a staff of professionals who will design, plant and provide follow-up maintenance advice. Southern States Landscaping Service has two locations in the Richmond area and will help rejuvenate an older landscape, construct an Oriental or colonial theme garden, or develop a landscape that is low-maintenance or that provides year-round color.

WATKINS NURSERIES

15001 Midlothian Tnpk.   *379-8733*

Watkins handles all kinds of landscaping and is equipped to transplant trees up to 25 feet in height. Its nurseries offer 1,000 varieties of hardy stock grown on 800 acres.

Interior Designers

The best way to find an interior designer is by word of mouth and by looking at work they have done for other people. You also will find samples of their work at annual exhibitions sponsored by organizations such as the Women's Committee of the Richmond Symphony. The Yellow Pages contain a list of more than 70 providers of residential interior decorating and interior design services in the Richmond area. For starters, here is a list of some of the ones that come highly recommended:

YVONNE PAYNE BANDAS

5805 Grove Ave.   *285-3563*

Yvonne Payne Bandas specializes in fine residential interiors, window treatments and antiquing. She is a member of the American Society of Interior Designers.

JANET BOURNE INTERIORS

P.O. Box 1273
Glen Allen 23060   *672-1251*

Janet Bourne is not wedded to any special style of furnishings or type of design. In her residential as well as commercial work she uses her creative ideas to tailor design to the personal tastes, preferences and lifestyle of the client.

CAROL PIPES INTERIOR DESIGN

1334 Gaskins Rd.   *740-1069*

About half of Carol Pipes' work is residential, and half is commercial. She has handled a lot of historic renovation projects. Her studio is in the far West End, and she is a member of the American Institute of Interior Designers.

CHADWICK ANTIQUES

5805 Grove Ave.   *285-3355*

Chadwick Antiques offers a complete interior design service, from one-room facelifts to complete whole-house projects. It handles English, American and continental furniture, paintings and antiques, does reupholstering and has a large fabric and wallpaper library.

DESIGN

105 E. Main St.   *644-5991*

Design and its two principals, Robert Watkins and DeVeaux Riddick, have been an important part of the Richmond interior design scene since the 1950s. They specialize in residential and commercial design, and their shop offers antiques, fabrics and drapes.

INDESIGN

2320 Francine Rd.   *272-9504*

Patricia W. Stockdon of Indesign specializes in residential interiors and accessories, especially for new homes under construction. She is a member of the American Society of Interior Designers.

J. TAYLOR HOGAN

308 Libbie Ave.   *282-4474*
Stony Point Shopping Center   *320-4620*

When you visit Taylor Hogan's shops in the West End or across the river in the

Stony Point area you will agree with his slogan of "A Touch of The Finer Things In Life." He has been in business for more than 30 years and offers a complete interior design service, from basic consultation to full-house treatments.

KUYKENDALL INTERIORS
3313 W. Cary St.   *359-0891*

The staff of this firm is capable of taking on any interior design challenge and specializes in residential work. It has branched out to Charleston, South Carolina, and Naples, Florida, and is opening an office in Palm Spring, California.

MARTIN
3325 W. Cary St.   *353-1400*

If you're searching for the eclectic, the contemporary, the New York feel, this is a good place to go. The firm has been in business for 12 years and has three interior designers on staff. It also operates a retail store.

MONTAGUE & O'FERRALL DESIGN, LTD.
2805 McRae Rd.   *330-7635*

Montague & O'Ferrall has helped many notable Richmonders solve interior design challenges. It also does a lot of out of town work at Sea Island and other locations. They favor the classic look with great fabrics, and they try not to be trendy. Hours are by appointment.

ROBERT RENTZ INTERIORS
3143 W. Cary St.   *358-1650*

Robert Rentz works with architects on homes from the ground up and also will take on just one room, if that is what you have. He favors the eclectic style, and the firm operates a retail store.

RICHMOND ART CO., INC.
101 E. Grace St.   *644-0733*

The Richmond Art Co. building, designed and built for the store in the 1920s, is one of Richmond's architectural gems. Here, in addition to furnishings and accessories that are a resource for many of Richmond's interior designers, you'll find the interior and lighting design services of William Lee Joel II, fellow of the American Society of Interior Designers. Richmond Art is very strong in both residential and commercial interior design and even provides lighting design assistance for other interior planning professionals.

STEDMAN HOUSE OF RICHMOND
5609 Patterson Ave.   *282-6888*

Stedman House offers the services of five members of the American Society of Interior Designers. They include names of individuals who have been synonymous with interior design in Richmond for more than a generation. Stedman House specializes in residential work, but does do some commercial work.

Interior design services also are available from these magnificent interior furnishings stores:

Thomas-Hines
3027 W. Cary St.   *355-2782*

Jack Thompson Furniture/Interiors
1224 W. Broad St.   *359-3551*

Inside
Commercial Real Estate

Greater Richmond saw enormous growth in the 1980s as office and industrial square footage more than doubled, sometimes at the rate of two to three million square feet a year. The region appears headed into another period of strong economic growth with the announcement by Motorola, Inc. that it has selected Greater Richmond as the site for a new $3 billion semiconductor plant. In addition 60 percent of major local companies say they expect to need new or expanded space over the next two years, and this doesn't take into consideration the real estate requirements of new firms moving to the area.

"Richmond, Virginia, has become one of the most powerful and appealing business environments in the U.S.," says the report of one of the largest commercial real estate firms. Greater Richmond's strategic mid-Atlantic location with one-day access to suppliers and major East Coast and Midwest markets, its position at the center of an important and growing urban-industrial corridor, and its low operating costs are major drawing cards. Couple this with a Fortune 500 corporate headquarters city lifestyle that attracts and helps keep valued employees, and you have a combination that offers enormous possibilities for growth and development.

Completion of I-295 and other new roads opens up vast new quadrants of land,

and completion of the floodwall is an accelerating factor in downtown/Shockoe Bottom renovation and adaptive reuse. Also, development is being pushed ahead on the new Virginia Biotechnology Research Park on a 22-acre site downtown just to the west of the Medical College of Virginia. This will enhance Richmond's growing importance as a center for biomedical and pharmaceutical firms.

GREATER RICHMOND PARTNERSHIP, INC.
901 E. Byrd St., Ste. 801   643-3227

If you want to explore and evaluate the Richmond area as a business location, the best place to start is with the umbrella economic development organization for the City of Richmond and for the metropolitan-area counties of Chesterfield, Hanover and Henrico. This public-private partnership has a staff experienced in working with companies large and small, and draws on the resources of a Business Information Center to provide statistical data that can be tailored to specific needs. The staff also can help put you in touch with people you will need, especially if you have a fast-track schedule.

The Greater Richmond Partnership works as a team with the Virginia Department of Economic Development and with economic development offices of the four local jurisdictions:

Chesterfield County Economic Development Office
9401 Courthouse Rd.   748-3963

Hanover County Economic Development Office
621 Air Park Rd.
Ashland   798-5798

Henrico County Industrial Development Authority
8011 Villa Park Dr.   264-1500

City of Richmond Economic Development Office
City Hall, 900 E. Broad St.   780-5633

Commercial Real Estate Brokers

There are about 50 commercial real estate brokers in the Richmond area. They include:

HARRISON & BATES, INC.
823 E. Main St.   788-1000

Harrison & Bates, Inc., founded in 1910, is one of the two largest commercial real estate firms in town. It sponsors the major commercial real estate event of the year — the annual Commercial Real Estate Showcase & Market Review — which packs the Richmond Centre every January for exhibits and for a multimedia presentation involving market analyses and prognostications.

MORTON G. THALHIMER, INC.
1313 E. Main St.   648-5881

The other major player is Morton G. Thalhimer, Inc., founded in 1913. It offers a comprehensive array of commercial real estate services and each year publishes a Commercial Real Estate Report that tracks office, retail, industrial and service-sector trends and reports on results of a corporate Future Outlook survey.

Among other firms involved in the commercial real estate market, there are at least seven standouts:

Goodman Segar Hogan Hoffler
707 E. Main St.   644-4066

Joyner & Company
2727 Enterprise Pkwy.   270-9440

Kiniry & Co.
700 E. Main St.   643-0611

Porter Realty Co., Inc.
1804 Dabney Rd.   353-7994

Property Resources of Virginia
7201 Glen Forest Dr.   285-7070

C. Porter Vaughan, Inc.
4912 Augusta Ave.   355-5733

Virginia Landmark Corp.
1807 Libbie Ave.   285-3935

Commercial Developers

About 60 commercial real estate developers, some part of multi-state operations and others locally based, have office, retail industrial and mixed-use projects in the Richmond area. Some of the more important ones include:

CHARTER PROPERTIES, INC.
9030 Stony Point Pkwy.   330-9400

Charter Properties pioneered the first office park in Charlotte in the early 1970s and is the developer or partner in multi-family, retail and office projects. Its office projects will total more than four million square feet when built out. Its mixed-use project in Richmond is **The Park at Stony Point**.

Plans for The Park at Stony Point include 1.1 million square feet of office space and a major regional shopping mall. Along a ridge overlooking the James River, the 281-acre park bisected by the Parham-Chippenham Connector is at the southern end of the Willey Bridge. It is convenient to downtown and to the af-

One of America's Major Corporate Centers

The Richmond area is one of the nation's largest Fortune 500 headquarters centers. Of the top 14 corporate headquarters locations in America, only Richmond and Atlanta are in the Southeast.

Most of Richmond's major companies have evolved from small beginnings. Some of the most fascinating corporate stories are these:

Ethyl Corporation

Floyd D. Gottwald joined Richmond's Albemarle Paper Manufacturing Company in 1918 as an export clerk and rose through the ranks to become president in 1941. By the early 1960s, he had raised Albemarle's net sales to about $44 million and its net worth to $25 million. Then, on November 30, 1962, following nearly a year of negotiation, Gottwald stunned the business world with Albemarle's acquisition of New York-based Ethyl Corporation — a company 18 times its size — for $200 million. "It was like a mom-and-pop grocery buying the A&P," said the then-president of Standard Oil of New Jersey. Forbes magazine described Gottwald as a businessman "with a passion for anonymity and an obvious flair for high finance." Headquartered in Richmond, Ethyl is a major player on the Fortune 500 list and, after spin-offs in recent years, today concentrates on Ethyl's original core business, petroleum additives. Spin-offs over the years have included Tredegar Industries, a producer of plastic film and molded products, First Colony Corp. (insurance) and Albemarle Corporation, a marketer of specialty chemicals. The last of Albemarle Paper was sold many years ago to a group headed by two former employees and became what today is James River Corporation.

Reynolds Metals Company

In its more than 50 years in Richmond, Reynolds Metals Company has mushroomed from a relatively small packaging producer into the nation's second-largest aluminum producer and one of its largest corporations. More than anyone else, the company and the Reynolds family "changed aluminum from an exotic industrial raw material into fabricated end products," noted Forbes magazine in 1974. The company introduced Reynolds Wrap household foil in Richmond in 1947. It pioneered aluminum siding for houses in the 1940s, the all-aluminum beverage can in the 1960s and nationwide aluminum recycling in the 1970s.

Circuit City Stores, Inc.

What has emerged as the nation's largest specialty retailer of brand-name consumer electronics didn't begin that way. When Samuel S. Wurtzel set out to sell television sets in 1949 from one-half of a tire store on W. Broad Street, Richmond had but one television station — and that didn't begin telecasting until 4:30 in the afternoon. Television was still very much of a novelty; sales resistance was difficult to overcome; and Wurtzel's Wards Company had to use all kinds of inducements. But within 10 years, the first store had become a chain of four, and the merchandise line was extended to include appliances. Further expansion pushed sales in 1966 to almost $23 million, up from less than $2 million in 1960. In the 1970s, the first of the gigantic warehouse-showrooms — now called Circuit City Superstores — put American electronics and appliance retailing on a new track. The early 1980s brought an ambitious expansion of Superstore locations and saw a merger with Lafayette Radio and Electronics Corp. In 1984, the corporate name was changed to Circuit City Stores, Inc., coast to coast. Circuit City's sales total about $5 billion annually.

James River Corporation

Brenton S. Halsey and Robert C. Williams founded James River Corporation in 1969 with the purchase from Ethyl Corporation of the former Albemarle Paper mill, which had one small paper machine and 100 employees. Through innovative management, new product development and energetic marketing, they not only made the old mill a success but guided James River Corporation through a multitude of acquisitions here and abroad. Sales have grown from $4 million to well more than $5 billion, and James River is now one of the largest papermakers in the world.

---

fluent areas of West End Richmond, Henrico County and Chesterfield County.

CHILDRESS KLEIN PROPERTIES, INC.
9100 Arboretum Pkwy.   330-3900

Childress Klein owns and manages extensive real estate holdings Chesterfield and Henrico counties and in the City of Richmond. They include:

The proposed 68-acre **Acropolis Corporate Centre** in Chesterfield County at the intersection of the Powhite Parkway and Coalfield Road, just ½ mile west of Va. 288. Envisioned with post-modern, neoclassical architecture, Acropolis will have more than 750,000 square feet of commercial space, including a 300-room hotel, when completed.

Southpark, in the City of Richmond, a 237,000-square-foot office-warehouse park at the intersection of I-95 and Bells Road with excellent access to the Port of Richmond's Deepwater Terminal.

DANIEL CORPORATION
951 E. Byrd St.   780-3030

Daniel Corporation, a major real estate development and management firm based in Birmingham, Alabama, has maintained a regional office in the Richmond area for more than 25 years. For many years it has owned and managed Imperial Plaza, an 852-unit high rise apartment community for senior citizens. In 1994 it opened Guardian Place, a 120-unit retirement community for senior citizens who want access to support services on an as-needed basis. Among its newest projects are:

Riverfront Plaza, a twin-tower, 20-story office complex with 950,000 square feet of Class A office space and five stories of underground parking. It has become a prominent landmark on the Richmond skyline. It is the home of the Greater Richmond Partnership, Dominion Resources, Arnold Finnegan Martin, Coopers & Lybrand and of other major corporate offices, accounting firms and insurance agencies.

Park Central, a 100-acre multiuse office and office/service park, is on Parham Road near I-95, I-295 and U.S. 301. The site is in an excellent location and is attracting a lot of interest. Five companies, including those in the printing and service industries, have built new facilities in Park Central recently.

FAISON ASSOCIATES
901 E. Cary St.   *344-3232*

Faison's portfolio exceeds $1.4 billion and it manages more than 20 million square feet of retail, office, warehouse and hotel property in 10 states. The Richmond office, its first full-service regional operation, opened in 1983. Regional projects include Virginia Center Commons and Southpark Mall, but the firm has made the biggest impact on the downtown skyline through its co-development, along with CSX, of the **James Center**.

The James Center, situated on 8.2 acres encompassing five city blocks and commanding an impressive view of the river, is a premier downtown business location that now includes three 20-story-plus towers with a total of 1.3 million square feet. Three more buildings, an additional 1.5 million square feet, are planned. CSX Corporation, Chesapeake Corporation and Central Fidelity Banks have their corporate headquarters here, and the complex is the home of two private clubs and of some of Richmond's biggest law and accounting firms.

FIGGIE PROPERTIES, INC.
1049 Technology Park Dr.
Glen Allen   *264-5840*

Figgie Properties Inc. is the real estate development division of Figgie International, Inc. and is active in the development and management of office, industrial, retail and residential centers throughout the United States. Its major local project is the **Virginia Center**.

In Henrico County on 1,250 acres strategically at the intersection of I-95, I-295 and U.S. 1, Virginia Center is a mixed-use office, residential, office/service and retail project. It includes a corporate center, Virginia Center Commons, the Virginia Center Technology Park (with facilities like those of Bergen Brunswig Drug Company), and The Crossings, one of the top five golf courses in the state.

INNSBROOK CORPORATION
4222 Cox Rd.   *741-8100*

Innsbrook Corporate Center, without doubt, the classiest of Richmond's premier, campus-like office parks, is at the intersection of I-64 and I-295 in western Henrico County near what is locally known as "Downtown Short Pump." Begun in 1981, its 800 acres include lakes and meticulously landscaped grounds that have evolved into a self-contained community that is one of the area's most prestigious business addresses. "Residents" of Innsbrook include corporate headquarters, offices of state associations and facilities such as GE Lighting's international customer service center and Virginia Power's operations center.

KOGER PROPERTIES
1500 Forest Ave.   *282-5461*

Koger is a company with a long history in the office park field. Its local **Koger**

Center is strategically in the West End at the intersection of Forest Avenue and Three Chopt Road.

THE LANDMARK
COMPANY OF VIRGINIA

3937 Deep Rock Rd. 270-7367

The Landmark Company of Virginia serves a niche in facilities that are 40 percent office and 60 percent warehouse. It builds in Deep Run Center in Henrico County, in Chesterfield Airport Industrial Park and Southport in Chesterfield County and in Ashcake Industrial Park in Hanover County.

LAVEER PROPERTIES

2112 W. Laburnum Ave. 359-7795

CenterPointe, covering 947 acres, is at the intersection of Coalfield Road, Va. 288 and the Powhite Expressway in Chesterfield County.

LINGERFELT
DEVELOPMENT CORPORATION

12 S. Third St. 644-9111

Home-based in Richmond, Lingerfelt Development Corporation has more than 30 years of experience and a portfolio of more than three million square feet of development — including Richmond's 220,000-square-foot Internal Revenue Service Eastern Regional Distribution Center completed under budget in a fast-track 3½-month time period. Lingerfelt has specialized in industrial, commercial and institutional projects including:

Fairgrounds Distribution Center, an 11-unit complex of buildings, ranging in size from 120,000 square feet to 288,000 square feet. The Center has spur tracks off the CSX main rail line and is convenient to the interstate highway system. It has proved popular for manufacturing as well as distribution operations. Tenants include FoxMeyer, a pharmaceutical distributor, Shelcore, Inc., a maker and international marketer of preschool toys, and the photofinishing plant of Konica Quality Photo East.

Eastport Business Park, a 98-acre business park adjacent to Richmond International Airport with access to CSX rail lines and to I-64 and I-295. Eastport is designed to meet the needs of service, distribution and light industrial operations.

LEADBETTER, INC.

405 Airpark Rd., Ashland 798-8301

Leadbetter, Inc., is a developer of Hanover County office, warehouse, industrial and retail property. It is able to provide space in existing buildings or, in cooperation with Leadbetter Construction Company, to meet the needs of a client looking for a custom-designed facility. Its major Hanover County project is **Hanover Industrial Air Park**, which was begun in the 1960s, and today covers more than 600 acres. Its convenient access to I-95 and other arteries and its attractive costs have drawn hundreds of tenants to its prime Hanover County location. Right at hand is Hanover County's airport.

MARK MERHIGE REAL ESTATE
BROKERAGE & DEVELOPMENT, INC.

114 Virginia St. 780-3140

While the firm is a smaller developer, it has created a niche for itself in rehabilitation of historic properties for residential, restaurant and office use. These projects have received awards from architectural and historic preservation groups. With offices in Shockoe Slip, the firm also handles commercial leasing and property management.

MEDIA GENERAL
DEVELOPMENT CORPORATION
333 E. Grace St. 649-6623

Atlee Station is a 236-acre corporate community being developed at the intersection of I-295 and U.S. 301 in Hanover County by Media General Development Corporation. The office park, with its lakes and 14-acre greenway, is ideal for corporate headquarters, research and development firms, operations centers and professional offices. It is here that Richmond Newspapers, Inc. has built its multi-million-dollar, high tech production and distribution center.

PARAGON GROUP, INC.
6800 Paragon Pl. 288-4444

A national real estate development and management company headquartered in Dallas and operating in 45 cities in 15 states, Paragon began construction of Richmond's **Paragon Place** in 1985. Paragon Place is strategically at the intersection of I-64 and West Broad Street near the headquarters of Reynolds Metals Company. The office park covers 44 acres. Paragon pulled off somewhat of a coup when it acquired the site in the mid-'80s. Development plans call for a density that is relatively urban, encompassing about 700,000 square feet.

RF&P CORPORATION
600 E. Main St., Ste. 2300 225-1600

Encompassing 850,000 square feet of office and warehouse space, **Greater Richmond Dabney Center** (including Brittons Hill) is RF&P's largest local commercial real estate development. Other properties include **The Arboretum** (375,000 square feet of elegant office space at the intersection of the Powhite Expressway and U.S. 60) and office buildings and parks at **Interstate Center** (126,000

square feet), **Commerce Center** (56,000 square feet) and the Kemper Building at Innsbrook (60,000 square feet). RF&P holdings also include industrial buildings (150,000 square feet) and a large quantity of developable acreage, and it is looking for acquisitions and build-to-suite opportunities.

ROBINSON & WETMORE, INC.
7301 Forest Ave. 288-0026

Robinson & Wetmore to date has developed properties in Norfolk, Chesapeake and Virginia Beach as well as here in Richmond. Its president began his career in mortgage lending, acquisitions, joint ventures and real estate development with Prudential Insurance Company. Richmond projects include Dumbarton Business Center I, an 80,000 square foot office-warehouse building in Henrico County and three buildings in Glen Forest, one a build-to-suit for Reynolds Metals and another a build-to-suit for Wang Laboratories.

ROBINSON SIGMA
COMMERCIAL REAL ESTATE, INC.
7100 Beaufont Springs Dr. 320-5500

Robinson Sigma, with offices here and in Norfolk and Hampton, leases and manages seven million square feet of commercial space — half retail, half office — including **The Boulders** at U.S. 60 and Chippenham Parkway. The 230-acre office park has proved popular and is growing. Contemporary office buildings at The Boulders include one which serves as the corporate headquarters of Tredegar Industries.

THE FRIEDLAND CO.
3951 Westerre Pkwy. 273-9300

The Friedland Company's Richmond-area projects, originally launched by Trammell Crow, include **Westerre**, **North Run Business Park** and **Northridge Business Park**. Westerre is near the I-64 and Gaskins Road interchange in western Henrico County. Time-Life Books' national customer service headquarters is one of the tenants at North Run Business Park, on Parham Road near I-95. The park provides a campus-like setting and is across the street from J. Sargeant Reynolds Community College.

Northridge Business Park is a 10-acre office/warehouse project just off I-95 at the Atlee-Elmont exit and just a few miles north of I-295 in Hanover County.

WOOLFOLK PROPERTIES, INC.
830 Southlake Blvd. 794-5888

Douglass K. Woolfolk has a longstanding interest in design and environment and often describes himself as a "frustrated architect." His three sons are now involved with him in The Woolfolk Companies, which cover a full range of real estate development, construction, sales, leasing and management services. Current projects include **Bellgrade Plantation**, a mixed-use development at the intersection of Robious and Huguenot roads, covering 161 acres of prime Chesterfield County land near the Richmond city limits. While more than half of the site is earmarked for residential use, the balance is office, office/service and retail.

WILTON REAL ESTATE & DEVELOPMENT CORP.
12095 Gayton Rd. 740-5489

The Wilton Companies are among the largest commercial real estate developers headquartered in Virginia. It has controlling interest in two million square feet of commercial real estate in the state. Its **Hermitage Industrial Center**, a ma-

jor commercial distribution complex, is in Henrico County.

Other Office and Business Parks

In addition, among the vast array of office and business parks of all sizes, these deserve special mention:

APPOMATTOX INDUSTRIAL CENTER
South of Ruffin Mill Road near the Walthall interchange on I-95 in Chesterfield County, Appomattox Industrial Center covers 250 acres.

ASHLAND BUSINESS PARK
The 187-acre business park is adjacent to Hanover County's college town of Ashland and offers quick access to I-95 and U.S. 1. Designed for commercial, retail and light industrial use, the park has a central heliport, jogging trails, picnic areas, and planned support facilities include those for child and senior care and for restaurants and lodging.

CHESTERFIELD AIRPORT INDUSTRIAL PARK
Covering 300 acres, the park has attracted some blue-chip tenants — Reynolds Metals Company's can division headquarters, Frito-Lay, Japanese-owned Maruchan Virginia and American Filtrona.

INTERNATIONAL BUSINESS PARK
It's one of the area's smaller business parks (73 acres total with nine acres still available), but it has a great location near Richmond International Airport and adjacent to I-64. Alfa-Laval selected it for its corporate headquarters and manufacturing plant.

LAKERIDGE COMMERCIAL PARK

Bordering I-95 in Hanover County, Lakeridge has an international flair with companies from England, Italy and Germany. It is attractively landscaped and is characterized by companies involved in research, manufacturing and/or distribution.

MIDLANTIC BUSINESS CENTER

Opened in 1990, Midlantic has infrastructure in place for development of 180 acres adjacent to the Chesterfield Airport Industrial Park.

MOOREFIELD OFFICE PARK

Covering 83 well-landscaped acres at Robious Road and Midlothian Turnpike, Moorefield has the Sheraton Park South hotel among it amenities.

OAKLEYS CENTER

Designed to accommodate finished site sales, build-to-suit projects and speculative buildings, Oakleys Center is on 33 acres just north of I-64 between Laburnum Avenue and Airport Drive.

RIVER'S BEND

River's Bend offers 400 new acres of prime Chesterfield County land on the west side of I-295 and north of Va. 10. It is planned for office and industrial use.

ROSLYN FARMS

Roslyn Farms covers 346 acres southeast of Ruffin Mill Road along the Walthall interchange on I-95.

TECHNOLOGY POINTE

At Innsbrook in western Henrico County, Technology Pointe is a 40-acre section of Innsbrook Technology Park. It is being developed to include about 450,000 square feet of flex product. The site has extensive frontage on I-295 and is reached via Cox Road from U.S. 250 (Broad Street).

WATERFORD

An office park, Waterford covers 260 acres at Old Hundred Road and the Powhite Expressway in Chesterfield County.

WEST CREEK

This 3,500-acre site is being developed by a team that includes CBR Associates, Inc. Projected construction over the next 30 to 40 years envisions 21 million square feet of commercial space. Buildings to date include the new home of the Psychiatric Institute of Richmond and the 20-acre lakefront headquarters of the Virginia Farm Bureau Federation. The massive West Creek sits in on Patterson Avenue in Goochland County adjacent to the Henrico County border. Motorola Inc. has signed an option to buy 230 acres in West Creek for a new $3 billion semiconductor plant, and it has a second option to buy an additional 140 acres.

WOODLAND CENTER

At Airport Drive and I-64, Woodland Center is a 67-acre business park that provides a Class A environment for distribution and light industrial companies seeking immediate access to Richmond International Airport and the interstate highway system.

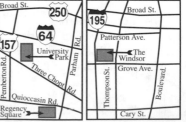

Inside
Retirement

Richmond appeals to many retirees because it's big enough to offer cultural activities, educational opportunities and second careers, yet small enough that transportation is relatively stress-free. It's also a short trip from here to nearby tourist destinations such as Williamsburg, Washington, D.C., the Shenandoah Valley, the Chesapeake Bay, ocean beaches and rivers.

About 112,000 people age 60 or older call Richmond home. Most are from the area or have family or friends who live here.

As the area's senior population increases, Richmond retirees are gaining influence as consumers and have more choices in housing and services than ever before.

To help seniors maintain an active and independent lifestyle, many retirement homes and communities in the Richmond area offer "assisted living" arrangements that allow residents to live independently, participate in activity programs and take advantage of services such as housekeeping, grounds maintenance, transportation, meals and personal services as needed.

For those who don't want to join a retirement community, some companies, such as Mature Options, cater to the needs of seniors who want to live at home but are unable to live independently.

For retirees who like being homeowners, but don't want all the work and worry, at least one development — Summer Hill at Stony Point — offers them an opportunity to own a home in a neighborhood that provides security and maintenance services, plus the fellowship, programs and services of a typical retirement community.

In the Richmond area, you'll also find numerous programs, clubs, support groups, publications and organized activities for seniors, including trips, golf groups, athletic competitions, walking clubs and dances. There are more than 100 retirement homes and communities here, and as many licensed nursing homes. In this section we've provided a sampling of some of the innovative and reputable retirement communities and organizations — this section does not include nursing homes. For more information about programs, services and housing options, we suggest that you start with the Capital Area Agency on Aging.

Organizations

CAPITAL AREA AGENCY ON AGING
24 E. Cary St.   343-3000

This private, nonprofit organization is part of a nationwide system developed as a result of the Older Americans Act and administered by the Virginia Department for the Aging. It's a great place to start when you need information about senior clubs, housing, home equity conversion, long-term care, social security, services and opportunities in the Richmond area for people age 60 and older. If the staff can't help you directly, they'll put you in touch with someone who can. In addition to its role as an information clearinghouse, the agency also provides some direct services such as a senior discount program, job referrals, home repairs and meals programs. Services are free, but donations are accepted.

COUNCIL OF SENIOR CITIZENS ORGANIZATIONS

President Helen Hulcher   262-3412
Margaret and John Farmer   358-2825

A group of retired people started this organization in 1962 to create an organization with clout on issues affecting older people. They provide guidance and leadership training for senior groups and speaker referrals on a variety of topics. They also offer information to individuals who want to get involved with local groups, primarily in Richmond.

AFFILIATED SENIOR CITIZENS OF METROPOLITAN RICHMOND

President Mozelle Salle Baxter   358-2837

This organization is made up of about 48 senior groups in Metropolitan Richmond. It helps new groups get started and provides activities and programs regarding senior issues such as the church's role with the elderly, and beauty and health.

CITY AND COUNTY RECREATION AND PARKS DEPARTMENTS

Richmond	780-4283
Chesterfield	748-1623
Hanover	798-8062
Henrico	672-5100

The Recreation and Parks departments of Richmond and each of the surrounding counties sponsor a variety of senior recreation programs and activities. Contact the nearest office for details.

VIRGINIA DEPARTMENT FOR THE AGING

Long-term Care Ombudsman Office
    (800) 552-3402

The Virginia Department for the Aging works primarily with statewide policy and legislation concerning tax relief, health care and transportation issues regarding elderly people. Most of the department's services are provided through the Capital Area Agency on Aging; however, the department's staff provides free, confidential counseling and complaint resolution concerning long-term care options.

MATURE OPTIONS

1910 Byrd Ave.   282-0753

Through Mature Options, Norah Knutsen, an experienced Gerontological Clinical Nurse Specialist, assists older adults and their families with the selection and management of long-term care services best suited to their individual needs. Norah works closely with you to explore a full range of options from in-home assistance or adult day care to assisted living arrangements or institutional care.

Retirement Communities

BRANDERMILL WOODS

14311 Brandermill Woods Tr.   744-0141
    (800) 552-6579

This continuing-care retirement community opened in 1986 and leases single-story cluster homes with attached garages and apartments to energetic couples who are typically in their early 70s. All levels

of care and a full range of services are available as residents' needs change. There are two three-story apartment buildings, cluster homes, a club house, health care complex and a nursing home. The health care complex includes assisted-living apartments and a 60-bed skilled, licensed nursing home. Located on about 40 acres, this community adjoins the larger residential community of Brandermill.

Residents enjoy the intergenerational mix of people in the neighborhood and bird watching in a natural country setting. They have access to the lake and walking paths, and membership in the Brandermill Country Club is available.

Services include security guards, medical alert buttons, up-and-about buttons, exterior and interior maintenance, transportation, trips, exercise and activity programs.

The average rent is $2,000 per month for two people in a two-bedroom home.

BRAXTON RETIREMENT COMMUNITY
Lakemere Dr. at Ironbridge Rd.   275-2689

About 5 miles from the Courthouse area, in Chesterfield County, Braxton Retirement Community offers home ownership without the hassle or worries of maintenance or security.

This 43-acre community features sidewalks, street lamps and a computerized security gate. About 30 single-family homes have been built since development began in 1992. When the community is completed, there will be about 150 homes on $1/3$-acre parcels of mostly open land. All homes are built by owner and developer W.S. Carnes, a Richmond area builder for more than 40 years.

Designed for active retirees, the community is conveniently located with easy access to the Richmond area via Chippenham Parkway and Route 10. Residents also enjoy walking trails and a fishing pond, and future plans include a clubhouse and recreational activities. No health care or other services are offered, but a list of providers is available.

Each resident has an access code that allows them to pass through the community's computerized security gate. Visitors use a phone at the gate to call residents, who open the gate via a remote telephone code.

Homes may be built for $140,000 or more, depending on the design and square footage. Homes range in size from 1,400 square feet to 2,500 square feet and feature quality construction using your plans or spec plans offered by the community. You must be at least 55 to live here. There is an annual $125 community fee.

THE GUARDIAN PLACE
1620 N. Hamilton St. 355-3013

Designed exclusively for seniors with moderate incomes, The Guardian Place features state-of-the-art accommodations for the elderly. The modern four-story brick building opened in 1994 with 120 independent living apartments. Studios and one- or two-bedroom apartments are available.

Developed by the United Methodist Family Services, the Guardian Place is the only retirement home in Virginia that was financed with tax credits. To qualify for special financing, a resident's annual income must not exceed an amount set annually by the Virginia Housing and Development Authority (VHDA).

The Guardian Place provides a community room, library and courtesy transportation for residents. A resident man-

ager is available 24 hours a day, and each apartment has emergency call buttons.

Residents enjoy the spacious grounds, garden plots, potluck dinners, luncheons, bridge parties and crafts. They also have convenient access to public transportation, shopping and nearby cultural attractions and colleges. Some residents are still employed or work as volunteers.

There is no entrance fee. Monthly rates range from $470 to $619 including utilities.

GINTER HALL WEST
12411 Gayton Rd. 741-9494

Located in a quiet residential area in the West End, Ginter Hall West provides personal assisted-living care for senior citizens. Constructed in 1987, the brick facility includes 128 rooms with the capacity for 236 residents. Services include 24-hour personal care, meals, activity programs, religious services, housekeeping, laundry, an emergency call system and a beauty salon/barber shop.

Ginter Hall West also provides a respite program to assist families with daily caregiving tasks. Stays may last two or more weeks. Respite Care residents receive the same services and amenities offered to permanent residents.

Monthly rates range from about $2,000 to $3,300, depending on the size of the apartment and number of occupants. Daily rates are also available. There is no entrance fee.

THE HERMITAGE
1600 Westwood Ave. 355-5721

Owned by Virginia United Methodist Homes, Inc., the Hermitage is an established continuing-care retirement community located on the edge of Ginter Park. The Georgian-style mansion was originally built as a private residence in

1911. Residential wings were added after it opened as a retirement home in 1949, and the 115-bed health care center was added in 1978. About 260 people of all faiths live here. One-, two- and three-room apartments are available for independent living. Assisted-living apartments are also available. Situated on seven acres of beautifully landscaped lawns, the Hermitage provides a full range of support services, a beauty shop, chapel, sundry store and banking.

Residents are very active in creative arts, music and religious activities and enjoy the attention of an active group of volunteers.

There is an entrance fee and a monthly rate of approximately $1,156 that includes meals, housekeeping, transportation, activities and other support services. Monthly lease contracts are also available.

IMPERIAL PLAZA
1717 Bellevue Ave.   264-1380

This retirement community near Bryan Park has it all — shopping, dining, a 278-seat theater, a beauty shop, even banking, and it's all in one complex with connecting corridors, so you don't have to venture outside in bad weather or go up or down any steps. There are three nine-story brick buildings and one 13-story building located in a parklike setting on 31 wooded acres. More than 800 independent living units from one-bedroom apartments to two-bedroom penthouses are leased on a yearly basis.

A full range of support services, transportation, security and emergency pulls are available. For those who need a little extra help, meals and personal services are provided residents in their private apartments in the Assisted Living Center. Licensed practical nurses are on duty 24 hours a day.

Built in the late 1960s, the buildings were recently renovated, and new carpeting and appliances installed.

A full-time activities coordinator keeps residents busy with song and dance shows, gardening, art classes, bus tours, shopping excursions, church services, bridge, pool, horseshoes, bingo and committee work. Residents also publish an in-house newsletter.

Monthly rents range from about $500 to $1,360 with additional charges for optional services.

LAKEWOOD MANOR
BAPTIST RETIREMENT COMMUNITY
1900 Lauderdale Dr. 740-2900

This campus-style, life-care community operated by Virginia Baptist Homes, Inc. is located in the West End on more than 50 wooded acres. It's home to about 400 people of all faiths who are typically in their late 70s and 80s. There are five three-story apartment buildings, a health care center and a community center, all connected by covered walkways. Residents choose from a variety of floor plans and apartment sizes. Meal service is provided, or residents may prepare their own meals; all apartments have kitchens.

A full range of security and support services is available. Lakewood Manor also provides a bank, convenience store, beauty and barber shop, activities room, woodworking shop, gardening areas, billiards and a library.

People who live here like to travel and participate in many cultural, social and religious activities.

The health care center provides physical and rehabilitative therapy, care for temporary illnesses, recuperation from hospitalization and long-term nursing care.

There is an entrance fee, and monthly fees range from $1350 to $1877 per month.

ST. MARY'S WOODS
1257 Marywood Ln. 741-8624

Located in the West End across from Gayton Shopping Center, St. Mary's Woods is a nonprofit retirement community sponsored by the Catholic Diocese of Virginia. Residents live in one- or two-bedroom apartments with kitchens and patios or bay windows.

Security and a full range of services are provided. Facilities include a medical/outpatient clinic, beauty and barber shop, dining room, library, chapel, whirlpool, activity rooms and a craft room equipped with a ceramic kiln.

In the Assisted Living Center, residents enjoy the same apartment selection and amenities with the addition of special services. The staff includes a full-time registered nurse and 24-hour nursing assistance.

Residents participate in exercise programs, art classes, religious studies, bingo, bridge, ceramics, movies and community service projects.

Monthly rates range from $1,259 to $2,487 and include services, utilities and meals.

SUMMERHILL AT STONY POINT
9250 Forest Hill Ave. 320-8312

This was the first and may be the only retirement community in the area where you can buy a home. To live here, you must be at least age 55 and capable of living independently. Situated on 19 partly-wooded acres beside a lake, Summerhill at Stony Point is within walking distance of the Stony Point Shopping Center. Arranged in clusters, 71 homes are available with one, two or three

bedrooms. All of the homes are one story, with brick or vinyl siding and cedar shake roofs. There is also a lodge with a private dining hall, exercise room, library, activity room and common area.

Residents enjoy the scenery, and it's not unusual to see their grandchildren fishing for bream and bass in the lake. Known as a place to hear live music, the community sponsors concerts at the lodge.

Operated by the Health Corporation of Virginia, the community provides a full range of support services including a full-time activity coordinator, security, emergency medical call buttons, interior and exterior maintenance, home repairs, transportation, emergency response, meals, home health care, nursing home services and a long-term care funding program. Residents have guaranteed access to the nursing home at Richmond Memorial Hospital, and recuperative care is available at the Westwood Transitional Care Unit.

Prices begin around $90,000.

THE VILLAGE AT STRATFORD HALL
2125 Hilliard Rd.   266-9666

The Village offers assisted living and companionship in a gracious, upscale environment. People who live here are usually surviving spouses in their 80s or 90s. Located in the Lakeside area, across from the Lewis Ginter Botanical Gardens, the two-story brick home includes 52 units.

A full range of support services are provided including meals, an activities program, a beauty shop, exercise equipment and an emergency call system.

Residents enjoy shopping, movies, music programs, bridge, dominoes, scrabble and a variety of activities.

There is no entrance fee, and monthly rates range from $1,600 to $2,700 depending on the size of the apartment and the number of occupants.

THE VIRGINIAN

300 Twinridge Ln.   *330-4252*

Located between Bon Air and Midlothian Turnpike in Chesterfield County, the Virginian offers 117 one- or two-bedroom apartments or studios for people age 55 or older who are capable of living independently. Most apartments have patios or balconies.

Facilities include craft and multipurpose rooms, billiards, a library, chapel, big-screen TV, lounge and exercise room.

Services include meals, transportation, housekeeping, planned activities and an emergency alert system.

Monthly rates range from about $1,000 to $2,000 and include basic services and utilities.

WESTMINSTER CANTERBURY

1600 Westbrook Ave.   *264-6000*

There is usually a waiting list of people who want to live in this life-care community, sponsored by the Presbyterian and Episcopal churches. Westminster Canterbury offers 385 independent-living apartments, 130 assisted-living apartments and 133 private rooms in the health care center. Individual cottages for independent living are also available through The Glebe, with separate rates and contracts for services.

On-site services and facilities at Westminster Canterbury include an indoor pool and fitness center, coffee shop, laundry, banking, beauty and barber shop, gift shop, catering, transportation, pharmacy, physical therapy, doctors' and dentists' office, clinic, library and chapel.

Entrance fees are required. Monthly rates range from $1,200 to $3,540 depending on the level of care, size of the apartment and number of occupants.

Inside
Historic Preservation

Plans to demolish and replace almost all of the old buildings in the city of Richmond with modern, high rise buildings were on the books by 1956, the same year the Historic Richmond Foundation was established by the Association for the Preservation of Virginia Antiquities (APVA).

Since that time, every major landmark in the city has been threatened, but the preservation movement in Richmond started early enough that today, whole city blocks and neighborhoods have been restored, creating a charming and unique historic ambience.

Thanks largely to the efforts of the **Historic Richmond Foundation**, the APVA, other preservation groups and concerned individuals, Richmond is one of the few cities that escaped wholesale demolition of its historic buildings during the 1960s. Credit is also due to Mary Wingfield Scott for drawing attention to the need for historic preservation through her lectures and books on Richmond, including *Old Richmond Neighborhoods*.

And, to the benefit of city government and businesses, historic preservation has proven to be economically successful as a source of tax revenue and as a major tourism draw.

Preservation began in earnest in 1956, when the Historic Richmond Foundation focused its efforts on saving and restoring the immediate area around St. John's Church in Church Hill. Since the neighborhood had become a rooming-house area, it was difficult to interest people in buying and restoring the property, but the Foundation was able to demonstrate what a restored block would look like. By the mid-'70s, restoration efforts spread to other blocks of Church Hill as people became more interested in returning to the culture of the inner city — a direct reaction to suburban life, evident in cities across the nation.

During the past few decades, Richmonders have become personally involved in historic preservation, and the movement is strongly felt throughout the city. For instance, when Old City Hall was up for sale, there was great fear that it might be destroyed. It took three years and loud citizen protest citywide to save it. Today, it's been completely restored and is used as an office building.

When the city decided to pave Monument Avenue with asphalt, Helen Marie Taylor literally stood in front of a steam roller to prevent it from happening. Following an outpouring of public sentiment, the avenue ultimately was paved with asphalt bricks to retain the original character of the famous street. (The bricks also cost less in the long run than asphalt.)

Other successful preservation efforts include the establishment of city historic districts and the restoration of Shockoe

The Trial of Aaron Burr

Andrew Jackson and Washington Irving were among the thousands who converged on Richmond in the summer of 1807, one of the hottest on record, for the treason trial of former Vice President Aaron Burr. Jackson, dressed in the attire of a backwoodsman, took to the public green repeatedly to loudly denounce the trial as "political persecution." Irving, then a young correspon-

dent for New York newspapers, sent off dispatches that were highly favorable to the accused. President Thomas Jefferson, bitterly antagonistic to Burr, refused to allow letters in his possession to be used in Burr's defense, claiming executive privilege. Although he finally permitted extracts to be made, echoes of this dispute would be heard almost 170 years later during the Watergate scandals when the Burr case would be cited in the struggle for the Nixon tapes.

Hotels and inns overflowed; some people sleeping three to a bed; and many camped in covered wagons and tents along the river bank. The trial was the most important of its kind in American history. It defined the terms of treason in

Aaron Burr

detail for the first time. It involved the influential and the famous as well as a power struggle between political parties and between the executive and judicial branches of government.

Through almost six months in Richmond, the cultured and handsome Burr became a darling of local society. This began on March 30, the day he was brought to Richmond for a preliminary hearing at the Eagle Tavern. Two men in the bar, apparently impressed with Burr's aristocratic manner, not only signed for his $5,000 bail, but gave him $1,000 to buy a wardrobe to replace the ragged clothes in which he had been arrested near Mobile.

Richmond's hospitality continued through the sessions of the grand jury and the trial itself, all held in the old House Chamber at the State Capitol. Burr became a sought-after guest of Richmond's prominent families and lawyer John Wickham even invited him to a dinner to which Wickham also invited Chief Justice John Marshall, who was to preside over his trial. He also invited other friends, some of whom would serve either on the grand or trial juries. Marshall claimed he did not know Burr would be invited, but the situation created quite a stir.

Even after the grand jury returned the indictment for treason on June 24, and although Burr was incarcerated in the city's vermin-infested jail for two nights, Richmond's hospitality continued. He was moved to a brick house at the corner of 9th and Broad streets where he was kept under guard for a period of time. Then he was moved to the newly-completed state penitentiary where he enjoyed a three-room suite with callers who every day brought an endless array of delicacies, gifts and messages.

The former vice president was charged with conspiring to establish an independent government west of the Alleghenies, thus threatening dismemberment of the Union.

The battle in the courtroom began on August 3. Counsel for the defense included illustrious barristers such as Wickham, Edmund Randolph and colorful Baltimore lawyer Luther Martin (known as "Old Brandy Bottle"). The prosecution included U.S. District Attorney George Hay and William Wirt, author of *The Letters of a British Spy*.

A major event in the whole tableau was the arrival of Gen. James Wilkinson, commander of the United States Army in the West. Although he was described as a "pensioned Spanish spy, confederate with Burr" and as "from the bark to the very core a villain," he was not indicted.

Most people believed Burr was almost certainly guilty of trying to set up some kind of government in the West. But the prosecution's case was torn to shreds when Chief Justice John Marshall ruled that in order to prove guilt it was necessary to show overt acts, with two witnesses present when each act was committed. The prosecution could do no such thing, and the jury on September 1 in an unusual verdict found Burr "not proved guilty . . . by any evidence submitted to us."

Even though Marshall directed the clerk to place the words "Not Guilty" on the record, Burr was not pleased with the less than clear-cut outcome. While he went forth a free man, Burr remained under a stigma for the rest of his life.

The long, hot summer and the heat of the trial had ended. Richmond taverns and inns emptied. Andrew Jackson got back on his horse and left for Tennessee. "Old Brandy Bottle" headed back to Baltimore. And one of the key issues, whether states that had voluntarily entered into a compact could in the same manner withdraw from it, would linger on until it was settled in a clash of arms 50 some years later — an episode in American history in which Richmond again would play a central role.

Five years later Wickham would build a magnificent neoclassical home on East Clay Street, today home of the Valentine Museum.

Slip, Jackson Ward, Monument Avenue, Franklin Street east of Belvidere, the State Capitol, the Ironfronts on Main Street in downtown and hundreds of other projects.

Eventually, the restoration of the old National Theatre Building, in the 700 block of E. Broad Street, and other nearby buildings is expected to stimulate further restoration and have a positive affect on the entire street.

There are also times, though, when historic preservation efforts conflict with individual property rights, prompting owners to fight back. Several years ago, in Hanover County, an extensive section of Civil War earthworks on private property was threatened by plans for a new subdivision. Preservationists wanted to save the earthworks, so the county stalled approval of the new development until the situation could be resolved satisfactorily. Unfortunately, the landowner thought that the earthworks were threatening the sale of his property. As a result, he bulldozed over many of the trenches, effectively ending his problem. In the end, the land was sold and only a small portion of the earthworks was saved.

For more information about historic preservation in Richmond, we recommend the book *Old Richmond Today* by Richard Cheek and John G. Zehmer, published by the Historic Richmond Foundation, and *The Architecture of Historic Richmond* by Paul S. Dulaney. Information about historic homes, buildings, museums and neighborhoods is included in this book in the Attractions and Neighborhoods chapters.

Several of the following organizations play a major role in historic preservation in the metropolitan area. The Valentine Museum, the Museum of the Confederacy, the Virginia Historical Society and other museums and cultural institutions in the area are also actively involved with preservation activities and outreach programs. There are also numerous neighborhood associations that establish and maintain historic districts to help preserve the architectural value and integrity of their property.

Organizations

HISTORIC RICHMOND FOUNDATION
2407 E. Grace St.   **643-7407**

The Historic Richmond Foundation was founded in 1956 by the Association for the Preservation of Virginia Antiquities (APVA) to purchase, restore and interest people in saving old buildings. Initial efforts focused on restoring the block of Church Hill around St. John's Church. The Foundation provides educational services and assistance to people who want to establish historic districts and purchases historic property either to save it from destruction or to demonstrate the value of restoration and preservation. Several years ago, Historic Richmond Foundation merged with Richmond on the James and expanded its activities to include heritage tourism programs and tours. In 1993 the Foundation sponsored the first Races at Marengo at historic Marengo estate in New Kent County. The steeple chase races are held each spring. Proceeds benefit the Foundation.

ASSOCIATION FOR THE PRESERVATION OF VIRGINIA ANTIQUITIES
William Byrd Branch
2300 E. Grace St.   **648-1889**

This is the local branch of the statewide preservation organization. APVA owns major historic landmarks and maintains them over a long period of time. Call for information about properties or tours.

CHESTERFIELD COUNTY HISTORICAL SOCIETY
Old Chesterfield County Courthouse
10011 Ironbridge Rd.   **748-1026**

Formed in 1981, the Chesterfield County Historical Society operates four historic sites at Chesterfield Courthouse, Museum, Old Jail and Magnolia Grange. It also sponsors Plantation Day in May. The society has about 1,000 members and was recently involved in an archaeological dig at Magnolia Grange. They discovered a kitchen, slave quarters, a smoke house and a well house. The well house was reconstructed, and the others were outlined. Society members also have recorded gravestone inscriptions in remote county cemeteries and helped save some earthworks from a residential development. The earthworks were later established as a focal point of a public park. The society has a genealogy committee, a photography collection and a research library at the Courthouse that are open to the public. Members publish a biannual brochure about the history of the county. The county owns the buildings maintained and operated by the Historical Society.

VIRGINIA DEPARTMENT
OF HISTORIC RESOURCES

221 Governor St. 786-3143

This state agency administers state and federal regulations for historic preservation and maintains archives of 60,000 historic properties throughout the state including historic districts, individual property and archaeological sites. Anyone interested in looking at the files should call first for an appointment. This department also has a curatorial laboratory and archives collections from sites throughout the state. The staff provides assistance to schools, libraries and museums interested in historic preservation. They also assist people with the establishment of state and federal historic districts and landmarks.

RICHMOND COMMISSION
OF ARCHITECTURAL REVIEW

Dept. of Community Development
City Hall, Rm. 510
900 E. Broad St. 780-6335

This eight-member commission is appointed by City Council to review exterior changes within the city's 45 old and historic districts including Shockoe Slip, Shockoe Bottom, St. John's Church and Jackson Ward. Four of the members are selected based on recommendations by the local chapter of the American Institute of Architects, the Historic Richmond Foundation, the Association for the Preservation of Virginia Antiquities and the Richmond Association of Realtors. The other members are appointed at-large from the community. Members serve for five years and may be reappointed once. Questions and inquiries should be directed to the Secretary of the Commission at the above-listed address or telephone number.

HANOVER HISTORICAL SOCIETY

Ann Cross 746 2377
P.O. Box 91
Hanover 23069 746-1733

Hanover County's Historical Society has an office and resource center at the Old Jail in Hanover Courthouse on the Green. The society collects historical information and objects related to Hanover County. It published *Old Homes of Hanover County* in 1983 as an outgrowth of a bicentennial project, and recently published another book, *Hanover County, Virginia: A Retrospective*, that documents the history of Hanover County through local newspaper articles. *A Sketch of the Early History of Hanover County,* also published by the society, documents Hanover County's contributions to the American Revolution. The society has about 300 members.

Cruise the James River on the *Annabel Lee.*

HANOVER HISTORICAL COMMISSION
Mike Fiore, Chairman
c/o Resource International
6160 Kings Charter Dr.
Ashland 23005   550-9201

The Hanover Historical Commission was established by the Board of Supervisors in 1988 as a resource committee for the board on historical information. In recent years, the commission established a tourism committee to develop ways to promote historic attractions in the county, and a preservation policy committee. It also established a land use and zoning committee to review proposed developments for their impact on historic sites and to advise the planning commission and the board of supervisors. A continuing education committee helps inform citizens about county history.

A few years ago, the commission obtained two matching grants from the state to do an historic architectural survey of 950 parcels in the county; it raised half of the county's matching funds. The survey included old homes, hotels, railroads, cemeteries and other historical sites. The results are used as an information resource and planning tool. A complete map set with an inventory of sites is under development.

The commission functions as an umbrella group for all county historic groups and related organizations. The Board of Supervisors appoints representatives for each of the county's districts. Members serve for one year and refer their opinions to the County Architectural Review Board.

HENRICO COUNTY HISTORIC PRESERVATION ADVISORY COMMITTEE
History and Historic Preservation Program
Human Services Building
Dixon Powers Dr.   672-5106

Established in 1990, this advisory committee is involved in updating the inventory of county historic sites. The History and Historic Preservation Program staff serves as support to the committee and oversees Meadow Farm, its archives, library and collections. The committee serves as a liaison between the County Board of Supervisors and citizens and consults with and advises the county manager, the director of recreation and parks and the board of supervisors to identify, interpret, rehabilitate, protect and preserve historic and cultural resources in Henrico County. Committee members serve one year and are appointed by the board of supervisors from each magisterial district. There is also a Henrico County Historical Society. For more information call 795-5781.

Inside
Monuments

Richmond is known as the City of Monuments, so naturally when people come here they want to see the parade of memorials to Confederate heroes on historic Monument Avenue.

With its tree-lined streets, beautifully landscaped mansions and parklike medians, Monument Avenue is one of the most beautiful streets in the world. From Allen to Belmont avenues, the intersections are studded with monuments to General Robert E. Lee, Confederate President Jefferson Davis, Commander Matthew Fontaine Maury and Generals Thomas J. "Stonewall" Jackson and James Ewell Brown "J.E.B." Stuart.

Their size and the fact that these magnificent monuments to Confederate heroes exist at all is intriguing. Where else in the world can you find such a collection of memorials to vanquished military leaders in the same country that defeated them? Their height and grandeur gives them an almost deity-like aura, reflecting the pride and respect Southerners had for these military strategists and the Southern ideals and values that they epitomized. They are also recognized as excellent examples of public sculpture.

Around the turn of the century, hundreds of people pulled wagons carrying the statues to their present sites. Each un-

Credit: Richmond Newspapers

The J.E.B. Stuart monument is one of the many famous sculptures on historic Monument Avenue.

veiling ceremony was preceded by a large parade with thousands of Confederate soldiers.

As much as they are a source of pride, the monuments have also been a source of controversy ever since the decision was made to place the first monument, the one to General Robert E. Lee, in the middle of a cow pasture in 1890.

Many residents were unhappy about the decision to place the statue of Lee outside the city limits on donated pasture land, instead of in Hollywood Cemetery, Capitol Square or another more distinguished area of the city. Imagine how strange it must have been to see the magnificent statue of General Lee guarding an open field in the middle of nowhere.

Even the design of the monument had to be altered because the Governor thought it should be at least as high as the monument to George Washington in Capitol Square.

But not everyone was in favor of the monuments. The *Richmond Planet* owner and editor, Councilman John Mitchell, Jr., an African-American, argued in council and through editorials published by the paper against city appropriations for the monument's unveiling. On the day of the unveiling, the paper said the whole proceeding handed down a "legacy of treason and blood."

The monument was also controversial in the North where the idea of a monument to a Confederate general created both positive and negative reactions. One Northern newspaper urged Congress to forbid the erection of any more monuments to Confederate heroes and the display of the Confederate flag. Another compared Lee to Benedict Arnold.

Controversy over location continued a few years later in 1894, when the Confederate Soldiers and Sailors Monument

was set on Libby Hill instead of at a preferred Monument Avenue site. Organizers were told that Monument Avenue was "for generals and other important heroes."

In keeping with that concept, the monument to Confederate President Jefferson Davis was erected on Monument Avenue instead of at a site in Monroe Park that had been selected by Mrs. Davis. The Monument Avenue site also provided a better vista for the monument and further encouraged residential development along Monument Avenue.

Ideas for other monuments have come and gone through the years, including one of a Confederate nurse by Salvador Dali, but none has been located on Monument Avenue since the monument to Commander Matthew Fontaine Maury was erected in 1929.

In recent years, the Richmond City Council considered a proposal to honor civil rights leaders from Richmond and Governor Doug Wilder, the first black governor in the nation, with memorials on Monument Avenue. The idea caused quite a stir among Richmonders and left them divided on local radio talk shows over who should be honored and where their statues should be located.

If you have trouble understanding all the passion and politics surrounding these bronze and stone sculptures, keep in mind the strong bonds that have traditionally linked generations of Southerners — their almost religious sense of pride in the past and the fact that building monuments was the preferred way to honor heroes then, as it still is today — at least to some people. They were also produced in an era when artists and craftsmen were readily available to design and create them.

In addition to those on Monument Avenue, you'll find more than 40 other statues and monuments in streets, parks and cemeteries throughout the Richmond area. Numerous stone markers tell stories of battles won and lost and other important happenings on or near Richmond soil.

Following are a few descriptions and stories. If you're interested in learning more about them, we suggest that you start with a guided bus, trolley or walking tour. (See our Getting Around and Attractions sections for more information on these tours.) You may also want to read about the development of the Lost Cause in Charles Wilson's *Baptized in Blood* and Gaines Foster's *Ghosts of the Civil War*, which explains the stages of monument building in the South after the Civil War.

Monument Avenue

ALLEN TO BELMONT AVENUES

Monument Avenue is famous for its parade of monuments to Confederate heroes including General Robert E. Lee, Commander Matthew Fontaine Maury, Confederate President Jefferson Davis and Generals Thomas J. "Stonewall" Jackson and James Ewell Brown "J.E.B." Stuart. All of the monuments are in the middle of intersections, aligned with the center of the parklike medians that divide the avenue. Since Monument Avenue is a busy street, the best way to see the memorials is to park and walk.

ROBERT E. LEE
Allen and Monument Aves.

This monument to Confederate General Robert E. Lee shows Lee on horseback gazing south. Lee's horse, Traveller, was not used for the monument because his appearance was not grand enough. The monument cost $77,000,

which was raised through the efforts of the Hollywood Memorial Association and the Lee Monument Association.

After much competition over where to put the statue — Hollywood Cemetery, Libby Hill, Capitol Square, Monroe Park or Gamble's Hill — it was finally decided that it should be located on donated land at the edge of the city. People weren't happy about putting it outside the city limits in a cow pasture. Until the early 1900s there were only a few buildings on the new Monument Avenue, but eventually, the city grew up around the monuments.

At the request of the governor, French sculptor Jean Antonin Mercie had to alter the design of the Lee Monument so that it was "not one inch lower" than the statue of George Washington in Capitol Square. The 21-foot-high bronze equestrian figure is mounted on a 40-foot-tall granite pedestal, flanked by two grey marble columns.

When it was erected in 1890, wagons carrying the statue were pulled to the site by hundreds of citizens. The unveiling was preceded by a parade that included 50 Confederate generals, 15,000 Confederate veterans and 10,000 citizens.

The bronze figure of Lee's horse also served for many years as a very active beehive that produced more than a ton of honey. In the spring, you could see clouds of bees swarming out of the horse's mouth.

MATTHEW FONTAINE MAURY
Belmont and Monument Aves.

Commander Maury, "the Pathfinder of the Seas," invented the explosive torpedo that wrecked more Northern vessels than any other cause. Erected in 1929, this William F. Sievers creation is an eight-foot-high seated bronze figure of

Maury atop a five-foot granite pedestal arranged in front of an 18-foot-high base that supports a nine-foot-wide bronze globe. At the base of the globe is a depiction of figures tossed by swirling waves, an allegorical tribute to Maury's study of ocean winds and currents. Of all Sievers monuments, this and the Jackson Monument are his favorites.

J.E.B. STUART
Stuart (Lombardy St.) and Monument Ave.

The Stuart Monument and the Davis Monument were unveiled almost simultaneously in 1907, part of a week-long Confederate reunion attended by about 18,000 veterans. It was not unusual for these ceremonies to receive the entire front page of the newspaper and for 15 or more additional pages to be devoted to related activities and personalities. Quite a ladies' man, the dashing cavalryman is portrayed astride his high-stepping horse with a jaunty plume in his hat. Created by sculptor Fred Moynihan, the approximately 15-foot-tall bronze figure sits atop a 7½-foot granite pedestal.

JEFFERSON DAVIS
Davis and Monument Aves.

Erected in 1907 during the same week the Stuart Monument was unveiled, this monument to Confederate President Jefferson Davis was originally planned for a site in Monroe Park selected by Mrs. Davis — the cornerstone had been placed there but was later moved to Monument Avenue. The monument was designed by William C. Noland and executed by Edward V. Valentine. A 7½-foot-high bronze figure atop a 12-foot granite pedestal stands in front of another bronze figure, Vindicatrix — an allegorical figure of the South — that is mounted on a 67-foot column. The grouping is encircled by a colonnade of 13 Doric columns.

STONEWALL JACKSON
Boulevard and Monument Ave.

The story goes that the Confederate veterans in the nearby Old Soldiers Home insisted that since Lee faced the South, Gen. Thomas J. "Stonewall" Jackson should face the North into the eye of the foe. Hence the expression that he faces "defiantly North." The unveiling of this statue in 1919 was preceded by a parade that included hundreds of Jackson's old soldiers. Designed by William F. Sievers, the 17½-foot-tall bronze equestrian figure is mounted on a 20½-foot granite pedestal.

A.P. HILL
Laburnum Ave. and Hermitage Rd.

Erected by the efforts of Pegram's Battalion, this monument to Confederate Gen. A. P. Hill was unveiled on Memorial Day, 1892, following an elaborate parade and ceremony. Hill's body was removed later from Hollywood Cemetery and placed under the monument. Created by William Ludwell Sheppard, the 9½-foot-high standing figure is mounted on a 24½-foot pedestal. Land for the monument was donated by Major Lewis Ginter.

BOJANGLES
W. Leigh and Price Sts. and Chamberlayne Pkwy.

Bill "Bojangles" Robinson was a famous black tap dancer from Richmond who starred in Broadway productions and motion pictures. His "dance on the stairs" was unique, and he was once named the "outstanding stage and screen star of the year." Erected in 1973, through the efforts of the Astoria Beneficial Club, this was the first monument in Richmond to honor a black citizen. The triangular park where it stands was renamed the Bill "Bojangles" Robinson Square. Robinson paid for a traffic light at the intersection where his statue now stands because there were so many accidents there. Once a millionaire, he gave generously to charities, but when he died there wasn't enough to pay his debts. Created by John Temple Witt, the nine-foot-tall aluminum figure of Bojangles dancing down a flight of steps stands on a six-foot-high black marble pedestal.

Capitol Square

There are many monuments in Capitol Square. Among them are:

Harry F. Byrd — Senator Byrd was a United States Senator and Governor of Virginia. Known for his "pay as you go policies," he is depicted carrying the budget in his left hand.

Stonewall Jackson — This statue was commissioned by a group of the Confederate General's admirers shortly after his death. The state paid for the pedestal and the cost to have it erected.

Dr. Hunter Holmes McGuire — Dr. McGuire was President of the American Medical and American Surgical associations and founder of the University College of Medicine, which later became the Medical College of Virginia.

George Washington — Thomas Crawford's equestrian statue of George Washington was unveiled on the first president's birthday in 1850. It was hauled from lower Main Street by thousands of people. Although art critics hold different opinions about the quality of Crawford's Washington, they rave over the marble statue of Washington by Jean Antoine Houdon inside the Capitol. Many regard it as the most priceless piece of marble in the United States and Virginia's greatest treasure.

Other Monuments in Parks, Cemeteries and Streets

CHRISTOPHER COLUMBUS
Byrd Park, at the south end of the Boulevard

Created by Ferruccio Legnaioli in 1927, this was the first Columbus statue in the South and the first monument in Richmond that was illuminated at night. The statue was sculpted, erected and financed entirely by Virginians of Italian birth.

CONFEDERATE SOLDIERS MONUMENT
Oakwood Cemetery, east of the Oakwood Ave. entrance

Erected in 1871 by the Oakwood Memorial Association, this granite obelisk on a seven-tiered pyramid-shaped base honors the 16,000 Confederate soldiers buried in Oakwood Cemetery.

CONFEDERATE SOLDIERS AND SAILORS
Libby Park at 29th St. and Libby Ter.

Created in 1894 by William Ludwell Sheppard, this bronze figure depicts a Confederate soldier standing atop a 73-

Some parents used to tell their children that Gen. Lee and Traveller came down from the monument at night so Traveller could have a drink of water and something to eat.

Insiders' Tips

foot granite column made of 13 stone cylinders representing the 13 Confederate states. The granite column is topped by an ornate Corinthian capitol. The stone used in the monument came from granite quarries on the southside of the James River. This monument was denied placement on Monument Avenue, a memorial site reserved "for generals and other important heroes."

HOWITZERS
Harrison St. at Park and Grove Aves.

Created in 1892 by William Ludwell Sheppard, a former officer in the Howitzers, this monument near the west edge of Virginia Commonwealth University, depicts a young artilleryman, "Number One," standing at the piece. The memorial to the cannoneers was sponsored by the Howitzer Association.

LIGHT INFANTRY BLUES
6th Street Plaza, 500 block of N. Sixth St.

Erected in 1978 between the Coliseum and 6th Street Marketplace, this 10-foot-high bronze figure depicts a soldier wearing the Blues' uniform with shako hat and feather plume. He is standing at parade rest, holding a 1903 Springfield rifle. Light Infantry Blues is a memorial to the National Guard unit of the same name, founded in 1789.

MEMORY, VIRGINIA WAR MEMORIAL
Virginia War Memorial, U.S. I at the north end of the Robert E. Lee Bridge
Open daily 7 AM to 10 PM

Memory, a statue honoring Virginian motherhood, is part of the Hall of Memory in the Virginia World War II, Korean and Vietnam War Memorial

perched on a bluff high above the James River. Created by Leo Friedlander in 1956, the 22-foot-high figure of a woman was carved from four blocks of Georgia marble. She symbolizes Virginian women gazing at the names of more than 11,000 Virginian soldiers who died during the wars engraved on the inside walls of the Shrine of Memory. A gas-fed torch of liberty burns at the base of the statue symbolizing the never-say-die spirit of patriotism. The shrine is a temple-like structure with a wall of columns on one side. Soil samples from American military cemeteries and memorabilia from 200 battlegrounds and battle seas where Americans fought are embedded in the floor. Many civic groups use a meeting hall that's located here.

CARILLON, DOGWOOD DELL
1300 Blanton Ave., Byrd Park

The Carillon is a 240-foot-high bell tower that pays tribute to Virginians who died in World War I. The first-floor gallery is often used for art exhibits, and the tower is sometimes used for climbing and rappelling demonstrations.

JAMES NETHERWOOD
Oakwood Cemetery, north of the Oakwood Ave. entrance

This is a late 1890s self portrait of James Netherwood, a local stone carver. He is depicted with his hat, a worn apron, his carving tools and a stack of granite blocks. The nine-foot-tall granite figure stands above a 20-foot grey marble column reportedly rejected for the Lee monument. A four-foot-high granite figure of Netherwood's wife, Nancy, is also in the plot.

Inside
The Arts

Richmond's lively music, arts and theater scene covers a full calendar of symphony, pops, ballet, opera, stage, street festivals, outdoor concerts, gallery openings and a week-long summer musicfest.

Like everything else in Richmond, the city's beginnings as an arts and cultural center didn't happen just yesterday. The city's first theater was built in 1786, and by the mid 1800s the stature of Richmond as a theatrical mecca was matched by only three other cities in the nation. It was during this period that Richmond audiences saw 24 English plays presented for the first time in America. The internationally famous actor Julius Brutus Booth made his U.S. debut here in 1821.

Thomas Sully, the portrait painter, lived and worked in Richmond from 1799 to 1806. The sculpture and painting talents of Edward V. Valentine and William L. Sheppard flourished here in the late 1800s. And Richmond has been the home of great writers.

One of the interesting footnotes to the city's cultural history is that Allan Hirsh, who grew up in the 800 block of W. Franklin Street, was the composer of the "Boola Boola" song of Yale University.

Today Richmond is the home of the South's preeminent museum, the Virginia Museum of Fine Arts, and of the internationally traveled Shanghai Quartet. Formed in Shanghai in 1982, the quartet has made its base here with the renowned music department at the University of Richmond since 1988.

To keep up with everything that's going on in Richmond's arts and cultural world you'll have to become an avid reader of the daily and weekend pages of the *Richmond Times-Dispatch* and of the weekly compendium of events published every Tuesday by *Style Weekly*.

Also, for scheduling information on fine arts and cultural events you can call Artsline, a 24-hour service of WCVE-FM. The phone number is 345-ARTS.

Here are highlights of some of the city's arts organizations and events.

ARTS COUNCIL OF RICHMOND
1435 W. Main St.   355-7200

The Arts Council of Richmond is a nonprofit organization dedicated to the support, promotion and encouragement of the arts in the metropolitan area. It publishes *Arts Notes*, *Arts Spectrum* (a directory of arts and culture in metropolitan Richmond) and a *Visiting Artists Directory*. The Arts Council is a great resource, and it is the local focal point of the nationwide Business Volunteers for the Arts program. The organization raises its own funds and sponsors exhibitions, the Run for the Arts, the Visiting Artists Program, the Children's Book Festival every spring, a pacesetting Partners in the

Arts arts-education collaborative in public schools, plus an annual two-day cultural event for children.

This latter event, the Richmond Children's Festival, is built each year around a different international cultural theme. This fall festival is held in Byrd Park. Singing, dancing, play areas, hands-on art and activities and special performances all combine to make this a great occasion for the young and young at heart.

DOWNTOWN PRESENTS. . .

550 E. Marshall St., Ste. 202   643-2826

This nonprofit organization sponsors and cosponsors a wide variety of festivals and events, primarily in the downtown area. Included are Easter on Parade, Friday Cheers, The Big Gig, the New Year's Eve celebration in Festival Park and the 2-Street Festival.

JUNE JUBILEE

June Jubilee is one of Greater Richmond's oldest and most popular arts and music festivals. Launched in the late 1970s by the Arts Council of Richmond, it now is coordinated by Downtown Presents in collaboration with local cultural and civic organizations. The outdoor festival, on a weekend in early June, draws thousands to events at Valentine Riverside, in Festival Park and in Shockoe Bottom. Local talent is in the spotlight in this celebration of the city, the summer and the arts. There's a potpourri of activities for everyone.

Where to Find the Performing Arts

You'll find the performing arts in downtown piazzas, in theaters, restaurants, clubs, concert halls and muse-ums scattered throughout the metropolitan area, at Dogwood Dell (a small-scale version of Wolf Trap near The Carillon in Byrd Park), at the Coliseum (a big-time gathering place for rock, rap and pop fans; call 780-4956 for information on upcoming concerts), at the Flood Zone (Richmond's premiere rock club; call 643-6006 for concert schedules) and at these three big-audience venues:

CARPENTER CENTER
FOR THE PERFORMING ARTS

525 E. Grace St.   782-3900

Almost $6 million was raised by the general public, business and foundations to renovate the old Loew's Theatre for this 2,060-seat performing arts center. Originally opened in 1928, it is an architectural classic of movie palace design, with an interior simulating a Mediterranean courtyard with starlit sky overhead. Symphony, opera and Broadway shows all play here, and it's a popular place for corporate annual meetings. The center is at the Grace Street entrance of Sixth Street Marketplace, and parking is available in decks nearby on Grace Street, Sixth Street and in other parking decks within a several-block radius.

CLASSIC AMPHITHEATRE ON
STRAWBERRY HILL

600 E. Laburnum Ave.   228-3213

This $2.3 million, 10,000-seat outdoor amphitheater at the State Fairgrounds at Strawberry Hill opened in 1992. Its season runs from April to October with country, rock and pop shows. Concerts have included those by Jimmy Buffett and Travis Tritt, Crosby, Stills & Nash, the Indigo Girls, Dolly Parton, Tina Turner, John Denver and Peter, Paul & Mary.

THE MOSQUE

6 N. Laurel St.   *780-4213*

This 3,667-seat theater dates back to 1927 when the opulent Near Eastern-style structure was built for use originally by Shriners. It has been known as the Mosque (although a name change is being considered as this book goes to press) and owned by the city since 1939. It is the home of the 10th oldest Wurlitzer organ in the United States, and its decor includes five Oriental murals and tiles imported from Spain, Italy and Tunis. It is here that you will find performances by national touring companies and orchestras, the annual sellout performances of *The Nutcracker*, plus a wide range of other major events like Garrison Keillor's "American Radio Hour" when it originates from Richmond. The Mosque is in the VCU area at the corner of W. Main and Laurel streets, and there is a parking deck across the street.

Theater

Greater Richmond's professional-level theater companies stage about 70 shows a year. In addition, there are lots of community theater groups. Theater companies include:

THEATREVIRGINIA

Boulevard and Grove Ave.   *367-0840*

Virginia's flagship professional theater, TheatreVirginia, performs in a 535-seat theater complex within the Virginia Museum of Fine Arts. It is a full member of the League of Resident Theatres and achieved Equity status in 1972. It produces a series of plays in a season that runs from September through June, with each play running for about a one-month period. Productions range from the classics to the contemporary. Subscription packages (including a Flex-Pak that allows theatergoers to pick any three shows they wish from a season) and individual-performance tickets are available. Dinner is available before the show in the Members Suite for members of the Virginia Museum and for season ticket holders. A statewide play-writing competition, New Voices for the Theatre, is sponsored by TheatreVirginia and is open to Virginia students in grades five through 12.

THEATRE IV

114 W. Broad St.   *783-1688*

Theatre IV is based in a two-stage complex at the magnificently renovated Empire Theatre. It offers a Broadway Series as well as a Family Playhouse (children's) and a Theatre Gym series of innovative works produced by invited artists. Its children's touring theater is the second largest in the nation and reaches an audience of nearly 720,000 in 26 states. In 1991 it staged the world premiere of Richmond-written and produced *Four Part Harmony*, a musical based on the true Vietnam experiences of American aviators including Richmonder Paul Galanti, who spent seven years in the Hanoi Hilton, and his wife Phyllis, who helped spearhead the national campaign to bring the American POWs home.

BARKSDALE THEATRE
AT HANOVER TAVERN

Hanover Courthouse, U.S. 301 N.   *559-4804*

The Barksdale is the Richmond area's oldest not-for-profit theater. It is housed in an 18th-century tavern where Patrick Henry once tended bar and where George Washington and Thomas Jefferson stopped during their many travels through the area. The theater presents a mix of musicals, comedy and dramatic performances. The theater seats 199 persons and is open throughout the year. The Barksdale was founded as America's first dinner theater. Dinner is still available, but is optional.

SWIFT CREEK MILL PLAYHOUSE
U.S. 1, Colonial Heights   748-5203

Housed in a 350-year-old grist mill, Swift Creek Mill Playhouse offers a range of fare and does an excellent job with musical comedies. It can be reached directly via U.S. 1 or via I-95 south. The Playhouse is open year around and has been popular with Richmond theatergoers for many years. Tickets may be purchased for dinner and theater or for the theater only. It also offers a daytime theater series for children.

RICHMOND ART THEATRE
359-3357

Performing at the University of Richmond or at Steward School, the Richmond Art Theatre season includes classic and contemporary plays and an annual Shakespeare Festival.

THEATRE VCU
10 N. Brunswick St., Box Office   367-1514

This is the theater company of Virginia Commonwealth University that offers undergraduate and graduate programs in theater. Theatre VCU showcases student and faculty work and annually offers four faculty-directed mainstage productions plus "thesis" productions that are usually student-directed. Performances are in the Shafer Street Playhouse and in the Raymond Hodges Theatre on the VCU Fan District campus.

THE UNIVERSITY PLAYERS
University of Richmond   289-8263

Like Theatre VCU, the performances of The University Players at the University of Richmond add spice and innovation to the city's theater season. The group is an arm of the university's theater department and presents a four-play season in the Camp Theatre at the Modlin Fine Arts Center at the University of Richmond.

NATIONAL TOURING COMPANIES
The Carpenter Center for the Performing Arts
Sixth and Grace Sts.   782-3900

The Carpenter Center is usually where you'll find national touring companies when they are in town. If this 2,000-seat theater isn't big enough, then performances are scheduled at The Mosque with its 3,000-plus seats. Each season brings about 20 road shows to Richmond. Broadway offerings in recent years have included *Evita*, *Annie*, *Gypsy*, Robert Morse in his one-man play about Truman Capote called *Tru*, and *Les Miserables*. Most road shows are marketed and announced singly except for the "Broadway Under the Stars" series that has included revivals of *Camelot* with Robert Goulet and *Sound of Music* with Marie Osmond.

THE GILPIN STAGE COMPANY
114 W. Broad St.   321-1147

This nonprofit group, formed in 1989 under the protective wing of Theatre IV, has been going through some rough financial times. It focuses on African-American artists and performs at the 80-year-old Empire Theatre and Little Theatre, on W. Broad Street near Belvidere.

RICHMOND THEATRE COMPANY FOR CHILDREN
111 N. Sixth St.   644-3444

The Richmond Theatre Company for Children is a nonprofit touring troupe that puts on more than 1,800 performances a year before an audience of nearly 60,000 children in six mid-Atlantic states. It plays daycare centers, festivals and libraries primarily before audiences in the 3 to 8 age group. Occasional performances are open to the ticket-buying public in Richmond.

THEATRE & COMPANY
226-6485

Formed by actor-director Tony Cosby, the well-known Richmond portrayer of the Rev. Martin Luther King, Jr., this non-profit touring company has presented *King and The Movement*, a play about King, before audiences in Richmond, other Virginia cities and Washington, D.C.

THEATRE AT THE
BOLLING-HAXALL HOUSE
J I I E. Franklin St. 643-2847

This is the resident company of the Woman's Club at its Bolling-Haxall House on Franklin Street. It offers two plays a year with emphasis on drawing room comedy.

HENRICO THEATRE COMPANY
P.O. Box 27032
Richmond 23273 672-5115

The Henrico Theatre Company is a volunteer organization sponsored by the Henrico Division of Recreation and Parks. Auditions are open to any interested person. The group usually presents four major productions a year — Broadway revivals, comedies and an annual one-act showcase featuring winners of its play-writing contest — in the Belmont Park Recreation Center at 1600 Hilliard Road.

HENRICO TEEN THEATRE COMPANY
P.O. Box 27032
Richmond 23273 672-5115

Also sponsored by Henrico's Division

of Recreation and Parks, this group of young actors makes its home with other county-affiliated theater companies at the Belmont Park Recreation Center, 1600 Hilliard Road. One play is presented each summer.

RICHMOND DEPARTMENT OF
RECREATION AND PARKS
900 E. Broad St. 780-8137

Two plays and one musical are produced each summer in the Festival of Arts at Dogwood Dell in Byrd Park. Springtime productions include dinner-theater presentations at the Carillon in Byrd Park. Presentations are under the guidance of the department's production specialist.

RICHMOND COMMUNITY THEATRE
3003 Collins Rd. 225-8623

This touring black-experience theater was founded in 1975 by Richmond playwright Marguerite Austin, its artistic director. Plays are directed by the founder's daughter, Dawnamaria Johnson.

CHESTERFIELD THEATRE COMPANY
P.O. Box 206
Chester 23831 748-0698

This is the area's oldest community theater (formerly known as the John Rolfe Players), and it is headquartered in the John Rolfe Playhouse at Shiloh and Centralia roads in Chester. It puts on plays three times a year, in the fall, winter and spring. Performances are staged in school auditoriums in Chesterfield County.

CHAMBERLAYNE ACTORS THEATRE
319 N. Wilkinson Rd. 262-9760

An all-volunteer group, Chamberlayne Actors Theatre is affiliated with the North Chamberlayne Civic Association. All auditions are open, and all volunteers are expected to strive for professionalism in their work. The group is dedicated to producing wholesome family-type, light shows three times a year with nine performances of each show. Performances are in the 200-seat North Chamberlayne Civic Association building at 319 N. Wilkinson Road in Henrico County. Steering committee chairman is John Ambrose.

RANDOLPH-MACON DRAMA GUILD
Randolph-Macon College
Ashland   *752-4704*

This student-run theater group is affiliated with the college's fine arts department and performs on campus in the 150-seat Old Chapel Theatre. Three major productions are usually staged each year.

VIRGINIA UNION
UNIVERSITY PLAYERS
1500 N. Lombardy St.   *257-5861*

This theater group at Virginia Union University presents several plays a year, some in collaboration with the university's music department and with Theatre VCU. Its productions are presented at various locations.

RICHMOND NEIGHBORHOOD PLAYERS
P.O. Box 535
Richmond 23204   *342-0960*

A volunteer community theater group, Richmond Neighborhood Players performs a three-show season at the McVey Theater at St. Catherine's School.

RICHMOND TRIANGLE PLAYERS
2033 W. Broad St.   *346-8113*

Devoted to plays with gay and lesbian themes, this troupe stages its productions in a cabaret space at Fielden's, a late-night club at 2033 W. Broad Street.

MYSTERY CAFE
Holiday Inn Koger
1021 Koger Center Blvd.   *649-2583*

If you like audience-involving whodunits, then be sure to head to the Chesterfield Room in the Holiday Inn at the Koger Executive Conference Center. It is here that you will find Mystery Cafe, Richmond's first major commercial venture into murder-mystery theater.

Other Theater

Other local theater and performing arts groups include: **Applause Unlimited** (a puppet, clowning and novelty theater group formed by master puppeteer Terry Snyder and former Ringling Bros. and Barnum & Bailey circus clown Christopher Hydert, 264-0299); **Curtains-Up Theatre** (essentially an African-American theater company, but it doesn't limit its plays to the black experience, 329-1912); **Encore! Theatre** (largely University of Richmond theater alumni, 747-7028); **Jazz Actors Theatre**, 780-8740; **Firehouse Theatre Project** (a nonprofit troupe devoted to the Meisner acting technique, 784-0000); **St. Bart's Players** (at St. Bartholomew's Episcopal Church, 747-9486); **Richmond: Out of Stock** (satirical revues and an accent on the outrageous, 353-8386); **Theatre With Children for Children** (the performing arts arm of the Community School of the Performing Arts at VCU, 828-2772); and **Virginia Historical Theatre** (Virginia history, 323-6477). New groups forming as this Insiders' Guides edition went to press include **Shoestring Productions**, 648-2948, and **Richmond Chamber Theatre** and **Company of Fools**, for which telephone numbers were not immediately available.

The **Music and Fine Arts Ministry** of the West End Assembly of God stages a biblical extravaganza, *The Master's Plan*, during Holy Week at the Carpenter Center. More than 200 people perform in this volunteer undertaking.

Music

RICHMOND SYMPHONY
300 W. Franklin St.   *788-4717*

For classical music lovers, the Richmond Symphony is the biggest game in town. It offers four major series and a number of special programs, in the process offering just about every kind of great music anybody would want. Its Masterworks series hones in on the classics and brings the world's great soloists to the city. Its tremendously successful Champagne Pops series thrills audiences with favorites from Broadway, Hollywood, the realm of popular music and from the best-loved classics. For its All Star Pops series you'll find the Symphony teaming up with the likes of Peter Nero, the Preservation Hall Jazz Band, Dionne Warwick and Donald O'Connor. Its Double Exposure series, launched in 1991-92, is performed at the VCU Performing Arts Center and gives concert-goers an opportunity to meet and talk with featured soloists and performers. If you enjoy great music best when you can wear casual clothes and munch on free pizza, then

the Symphony's Kicked Back Classics performances at The Flood Zone are made just for you.

VIRGINIA OPERA
300 W. Franklin St.   *643-6004*

One of only two statewide opera companies in the United States and one of the nation's fastest-growing regional companies, the Virginia Opera presents a full season at the Carpenter Center for the Performing Arts each year, often playing to soldout houses. In a season that runs from October to March you'll find offerings that range from things like *Carmen* and *Tosca* to *Porgy & Bess*. In addition to traditional repertoire, the Virginia Opera is one of a handful of companies in the nation that explores new ground and brings brand new operas to its audiences.

VOCAL ARTS
ASSOCIATION/OPERA THEATRE
7333 Hermitage Rd.   *266-0548*

This group offers training and programs for area singers in opera, recitals, pageants and national auditions. Singers receive lessons, coaching and performance opportunities.

HENRICO COMMUNITY BAND
P.O. Box 27032
Richmond 23273   *672-5115*

The band room at Tuckahoe Middle School, 9000 Three Chopt Road, echoes with brass, woodwinds and percussion when this community ensemble of about 40 members strikes up for rehearsals on Thursday evenings. Its an all-volunteer group that has a lot of fun.

RICHMOND POPS
8909 Elm Rd.   *272-5141*

Directed by Frank Rowley, who at age 17 played under the direction of John Philip Sousa in a high school band, this is the only professional concert band in the area. It offers music from Broadway shows, opera, classical, swing and jazz. Outdoor performances in the style of the Boston Pops include those on July 4 at Innsbrook and on Easter Sunday at "Windsor" in Windsor Farms. It also performs with the Concert Ballet of Virginia. Rehearsals are held Tuesday nights at the Tuckahoe Presbyterian Church, 7000 Park Avenue.

RICHMOND CLASSICAL PLAYERS
903 Forest Ave.   *288-6065*

Specializing in string music from the Baroque to the contemporary, Richmond Classical Players performs at Trinity United Methodist Church.

RICHMOND CONCERT BAND
740-1654

This is a nonprofit, all-volunteer organization that encourages the appreciation of concert band music. No auditions are required. Rehearsals are held Tuesday nights at the Tabernacle Baptist Church. The band performs at Dogwood Dell, the State Fair and for special events.

HANOVER CONCERT BAND
Daytime 730-9146
Evenings 271-0647

This band meets Tuesday evenings at Enon Methodist Church and plays at community events including the Fourth of July celebration in Ashland.

RICHMOND PHILHARMONIC
5511 Staples Mill Rd., Ste. 103   *233-2864*

The Richmond Philharmonic presents four concerts a year and works to provide local musicians with an opportunity to develop and display their talents in concerts and chamber programs. Inquiries about membership are invited. Rehearsals are held Monday nights at Ginter Park Presbyterian Church, 3601 Seminary Avenue. The Chamber Ensembles of the Richmond Philharmonic (CHERP) plays at weddings, parties and business functions, and bookings may be arranged by calling Dr. Robert Wagenknecht at 748-1765.

THE BIG GIG
550 E. Marshall St., Ste. 202   *643-2826*

The Big Gig, Richmond's Summer Musicfest, is an annual two-week extravaganza consisting of more than 50 daytime and evening concerts held throughout the city. Sponsored by Downtown Presents and the Virginia Union University Department of Music, it is a celebration of music designed to appeal to a broad audience. It takes place in July, and most performances are held outdoors in casual settings such as historic gardens and city parks, inviting audiences to dress comfortably, to relax on blankets or in lawn chairs and to enjoy concerts by renowned musical artists. Performances range from those by jazz artists Charlie Byrd, Ahmad Jamal and George Shearing, to Mario Bauza's 20-piece Afro-Cuban Orchestra, with some Gilbert and Sullivan and classic Bach on the opposite spectrum. All but five concerts are free of charge. Its ticketed series, called Celebrity Spotlight, has offered performances by Tony Bennett, Ruth Brown and Bobby "Blue" Bland, Regina Belle, Emmylou Harris, country singer Kathy Mattea, flutist Herbie Mann and a Scottish concert with pipers and dancers.

FRIDAY CHEERS
Festival Park (downtown)   *643-2826*

Sponsored by Downtown Presents, Friday Cheers is a series of free Friday evening concerts featuring performances by local and regional pop groups in Festival Park between Sixth Street Marketplace and the Coliseum. The weekly outdoor concerts run from May through September. Refreshments are on sale, and the events draw enormous crowds of young people who come to socialize, listen to music and celebrate the workweek's end.

2 STREET FESTIVAL
Jackson Ward 643-2826

"2 Street," or Second Street north of Broad, once was the focal point of African-American business and nightlife in Richmond. It is now undergoing a rejuvenation, but the old days are recalled in the annual 2 Street Festival sponsored by Downtown Presents every fall. Music is important and, especially if you like jazz, this is the place to be.

JUMPIN'
The Virginia Museum
Boulevard and Grove Ave. 367-8148

This popular Thursday evening series in the Virginia Museum of Fine Arts' sculpture garden is a perennial summertime favorite and offers a broad range of music including Cajun, jazz, rhythm and blues and Caribbean. The event is as much social as it is musical, and tickets usually sell out well in advance of each week's event.

FAST/FORWARD
The Virginia Museum
Boulevard and Grove Ave. 367-8148

Presented by the Virginia Museum of Fine Arts, Fast/Forward offers performances by innovative dancers, choreographers and musicians. If you like the cutting-edge and the experimental, you'll find it in these performances that are staged at the museum from September through May.

WORLD MUSIC AND PERFORMANCE
The Virginia Museum
Boulevard and Grove Ave. 367-8148

Also at the Virginia Museum, this series includes four music and dance performances annually, usually with an ethnic theme.

MARY ANNE RENNOLDS CONCERTS AT VCU
VCU Performing Arts Center
922 Park Ave. 828-4019

Sponsored by the music department at Virginia Commonwealth University, the Mary Anne Rennolds Concerts bring to Richmond some of the world's finest chamber music. The series includes six concerts annually.

GELLMAN ROOM SERIES
101 E. Franklin St. 780-4740

This concert series, performed in the Gellman Room at the Richmond Public Library, is a fixture on the Richmond scene. Concerts are scheduled the second Saturday of each month from October through April.

INTERNATIONAL FOOD FESTIVAL
Richmond Centre
400 E. Marshall St. 783-7300

True, the spotlight here is on ethnic food and delicacies from all over the

Performances of *The Nutcracker* are an essential part of the December holiday season in Richmond.

world. But its also a good place to absorb a multi-cultural cornucopia of music, dance and other offerings from exotic locales. The event is usually held in September.

SHANGHAI QUARTET
AT UNIVERSITY OF RICHMOND
289-8277

Formed in Shanghai in 1982, this internationally-acclaimed quartet has been in residence at the University of Richmond since 1989. Its concerts, providing lovers of great music with a unique opportunity, are performed during the fall and winter months.

The renowned music department at the University of Richmond also offers a full season of other concerts, all free, featuring guest artists and a wide variety of music from September through April. The university's orchestra welcomes community participation.

RICHMOND
CLASSICAL GUITAR SOCIETY
741-6258, ext. 3460

Dedicated to promoting interest in classical guitar, this group offers concerts by local and national guitarists throughout the year.

RICHMOND JAZZ SOCIETY
P.O. Box 25723
Richmond 23260   *643-1972*

This nonprofit society, dedicated to the preservation and promotion of jazz, presents local and national jazz artists in concert. Meetings are held monthly and feature guest artists and speakers.

AFRICAN-AMERICAN
HERITAGE CHORALE
P.O. Box 25714
Richmond 23260   *783-0904*

This professional ensemble of 20 sing-

ers specializes in music by African-Americans although music by European composers is also included in its programs throughout the community.

RICHMOND SYMPHONY CHORUS
8413 Volanda Rd.   *270-6344*

This chorus, conducted by James Erb, performs with the Richmond Symphony and with the Richmond Ballet. Auditions are held periodically. Rehearsals are Tuesday evenings at Ginter Park Presbyterian Church, Walton and Seminary avenues.

THE VIRGINIANS
Gary Poehler weekdays at   *288-6993*

Formerly the Tobaccoland Chorus, this 110-member chorus is the Southern Division champion of the Mid-Atlantic District of the international Society for the Preservation and Encouragement of Barbershop Quartet Singing in America. The group gives a spring and two summer concerts in Dogwood Dell and performs in competitions and at conventions, benefits and private functions. Rehearsals are on Tuesdays at 7:15 PM at Derbyshire Baptist Church. New members are welcome.

SWEET ADALINES INTERNATIONAL
Greater Richmond   *282-7464*
Richmond Encore   *231-3158*
Prospective Rivah Crossings   *781-0186*

This women's group teaches and performs barbershop-style four-part harmony. There are three local chapters: the Greater Richmond Chapter, which rehearses Tuesday evenings; the Richmond Encore Chapter, which rehearses Thursday nights at 7809 Woodman Road; and the Prospective Rivah Crossings Chapter, which rehearses Thursday nights at the Hanover Auction House, 6220 Mechanicsville Turnpike.

RICHMOND CHORAL SOCIETY

Centenary United Methodist Church 264-3283

The 100-voice Richmond Choral Society was founded in 1946 to perform fine choral music. It presents three concert a year. A holiday concert is performed in December, a program of masterworks in early spring and a pops concert in the early summer.

VIRGINIA CHORAL ENSEMBLE

Cedar Street Memorial
Baptist Church 737-2380, 233-2841

This ensemble specializes in gospel music and is directed by Leroy Braxton. It tours the state and has recorded three albums.

THE VOLUNTEER CHOIR

P.O. Box 25793
Richmond 23260 353-7682

Directed by Larry Bland, this 100-voice chorus has recorded four albums. Its repertoire includes progressive gospel music, traditional spirituals, Broadway show tunes and popular songs. It rehearses Saturday nights at Second Baptist Church and sings at the 11 AM service every fourth Sunday and at community events including the Easter Parade on Monument Avenue. In the course of these performances, the chorus strives to promote better understanding among diverse groups and to encourage better race relations.

AMERICAN GUILD OF ORGANISTS

288-2867

The Guild's fall, winter and spring concerts, often including orchestra accompaniment, are performed in area churches.

OTHER MUSIC

Information on the concert seasons and on student-faculty-community orchestras and ensembles at local colleges and universities is available by calling the University of Richmond at 289-8277, Virginia Commonwealth University at 367-1166, Virginia Union University at 257-5665 and Randolph-Macon College at 752-4721.

Free summertime outdoor concerts include the Boulders Family Concert Series sponsored by the Chesterfield Parks and Recreation Department, 748-1623, at the Boulders office park; the Innsbrook After Hours Concert Series, 746-1007, in the Pavilion at W. Broad Street and Cox Road; the Life of Virginia Concerts on the Lawn at Brookfield, 281-6699; Musical Mondays at Maymont, 358-7166; and the Ukrop's Community Pride Cultural Series, 222-6484, at the Bill Robinson Playground. Also there are Tuesday Tunes in the plaza at Main Street Centre, Plaza Pizazz at Nations Bank Center and Jazz at the Riverside at Valentine Riverside.

Local churches also have active concert series beginning in the fall and running through the spring. Featuring local, regional and nationally known artists, they include St. James's Episcopal Church, 355-1779; River Road Baptist Church, 288-1131; St. Paul's Episcopal Church, 643-3589; and Second Presbyterian Church, 649-9148, which alternate as locations for noontime Midday Music concerts on Wednesdays; and Bon Air Presbyterian Church, 272-7514.

Other music groups in the Richmond area include:

Richmond Chamber Players	730-1448
Richmond Music Teachers Association	359-2100
Richmond Renaissance Singers	359-2475
Richmond Theological Center	
Consortium	359-5031
VCU Choral Arts Society	367-1166

Ballet and Dance

THE RICHMOND BALLET
614 N. Lombardy St.   *359-0906*

The Richmond Ballet is the state ballet of Virginia and is the Commonwealth's only professional ballet company. It produces a full Richmond season — including *The Nutcracker*, which plays every December to packed houses in an ever-expanding string of evening and matinee performances — and it tours throughout Virginia and the Southeast. The company's expansive repertoire includes works of some of the most influential choreographers of the 20th century, full-length classical ballets and exciting new works by some of today's brightest young choreographers. The School of the Richmond Ballet, the company's official training affiliate, provides instruction to more than 700 students. Classes in ballet, creative movement and jazz are offered to children, teens and adults.

THE CONCERT BALLET OF VIRGINIA
P.O. Box 25507
Richmond 23260   *780-1279*

The Concert Ballet of Virginia is a civic ballet company and is Richmond's oldest. It is based at the Bolling-Haxall House, 211 E. Franklin Street. It traditionally presents a fall program, a touring *Nutcracker*, a concert with the Richmond Pops and a spring performance. The dancers number about 65, including 30 members of a junior company. It also has an adjunct company, Concert Ballet Contemporary.

FAST/FORWARD
The Virginia Museum
Boulevard and Grove Ave.   *367-8148*

This "cutting-edge" music and dance series presented by the Virginia Museum's 20th-century art department usually includes two dance programs each year.

EZIBU MUNTU
AFRICAN DANCE CO., INC.
P.O. Box 62
Richmond 23201   *321-6417*

This ensemble of dancers and drummers celebrates the richness of many African cultures through dance, rhythm, rituals and song. The group tours and offers performances, workshops, classes, lectures and demonstrations.

VCU DEPARTMENT OF
DANCE AND CHOREOGRAPHY
1315 Floyd Ave.   *367-1842*

Virginia Commonwealth University's Department of Dance and Choreography annually stages a series of student/faculty dance programs and booked events, usually at the VCU Dance Center.

OTHER DANCE GROUPS

Some of the other local dance groups and organizations include the Anoush Armenian Dance Group (Ms. Armikhanian at 741-7533), the Scottish Country Dancers of Richmond (Mr. Fogg at 740-4404), Women of Selket (Middle Eastern, Linda Hollett at 264-1091), Israeli Dancers (Page Luxmore at 285-3151), the International Folk Dance Club (Linda Salter at 360-2630), Richmond Square and Round Dance Association (June Dvorak at 329-4704), U.S. Amateur Ballroom Dancers Association, Richmond Chapter (Debbie Hood at 276-2049), Richmond Swing Dance Society (Rob Clark at 262-0692), Traditional American Dance and Music Society (Catherine Farmer at 359-0497), Festival Folk Dance Club (Mary Jean Linn at 643-6707), Colonial Dance Club (Linda

Macdonald at 744-3264), Elegba Folklore Society (Janine Bell at 644-3900) and Virginia Bop (Ms. Beistel at 739-0229).

Museums and Galleries

THE VIRGINIA MUSEUM OF FINE ARTS

Boulevard at Grove Ave.   367-0844

When *Vanity Fair* wrote up the opening of the Virginia Museum's new 90,000-square-foot West Wing in the mid-1980s, the magazine's "Best Fetes" column noted the presence of pop artist Andy Warhol, writer Tom Wolfe and well-known artists such as Julian Schnabel, Richard Estes and George Segal. The event was covered by French, Italian, British, German and U.S. network television. All of this perhaps gives some indication of the reputation that has been attained by The Virginia Museum of Fine Arts. It is unexcelled in the South, and it is without question the star in Richmond's cultural crown. Its permanent collections range from the opulent art of the Czars and the works of old masters to one of the greatest assemblages of American 20th-century decorative art and the nation's finest collection of art of Tibet, Nepal and India. If you have even just a remote interest in art, the Virginia Museum should be number one on your list.

THE ANDERSON GALLERY

907½ W. Franklin St.   367-1522

The Anderson Gallery is the Museum of the Arts of Virginia Commonwealth University which has one of the largest art schools in the nation. The gallery is known here and abroad for exhibiting the work of nationally and internationally renowned artists, emerging figures and regional names. Its catalogs and publications are award-winners, it offers free lectures open to the public, and it has a most unusual museum store.

LORA ROBINS GALLERY

University of Richmond   289-8237

Displays here sparkle with gems, jewels, minerals, seashells and corals, fossils and cultural artifacts. Larger items include a 1,700-pound amethyst geode, a giant, man-eating clam shell from Australia's Great Barrier Reef, and a three-foot-high alabaster model of the Taj Mahal. The gallery, as its brochure says, is designed to "create an awareness, appreciation and understanding of the handicraft of nature." This it does, in room after room. The Lora Robins Gallery is a gem of a museum that has received too little attention for too long.

MARSH GALLERY

University of Richmond   289-8276

In faculty size and student enrollment, the University of Richmond's art department is small compared with VCU's, but the Marsh Gallery nevertheless takes very seriously its mission to show a wide range of significant art. Its exhibition program grows more ambitious every year and focuses, one at a time, on prominent artists.

ARTSPACE

6 E. Broad St.   782-8672

This nonprofit co-op gallery has evolved into a focal point for area art — especially figurative work and cosmic themes — that is both thoughtful and challenging. Most shows combine two or three artists whose works deal with similar themes.

EVELYN CHRISTIAN GALLERY

201½ N. Belmont Ave.   225-8900

This gallery serves corporations and interior designers from an exclusive stable of approximately 50 artists from throughout the country. Exhibitions feature gallery regulars as well as newcomers.

CUDAHY'S GALLERY
1314 E. Cary St.   *782-1776*

Cudahy's features three floors of paintings, prints and crafts. Most of the artists have Virginia roots, but the gallery often expands to include talent from the mid-Atlantic and southeastern parts of the nation. The gallery also operates a portrait service and exhibits samples of work by dozens of portrait painters who work on commission.

ELEGBA FOLKLORE SOCIETY CULTURAL CENTER
114 E. Franklin St.   *644-3900*

Photography and art exhibitions with an African-American perspective are featured here throughout the year.

ERIC SCHINDLER GALLERY
2305 E. Broad St.   *644-5005*

One of Richmond's oldest art enclaves, the Eric Schindler Gallery is in the historic district of Church Hill and carries an eclectic mixture of wares. Along with paintings by Parks Duffey of life in the Caribbean done in 1989 and work by other artists, you'll find 16th-century engravings, reproductions of 18th-century architectural prints, old books and even pieces of historic memorabilia.

GALLERY MAYO
5705 Grove Ave.   *288-2109*

This gallery specializes in 19th- and early 20th-century American art. It has a number of exhibitions each year. These sometimes are organized around a theme but often are a miscellany of the gallery's new acquisitions. Gallery Mayo is amid

The Shops on the Avenues at Libbie and Grove avenues in the West End.

MARTHA MABEY GALLERY
3433 W. Cary St.   *353-7053*

The Martha Mabey Gallery of contemporary art features paintings, original prints, sculpture and hand-painted furniture by local, regional and international artists. Folk art, modern Chinese paintings, portraits and watercolors are specialties.

REYNOLDS GALLERY
1514 W. Main St.   *355-6553*

Reynolds-Minor began as a small downtown gallery with shows combining major New York talents with mainstream artists from Washington and Virginia. Since moving to The Fan area, the two-floor space has become one of the city's most popular commercial galleries. It emphasizes works on paper by star artists and some of the area's most prominent talent.

1708 GALLERY
103 E. Broad St.   *643-7829*

This nonprofit contemporary art gallery is artist-owned. Perhaps the most "in" place to be on the Richmond art scene is at opening receptions here, which usually are held on the first Friday in the month. Community outreach includes "Art Pros" mentorships and "Gallery in the Schools." Volunteer involvement is welcomed.

LAST STOP GALLERY
1719 E. Main St.   *788-4540*

Located in Shockoe Bottom, this gallery has gradually reduced the complete attention it gave to African-American art and now is more multicultural in its offerings.

ARTS IN THE SQUARE

550 E. Grace St.   *648-8015*

In 6th Street Marketplace, this 8,700-square-foot art gallery and working studio houses local artists involved in a variety of media. Changing exhibitions are accompanied by a host of special events, workshops, programs for children and music and performing arts.

RENMARK & ASSOCIATES

18 W. Broad St.   *788-1644*

This gallery features fine antique prints from the 16th to the 19th century. Botanical, architectural, wildlife, sporting and landscape art is offered.

UPTOWN GALLERY

1305 W. Main St.   *353-8343*

Here you'll find the work of 30 artists who not only produce the art but staff the gallery. The group works in a diversity of styles and media including oil, acrylic, watercolor, pastel, pen and ink, charcoal, collage, stone, metal and clay. Art classes and workshops also are offered. Artist members of the gallery include well-known local names.

Other Galleries

Other commercial galleries include Very Richmond Galley at 316 N. 24th Street, Stepping Stone Gallery at 5707 Grove Avenue, Suitable for Framing at 5800 Grove Avenue, Barber Gallery at 5812½ Grove Avenue, Heidemann Gallery at 600 E. Main Street, RJS Gallery at 3218 W. Cary Street, Robinson's Unlimited Gallery at 212 W. Broad Street and Wentworth Gallery at Regency Square.

In addition, you'll find exhibitions in a variety of other places. These include shows by area art clubs and artists in the small gallery just off the main lobby of the Crestar Bank at 11th and Main streets, exhibitions by area photographers at the Richmond Camera Shop at 217 E. Grace Street, shows featuring area art and photography at the Jewish Community Center at 5403 Monument Avenue, exhibitions of folk art at the Meadow Farm Museum in Henrico County, exhibitions in the first- and second-floor galleries at the Richmond Public Library at 101 E. Franklin Street, and exhibitions by Virginia artists in the second-floor lobby of the NationsBank Center at 12th and Main streets, in the James Center I lobby at 901 E. Cary Street, in the lobbies of the WRIC-TV building in Arboretum Place, and occasionally at the Virginia Eye Institute on the north end of the Huguenot Bridge.

Art Associations

Art association include Bon Air Artists Association, 378-5859; Ginter Park Art League, 264-8536; Hanover Art League, 994-2993; James River Art League, 232-3100; Lee Artist Association, 769-2731; Metropolitan Artist Association, 346-9225; Richmond Artist Association, 353-5166; and Tuckahoe Art League, 288-3931.

Crafts

ARTS IN THE PARK

1112 Sunset Ave.   *353-8198*

Arts In The Park, held the first weekend in May in Byrd Park, is the largest outdoor arts and crafts show on the East Coast. The nationally rated arts show, now in its third decade, is sponsored by the Carillon Civic Association and draws artists and craft people from 38 states. Admission is free, and there is free parking at the nearby University of Richmond Stadium with free shuttle bus service to and from the stadium. More than 100,000 people turn out for the show each year. It is a must on any art lover's calendar.

THE HAND WORKSHOP/
VIRGINIA CENTER FOR THE CRAFT ARTS
1812 W. Main St. 353-0094

The Hand Workshop is a nonprofit center for the visual arts. Since 1962 it has offered art classes for children, teen-agers and adults and art exhibitions by prominent regional and national artists. The Hand Workshop also sponsors the annual Richmond Craft and Design Show, featuring selected artists from across the United States. Individual and household memberships are available and include discounts on activities. Classes and workshops cover a wide spectrum from pottery and metalworking to printmaking and sculpture. It has partnership programs with local public schools and offers scholarships to talented teens.

RICHMOND PRINTMAKING WORKSHOP
1529 W. Cary St. 355-4677

Since its opening in 1978, the Richmond Printmaking Workshop has had two goals: to support the making of contemporary art through the mediums of printmaking and papermaking and to provide the public with an opportunity to learn about and contribute to that art. Independent and nonprofit, the workshop is the only organization of its kind in Virginia open to the public. The workshop has 1,700 square feet of studio space and facilities for etching, monoprinting, relief printing, lithography and papermaking. It offers classes and lectures in printmaking, papermaking and the book arts and provides studio facilities at affordable rates for independent work. Limited edition portfolios

by outstanding Virginia artists are published and visiting artists from around the country give lectures, demonstrations and classes. Memberships are available in several categories for an annual fee.

. . . BUT IS IT ART?
3026 W. Cary St. 278-9112

A group of fairly young craft artists has opened this gallery as a cooperative effort. A suite of small rooms displays their works.

GERRI'S CRAFTS
6th Street Marketplace 775-2288

Handcrafted offerings here include cross-stitch and wooden items, wreaths and dolls. Parking deck tickets are validated with a minimum purchase.

GLASS MARKET
107 N. 17th St. 788-1498

Here you'll find a gallery of stained-glass art as well as all of the stained glass supplies and tools you'll need if you want to do it yourself.

GLASS REUNIONS
1307 E. Cary St. 643-3233

This craft shop is in Shockoe Slip. It is Richmond's premier craft gallery specializing in blown and stained glass.

GLASS BOAT, LTD.
3220 W. Cary St. 358-5596

This place calls itself "a zastic storfluzen" of home accessories, gifts, clothing items and sterling silver jewelry. With a description like this, who could resist taking a look at its wares?

ELEGBA FOLKLORE SOCIETY
114 E. Franklin St. 644-3900

Across the street from the Richmond Public Library and next door to the Linden Row Inn, this craft shop features a collection of contemporary artwork, hand crafts, original cards, and familiar and exotic gift items.

RICHARD STRAVITZ

2422 Grove Ave.   *353-0615*

Richard Stravitz is a sculptor and works in bronze. If you're looking for art for your home or office, or if you want to explore a commission, it will be well worth your time to see his work.

STS ORIGINALS

108 N. Sixth St.   *648-4657*

Here you'll find fine art greeting cards, original paintings, prints, sculpture, pottery, African and Indian imports, wearable art and calligraphic services.

There are more than 200 craft, hobby and special interest groups in the Richmond area ranging from the Needlepoint Guild and the Bonsai Society to the Richmond Craftsman's Guild and the Weavers Society. You can find a listing of many of these organizations in the "Discover Richmond" section published in a Sunday edition of the *Richmond Times-Dispatch* in early August. It is available for purchase separately at the front desk of the newspaper office at 333 E. Grace Street.

Writer's Groups

Richmond has a great literary heritage going back to the days of Edgar Allan Poe. While many Richmond writers prefer to work on their own, others find support and encouragement by becoming affiliated with various writers' groups and clubs. Some of these organizations include:

Virginia Writers Club	*358-0905*
National League of American	
Pen Women	*744-8229*
Virginia Romance Writers	*744-1447*

NEW VIRGINIA REVIEW, INC.

1306 E. Cary St.   *782-1043*

New Virginia Review is a statewide not-for-profit organization dedicated to encouraging writers and readers of contemporary literature in Virginia. Programs include a book and author tour, a writing contest, fellowship residencies for writers at the Virginia Center for Creative Arts, a newsletter and an annual anthology. Poetry, fiction and essays are eligible for consideration for publication in its *New Virginia Review* magazine, which is printed three times a year and is available in bookstores or by subscription.

Alternative Films

Some of the most thought-provoking and unusual films in town are shown at local universities. The Alternative Film Series at Virginia Commonwealth University presents movies in the Business School Auditorium and showings are open to the public for a $2 fee. Films at the University of Richmond are shown in the Adams Auditorium of the Boatwright Memorial Library and are free. All foreign-language films are shown with English subtitles. Schedules of upcoming films are available by calling Virginia Commonwealth University at 367-0100 or the University of Richmond at 289-8000.

Different Cinemas

BYRD THEATRE

2908 W. Cary St.   *353-9911*

Built in 1928, this is Richmond's last old-time movie palace, replete with an original Wurlitzer theater organ. Its specializes in good movies and 99¢ admissions specials. In 1985 it restored its stage and began producing annual Easter and

Christmas shows starring the Byrdette chorus line. The stage shows were reintroduced in 1992 after a several-year hiatus. The fall of 1992 also brought four jazz artists to the Byrd's stage in "Live at the Byrd: Fall Jazz Series."

CINEMA & DRAFT HOUSE
8809-C W. Broad St. 747-6300

This is the place to go if you want to munch and sip while you take in a movie.

A special on certain weekdays offers all-you-can-eat pizza.

GRACE ST. CINEMAS
812 W. Grace St. 257-0271

On W. Grace Street in the VCU area (and in the home of the old Biograph), this twin theater specializes in art films, documentaries and classics.

Credit: Metro Richmond Convention and Visitors Bureau

The gardens of Agecroft Hall, a 15th-century manor house that was moved from Lancashire England to save it from destruction.

Inside
Attractions and
Other Fun Things To Do

You'll find an abundance of historical attractions, architecture, plantations and battlefields in the Richmond area plus some dynamic family-oriented cultural centers, parks and museums. We also have a calendar that's packed with events and festivals.

The newest attraction is the **Valentine Riverside** history park and museum complex at Tredegar Ironworks on the James River beside the Kanawha Canal. Visitors can explore the development of Richmond during the last four centuries through exciting new exhibits, costumed interpreters and state of the art sight and sound technology. Valentine Riverside uses the site of the historic ironworks and restored turn-of-the-century machinery to bring to life the role of the river, industry and technology in the development of Richmond.

Although Richmond is probably best known for its Civil War battlefields and monuments to Confederate heroes on Monument Avenue, the city also played an important role in the Revolutionary War and Colonial times. It was at St. John's Church in Church Hill that Patrick Henry gave his famous liberty or death speech.

At our museums and cultural centers, children, as well as adults, will enjoy intriguing programs and hands-on exhibits, not just a lot of dusty artifacts. On special weekends, costumed interpreters and living history programs help bring Richmond's heritage to life.

There's something here for everyone. We've got walking tours, bus tours, trolley tours, aerial tours and horseback tours. You can stroll through beautiful parks and gardens or ride a world-class roller coaster at Paramount's Kings Dominion Theme Park. You can even go whitewater rafting down the James.

Locals who think they've seen it all may be surprised. Paramount's Kings Dominion has added new rides, shows and attractions; the Black History Museum and Cultural Center of Virginia has expanded; and the Virginia Historical Society has added new exhibit areas in the Center for Virginia History at Battle Abbey.

If you're here for a visit, we hope you'll enjoy our city as much as we do. If you're a resident and it's been a while since you explored the many attractions offered here, we hope you'll find time to take a fresh look.

To help you find your way around, this section provides information about shows, where to get tickets, Civil War attractions, museums, historic homes and buildings, black history attractions, riverfront attractions and tours. Information on the arts, sports and annual events is provided in separate chapters.

General Information

RICHMOND VISITORS CENTER
Robin Hood Rd. and the Boulevard
358-5511

This visitors center next to The Diamond offers souvenirs and literature on attractions in the area. You can also make reservations at area hotels and buy tickets for Paramount's Kings Dominion here. Children will enjoy playing on the train and the aviation exhibits at Travelland, just outside the center.

METROPOLITAN RICHMOND CONVENTION AND VISITORS BUREAU
6th Street Marketplace
550 E. Marshall St.   *782-2777*

You'll find lots of information and literature here about places to go and things to do in the area. If this location is not convenient for you, try the Visitors Center on Robin Hood Road. There's also a visitors center at the Richmond International Airport, 236-3260, and a toll-free number for Richmond area hotel reservations (800) 444-2777. Discounted rates for lodging are available for walk-in customers only.

BELL TOWER, VIRGINIA INFORMATION CENTER
Capitol Square, Ninth and Franklin Sts. 786-4484

Travel counselors at the Bell Tower will provide you with free information about attractions in the area and throughout the state.

METROPOLITAN RICHMOND CHAMBER OF COMMERCE
201 E. Franklin St.   *648-1234*

The Chamber of Commerce provides information and literature about the area for new residents. Call for more information.

Shows

There are quite a few theaters and several major entertainment centers in the area that offer a variety of shows, performances and concerts. We've provided a list of them as well as ticket outlets for your convenience. You'll find more information about the performing arts in our Arts chapter.

Barksdale Dinner Theatre	537-5333
Carpenter Center For the Performing Arts	782-3900
Richmond Ballet	359-0906
Richmond Coliseum (Upcoming Events)	780-4956
Richmond Mosque	780-4213
Richmond Symphony	788-1212
Strawberry Hill (State Fairgrounds) Classic Amphitheatre Concert Line	228-3213
Fairgrounds Calendar	228-3283
Horse Events	228-3238
Swift Creek Mill Playhouse	748-5203
Theatre IV	344-8040
Theatre VCU	367-6026
Theatre Virginia	367-0831
University of Richmond Theatre	289-8271
Virginia Opera	644-6004

Concert Information

WRXL Concert Line	345-1020
WVGO Concert Information	345-0106

Tickets

Civil War Attractions

An overview of Richmond and the Civil War is provided in a separate chapter of this book (see our Civil War chapter). We hope it will help you understand the significance of these attractions. Information about the monuments is also in a separate chapter (see our Monuments chapter).

There are self-guided tours through most of these attractions, but if you want the inside story and a thorough interpretation, we suggest you contact Richmond Discoveries, a tour company that specializes in Civil War tours. For a different perspective, you may want to try an aerial tour of the battlefields and entrenchments offered by Historic Air Tours of Williamsburg. Civil War theme tours are also provided by several other tour organizations. For more information see Tours in this section.

In addition to the following attractions, you may also wish to visit Hollywood Cemetery and Meadow Farm at Crump Park.

MUSEUM AND WHITE HOUSE OF THE CONFEDERACY

12th and E. Clay Sts.   649-1861

The world's largest collection of Confederate artifacts and documents is housed here. You'll be amazed at the collection of Confederate flags and Civil War weapons as well as the personal effects of military leaders. The museum also offers chronological exhibits documenting the history of the Civil War through battles, leaders and the roles of social groups.

A new exhibit, In the Shadow of Ruins, examines how Southern women mourned dead family members and friends. The exhibit includes artifacts such as jewelry and invitations to memorial services. Another exhibit, From Sunup to Sunup, examines slave life in the Antebellum South and includes slave-made artifacts such as quilts, baskets, tools and toys.

Throughout 1996, the museum will celebrate its centennial with special events and a new exhibit on women in the South during the Civil War years. The exhibit will look at women of all races and social classes and the roles they played from 1861 to 1890.

The museum also developed a traveling exhibit on African-American Life in the Antebellum South that won national media attention a few years ago. The exhibit includes manacles and leg irons worn by slaves, photographs, clothing, letters and other artifacts that represent slave life and the development of a culture within a culture during this time period. The exhibit is still on tour and will return to the museum in a few years.

Next to the museum is the restored White House of the Confederacy, home of Jefferson Davis. Furnishings and decorations vary with the seasons. The home is shown in summer dress from May to mid-September with slip covers on the furniture and mosquito netting over chandeliers and beds. From Thanksgiving until early January, it's decorated for Christmas. During the summer, living history interpreters talk to visitors outside the house daily. Guided tours are available.

Admission is $4 for either the museum or the White House. Combination tickets cost $7. Children younger than 7 are admitted free. Children age 7 to 12 pay $2.25 for the museum and $3.50 for a combination ticket.

RICHMOND NATIONAL
BATTLEFIELD PARK
226-1981

The National Park Service protects this Civil War site and in so doing preserves the memory of those who fought and died for a cause they believed to be right and just. The park includes 10 park areas related to the 1862 and 1864 Civil War battles fought around the city of Richmond. There are two visitor centers and one exhibit shelter.

Sites related to the 1862 Seven Days Battles include Chickahominy Bluffs, Beaver Dam Creek, Gaine's Mill (Watt House) and Malvern Hill. Ulysses S. Grant's 1864 campaign is represented at Cold Harbor and Fort Harrison.

We suggest you start at the Chimborazo Visitor Center for an introduction to the history of the 1862 to '65 defense of Richmond. Detailed driving tour maps of the battlefields are available here. The complete tour involves about a 100-mile drive and will take one to four hours, depending on how many battlefields you wish to see. If possible, try to spend some time walking in the battlefield areas — it's the best way to understand the significance of the sites. There are no fees.

Living history programs and reenactments are performed on special occasions to enhance visitors' understanding of the events that took place at these sites. There are also bus tours of the battlefields, candlelight walking tours of Fort Harrison and the Cold Harbor Campaign, weekend walks and talks, and a Junior Ranger program for children ages 6 to 12.

CHIMBORAZO VISITOR CENTER
3215 E. Broad St.   *226-1981*

At the site where one of the Confed-eracy's largest hospitals once stood, visitors can now view exhibits, a slide program and a film about the battles around Richmond. There is also a battlefield tour on video tape available for rent or sale.

FORT HARRISON VISITOR CENTER
Rt. 5   *226-1981*
(About 8 miles east of Richmond)

Exhibits and signs along a self-guided trail through Fort Harrison provide details of the battle and the fort. Picnic facilities are available.

COLD HARBOR EXHIBIT SHELTER
Rt. 156   *226-1981*
(About 10 miles northeast of Richmond)

The well-preserved trenches along this 1.25-mile tour road are good examples of Civil War field fortifications. A narrated exhibit in the shelter explains the significance of the battle action and strategies. The Garthright House, used as a field hospital, and the Watt House, used as a Union headquarters, are nearby. Picnic facilities are available.

Black History Attractions

BLACK HISTORY MUSEUM
AND CULTURAL CENTER OF VIRGINIA
00 Clay St.   *780-9093*

This 19th-century house serves as a center for art exhibits, research and other cultural activities related to Virginia's black history and culture. Exhibits on Second Street and Bojangles are currently on display.

This house in Jackson Ward was originally built as a residence in 1832. It later served as the Black Public Library and as a high school.

Tour guides are available on request. Admission is $2 for adults and $1 for seniors and children.

VISIT VIRGINIA'S PREMIERE
CIVIL WAR ATTRACTION

The Museum and White House of the Confederacy is the single most important destination for anyone interested in the Civil War and the Confederacy. The Museum maintains the world's largest and most comprehensive collection of Confederate arms, flags, uniforms, art and documents. Adjacent to the Museum is the White House, President Jefferson Davis' Civil War home, which has been restored to its elegant Victorian appearance.

Monday - Saturday 10:00 to 5:00, Sunday 12:00 to 5:00

Twelfth and Clay Streets   Richmond, Virginia 23219   (804) 649-1861

MAGGIE WALKER
NATIONAL HISTORIC SITE

110½ E. Leigh St.   780-1380, 226-1981

Maggie Walker was a famous black woman who rose from poverty and overcame a physical handicap to become a successful banker, newspaper editor and influential civic leader. The daughter of an ex-slave, she founded The St. Luke Penny Bank and was an early advocate of black women's rights. The bank today is known as Consolidated Bank and Trust, the oldest surviving black-operated bank in the country.

Park rangers conduct guided tours of the 22-room house in historic Jackson Ward, where the Walker family lived from 1904 to 1934. Built in 1883, the dwelling has been restored and decorated to appear as it did in 1930. The site is operated by the National Park Service.

Groups of five or more need to make advance reservations. Parking is available in the neighborhood or at a public lot at Fourth and Leigh streets. Admission is free.

Museums, Historic Homes and Buildings

AGECROFT HALL

4305 Sulgrave Rd.   353-4241

This 15th-century Tudor-style manor house surrounded by magnificent gardens was moved here from Lancashire, England, to save it from destruction. It's furnished with period furniture, tapestries, decorative arts and everyday objects of life in 16th- and 17th-century England. Guided tours are offered and last about 45 minutes.

Shop for fresh vegetables at the Farmers Market.

Insiders' Tips

Top 10 Attractions in the Richmond Area

1) Paramount's Kings Dominion (more than 2 million)
2) Virginia Museum of Fine Arts (290,347)
3) Science Museum of Virginia/Virginia Aviation Museum (264,534)
4) Richmond Battlefield Park (208,175)
5) Virginia State Capitol (173,594)
6) The Valentine Museum/Riverside (92,333)
7) The Museum and White House of the Confederacy (75,344)
8) Richmond Children's Museum (74,009)
9) Maymont House/Maymont Nature Center (60,290)
10) Lewis Ginter Botanical Gardens (34,318)

(The ranking is based on attendance figures reported by the attractions from January to December, 1994. Source: Metro Richmond Convention and Vistors Bureau.)

Outside, you can wander through a formal garden, an English Knot Garden, an herb garden, a fragrance garden and a sunken garden, all in a spectacular rolling landscape overlooking the James River. The gardens are especially beautiful from late March until early October. A special spring bulb display is usually planned for April. Picnics and pets are not permitted. Consider combining your visit with a trip to the Virginia House next door.

Admission is $4 for adults; $2 for students; $3.50 for seniors; and children younger than 6 are free.

BETH AHABAH
MUSEUM AND ARCHIVES
1109 W. Franklin St.   *353-2668*

This is the only Jewish museum and archives in the area. It provides a source for genealogical and historical research on Richmond's Jewish heritage. It also offers changing exhibits on religious and ceremonial objects, holidays and histori-

cal events. Trained docents give tours and provide assistance. Parking is available in a lot off Birch Street. Look for the sign. Admission is free with a suggested donation of $2.

CHESTERFIELD COUNTY
MUSEUM COMPLEX
Chesterfield Historical Society
Chesterfield Courthouse   *748-1026*

Take a walking tour of this complex and wander through the Old Courthouse built in 1917, Magnolia Grange, a Federal-style plantation home built in 1822, the Chesterfield County Museum and the Old Jail. Magnolia Grange charges admission. Entrance to other sites is free or by donation. Parking is available in front of the Old Courthouse and Magnolia Grange. There are several fast-food restaurants nearby, or you can enjoy more relaxed dining at Houlett's Tavern next to Magnolia Grange.

The complex is on Rt. 10 (Ironbridge Road) at Chesterfield Courthouse near I-

95, Rt. 288 and Chippenham Parkway. Guided tours are available. Library assistants are on duty daily.

CHESTERFIELD COUNTY MUSEUM

6805 W. Krause Rd.
Chesterfield Courthouse   748-1026

Built as a replica of the county's Colonial courthouse of 1750, the museum portrays the development of Chesterfield from an agricultural county to a suburban community. Its collections include prehistoric fossils, artifacts from the Indians native to the area, items related to Sir Thomas Dale's English Settlement of 1611 and 18th-century French Hugenot settlers, as well as items portraying the devastation of the Revolutionary and Civil War battles. Exhibits also depict early schools, churches, a country store and mining and railroad exhibits.

Admission is $1 for adults, 50¢ for students.

MAGNOLIA GRANGE

10020 Ironbridge Rd.   796-1479

Named after a circle of magnolia trees that once graced its front lawn, this 1822 Federal-style plantation house was built by William Winfree. Magnolia Grange is noted for its elaborate ceiling medallions as well as the sophisticated carving on mantels, doorways and windows. It's decorated and furnished according to the style of the 1820s. Tours include both floors. Adult admission is $2; seniors $1.50; and students $1.

THE OLD COURTHOUSE

Ironbridge Rd.   748-1026

Designed in the Colonial Revival style, the Old Courthouse was built in 1917 to replace the Colonial Courthouse of 1749. Features include a Roman Doric portico and a domed octagonal belfry. Today it serves as the headquarters of the Chesterfield Historical Society. Visitors may use the research library. A film and changing exhibits on Chesterfield's history are offered for the public.

THE OLD JAIL

Ironbridge Rd.   748-1026

Children enjoy visiting the Old Jail and a replica of an old pillory where offenders were exposed to public scorn. Next to the Chesterfield County Museum, the jail was built in 1892 and used for prisoners until 1962. Today it depicts the life of prisoners during the 1800s and the first half of this century. The Old Jail also includes historical exhibits of the police and fire departments.

HENRICUS PARK/CITIE OF HENRICUS

Chesterfield County   768-5252
24-hour Information Line   751-INFO

Development of the partial reproduction of the Citie of Henricus, a 1600s town on the James River in Chesterfield County, is beginning to take shape. Henricus, now known as Farrar's Island, was established by Sir Thomas Dale in 1611 when the London Company sought a better location than Jamestown for its colony. This second English settlement was wiped out in 1622 by an Indian massacre.

The site now includes a palisade with watchtowers, a storehouse, a necessary building and commemorative monuments. Future development plans include the construction of the first church established in America and what is believed to be the nation's first hospital.

A 2.5-mile round-trip hiking trail through Henricus Historical Park offers spectacular views of the river, and commemorative markers relate interesting tidbits of history. The trail is well-shaded, and there are plenty of benches for resting or picnicking.

On Citie of Henricus Publick Day, celebrated on the third Sunday in September each year, the park sponsors a historic re-enactment of the lives of the settlers, a 17th-century Church of England morning prayer service, games, food and tours. Old-fashioned games such as hoop-rolling, bowling, stilt-walking and tree-stump checkers take you back to a simpler time. Visitors will also enjoy Indian storytelling and puppet shows, and they can try their skill at candle-making or building a wattle and daub hut with a thatched roof.

To get here from Route 10, take the Old Stage Road and follow the signs to Dutch Gap Landing at the end of Coxendale Road.

COURT END

Court End, in the heart of the city, includes a six-block area that's rich with museums, historic homes and other buildings of historic and architectural significance. Sites include the State Capitol and Executive Mansion, the John Marshall House, the Wickham House, the Museum and White House of the Confederacy, the Egyptian Building, Old Richmond City Hall, Monumental Church, St. Paul's Episcopal Church and the former African Baptist Church. Self-guided walking tour maps and block tickets are available from the Valentine Museum or the Museum of the Confederacy. Several guided walking tours are also available. (See Tours in this chapter.)

JOHN MARSHALL HOUSE
Ninth and Marshall Sts.   *648-7998*

The great Chief Justice John Marshall built this 2½-story brick house in downtown Richmond between 1788 and 1790. He lived here until his death in 1835. Now owned by the City of Richmond, the residence has been restored to its original appearance and includes original furnishings and household objects once owned by Marshall. Architecturally, the house combines Federal characteristics with early Georgian elements. Parking is available in metered spaces and nearby public lots. The house is maintained and administered by the Association for the Preservation of Virginia Antiquities. Admission is $3.

THE VALENTINE MUSEUM
1015 E. Clay St.   *649-0711*

This urban history museum is an excellent place to begin a tour of the city. As the museum of the life and history of Richmond, the Valentine features nationally recognized exhibitions focusing on various aspects of the city's past and its diverse population. A major attraction at the museum is the Valentine's 1812 Wickham House, featuring the nation's only known set of neoclassical wall paintings. Guided tours of the fully restored house are offered hourly.

The museum's collections include one of the best costume collections in the nation, examples of decorative arts, industrial arts, paintings, prints, watercolors and photography. The museum also has the most complete library of printed material relating to the city.

You can enjoy breakfast or lunch in Wickham's Garden Cafe. Free parking is available in a lot behind the museum. Just look for the boot-shaped sign. Group discounts and tours are available. Admission to the house and museum is $5 for adults, $4 for seniors and students and $3 for children age 7 to 12.

EDGAR ALLAN POE MUSEUM
1914-16 E. Main St.   *648-5523*

To celebrate the 150th anniversary of

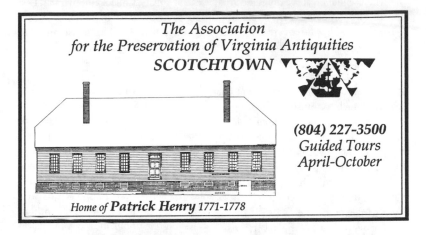

The Association
for the Preservation of Virginia Antiquities
SCOTCHTOWN

(804) 227-3500
Guided Tours
April-October

Home of **Patrick Henry** *1771-1778*

"The Raven," the museum will sponsor a variety of special events throughout 1995 including special readings, wine tastings and literary performances. There will also be a special Poe Festival with performances, readings and a scholarly symposium at Agecroft Hall in October. On Halloween, you can immerse yourself in the macabre world of Poe with a candle-light tour of the museum and special readings guaranteed to send shivers down your spine.

The museum occupies five buildings that open onto enclosed gardens. You can visit the Raven Room and see many artifacts of literary artist Edgar Allan Poe. The Old Stone House, built in 1737, is the oldest standing building in the original boundaries of the city. Tours are given every hour. Admission is $5 for adults, $4 for seniors and $3 for students. Call for group information.

HANOVER COURTHOUSE

U.S. 301   *537-5815*

Fifteen miles north of Richmond, this historic brick courthouse has been in continuous use since it was built in 1735. It was the site of Patrick Henry's first case,

Parsons Cause, and is still used today for ceremonial purposes. Tours are available by appointment.

LEWIS GINTER BOTANICAL
GARDENS AT BLOEMENDAAL

1800 Lakeside Ave.   *262-9887*

Garden and nature lovers will delight at the beauty of this botanical garden where thousands of plant species are artfully arranged across 80 acres to provide spectacular displays throughout the year. Bloemendaal is known for its extensive collection of daffodils, day lilies, rhododendrons and azaleas. You'll also enjoy seasonal floral displays and a cottage garden planted with herbs and species roses surrounding a charming Victorian manor house that now serves as a visitor center, gift shop and staff office building. Originally built in 1888 as a bicycle club, the home was expanded in 1901 and used as a children's hospital until it became a residence in 1906. Lewis Ginter's niece, Grace Arents, lived here until she died in 1928.

A major effort to further develop the gardens began several years ago. Recent improvements include a new lake in front of the house that creates a dramatic vista and the Henry M. Flagler Perennial Garden which features three acres of perennials in a garden masterfully choreographed to provide displays of color throughout the year. Visitors will enjoy strolling through the series of garden "rooms" which comprise the Flagler garden. A stone pavilion at one end of the display's central lawn is used for outdoor concerts and performances. The new Lucy Paine Minor Memorial Garden offers a gazebo with a charming display of daffodils, day lilies, a cryptomeria and a study garden of the lilies.

Surrounded by an Oriental-style garden, the new Japanesque-style Lora Robins Tea House opened in 1993 and serves lunch throughout the year.

Other development efforts include the Martha and Reed West Island Garden in the lagoon in front of the Tea House planted with Venus's flytraps, pitcher and bog plants; and a children's garden area planted with vegetables and flowers from Asia, Africa and North and South America. Interactive hands-on planting activities and programs are offered.

Long-range plans call for the development of several glass conservatories and houses, a garden of the plant kingdom, an English woodland garden along the lake and a water garden in and around the lake and lagoon.

Lewis Ginter Botanical Gardens offers a variety of workshops, basic gardening classes, lectures, tours and everything from concerts to camps for kids. Allow yourself about an hour for a self-guided tour through the gardens, and wear good walking shoes for grassy and pebbled paths. Maps and information are available at the admissions booth. Guided tours for groups are available in the fall and spring by appointment. Admission is

several dollars. Call for current rates. Discounts are available for seniors and children age 6 to 12. The house and Tea House may be rented for special occasions.

MAYMONT
1700 Hampton St.   358-7166

This 100-acre Victorian estate celebrated its 200th anniversary in 1993. With its Romanesque house, arboretum with mature exotic trees, formal Italian garden, Japanese garden, carriage rides, nature center, animal habitats and children's farm, Maymont is without question one of our most favorite places in the city. There's something for everyone here. History, architecture and decorative art lovers will be impressed by the mansion's original contents. It was once owned by the Dooleys, a wealthy couple that collected objects from all over the world. Nature and animal enthusiasts will enjoy the nature center, the children's farm, the bison, aviary and other wildlife habitats. Arborists, strollers, walkers and picnickers will enjoy the landscaped grounds, walking paths and the variety of beautiful old shade trees. You can even ride in a turn-of-the-century horse-drawn carriage.

Guided 30-minute tours of the house are offered in the afternoon until 4:30 PM. Tram tours of the gardens are also offered and take about 45 minutes to an hour. Self-guided tour information is available at the Nature Center. Special garden tours and group tours are also available, but you'll need to make reservations at least two weeks in advance.

Maymont is in the middle of the city on the north bank of the James River, just east of the Boulevard Bridge and south of Byrd Park. If you're interested in the house tour, carriages, Nature Cen-

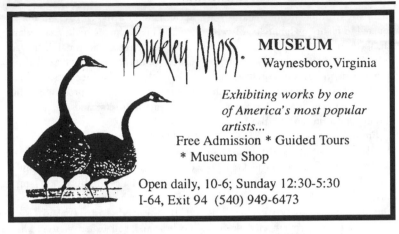
ter, arboretum, Italian or Japanese gardens, use the Hampton Street entrance. If you want to see the children's farm and animal habitats, use the Spottswood entrance.

Food and drink concession stands are open spring, summer and fall. Bicycles, pets, alcohol, kites and automobiles are not allowed in the park. Dress comfortably for walking, as the terrain is hilly and some of the slopes are quite steep. The grounds are open daily and close at night. The mansion, emporium, Nature Center, barn and gift shop are closed on Monday. Admission is free, but a $3 donation is suggested for the house tour. Fees are charged for carriage and tram rides.

MEADOW FARM AT CRUMP PARK

3400 Mountain Rd.   Weekdays: 672-9496
Glen Allen   Weekends: 672-1367

Open March through early December, Meadow Farm is a 19th-century living history museum where costumed interpreters re-create life on Dr. John Mosby Sheppard's middle-class farm in the 1860s, just before the outbreak of the Civil War. Unlike many historical attractions, this one is unique because it focuses on the middle class instead of the rich and famous.

This is a great place to visit with children. There's something for everyone — picnicking, history, hiking, fishing and good old-fashioned fun. You can tour the farmhouse, barn, a 19th-century doctor's office, blacksmith's forge, smokehouse, kitchen, orchard and crop demonstration fields. Sometimes you can smell the aroma of cobblers and biscuits baking over a hearthfire in the kitchen, and in the barnyard, you'll find a pig, chicken, sheep, cows and ducks.

Living history events and re-enactments throughout the year create a lot of excitement and activity here on weekends. Events include Sheep to Shawl in April, the Civil War Encampment and Battle in late May, Civil War Days in September, the Harvest Festival in October, and the Yuletide Feast in December.

Meadow Farm's 50 acres of pasture and woodlands also provide a natural environment for a wide variety of plants and animals. There are about 2 miles of nature trails where you'll discover delightful opportunities to see hawks, quail and deer. Formerly the home of Gen.

Sheppard Crump, Meadow Farm was donated to Henrico County by his wife, Elizabeth Adam Crump, in 1975.

Exhibits such as historical photographs of Henrico County, quilts and folk art are displayed in the orientation center and changed periodically. A video about the farm and a gift shop are also available.

From downtown, take I-95 N. to I-295 W. (Exit 36). Take the Woodman Road S. exit to Mountain Road. Go right and follow the signs. There are plenty of parking spaces. Picnic tables and playground equipment are available at nearby Crump Park. The farm is open daily most of the year. The orientation center is closed on Monday. Call for information about hours and winter closings. Admission is free.

OLD CITY HALL
10th and Capitol Sts.

This 1894 Victorian Gothic architectural masterpiece was saved from destruction by the Historic Richmond Foundation. It's now used as an office building. If you are in the area, it's worthwhile to walk through the lobby to see the elaborate interior.

RICHMOND CHILDREN'S MUSEUM
740 Navy Hill Dr.   643-KIDO, 788-4949

This museum provides hands-on learning experiences for children to expand their awareness of and respect for the diverse world in which we live — its art, nature and peoples. Kids ages 2 to 12 come here to explore and be creative. They can play in a grocery store, doctor's office or television news studio and see themselves on camera. While mom and dad watch, they can try their skills at Computers for Kids, dress in costumes and act out their fantasies on stage. They can even put on a miner's hat and go

spelunking in a special cave. In the art studio, children paint, make collages and create masterpieces. Seasonal themes focus on cultures throughout the world and offer a full slate of related activities. The whole family will enjoy professional music, drama, puppetry and dance performances.

The museum also sponsors nature programs, cooking demonstrations, art exhibits, storytelling, a theater group for children and Peanut Butter 'n Jam, a summer concert series for families.

Be sure to bring a camera and flash or a videocam. If you want to go somewhere for lunch, you can walk to the 6th Street Marketplace. There are lots of casual places to eat there.

The museum is on Navy Hill Drive, formerly known as Sixth Street, off Jackson Street near I-95 and I-64 in downtown Richmond. Parking is free. Admission is $2.50 for children and $3.50 for adults. Children younger than 2 are admitted free.

SCIENCE MUSEUM OF VIRGINIA
2500 W. Broad St.   367-1013
Event Line   367-0000
24-Hour Skywatch Information   36STARS

The Science Museum of Virginia, in the historic Broad Street Train Station, offers more than 250 hands-on exhibits and participatory programs to encourage visitors to explore the exciting world of science. The museum also offers OMNIMAX films projected on a five-story-high screen in the Ethyl Universe Theatre. The sensation of being part of the movie action is so strong, you'll feel like you've been on a ride at an amusement park.

Planetarium shows are also available. Interactive exhibits feature astronomy, aerospace, chemistry and physics, computers, crystals, electricity, illusions and telecommunications. You'll also see one of the world's largest pendulums, suspended from the center of the dome in the rotunda, which demonstrates the rotation of the earth.

Special events and activities are offered every weekend, and special exhibits are scheduled periodically. The second Saturday of each month is Super Second Saturday with special events and projects for 3- to 10-year-olds.

In the spring, the museum usually offers a major visiting exhibit. Popular displays in recent years include giant robotic dinosaurs, sea creatures and bears. In March 1995, a special weekend exhibit entitled Bay Days celebrates the sights and sounds of the Chesapeake Bay. In November, the museum presents the Model Railroad Show, and December features Joy From the World with down and trees and holiday customs from around the world as presented by representatives of Richmond's international community.

This is a great place to go as a family. It's also neat to just walk around the historic old train station with its domed ceiling and interesting spaces. Weekday afternoons and anytime in September and January are good times to visit if you want to avoid the crowds. Spring is typically a very busy time with a lot of school groups. Allow yourself plenty of time to see everything. You can easily spend half a day here. Lunch is available at the Cosmic Cafe inside the museum. There are several fast-food restaurants nearby, or you can pack a picnic lunch and eat on the grounds. Picnic tables are provided, and there are a few vending machines. Admission to the exhibit area is $4 for seniors and youths and $4.50 for adults. With one theater show, admission is $6 for seniors and youths and $6.50 for adults.

SCOTCHTOWN

Rts. 54 and 685
Hanover County   227-3500, 883-6917

One of Virginia's oldest plantations, Scotchtown in western Hanover County about 9 miles west of Ashland was Patrick Henry's home during the Revolutionary War from 1771 to 1778. The restored wood-frame Colonial home was built between 1717 and 1719 and is furnished with authentic 18th-century antiques. You can see the kitchen, which is in a separate building; the basement, which includes a small museum and wine cellar; and the dry well, which was used to keep meat and other perishable food fresh before there were refrigerators. The house is surrounded by about 40 acres of farm and woodland. Tours are conducted by docents.

Costumed guides and living history presentations are offered at special events such as the Scottish Festival and Games in May. Also, during the first full weekend in December, Scotchtown presents candlelight tours of the house, plays and special decorations illustrating Christmas customs in the 18th, 19th and 20th centuries. Refreshments and wreath-making classes are also offered.

This is another great place to take the kids and have a picnic. Some tables and benches are provided. Scotchtown is open April through October. Group tours are available year round. Call for reservations. Scotchtown is operated by the Patrick Henry Scotchtown Committee in cooperation with the Association for the Preservation of Virginia Antiquities. Admission is $5 for adults and $2 for children age 6 to 12.

St. John's Church

2401 E. Broad St.   *648-5015*

Relive Patrick Henry's famous "Give me liberty, or give me death" speech at this historic church in a restored section of Church Hill. The oldest church in the city, St. John's has served a congregation for more than 250 years.

From Memorial Day to Labor Day, free re-enactments of the Second Virginia Convention of 1775 are held every Sunday at 2 PM. Actors portray 11 patriots including George Washington, Thomas Jefferson and, of course, Patrick Henry. Seating is limited, so try to arrive by about 1:30 PM. Costumed interpreters conduct tours and assist visitors. The graveyard surrounding the church includes the graves of Edgar Allan Poe's mother, George Wythe and several governors. Photographers may find that the sun is a problem since the church faces north; you may want to bring a special lens. Admission is $3 for adults, $2 for seniors, $1 for youths ages 7 to 18. Tours are offered from 10 AM to 3:30 PM Monday through Saturday and on Sunday from 1 PM to 3:30 PM.

State Capitol and Capitol Square

Ninth and Grace Sts.   *786-4344*

A free 20-minute tour of the historic Capitol building is a favorite among school children and visitors. In the Rotunda you'll see numerous statues, including Virginia's most treasured work of art: the famous statue of George Washington by Jean Antoine Houdon. Look up, and you'll see the unusual interior dome with skylights that was built about 20 feet below the A-line roof. You'll also see the Old House of Delegates Hall where Aaron Burr was tried for treason in 1807 and the former Senate Chamber where a number of famous paintings are displayed.

Built in 1788, the Capitol was the first public building in America built in the Classic Revival style of architecture. Thomas Jefferson influenced the design and secured the services architect Charles-Louis Clerisseau who modeled the building after the Maison Caree, a Roman Temple built in Nimes, France.

The Executive Mansion, home to Virginia's governors since 1813, is in Capitol Square just east of the Capitol. The Old Bell Tower, built in 1824 for the Virginia Public Guard, is also on the grounds. It's now used as a visitors center.

The grounds are always open and include two spring-fed fountains and numerous statues to famous Virginians. (See the Monuments chapter.) Many people enjoy picnicking here on the grass. During the summer, there's often lunch-hour entertainment in front of the Bell Tower.

If you want to see your representatives at work, visit a session of the General Assembly held for 60 days in even years and for 30 days in odd-numbered years. Sessions begin in mid-January. Space in the galleries is limited to about 80 to 100 people. To get in, you'll need a pass from the Capitol hostesses on the second floor in the Rotunda. Just give the pass to the doorman. If the galleries are full, you can watch the sessions on closed circuit TV in House Room 4 or Senate Room 4.

Tuckahoe Plantation

784-5736

Seven miles west of Richmond on River Road, you'll find Tuckahoe, considered the finest existing early 18th-century plantation in America. Built by Thomas Randolph in 1712, the grounds include the school where Thomas Jefferson studied. It's open for tours by appointment only. Admission is $5 for groups of fewer than 10 people; $3.50 for groups of 10 or more. Admission to the grounds only is free with a suggested donation of $1.

VIRGINIA AVIATION MUSEUM
5701 Huntsman Rd.   *236-3622*

Next to Richmond International Airport, this museum, now a division of the Science Museum of Virginia, displays an extensive collection of vintage and historically significant aircraft as well as navigation devices and memorabilia dating from 1914 to World War II. There's also a special exhibit dedicated to Adm. Richard E. Byrd. A new wing is also open where visitors can occasionally see planes being restored.

In May, the museum sponsors "Toss Across America," where you can learn and practice the art of tossing a boomerang. In June, the museum presents "Flight Day" with special activities, planes and children's activities.

Admission to the museum is $3.50 for adults; $2.50 for seniors and children older than 4.

VIRGINIA HISTORICAL SOCIETY
CENTER FOR VIRGINIA
HISTORY AT BATTLE ABBEY
428 N. Boulevard   *358-4901*

The Virginia Historical Society Center for Virginia History was built in 1914 as a memorial to Confederate soldiers who died during the Civil War and today houses the world's largest and most comprehensive collection of Virginia history. Here, you can visit seven galleries and see changing and permanent exhibits depicting and recounting state history. One of the newest exhibits explores the life of Pocahontas. Another major 1995 exhibit, Virginians as Americans, examines Virginia history from the 16th through the 19th centuries. You can also conduct historical and genealogical research in the library.

The center's collections include the largest portrait collection in the South, significant photography archives, the world's largest collection of Confederate-manufactured weaponry and thousands of museum objects. Docents are available for group tours.

For a full day of art, history and science, combine a visit here with a trip to the Virginia Museum of Fine Arts next door and the Science Museum of Virginia on nearby W. Broad Street. Parking is available in front of and behind the building or on the street. Admission is $3 for adults, $2 for students.

VIRGINIA HOUSE
"AN AMERICAN COUNTRY PLACE"
4301 Sulgrave Rd.   *353-4251*

Original materials used to build this beautifully reconstructed English manor home date back to 1124. This castle-like home next to Agecroft Hall in Windsor Farms is furnished with antiques and tapestries. Breathtakingly beautiful gardens slope down toward the river. A major spring bulb display is usually planned for April. Tours are available. Owned and operated by the Virginia Historical Society, the house is open daily. Admission is $4 for adults and $2 for students and children.

VIRGINIA MUSEUM OF FINE ARTS
2800 Grove Ave.   *367-0844*
Tours and Group Visits   *367-0859*

This museum presents a panorama of world art from ancient times to the present and has gained an international reputation for its collections. Outstanding features include one of the nation's leading collections of the art of India,

Nepal and Tibet; the Lewis collections of American paintings since World War II, and art nouveau and art deco objects; a collection of Easter eggs and objects created by master jeweler Peter Carl Faberge; Goya's portrait of Gen. Nicolas Guye; a rare marble statue of Caligula; Monet's "Irises by the Pond"; and the Mellon collections of British sporting art and French impressionist and post-impressionist art.

While you're here, you can have lunch in the cafeteria or on the patio. And, be sure to visit the gift shop. You'll find an extensive selection of gifts, books and crafts. The museum also offers many wonderful programs and classes. For more information about the museum, see our chapter on The Arts. Admission is free; a $4 donation is suggested.

WILTON HOUSE MUSEUM
215 S. Wilton Rd.   282-5936

At this 18th-century plantation house, you can experience the elegance of Colonial architecture and interiors and learn about the daily struggle for survival faced by the forbearers of our country.

Perched on a bluff overlooking the James River, the house is one of the finest examples of the early Georgian style as built in Virginia. The interior paneling is especially noteworthy, and there's a spectacular view of the James River Gorge from the gardens. Eagles are frequently sighted here, so birdwatchers may get a special treat. This attraction is off the beaten path, and tours are conducted by trained docents as visitors arrive. You

won't have to wait for a tour. Wilton Road is south of the 5400 block of Cary Street. Admission is $4 for adults, $3 for seniors and $2 for students. Children younger than 6 are free. Group rates are available.

Riverfront Attractions

ANNABEL LEE
4400 E. Main St.
Intermediate Terminal   644-5700

This 350-passenger paddlewheel river boat replica is the only showboat in town. Departing from the intermediate terminal, the *Annabel Lee* offers dining, entertainment and narrated tours of historical points of interest along the James River east of Richmond. Meals are served buffet-style and two full-service bars are available.

The lunch cruise travels about 10 miles down river, and the dinner cruise travels about 15 miles. The trip features live music and narrated commentary about the river. On Tuesdays, the plantation/brunch cruise travels about 25 miles and docks at Westover Plantation. The cruise includes tours of the gardens at Westover and full tours of Berkeley and Evelynton plantations. You return by motor coach. Party cruises are offered some Saturday nights from 11 PM to 1 AM and include appetizers, a DJ or live band and dancing.

People usually wear nice casual to dressy attire for evening cruises. In the afternoons, people dress more casually in sports clothes. Be sure to wear comfort-

Down The Lazy River

Leave the city skyline behind and journey back in time as you head down the James River on Richmond, Virginia's most popular attraction, The Annabel Lee.

ANNABEL LEE

4400 E Main Street 222-5700

able walking shoes for the plantation cruise and tours.

You may pick up your boarding pass at the ticket booth and begin boarding about 30 minutes before departure time. Free parking is available at the pier.

The *Annabel Lee* has two fully enclosed climate-controlled decks and an open Starlite Deck. She sails rain or shine. Reservations are required. Occasionally you may be able to buy a ticket the day of the cruise if space is available. Chartered trips are available for weddings, parties, corporate outings and special events. Ticket prices vary depending on the trip and the meals involved. Adult tickets begin at $15, and children's tickets begin at $9.95.

CANAL WALK
10th and Bank Sts.

This downtown waterfront attraction

begins at 10th and Bank streets and ends at the James River Plaza. Information provided by historic markers and kiosks tells the history of the riverfront. An additional half-mile riverfront pedestrian path along Tredegar Street from Seventh Street west to the Lee Bridge was completed recently.

GREAT SHIPLOCKS CANAL PARK
Dock and Pear Sts.

This is the site of the lowest of the Kanawha Canal Locks. The stone lock was completed in 1854. An interpretive display provides visitor information.

JAMES RIVER AND KANAWHA CANAL
12th and Byrd Sts.

Conceived by George Washington as a way to open trade with land to the west, the Kanawha Canal was the first commercial canal system in North America.

Washington oversaw the initial construction of the project. The canal opened in 1790 between Richmond and Westham. A narrated slide presentation tells the story to visitors.

RICHMOND RAFT COMPANY
4400 E. Main St.   222-7238

"Get set to get wet . . . you'll get soaked." That's their slogan, and this is definitely one of the most exciting and fun ways to explore the James River. This full-service outfitter offers various scenic trips on the Falls of the James through the center of the city. It's the only urban whitewater run in the country. You don't have to be experienced; your guide will teach you along the way.

The Fall of the James single-day paddle raft excursions are offered March through November. The full trip takes about six hours and includes the upper and lower sections of the river. Lunch is provided. The short trip lasts about three hours and includes the lower section of the river.

The trips are always exciting, but the fastest rides are in the spring when water levels are typically at their highest. The summer months are warmer and more conducive to swimming and sunning along the way, and the fall is the most scenic time. Rides are not recommended for children younger than 12. Trip costs range from $25 to $45. Discounts are available for groups of 18 or more.

VALENTINE RIVERSIDE
Tredegar Iron Works
470 Tredegar St.   649-0711

This history park and museum complex at the historic Tredegar Iron Works offers exhibits, a theater show, a discovery room for youngsters, touch-screen computers with photographic images, costumed historic interpreters, a Sound and Light Show and much more. See the related sidebar in this chapter for details.

Other Points of Interest

FARMER'S MARKET
17th and Main Sts.

You'll find pepper strings, onion braids and some of the freshest fruit and produce in town at this colorful, open market in Shockoe Bottom. Local farmers have sold their produce here for more than 200 years. The market is now covered with a roof, and signs marking the historic district have been erected.

HOLLYWOOD CEMETERY
Albemarle and Cherry Sts.

This historic graveyard features numerous statues and monuments as well as the graves of U.S. Presidents James Monroe and John Tyler, Confederate President Jefferson Davis, Confederate General J.E.B. Stuart and 1,800 Confederate soldiers. Richmond Discoveries offers a guided walking tour here every Sunday. See their listing in this chapter under "Tours."

OAKWOOD CEMETERY
3101 Nine Mile Rd.

This is the final burial place for 16,000 Confederate soldiers. It was also the burial site for Union Colonel Dahlgren until his father sent President Jefferson Davis $100 in gold to have his son's body sent home for final burial.

SHOCKOE CEMETERY
Hospital St.

This is one of the oldest municipal cemeteries in the nation. Here, you can see the graves of Chief Justice John Marshall, Revolutionary War hero Peter

Francisco and Elizabeth Van Lew, a Union spy who lived in Richmond during the Civil War.

Other Fun Things to Do

CITY HALL OBSERVATION DECK
Ninth and Broad Sts.   780-5747

The top-floor skydeck of City Hall offers one of the best panoramic views of the city and the James River. Perched 19 floors above the ground, the deck is open daily.

MONEY MUSEUM
Federal Reserve Bank of Richmond
701 E. Byrd St.   697-8108

Explore the history of money through items once used for barter such as animal pelts and tobacco, gold and silver bars and certificates. Artifacts related to the production and safekeeping of money are also on display. The museum is on the first floor of the Federal Reserve Bank building and is open Monday through Friday from 9:30 AM to 3:30 PM. It's closed on bank holidays. Admission is free. Groups of 20 or more need to make an appointment.

THE OLD DOMINION RAILWAY MUSEUM
102 Hull St.   233-6237

Near the 14th Street Bridge in the old Hull Street Passenger Station, this museum features artifacts and photographs related to the history of railroading in Richmond. A small steam locomotive and baggage car are on display. Special programs such as Civil War railroading and interpretive hikes along the flood wall are also offered. The museum is open Monday through Saturday from 11 AM to 4 PM and Sunday 1 PM to 4 PM. Admission is free. Group tours are available.

PARAMOUNT'S KINGS DOMINION
Rt. 30 and I-95   876-5000
Doswell

If you love rides and getting wet, this is the place to go. Paramount's Kings Dominion is a 400-acre family entertainment park with seven different theme areas "where the magic of the movies meets the thrills of a lifetime."

In 1995, Nickelodeon, the No. 1 network for kids, brings its wild, messy, hands-on entertainment to the park in a new three-acre area with lots of Green Slime. Everyone can participate in the

"Mega Mess-a-Mania" game show featuring stunts and challenges from "Double Dare, What Would You Do?" and other hit Nickelodeon game shows. There's a "Guts"-style obstacle course for kids, a Green Slime maze and a Gak kitchen for making fresh gooey batches of the stuff.

In Wayne's World, an "excellent" theme area, guests can experience the thrilling new Hurler roller coaster that exceeds speeds of 50 mph and includes four high-speed turns. Wayne's World visitors will feel like they're actually on the Hollywood set of the *Wayne's World* films, beginning with a realistic streetscape that recreates Wayne and Garth's hometown and a replica of the set for Wayne's Basement Studio. There's also Stan Mikita's Restaurant and the Rock Shop music store.

Visitors can also experience the thrill of high-speed professional auto racing at the Days of Thunder racing simulator; a dazzling new ice show that features 11 talented skaters performing to popular Paramount movie themes; a unique children's restaurant; Busytown Cafe, themed around characters from Richard Scarry stories; and walk around movie characters such as Wayne and Garth, Klingons, Vulcans, Romulans and Bajorans, along with Hollywood-style characters and well-known Hanna-Barbera characters.

Throughout the park, you'll find more than 40 rides, including six unique world-class roller coasters. Four popular ones are the Shockwave, a stand-up roller coaster; the Anaconda, a looping ride with an underwater tunnel; the Grizzly, a ferocious wooden roller coaster; and the Rebel Yell, a twin-racing roller coaster with one train traveling forward and one train traveling backward. There's also the Scooby Doo Coaster in Hanna-Barbera Land for younger children. Other popular attractions include the White Water Canyon raft ride, the 330-foot replica of the Eiffel Tower and Hurricane Reef water park with six acres of water slides, meandering raft rides, splash areas and wading pools for little ones.

When you need a break from the rides, you can see live performances and animal shows. The park also has evening fireworks shows, musical street parties and concerts.

Be sure to bring your swimsuit for the water park, and plan to take your time. Arrive early and spend the day. Many people pack a picnic lunch and eat in the park areas just outside the entrance. There's a lot of walking, and it gets hot, so dress comfortably. Season passes for individuals and families are a bargain for locals who like to come here often.

Discount tickets are offered by many companies and employers in the area. Just ask at work and watch the ads. Admission is $27.95 for ages 7 and older; $19.95 for ages 3 to 6. Children age 2 and younger are free. Season passes may be purchased by calling (800) 553-7277.

The park is open daily from Memorial Day weekend through Labor Day.

Insiders' Tips

Movies filmed in Richmond include *A Woman Named Jackie*, *Doc Hollywood*, *Love Field*, *Miss Rose White* and *True Colors*.

Valentine Riverside

Open since the summer of 1994, Valentine Riverside is expected to become a major tourist and educational draw that will spur the growth and redevelopment of the city's river front.

On the James River beside the Kanawha Canal at the historic Tredegar Iron Works, one of America's earliest factories and the principal iron supplier and arsenal of the Confederacy, this multi-faceted $26 million history park and museum complex offers more than you can access in one day.

Inside the Tredegar Pattern Building at the entrance to the park, visitors will see a theatre show about industry, exhibits and special programs. Windows on Richmond: Reflections on a Nation, for instance, depicts how European immigrants, African Americans, people of vision such as Patrick Henry, Gabriel, Edgar Allan Poe and Maggie Walker, and people of skill such as John Wickham, Mary Randolph and Henry Carter Osterbind, lent their talents over time to collectively transform the settlement on the James into the great city of Richmond. A horizontal map displays the geography of how the city has grown since the first settlement in 1607 and how it fit into the world. A new exhibit, America's Reconstruction: People in Politics after the Civil War, will open in November 1995.

A discovery room for young visitors encompasses the second floor. Here you'll find Legos, building sets, Lincoln Logs and other games and toys. Parents may check-in their children and leave them here if they want time to explore on their own.

On the third floor, special touch-screen computers with photographic images offer historical and panoramic views of the river and the city to show how human settlement transformed the landscape. Visitors may select a year or an event, such as the burning of Richmond during the Civil War, and witness the changes in the skyline as buildings are built, destroyed and built again.

Costumed historic interpreters portraying workers, entrepreneurs, managers and a worker's widow talk to visitors about life in the early 1900s, and you'll see historic machinery in operation including a waterwheel and flume, foundry crane, bulldozer press, working models of turbines and the rolling mill that produced plates for the *Monitor* and the *Merrimack*.

Raft rides, a 1930s-style carousel, a 1920 trolley, locomotive and caboose, and modern tot lot with pulley-operated sand and water works add a sense of excitement and adventure guaranteed to make learning about history fun. In cooperation with Richmond Raft Company, Valentine Riverside offers visitors a chance to raft the James — with or without rapids. Rafts accommodate about a dozen people, and the ride lasts for about 30 minutes.

Bicycles and box lunches are available for those who want to ride along the Canal Walk, and learn more about the river. Maps and helmets are provided and interpretive signs are located at points of interest along the 20-block route between Seventh and 27th streets.

In the evening, the Sound and Light Show projected on the Pattern Building portrays the changes that occurred at Tredegar and in Richmond during the past centuries. The 20-minute show is big, loud and dramatic. Underground speakers literally shake the ground during thunderous battle scenes.

Valentine Riverside also offers shuttle transportation to and tours of Valentine Court End, Belle Isle, Hollywood Cemetery and Shockoe Slip. A Richmond Highlights tour and theme tours on the Civil War, African-Americans and Industry are also available. Shuttle transportation is provided so visitors may leave their cars securely parked at Valentine Riverside.

Indoor and outdoor dining is available at the Electric Skyline Cafe in the Origins Building which originally housed offices at Tredegar Iron Works. Portions of the Electric Skyline Exhibit, featuring neon signs and advertising designs once displayed in the city, are incorporated into the decor. Several additional outdoor dining areas are scattered throughout the park.

A special monument serves as focal point of the park and recognizes the important influence African-Americans had in the history of the city. An iron grid tower with a soapstone sculpture of a gourd dipper rises above a 20-foot pool surrounded by slate and filled with African fish and plants.

Ethyl Corporation made the Valentine Riverside project possible by giving the Valentine Museum use of the site and the Tredegar Iron Works building. The local Fortune 500 company also contributed $600,000 for a feasibility study and made an $8 million challenge commitment. Numerous corporations, foundations and individuals have also contributed to the project.

To get here from downtown Richmond, turn right on Seventh Street by the Federal Reserve, then right again at the fountain onto Tredegar Street. Continue to the Tredegar Iron Works and follow the signs for parking.

Admission is $5. Children age 3 and younger are free. Fees for bikes, motor tours and raft rides are not included. Call for details about daily schedules and rates. The Sound and Light Show and raft rides are offered daily as weather permits.

It's open only on weekends from the end of March until Memorial Day, and from Labor Day until October. The park is closed a few days each season for special events, so it's best to call first to make sure it's open the day you plan to visit.

RICHMOND COLISEUM

601 E. Leigh St.　　　　*Office: 780-4970*
　　　　　　　　　　　　　　　Events: 780-4956

In the downtown area near Broad, Fifth and Seventh streets, the coliseum hosts a variety of major spectator events including college sports, Richmond Renegades Hockey, WWF wrestling, the Ringling Bros. & Barnum and Bailey Circus, concerts, tractor pulls and more. Food is available nearby at the 6th Street Marketplace, and there are concession stands inside the coliseum. Be aware that you cannot leave and get back inside unless you buy another ticket.

VIRGINIA FIRE AND POLICE MUSEUM
(Steamer Company No. 5)
200 W. Marshall St.　　　　　*644-1849*

Built in 1849, this is Richmond's only surviving firehouse from the Civil War period, and it's one of the oldest firehouses in the country. The museum features Italianate architecture and hand-drawn, horse-drawn and early motorized fire-fighting apparatus. A 19th-century working police station with jail cells is under development. More than 100,000 school children are trained in fire safety here each

year. The museum is open Monday through Saturday from 10 AM to 4 PM. Suggested donations for admission are $3 for adults and $1 for children. Police and fire personnel are admitted free.

Tours

PLANTATION/BRUNCH CRUISE
Annabel Lee
4400 E. Main St.　　　　　*222-5700*

Enjoy a buffet brunch while you cruise down the James River to Plantation Row for tours of Westover, Berkeley and Evelynton plantations. This tour is available only on Tuesdays.

COURT END PASS

Self-guided tour maps and admission passes to the historic homes and museums in Court End are available from the Valentine Museum, the Museum of the Confederacy and the John Marshall House. Block tickets are $11 for adults, $10 for seniors and $5 for ages 7 through 12. Group rates are available.

HISTORIC AIR TOURS
Williamsburg　　　　　　*253-8185*
　　　　　　　　　　　　(800) VABYAIR

These guided aerial tours of battlefields, entrenchments, plantations and other Civil War sites around Richmond or Petersburg offer a unique perspective for history buffs. You'll find out how topography influenced troop movements, and you'll trace the actual paths of the soldiers. Guides are well-versed in Civil War history, and the tours are offered in cooperation with the National Battlefield Park Service and the Museum of the Confederacy. The tours last about an hour and include major plantations and commentary on the Richmond skyline. You'll see 19th-century river docks, railway lines, monuments, historic cemeteries and neighborhoods. Advance reservations are suggested but are not necessary. You may be able to fly the same day you call if space is available. The cost of the tour is about $60 per person and includes admission to the Museum and White House of the Confederacy. All flights leave from the Williamsburg-Jamestown Airport. The planes can carry up to five passengers plus a pilot.

HISTORIC RICHMOND TOURS
780-0107

General and themed tours of the city are offered daily by Historic Richmond Tours. Van tour passengers are picked up at major hotels and at the Robin Hood Road Visitors Center. Themed tours include the Civil War City, Civil War Battlefields, downtown Richmond, the canal system, historic Church Hill and Hollywood Cemetery. Reservations are required. Step-on guides, meeting and convention services are also available.

LIVING HISTORY ASSOCIATES
1100 W. Franklin St.
Second Floor   *353-8166*

Skilled interpreters in modern or au-

thentic historical clothing help bring history to life for a variety of tours and events. The staff includes professional historians, teachers, museum staff members, writers, musicians, historical interpreters and others who have a love for history and know how to make it interesting. These are the people you see at special museum events and in advertisements. They offer walking tours, private tours, color guards with fife and drums and other living history entertainment for schools, special events, children's programs, dinners, lectures and more. Step-on motor coach guide service and other convention and tour services are also available, including arrangements for lodging, meals and transportation. Activities and programs can be custom designed to meet your needs. Make reservations and special requests as far in advance as possible. Location and technical advice for filmmakers is also available.

NATIONAL RAILWAY HISTORICAL SOCIETY
231-4324

If you really like to plan ahead, you can book a ride on the Autumn Leaves Special. This is a daylong trip on one of the largest steam-engine trains in operation today, built in 1950. Trips are sponsored by the Old Dominion Chapter of the National Railway Historical Society and will be offered again after refurbishing is completed. Call for information about upcoming trips and schedules.

Insiders' Tips

Attend gala events at the Virginia Museum.

Quoth the Raven, 'Nevermore'

To celebrate the 150th anniversary of "The Raven," the hair-raising poem that made Edgar Allan Poe famous, the Poe Museum will sponsor special readings, wine-tastings and activities throughout 1995.

First published by *The Evening Mirror*, a New York weekly, on January 29, 1845, "The Raven" was introduced by the newspaper as "the most effective single example of 'fugitive poetry' ever published in this country, and

unsurpassed in English poetry for subtle conception, masterly ingenuity of versification, and consistent sustaining of imaginative lift and 'pokerishness'" (which meant something like spooky). "The Raven" was an immediate success and brought Poe national and even international acclaim.

Poe spent his boyhood in Richmond. He came here with his actress-mother, Elizabeth Arnold Poe, who appeared at the Richmond Theatre. She died at age 24 from tuberculosis in 1811. Poe, who then was just 2 years old, went to live with Frances and John Allan. He took Allan as his middle name, but rarely used it. He usually signed his name Edgar A. Poe.

Edgar Allan Poe

His first journalistic job was editing the *Southern Literary Messenger* at 15th and Main streets in Richmond. A stinging critic and master storyteller, Poe soon became a household name. People knew who Poe was and knew about his black bird. Children followed him down the street quoting "'nevermore,' 'nevermore.'"

He spent his life creating more than 200 poems, short stories and other writings, but "The Raven" gave him a reputation as a fine writer. It is said that he enjoyed the attention and the publicity, but didn't care much about money. His work was art for art's sake, and he lived most of his live in poverty. He was paid $15 for "The Raven," a fair price at the time, but without the copyright protection writers enjoy today, he received nothing for the numerous reprints, parodies, imitations, songs or pictorial representations it inspired.

One of the most misunderstood writers in American literature, Poe was ahead of his time. He was also a binge drinker which contributed to his image problem. After Poe died in 1849 at the age of 40, he was maligned by self-serving critics who exaggerated the negative aspects of his work and his life. Even today, the idea of Poe as a drug addict, drunkard and manic depressive is so entrenched, many visitors to the Poe Museum still arrive with that concept — a view that the museum pledges to dispel.

The French poet Charles Baudelaire translated many of Poe's works and helped to change Poe's reputation. Today, more objective critics say that Poe was a meticulous writer who could not have produced the work he did if he were in a chronic disturbed or drugged state. His many accomplishments show him to be one of America's finest and most influential writers — he created the modern detective story, helped develop science fiction as we know it today, and set the standards for literary criticism in 19th-century America.

His writings include: "The Fall of the House of Usher," "The Pit and the Pendulum," "The Black Cat," "Eureka," "The Tell-Tale Heart," "Tamerlane and Other Poems," "The Gold Bug," "The Murders in Rue Morgue" and "Ligeia," a short story he considered his best.

RICHMOND DISCOVERIES, INC.
8620 Varina Rd.   795-5781

This company offers regularly scheduled guided walking tours of city areas on a variety of themes and custom tours for groups. They specialize in Civil War tours. Guides wear costumes on request.

From March through October, you can join a walking tour of Hollywood Cemetery the last Sunday of each month at 2 PM, or a tour themed around the Civil War on Sundays in the spring and fall. Reservations for these tours are not necessary. Call to find out locations and times. Families are encouraged to participate. There is no charge for children accompanied by an adult.

Richmond Discoveries is the group that sponsors the annual Memorial Day Heritage Weekend and the commemorative parade that goes down Monument Avenue and ends with a ceremony in Hollywood Cemetery.

RICHMOND ROUNDABOUT, INC.
211 W. Hillcrest Dr.   282-5909

This tour company will take your group to well-known historic sites or to places off the beaten path. If you want something different, Richmond Round-about specializes in uncommon, unusual or unexpected tours.

WINNING TOURS
1831 Westwood Ave.   358-6666

This company offers a variety of guide services and tours.

Bus Tours

All of these local companies provide group bus service and touring arrangements for attractions in the area and to other nearby destinations.

JAMES RIVER BUS COMPANY
1017 W. Graham Rd.   321-7661

TOURTIME AMERICA
I-95 at Atlee-Elmont Exit   550-1287

VIRGINIA COACH LINE
2116 W. Cary St.   359-1112

WINN BUS LINES
1831 Westwood Ave.   358-6666

Major Event Facilities

The Mosque, Coliseum, Farmer's Market, Richmond Centre for Conventions and Exhibitions and the Arthur

LORA ROBINS GALLERY
OF DESIGN FROM NATURE
Richmond Way
UNIVERSITY of RICHMOND

COLLECTIONS OF MINERALS, JEWELS, SEASHELLS AND OTHER WORKS OF, AND FROM, NATURE'S ART

Hours: Monday-Friday, 10 AM-4 PM
Saturday-Sunday, 1 PM-5 PM
The Gallery will be closed when engaged
for private events

Open to the public without charge.
Parking adjoins the Gallery.

FOR INFORMATION CALL 289-8237

BEHIND EVERY GREAT EXPLORER, THERE'S A REALLY GREAT GUIDE.

All of history's great explorers knew it. To get where you want to go, you need a guide that really knows the territory. Before you begin to explore the wonderful world of Richmond's Downtown, make sure you have your copy of our comprehensive "Do The Town" guide. It's chock full of information on the things you'll want to know about Downtown. Great restaurants to suit your tastes and pocketbook. Not-to-be-missed museums and attractions. Top-flight sports and performing arts. Places to get a great new "do," buy a rare antique or take a chance in the Virginia Lottery. All in one compact book that includes an easy-to-follow map to help you plot your course around Downtown.

Come explore the wonderful world of Richmond's Downtown. And discover just how much fun a great city can be.

For your FREE copy of our "Do The Town" guide, write, phone or fax:

**Downtown Richmond, Inc.
700 East Franklin St., Suite 810
Richmond, VA 23219
(804) 643-2824
Fax (804) 649-3435**

Ashe Jr. Athletic Center are operated by the Richmond Department of Parks and Recreation.

RICHMOND COLISEUM
780-4970

This arena-style facility at Seventh and Leigh streets in downtown can seat more than 12,000 spectators and is frequently used for sporting events and music concerts. The home of the Richmond Renegades, the Coliseum's main floor can be converted into an ice rink.

THE RICHMOND CENTRE FOR CONVENTIONS AND EXHIBITIONS
783-7300

You can rent the entire facility or just a meeting room at the Richmond Centre at Fifth and Marshall streets. The Centre is within walking distance of the Coliseum and major hotels.

THE MOSQUE
780-8226

In the Fan at 6 N. Laurel Street, the Mosque seats 3,667 and has one of the most popular stages in the area for music and theatrical performances. It also has a Grand Ballroom and smaller rooms available for rent.

ARTHUR ASHE JR. ATHLETIC CENTER
780-6131

This athletic center at 3001 N. Boulevard seats 6,200 spectators and is available for sports events, dances and other functions.

Credit: Richmond Newspapers

*Attending Strawberry Hill Races is an annual rite of Spring
for many Richmonders.*

Inside
Annual Events

Richmonders turn out in great numbers for events, parades and festivals, especially the Richmond Children's Festival, Strawberry Hill Races, Camptown Races, June Jubilee, the BIG Gig, the State Fair, the International Food Festival and the Jaycee's Christmas Parade.

We love an excuse to party, and we've got a festival for everything, especially food. There's a tomato festival, a pork festival, a watermelon festival, oyster festivals, Virginia food festivals, Greek food festivals and International food festivals. There's even the new "A Taste of Richmond" festival that offers tempting samples from a variety of area restaurants.

Since many of our popular events are related to the arts, we've described those in our Arts chapter. Some are described in our Sports chapter, and we've explained some other popular ones here. We know that's a little confusing, so a complete calendar of annual events is included at the end of this chapter to pull it all together for you in one place.

A DAY IN THE PARK WITH A FRIEND
Carillon, Byrd Park
Richmond Newspapers, Inc. 649-6738

Sponsored by Richmond Newspapers, this August event features exhibits and demonstrations by local law enforcement, fire and community service organizations. You'll get to know the people behind the badges, and you'll see parachute jumping, police dog shows and dozens of other lifesaving and rescue operations. Kids can climb on fire engines, sit on police motorcycles and get fingerprinted. There's lots to do and see. Admission is free.

COMMUNITY LEARNING WEEK
1500 N. Lombardy St. 257-5646

Community Learning Week, in mid-January, is the nation's only weeklong series of events, conferences and workshops built around the life and philosophy of the Rev. Dr. Martin Luther King Jr. This event is hosted by Virginia Union University and is sponsored by more than 75 business, civic and social organizations.

EASTER ON PARADE
Downtown Presents. . . 643-2826

Several blocks of Monument Avenue in the Fan District are sectioned off for this old-fashioned Easter parade among the monuments. If you like people-watching, you don't want to miss this one. Join the crowd, stroll down the avenue and enjoy the sights and entertainment. The porches of elegant mansions become stages for some of the area's best jazz, bluegrass and Dixieland musicians, while roving characters and performers provide delightful entertainment everywhere you look. Children are welcomed with special activities including carousel and

Ferris wheel rides, face-painting, bonnet decorating and more. Be sure to bring your camera for the annual bonnet contest usually held in front of the Davis monument. Pets and coolers are not allowed. Event maps are available from food vendors and the information booth.

FESTIVAL OF THE ARTS
Dogwood Dell/Carillon
Byrd Park   780-5733

Free concerts, dances and dramatic performances are offered at this multitiered, grassy outdoor amphitheater each summer during the Festival of the Arts. Bring a picnic supper, a blanket or lawn chairs and relax under the evening stars. You'll see everything from rock 'n' roll to classical ballet. It's great family entertainment. Once you get to the park, just head for the Carillon. It's a 240-foot Georgian bell tower that pays tribute to Virginians who died in World War I. There's room for about 3,000 people, but come early to get the best seats and room for your spread.

THE FIRST THANKSGIVING
Berkeley Plantation   272-3226

Spend the day at this beautiful plantation on the James and watch an outdoor drama commemorating the events of the first official Thanksgiving celebration held in this country. It wasn't at Plymouth, it was here. You'll enjoy living history performances, dancing and demonstrations by representatives from local Indian tribes and live musical entertainment. You'll also find Southern-style food and an arts and craft show featuring some of the finest artisans in the area. The celebration is held the first Saturday in November. Admission to the event includes a tour of the plantation house and gardens.

HISTORIC GARDEN WEEK IN VIRGINIA
12 E. Franklin St.   644-7776, 643-7141

The last full week in April, hundreds of private homes and gardens throughout the state are open for tours as part of Historic Garden Week, sponsored by the Garden Club of Virginia. In the Richmond area, about 15 to 20 homes are open each year for about three days during the tour period. Cosponsored by the Historic Richmond Foundation, this tour marks the only time many homes and shrines, including Westover Plantation, are open to the public. Proceeds are used to help restore historic grounds and gardens throughout the state. A guidebook with information about tour locations and schedules is available March 1 from the Garden Club of Virginia. The guidebook also includes information about other historic landmarks and shrines in the state.

Admission usually ranges from about $12 to $15 for block tours. Admission to individual homes is about $2 to $4. Richmond area tours are sponsored by the Boxwood Garden Club, James River Garden Club, Three Chopt Garden Club and Tuckahoe Garden Club of Westhampton.

MAYMONT FLOWER AND GARDEN SHOW
Maymont Foundation   358-7166

In midwinter, the Maymont Flower and Garden Show offers a refreshing preview of spring. Held each February at the Richmond Centre in downtown Richmond, this is Virginia's largest flower and garden show. You can stroll through uniquely designed blooming indoor landscapes featuring tens of thousands of trees, flowers and shrubs. Full-size ponds, gazebos, fountains and garden statuary are also displayed, and landscape designers and contractors are available to answer your questions. You'll find every imaginable flower or garden-related item on display or for sale including lights, furniture, ornaments, baskets, handcrafts, flags, sculpture, flower pots, books, tools and more. Numerous gardening and horticultural associations and organizations have exhibits, and educational topics are presented by well-known speakers. The best time to go to avoid the crowds is around 6 PM. Proceeds benefit the Maymont Foundation.

NATIVE AMERICAN INDIAN POW WOW
Strawberry Hill   *228-3200*

This is an authentic Native American Indian Pow Wow open to the public. The first one in 1991 was so successful, the organizers decided to make it an annual event each November. You'll see Indian dancing, costumes, craft-making and competitions. Admission fees vary.

SOUTHERN WOMEN'S SHOW
Charlotte, N.C.   *(704) 376-6594*

Each spring, the Southern Women's Show arrives at the State Fairgrounds on Strawberry Hill with four days of learning, shopping and tasting. Don't miss this chance to see fashion shows, hear expert financial advice, visit boutiques, attend educational seminars and discover art and home decorating ideas and techniques. You can even have a professional makeover and a quick health check.

STRAWBERRY HILL RACES
Strawberry Hill   *228-3200*

This steeplechase is one of the biggest annual events in the area and has become Richmond's rite of spring. Proceeds benefit local charities. The Richmond Symphony was selected to be the lead benefactor in 1993, replacing the Historic Richmond Foundation, which benefited from the races for more than a decade. The Symphony plans to use the proceeds to expand its youth and school programs throughout Virginia.

Held in April, the races are preceded by balls, carriage parades and parties. The day of the races, people have elaborate themed tailgate parties, and many dress in fashions or costumes to complement their party themes. It's a big reunion for locals, and you'll see just about everything from sunbathers guzzling beer to Rolls Royces and people dressed in top hats and tails sipping French champagne. Be sure to walk around the infield to see it all. Prizes are awarded for the best tailgate parties. Call in advance to reserve a space or to enter the tailgate competition.

STATE FAIR
Strawberry Hill   *228-3200*

Every September, the State Fair returns with something for everyone. There are craft displays, blue-ribbon winners, livestock displays and demonstrations, midway rides and games, Italian sausages and corn dogs, big-name entertainment shows, magic shows, side shows, a circus and lots and lots of exhibits by companies and organizations from all over the state. Many employers and companies offer discount tickets. Ask at work or watch the ads.

Celebrate the Fourth of July by watching the fireworks display at the Diamond and by going to the country music concert on Brown's Island.

Insiders' Tips

• **349**

TACKIEST CHRISTMAS DECORATIONS TOUR

Every year, some holiday enthusiasts go to extremes to decorate their homes. Some have so many lights, they have to generate their own electricity, and you have to wonder where they store all the trains, carolers, candy canes and Santas. Watch the *Richmond Times-Dispatch* for a description and map of the tour. Some of the homes are so popular, you actually have to wait in traffic to see them. Others have so much to see, you'll want to park and walk around for a closer look.

THE RACES AT MARENGO

Historic Richmond Foundation   643-7407

Relive the elegance of an earlier time and enjoy a picturesque day in the country with the excitement of horse racing at The Races at Marengo. Held each May, the growing event attracts more than 7,500 visitors. Proceeds benefit the Historic Richmond Foundation's preservation projects in Richmond. Just 30 minutes from Richmond, the races are held at a new steeplechase course in New Kent County at Marengo, a historic plantation overlooking the Pamunkey River. The house is the centerpiece of the track that dips down by the river, rises dramatically at a point called Heartbreak Hill and levels off around the final turns to the finish. Owned by Mr: and Mrs. E. Taylor Moore Jr., Marengo was named for the site of Napoleon's victory over the Austrians in 1800, the second battle of his Italian campaign. Built in 1817, Marengo still has its original Federal house and several outbuildings.

Activities at the races include a parade of antique carriages and competitions for the best tailgate and corporate tent parties and the most elegant hat. Tailgate parking, box seats and picnic spots

are available. Call for reservations and tickets.

A TASTE OF RICHMOND

Richmond Newspapers, Inc.   649-6085

Designed to showcase the delicious and varied cuisine of area restaurants, this annual event offers visitors a chance to sip and nibble their way through dozens of booths operated by some of the finest, most creative and unusual restaurants in the area. Live music, children's activities and games add to the weekend of festivities. Sponsored by Richmond Newspapers, Inc., A Taste of Richmond is usually held on Brown's Island in May.

SECOND STREET FESTIVAL

Downtown Presents. . .   643-2826

This two-day festival on Richmond's historic Second Street celebrates the culture and heritage of Richmond's African-American community and serves as a reunion for many who lived and worked here or frequented the area. You'll find jazz, ragtime, gospel music, and music from 1920 through 1950, plus dramatic performances, children's activities, dancing in the street, and ethnic food such as chitterlings, pig's feet, fish, fried chicken, collard greens and more. Vendors sell African-American clothing, jewelry, prints and other wares. Admission is free.

URBANNA OYSTER FESTIVAL

Urbanna   758-5540

We're cheating on this one because it's not a Richmond area event, but since so many Richmonders go to this festival we thought it should be included. In fact, this festival is so popular that the water pipes under the streets broke from the weight of the crowd several years ago. It's more spread out now and not as crowded as it used to be. This festival is held the

2nd Street

Once called The Deuce, 2nd Street was the hub of a vital African-American business community anchored by seven African-American banks in Jackson Ward from Broad to Jackson streets. It was also a place for nightclubs and nip joints.

During its heyday from the 1920s to the '40s, locals and students from Virginia Union University would meet for dinner at Slaughter's and catch a midnight show. Entertainers including Laverne Baker, the Five Satins and the Five Keys often appeared at the Hippodrome Theatre — the heart of 2nd Street. Although the nightclubs were illegal, those who remember them say there was never any trouble.

Sundays on 2nd Street presented a different face. The Elks Home had a parade and people dressed up in their best clothes and strolled from Broad to Duvall Street.

Credit: Richmond Newspapers

This gentleman is one of many participants in the 2nd Street Festival.

To celebrate the history of 2nd Street and focus attention on the restoration of Jackson Ward neighborhood, the 2nd Street Festival has been held each year since 1989. The first festival was staged as an event for the opening of 2 Street, a film produced by Richmond Renaissance, the Valentine Museum and the Black History Museum. The festival was so popular, it's been held every year since. Festivities now spread across four blocks.

The two-day event features arts, crafts, African-American cuisine, live music, films in the Hippodrome Theatre, children's activities and walking tours. The aroma of down-home cookin' fills the air, and African rice, chitlins and bologna burgers are sold along with cotton candy and other festival foods. The crowd moves to irresistible funky rhythms, while ragtime, blues, soulful gospel music and jazz performances pay tribute to a rich heritage of music.

As many as 40,000 people attend the festival, held on Second Street from Marshall to Leigh Street, and on the two blocks of Clay Street just east and west of 2nd Street. Admission is free.

Festival-goers may also visit the Maggie Walker House, at 110½ Leigh Street. Maggie Walker founded the St. Luke Penny Savings Bank and was the first woman bank president in the United States. Her bank and two other African-American banks merged to become the Consolidated Bank and Trust Company. The house where she lived was restored in 1985 and is now operated by the National Park Service. As much as it is a notable historic attraction, the festival also serves as a symbol of the revitalization of the neighborhood.

Other attractions in the area include the Black History Museum and Cultural Center, the former Eggleston and Slaughter hotels and the Consolidated Bank and Trust Company.

first weekend in November every year. Oyster fans will find raw, steamed and roasted oysters, oyster stew, oyster fritters and fried oysters. If you don't like oysters, the crab cake and soft shell crab sandwiches are good bets, and there's lots of other food to eat. You'll also find an art show, crafts, a few amusement rides and tours of tall ships docked in the harbor. The Saturday afternoon parade features numerous high school bands, Shriners and literally every fire department within driving distance (you won't believe the sirens!). Try to get there before 9 AM on Saturday if you want to park anywhere close. Visit on Friday to avoid the crowds and miss the parade.

Annual Events

This is a month-by-month listing of some favorite annual events enjoyed by Richmonders. We've described some of the most popular ones in our chapters on The Arts, Attractions and Sports. Call for more information and schedules.

January

BASSARAMA
Strawberry Hill   228-3200

COMMUNITY LEARNING WEEK
1500 N. Lombardy St.   257-5646

GREAT SOUTHERN WEAPONS SHOW
Strawberry Hill   737-0484

February

RICHMOND ACADEMY OF
MEDICINE AUXILIARY ANTIQUE SHOW
Science Museum   740-7892

MAYMONT FLOWER & GARDEN SHOW
Richmond Centre   783-7300

CIAA MEN'S BASKETBALL
TOURNAMENT
Richmond Coliseum   780-4956

ASTRO CERAMISTS & DOLL SHOW
Showplace   225-8877

RICHMOND BOAT SHOW
Strawberry Hill   228-3200

March

RICHMOND HOME SHOW
Strawberry Hill   228-3200

WINSTON CUP RACE WEEKEND
Richmond International Raceway   329-6796

ST. PATRICK'S DAY PARADE
                                  266-0444

VIRGINIA SPRING SHOW
Showplace   225-8877

VIRGINIA-CAROLINA
CRAFTSMAN SPRING CLASSIC
Strawberry Hill   228-3200

CHILDREN'S BOOK FESTIVAL
Various locations   335-7200

CAA MEN'S BASKETBALL
TOURNAMENT
University of Richmond   289-8384

RICHMOND INTERNATIONAL AUTO
SHOW
Richmond Centre   783-7300

BIZARRE BAZAAR SPRING MARKET
Strawberry Hill   228-7555

GOLF SHOW
Richmond Centre   783-7300

April

D&S DOLL SHOW
Strawberry Hill   228-3200

STRAWBERRY HILL RACES
Strawberry Hill   228-3200

EASTER ON PARADE
Monument Ave.
Downtown Presents. . .   643-2826

FAMILY EASTER
Maymont Park   Various [illegible]

HERBS GALORE
Maymont Park   358-7166

RICHMOND BRAVES OPENING DAY
The Diamond   359-4444

CHILI COOK-OFF
Strawberry Hill   228-3200

HISTORIC GARDEN WEEK IN VIRGINIA
Various locations   644-7776

THE SOUTHERN WOMEN'S SHOW
Strawberry Hill   228-3200

CENTRAL VIRGINIA
AZALEA FESTIVAL PARADE
Forest Hill Park   233-2093

HERITAGE FESTIVAL
Poor Farm Park   798-8062

VIRGINIA CERAMISTS SHOW
Showplace   225-8877

VIRGINIA STATE HORSE SHOW
Strawberry Hill   228-3200

THE GREAT SOUTHERN WEAPONS FAIR
Strawberry Hill   737-0484

CIVIL WAR SHOW
Strawberry Hill   228-3200

May

TOUR DUPONT
Downtown   354-9934

THE RACES AT MARENGO
New Kent County   643-7407

ARTS IN THE PARK
Byrd Park   353-8198

CIVIL WAR ENCAMPMENT & BATTLE
Meadow Farm   672-5106

MEMORIAL DAY HERITAGE WEEKEND
Living History
(various locations)   353-8166

PLANTATION DAY
Magnolia Grange   796-1479

CAMPTOWN RACES
Graymont Park
Ashland   798-5314

SCOTCHTOWN FESTIVAL
Scotchtown   227-3500

JAMES RIVER WINE FESTIVAL
Brown's Island   359-4645

HOOP IT UP
Festival Park area   643-2826

June

BEACH MUSIC FESTIVAL
Jaycees, Strawberry Hill   644-9607

DOGWOOD DELL FESTIVAL OF THE ARTS
Dogwood Dell   780-5733

FAMILY CRAFTFAIR
Deep Run Park   672-5134

JUNE JUBILEE
Downtown   643-2826

JUMPIN'
Virginia Museum of Fine Arts   367-0844

GREEK FESTIVAL
Greek Orthodox Cathedral   355-3687

ASHLAND STRAWBERRY FAIRE
Randolph Macon College   798-9219

REENACTMENT AT COLD HARBOR NATIONAL BATTLEFIELD PARK
771-2808

VIRGINIA AVIATION MUSEUM FLIGHT DAY
236-3622

July

THE BIG GIG, RICHMOND'S INTERNATIONAL FESTIVAL OF MUSIC
643-2826

FOURTH OF JULY EXTRAVAGANZA
Chesterfield Fairgrounds   748-1623

FOURTH OF JULY CELEBRATION & PARADE
Maymont Park   358-7166

OLD FASHIONED FOURTH
Meadow Farm   672-5134

FOURTH OF JULY AT THE DIAMOND
The Diamond   359-4444

FOURTH OF JULY AT INNSBROOK
Innsbrook   965-7922

JUMPIN'
Virginia Museum of Fine Arts   367-0844

USA SPORTS CARD CLASSIC
Strawberry Hill   228-3200

August

VIRGINIA FOOD FESTIVAL
Strawberry Hill   228-3200

LIVING HISTORY ENCAMPMENT
Cold Harbor Battlefield   226-1981

JUMPIN'
Virginia Museum of Fine Arts   367-0844

SENIOR CITIZENS ARTS & CRAFT SHOW
Byrd Park   780-5733

CARYTOWN WATERMELON FESTIVAL
Carytown   741-0387

A DAY IN THE PARK
Richmond Newspapers, Inc.   649-6738

September

MILLER 400 RACE WEEKEND
Richmond International Raceway 329-6796

INTERNATIONAL FOOD FESTIVAL
Richmond Centre   783-7300

HENRICUS PUBLICK DAYS
Henricus Historical Park   748-1161

CIVIL WAR DAYS REENACTMENT
Meadow Farm   672-5106

STATE FAIR OF VIRGINIA
Strawberry Hill   228-3200

**CHRISTMAS IN SEPTEMBER
ARTS & CRAFT SHOW**
Dorey Park   672-5100

October

SECOND STREET FESTIVAL
Downtown Presents. . .   643-2826

RICHMOND CHILDREN'S FESTIVAL
Arts Council   355-7200

BLACK EXPO
Richmond Centre   783-7300

CENTRAL VIRGINIA PORK FESTIVAL
Strawberry Hill   228-3200

RICHMOND NEWSPAPERS MARATHON
                                       649-6325

SEAFOOD FESTIVAL
White House Station
St. Peter's Church   932-4846

FESTIVAL OF INDIA
Richmond Centre   783-7300

**GREAT PUMPKIN PARTY,
SHOCKOE SLIP HARVEST FESTIVAL**
Meadow Farm   672-5134

**AUTUMN HARVEST
GRAND ILLUMINATION PARADE**
W. Broad St.   266-6808

OKTOBERFEST
Strawberry Hill   228-3200

November

URBANNA OYSTER FESTIVAL
Urbanna   758-5540

JOY FROM THE WORLD AND MODEL RAILROAD SHOW
Science Museum of Virginia   367-6792

FIRST THANKSGIVING FESTIVAL
Berkeley Plantation   747-1537

ASHLAND HOLIDAY PARADE
Ashland   798-9219

NATIVE AMERICAN INDIAN POW WOW
Strawberry Hill   228-3200

VIRGINIA-CAROLINA CRAFTSMEN CHRISTMAS CLASSIC
Strawberry Hill   228-3200

VIRGINIA CHRISTMAS SHOW
Showplace   225-8877

RICHMOND CRAFT SHOW
Richmond Centre   783-7300

THE GREAT SOUTHERN WEAPONS FAIR
Strawberry Hill   228-3200

December

JAYCEES CHRISTMAS PARADE
Broad St., Downtown   644-9607

GRAND ILLUMINATION
James Center   344-3232

MAYMONT'S CHRISTMAS OPEN HOUSE
Maymont Park   358-7166

FAN DISTRICT HOUSE TOUR
Various locations   355-0892

CHURCH HILL HOUSE TOUR
Various locations   649-3519

EXECUTIVE MANSION OPEN HOUSE
Capital Square   786-2220

CAPITAL CITY KWANZA FESTIVAL
Festival Park or Jackson Ward   643-3826

CHRISTMAS AT AGECROFT HALL
353-4241

CHRISTMAS IN COURT END
Court End   649-0711

SCOTCHTOWN'S CHRISTMAS CANDLELIGHT TOUR
Scotchtown   227-3500

TACKIEST CHRISTMAS DECORATIONS TOUR
Details in the Richmond Times-Dispatch

YULETIDE FEST
Meadow Farm   672-5100

NEW YEAR'S EVE PARTY IN FESTIVAL PARK

BIZARRE BAZAAR
Strawberry Hill   228-3200

Inside
Kidstuff

Children can exercise their bodies and stretch their imaginations at some very special places and events in the area. You'll also find amusement parks, sporting events, festivals and parades that the whole family will enjoy. This list is intended to help you identify places where your kids might like to go. The headings correspond to chapters in this book where you'll find more information.

Attractions and Fun Things To Do

Richmond Children's Museum
Science Museum Of Virginia
Paramount's Kings Dominion

Rafting on the James River
Meadow Farm at Crump Park
Scotchtown
Maymont
Chesterfield County Museum —
    The Old Jail
St. John's Church
State Capitol
Travelland
Virginia Museum of Fine Arts
Valentine Riverside
National Battlefield Parks
Museum and White House
    of the Confederacy
Money Museum, Federal Reserve
    Bank of Richmond
Steamer Company No. 5

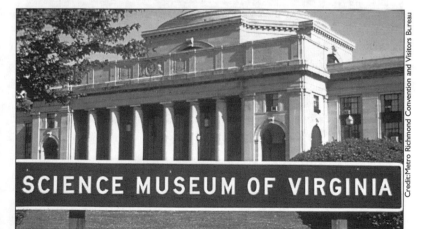

Credit: Metro Richmond Convention and Visitors Bureau

The Science Museum of Virginia offers numerous hands-on exhibits for children and adults to explore.

Sgt. Santa — A Year-Round Tradition

Every year around Christmas, Santa appears in all shapes and sizes at malls and Santa houses throughout Richmond. But there's one very special old elf with a snowy white beard and sergeant stripes on his sleeves who stands out from the rest.

Known as Sgt. Santa, former Richmond Police Officer Ricky Duling began playing Sgt. Santa in 1972 when he drove his police car through low-income neighborhoods during the Christmas season and gave boxes of candy to children. With his long white beard, which he grew for undercover work, he was a natural look-alike for the "real" Santa.

During the Christmas season, Sgt. Santa and his helpers provide thousands of packages, containing gifts such as comic books, candy, cookies and toys for children who otherwise may not receive gifts.

When Duling retired after 35 years as a city policeman, he made his role as Sgt. Santa a full-time avocation. Volunteers from civic clubs and scout troops joined him in helping people year round, as well as at Christmas. The group has helped families who were left homeless as a result

Credit: Richmond Newspapers

Sargeant Santa listens to a child's Christmas list.

of fires and given toys and food to a number of others. They've also helped furnish immigrants with furniture. Area merchants have joined the effort, donating items and collecting and matching donations from their customers.

In addition to his charitable giving, Sgt. Santa fulfills the customary responsibilities of any respectable Santa. He sits on Santa thrones, listens to wish lists, rides in parades and poses for photos.

If you're looking for the "real" Santa, try Santaland in the old Miller & Rhoads building downtown, home of Richmond's legendary Santa. (He's been visited by generations of Richmonders who swear he's the "real" guy.) You can also find Santa at Azalea Mall, Chesterfield Towne Center, Cloverleaf Mall, Fairfield Commons Mall, Regency Square, The Shops at Willow Lawn and Southpark Mall. Virginia Center Commons has a signing Santa who even makes time in his busy schedule to find out what your pet would like for Christmas. You'll also find Santa at numerous special events, museums and parades throughout the area. Watch the newspaper for details.

The Play Factory
Gymboree
The Laserzone
Strawberry, Blueberry, Blackberry and
    Pumpkin Picking at Area Farms
Dorey Park
Byrd Park
James River Park
Belle Island, Foot Bridge
Pocahontas State Park

Entertainment and Shows

Richmond Coliseum Events
Theatre IV Productions
The Nutcracker
Special Events At Local Libraries
Peanut Butter 'n Jam Summer Concerts
    (Richmond Children's Museum)
Friday Cheers, 6th Street
    Marketplace

Annual Events and Festivals

Festival of the Arts, Dogwood Dell
Richmond Children's Festival
June Jubilee

A Day in the Park With a Friend
Easter on Parade
The First Thanksgiving at Berkeley
Native American Indian Pow Wow
State Fair of Virginia
A Taste of Richmond
2nd Street Festival
Jaycees Christmas Parade
St. Patrick's Day Parade
Ashland Holiday Parade
Ashland Strawberry Faire
Tackiest Christmas
    Decorations Tour
Children's Book Festival
Memorial Day Heritage
    Weekend Events
The BIG Gig
Fourth of July Celebrations
    at Various Locations
Great Pumpkin Party, Shockoe Slip

Spectator Sports

Richmond Braves Baseball
Renegades Hockey
College Basketball and
    Football Games

Don't miss the cave at the Richmond Children's Museum.

Insiders' Tips

Richmond Newspapers Marathon
Tour DuPont

Nearby Attractions/Daytrips

Williamsburg, Busch Gardens,
    Water Country USA
Jamestown
Yorktown

Nauticus, The National Maritime
    Center in Norfolk
Monticello
Shenandoah Valley
Washington, D.C.
Virginia Living Museum,
    Newport News
Virginia Beach
The Rivah

Inside
Daytrips

Richmond's central location makes it an ideal starting point for daytrips. You can drive to nearly every part of the state within a few hours. To the east, you can visit the ocean, the Chesapeake Bay, Colonial Williamsburg, the Eastern Shore and the James River Plantations. To the west, you'll find the Shenandoah Valley, the Blue Ridge Mountains and Jefferson's Monticello. To the north is Washington, D.C., and to the south, you can explore Civil War area and more than 250 years of history in Petersburg.

Virginia is rich with a variety of attractions and scenic places. In this section we've included a few of our favorite destinations. The Eastern Shore and the Highlands of Southwest Virginia are also interesting areas to visit, especially for nature lovers, but you'll need to allow more than a day for a trip.

For more information and maps, we suggest that you start with the Virginia Information Center at the Bell Tower in Capitol Square, 786-4484, or contact the Virginia State Tourism Development Group, 1021 E. Cary Street, 786-4484. Insiders' Guide books are also available on some of these areas. A complete list of Insiders' Guide titles and information about how to order them is included in the back of this book.

Berkeley Plantation is the oldest three-story home in Virginia.

Credit: Richmond Newspapers

Plantations

Several Colonial plantations on the James River, southeast of Richmond on Route 5 in Charles City County, are historically and architecturally interesting. You can also enjoy beautiful views of the river from artistically landscaped lawns and gardens. Or, take a cruise on the *Annabel Lee*, a paddlewheel riverboat, and see them from the river the way the colonists did. There's more information about the *Annabel Lee's* Plantation Cruise in the Attractions and Events chapters. You can also call Virginia Plantation Country in Hopewell, 733-2400, for more information about river cruises, tours and nearby attractions, shopping and accommodations.

BERKELEY PLANTATION
829-6018

Built in 1726 by Benjamin Harrison IV, Berkeley is the oldest three-story brick home in Virginia. Harrison's son, the second owner of the plantation, was a signer of the Declaration of Independence and a governor of Virginia three times. William Henry Harrison, the ninth president of the United States, and Benjamin Harrison, the 23rd president, are descendants of Benjamin Harrison IV. Berkeley is also known as the site of America's first Thanksgiving, which took place in 1619. A festival commemorating the event is held here each year in November. Tours are available of the house and gardens.

EDGEWOOD
829-2962

This 1849 Gothic Revival mansion is now open for tours and as a bed and breakfast inn. The house features six bedrooms filled with antiques, a freestanding spiral staircase in the grand hall and 10 fireplaces. The grounds include a mill built in 1725. According to legend, you can still hear the footsteps of a woman who once lived here as she searches for her lover who never returned from the war. Reservations are required for tours and rooms.

EVELYNTON
829-5075

This was the home of Edmund Ruffin who is credited with firing the first shot of the Civil War at Fort Sumter. It's been the home of the Ruffin family since 1847. The property was originally part of Westover Plantation, and the house features examples of decorative arts from the great houses of Virginia. The house and gardens are open for tours and are available for catered occasions such as weddings, receptions and corporate meetings.

NORTH BEND PLANTATION
12200 Weyanoke Rd. (After 5:30 PM) 829-5176 Charles City

Built in 1819, North Bend Plantation is one of the oldest bed and breakfast buildings in the area. About a mile off Route 5 on Weyanoke Road, the Greek Revival plantation house is on the National Register of Historic Landmarks and is also a designated Virginia Historic Landmark. Ridgely and George Copeland are the third generation of the family to own the home, and they still cultivate the plantation's 250 acres. In 1864, Union General Phil Sheridan used North Bend as his Civil War headquarters. Union breastworks still exist on the grounds. Special possessions displayed to visitors include a fine collection of old and rare books, colonial antiques from related early James River plantation families and an antique doll collection. North Bend is also available for weddings and receptions.

SHERWOOD FOREST
829-5377

Built in 1730, this 300-foot-long frame house looks similar to the way it appeared in 1845 when it was renovated by former President John Tyler. The home was also owned by President William Henry Harrison. Original 18th-century furnishings throughout the house include heirlooms of the Tyler family, descendants of whom still live here. A 12-acre garden features more than 80 varieties of century-old trees. Mansion or garden tours are available. Reservations are preferred for mansion tours. It's shown by appointment only on weekends.

SHIRLEY
829-5121

Founded in 1613, Shirley is the oldest plantation in Virginia and has been the home of the Hill-Carter family for 10 generations. Anne Hill Carter, mother of Gen. Robert E. Lee, was born and married here, and Lee received part of his schooling here. The present mansion was completed in 1738 and appears for the most part in its original state. An architectural treasure, the mansion features a three-story circular staircase with no visible means of support, carved walnut staircases, superb paneling and elegant carved detailing. The 10th generation of the original family now oversees the farm and house. Tours are offered daily.

WESTOVER
795-2882

Built in 1730, Westover is one of the finest examples of Georgian architecture in America. This was the home of William Byrd II, the founder of Richmond and Petersburg. The grounds are open daily. The house is closed except during Historic Garden Week.

Wineries

There are a number of wineries and vineyards within driving distance of Richmond that are open for tours or festivals. For a free list write: Virginia Wine Marketing Program, Virginia Department of Agriculture and Consumer Services, Division of Marketing, P.O. Box 1163, Richmond 23209; or phone 786-0481.

Williamsburg, Jamestown and Yorktown

COLONIAL WILLIAMSBURG
(800) HISTORY

This is the largest restored 18th-century town in America. Once the capital of Virginia, Colonial Williamsburg has been restored to appear as it did in Colonial times during the Revolutionary War and the formative years of our country.

It's literally a city within a city. Costumed interpreters reenact daily life in such detail, and the homes and gardens are so authentic that you'll think you've stepped back in time. Christmas is especially beautiful with all the natural decorations. The holiday season begins with the Grand Illumination celebration the first week of December.

When you need a break from history, the whole family will enjoy a visit to Busch Gardens — The Old Country, a quality theme park with rides, entertainment, shows and themed areas modeled after European countries. School-age children and teenagers will also like Water Country USA, a water park with several acres of slides, rides and water activities.

If you like to shop, you'll find bargains on designer clothing and accessories at the Williamsburg Outlet Mall and designer fashions for men, women and

Thomas Jefferson's home, Monticello, is regarded as a pillar of Virginia's architectural history.

children at Berkeley Commons. The Pottery Factory is also a popular place to shop for bargains on glassware, pottery, dishes, baskets, plants, lamps, craft items and lots of other things.

You can't do it all in one day. Be sure to allow yourself several days to explore the attractions and shopping in this area, or plan frequent visits. Williamsburg is off I-64 E., about 50 miles east of Richmond. For more information write the Williamsburg Area Convention and Visitors Bureau, P.O. Box Drawer GB, Williamsburg 23187.

JAMESTOWN SETTLEMENT
229-1607

Previously known as Jamestown Festival Park, Jamestown Settlement features a recreation of a Powhatan Indian village, the replicas of three ships and James Fort. Exhibits focus on the native Indians who lived here in 1607, when the colonists established Jamestown as the first permanent English colony in America.

The park is about 60 miles from Richmond. Take I-64 E. to exit 57A. It's just off Route 31, about 6 miles southwest of Williamsburg.

YORKTOWN
887-1776

At the site where America won her independence, the Yorktown Victory Center features Revolutionary War exhibits plus an outdoor encampment with historic interpreters. Yorktown is about 75 minutes east of Richmond off I-64 near Williamsburg.

Fredericksburg

Civil War enthusiasts will want to spend some time in Fredericksburg touring the battlefields at Chancellorsville, the Wilderness and Spotsylvania Court House.

Other visitors may enjoy browsing through the quaint shops and restaurants in the picturesque historic district. You can also tour Kenmore, the home of George Washington's sister, and the Mary Washington House, which he bought for his mother.

If you like to shop, you may want to combine a trip here with a trip to Potomac Mills, one of the world's largest outlet malls. Potomac Mills is north of Fredericksburg, about 30 miles south of Washington, D.C.

Fredericksburg is about 60 miles north of Richmond off I-95. You can also take the train. For more information, contact the Visitor Center at 706 Caroline Street, (703) 373-1776.

Monticello

Monticello, the home of Thomas Jefferson, is about 70 miles west of Richmond near Charlottesville. The tour of this Jefferson-designed architectural treasure is interesting to school-age children as well as adults. The garden tour offers stunning views of the mountains and countryside as well as an interesting variety of herbs, flowers, vegetables and other plants. Start your visit at the Thomas Jefferson Visitors Center, exit 24 off I-64, 295-8181. Picnic facilities are available.

Petersburg

Just 22 minutes south of Richmond along the Appomattox River, the historic city of Petersburg is rich with Civil War history and is enjoying a period of growth following its rapid recovery from the devastation that occurred in August 1993, when a tornado ripped through the area. Although Old Towne Petersburg suffered extensive damage, most structures have been restored and are back in operation; the Appomattox Iron Works is still undergoing restoration. Many new antique shops, boutiques and restaurants are moving into the area.

Life before and during the Civil War is documented at the Siege Museum and at the Petersburg National Battlefield Park, which includes the site of the Battle of the Crater and a map presentation showing troop movements during six major battles. The City Point Unit of the battlefield has wayside exhibits and features Gen. Ulysses S. Grant's winter headquarters. The Five Forks Unit shows where Grant's forces captured Petersburg's railroad lines, a week before Gen. Lee surrendered his troops at Appomattox.

Once restorations are complete, visitors to the Appomattox Iron Works, the industry that helped Petersburg recover after the Civil War, will see the original machines in operation. There's also a working blacksmith shop, sawmill, machine shop and pattern shop. Costumed interpreters explain the iron-casting process.

In Old Towne you'll find one of the nation's best collections of antebellum buildings, tobacco warehouses and early 19th-century store fronts as well as an abundance of antique galleries, boutiques, craft shops, restaurants and sidewalk cafes. A destination in itself, French Betsy's Orleans House offers New Orleans-style dining and entertainment. The popular restaurant features dining areas themed after the Mardi Gras, Bourbon Street and the French Quarter to name a few. Courtyards, fountains, wall murals and street scenes capture the romantic, colorful ambiance of New Orleans and transport you to another place.

Other points of interest include the 1735 Blandford Church with its 15 magnificent Tiffany windows and graveyard where more than 30,000 Confederate soldiers are buried; the 1817 Farmers Bank, the second-oldest bank in the country; the Trapezium House, built in 1815 with no right angles; the 1823 Centre Hill Mansion, filled with decorative arts; the U.S. Slo-pitch (Softball) Hall of Fame; and Battersea, a 1770 Palladian-style mansion that is open for tours by appointment only. There's also a flea market every weekend in the old railroad station.

For more information, stop at the Visitors Center, Cockade Alley, in Old Towne or call 733-2400 or (800) 368-3595.

Hampton

Visitors to this waterfront city near Williamsburg and Virginia Beach, can tour the world's largest naval base, watch an IMAX film on a five-story screen at The Virginia Air and Space Center, or go for a spin on a restored 1920 carousel at the Hampton Carousel. Fort Monroe, America's only active-duty moat-encircled fort, offers walking tours, and the Grandview Nature Preserve provides a pristine 578-acre estuary and wildlife refuge — a great place for hiking, beachcombing and bird-watching. There's also a self-guided tour of seven African-American heritage sites. For more information, visit the Hampton Visitor Center, 710 Settlers Landing Road at Eaton Street, or call 727-1102 or (800) 800-2202.

Antiques, Shopping, Restaurants, Museums, Bed & Breakfast

PETERSBURG

Located along the Appomattox River, Old Towne
Petersburg is filled with antique galleries, boutiques,
craft shops, restaurants, and sidewalk cafes. 250 years
of history unfold in the six Petersburg museums, including
the 1735 Blandford Church with its fifteen Tiffany windows.
Stay the night in one of our many modern travel lodges or
bed & breakfast inns. For more information:

Petersburg Visitors Center
Post Office Box 2107,
Petersburg, VA 23804
or call: 1-800-368-3595
in Virginia call: (804) 733-2400

Newport News

About 75 miles southeast of Richmond, Newport News has one of the world's largest shipyards; the James River Golf Museum; the War Memorial Museum of Virginia, commemorating World Wars I and II and the Korean and Vietnam Wars; and the Virginia Living Museum, featuring a zoo, an aquarium and natural history displays.

You'll also find the Mariners' Museum to the north of the downtown area, where you can see ship models, whaling gear, figureheads and thousands of other marine objects.

To get here, take I-64 E. from Richmond. Call (800) 333-RSVP or 873-0092 for information.

Norfolk-By-The-Sea

One of the newest attractions here is Nauticus, The National Maritime Center with scores of ingenious exhibits and programs. A virtual reality flight simulator provides a realistic 3-D experience, and you can take a ride on a real subma-

rine. There's also a touch pool where you can pet a shark and other marine creatures, a 600 ft. deep water pier, interactive videos on navigation, reef diving and more, and multimedia films. Another popular attraction in Norfolk is Waterside, a festival marketplace that was recently expanded and now includes more than 125 shops, ethnic eateries, an amphitheater and a brick promenade along the edge of the Elizabeth River.

You can also take a self-guided driving tour of major attractions in the area by following the blue and gold Norfolk Tour signs. Along the tour, you'll see the Chrysler Museum, the botanical gardens, the zoo, historic homes and the world's largest naval base.

For more information, call the Norfolk Convention and Visitors Bureau or stop by one of the Visitors Centers at 236 E. Plume Street at the end of Fourth View Street in Ocean View or at The Waterside. Call (800) 368-3097.

Washington, D.C.

The nation's capital city is just 110 miles north of Richmond, straight up I-

95. There's an abundance of government buildings, museums, galleries, the National Zoo, entertainment and shopping. Some of our favorite places include the White House, the Smithsonian Institution, the Air and Space Museum and nearby Georgetown. There's so much to see and do, we can't possibly list everything here, but we can give you some traveling tips. Traffic is bumper to bumper on I-95 during morning and afternoon rush hours, so it's a good idea to plan your trip to avoid driving during those times. If you'd rather not drive, you can take a train from Richmond and get around pretty easily by subway or bus. Call (202) 659-5523 for information.

Northern Virginia

In Northern Virginia, just south of Washington, D.C., you can tour Mount Vernon, George Washington's home; Gunston Hall, home of George Mason, author of the Bill of Rights; Arlington National Cemetery; and historic battlefields. You can drive through beautiful rolling countryside and horse farms, visit wineries and vineyards, dine at charming old country inns and spend the night at historic bed and breakfasts.

You can also spend a relaxing weekend walking around Old Towne Alexandria, a historic seaport city on the Potomac River next to the nation's capital. There are interesting museums, quaint old homes, cobblestone streets, boutiques, art galleries, excellent restaurants and world-class hotels. For more information, contact the Alexandria Convention and Visitors Bureau, (703) 838-4200. You may also call (202) 659-5523.

The "Rivah" And The Bay

Just about everyone who lives in the Richmond area has been to the "Rivah." That's river pronounced with a Richmond accent, and it could mean any one of about 10 different rivers that empty into the Chesapeake Bay, or it could mean the Bay itself. Whatever it means, it's the thing to do during the summer and on weekends.

Many families have vacation homes on the Potomac, Rappahanock, York, Mattaponi, Pamunkey, James, Piankatank, Chickahominy or Wicomico rivers. It's not unusual for several generations of relatives to share ownership in a river place and gather there for big family reunions. If you're not lucky enough to have your own place, you can rent one. Just ask around or look for the ads in the newspaper.

Most of these vacation homes are in quiet river communities where you provide your own entertainment and feast on Chesapeake Bay blue crabs, oysters, rock fish and Southern-fried hush puppies. You can go fishing, crabbing, boating, sailing or skiing. Or, you can spend a lazy day on a breezy porch with a good book or a deck of cards. Some people like to go swimming, but you have to watch out for the stinging nettles in the hot summer months.

You'll find hundreds of popular places all along the rivers and by the Bay. Some of our favorites include Lanexa, Coles Point, Gloucester Point, Smith Point, Kilmarnock, Irvington, Windmill Point, Deltaville, Reedville, Gwynn's Island, Mathews, Colonial Beach, Sandy Point, Sting Ray Point, Urbanna and Wicomico Church.

If you have a boat, you don't necessarily need a place to enjoy the river. You'll see a lot of people leaving town on the weekends pulling speed boats, fishing boats and ski boats behind them. They're heading for public and private boat docks, yacht clubs and marinas. Frequent boaters can rent slips or trailer spots.

Virginia Beach

About 110 miles southeast of Richmond, Virginia Beach is the closest ocean beach for swimming, surfing and sunbathing. It has more miles of beach than any other city in the country, and there's a long boardwalk with spectacular views of the Atlantic Ocean and plenty of room for strolling, walking and bicycling. Be sure to allow time for the bumper boats and other amusements at Ocean Breeze Fun Park.

You can also go exploring and hiking at the nearby Back Bay National Wildlife Refuge, False Cape State Park and Seashore State Park and Natural Area. Families will enjoy a visit to the Virginia Marine Science Museum where children can explore hundreds of hands-on exhibits. Other popular attractions include the Virginia Beach Center for the Arts and the Cape Henry Lighthouse. Call (800) 446-8038 for information.

Shenandoah Valley

Just 1½ hours west of Richmond, you can drive along the highest crests of the Blue Ridge Mountains and enjoy majestic vistas and valley overlooks on the Skyline Drive and the Blue Ridge Parkway. The drive is always beautiful, but the best time to go is in the fall when the colors of the leaves are at their peak. To get here, take I-64 W. from Richmond and proceed west past Charlottesville to the Afton-Waynesboro exit at U.S. 250. You'll find yourself at the confluence of Skyline Drive and the Parkway.

If you love the outdoors and beautiful scenery, you'll want to come here often. You can hike, fish, camp and picnic in the Shenandoah National Park and the George Washington National Forest. There are also eight caverns open for tours including the Endless, Luray, Grand, Skyline, Massanutten, Shenandoah, Natural Bridge and Dixie caverns.

Military history lovers will enjoy visits to Robert E. Lee's office at Washington & Lee University in Lexington, Virginia Military Institute and New Market Battlefield.

Other points of interest include the multimillion-dollar Virginia Horse Center in Lexington, the Museum of Frontier Culture in Staunton, Walton's Mountain Museum in Schuyler, the Apple Blossoms Festival in Winchester and the annual Jousting Tournament at Mt. Solon. Contact the Virginia Tourism Development Group for more information. Call 786-4484.

Inside
Airports

Richmond International Airport (RIC) is convenient to downtown (about 10 minutes via I-64) and is served by 11 airlines offering more than 160 nonstop flights daily to and from 19 destinations including New York, Chicago, Boston, Dallas and Atlanta, and more than 60 direct-service flights to more than 30 destinations including those on the West Coast and in Canada. Twice-per-week, nonstop scheduled charter service is available to Freeport, Bahamas.

More than $42 million has been put into passenger comforts in recent years, and now the airport is probably one of the most user-friendly in the nation. Facilities include an international arrivals terminal serving charter carriers, a teleconferencing center and a fully staffed Metropolitan Richmond Convention and Visitors Bureau Information Center.

The airport does a booming air freight business, provides general aviation services, is home of a U.S. Customs Service staff of six, leases more than 200 acres for military aviation and is the site of the Virginia Aviation Museum that focuses on the "golden years" of flight between the two world wars.

Passenger services include a restaurant and lounge, a cappuccino bar, shops, car rentals, ground transportation, convenient and inexpensive parking, banking and money exchange facilities, photocopying and facsimile facilities, overnight express shipping services, meeting and conference room facilities, hotel reservation services and a complete travel center.

Major Airlines

Six major airlines serve Richmond International.

AMERICAN AIRLINES
(800) 433-7300
American provides daily nonstop and direct service plus connections through its Dallas/Fort Worth hub.

CONTINENTAL AIRLINES
(800) 525-0280
Continental offers daily service to New York/Newark, Cleveland, Greensboro and to 28 connecting locations.

DELTA AIR LINES
(800) 221-1212
Delta offers daily nonstop and connecting service via its Atlanta and Cincinnati hubs.

NORTHWEST AIRLINES
(800) 225-2525
Northwest provides daily nonstop service to Northwest's largest domestic and international hub in Detroit.

USAir
(800) 428-4322

Daily nonstop service connects Richmond with hubs at Baltimore, Philadelphia, Pittsburgh and Charlotte. USAir also has nonstop service to Boston and New York (LaGuardia).

United Airlines
(800) 241-6522

United offers daily nonstop service to Chicago/O'Hare.

Regional Airlines

Five regional airlines serve Richmond International.

American Eagle
(800) 433-7300

American Eagle offers daily nonstop service to the airline's Raleigh/Durham hub.

Comair
(800) 221-1212

A commuter affiliate of Delta Air Lines, Comair provides service to and from Delta's Cincinnati hub.

Continental Express
(800) 525-0280

Service to and from Greensboro is offered by Continental Express.

United Express
(800) 241-6522

United Express has nonstop service to the airline's Washington/Dulles hub.

USAir Express
(800) 428-4322

USAir Express offers nonstop daily service to the airline's Philadelphia and Baltimore hubs.

General Aviation Services and Charters

Corporate hangars are leased and maintained at Richmond International Airport by Richmond-area businesses. In addition, several charter and aviation service firms are located at the airport.

Aero Industries, 222-7211, is a full-service aviation center that offers fueling, service, maintenance and avionics at its Executive Terminal. Rental planes and planes for charter are available, and private planes can be refueled and stocked with food. A flight school operates with two full-time instructors on staff. Arrangements can be made to have rental cars waiting at the terminal on arrival.

Richmond Jet Center, 226-7200, is a terminal for corporate and private aircraft. The company provides its clients with fuel, maintenance and avionics services. Arrangements can be made to have planes restocked with food and to have rental cars waiting at the terminal upon arrival.

Aviation Specialists, Inc., 222-4122, handles aerial inspections of power lines and pipelines and does aerial photography. Aviation Specialists is not in the charter business, but you can call to arrange an airplane ride.

Plan a daytrip to Skyline Drive in the fall when leaf colors are at their peak.

Insiders' Tips

Million Air Richmond, 222-3700, is a full-service fixed base operation offering fuel, avionics, maintenance and corporate hangars. It also offers charter service.

Martinair, 222-7401, provides non-scheduled charter service in and out of Richmond International. Air ambulances for medical emergencies or organ transportation are available. Arrangements can be made to have a plane ready within an hour. The company can fly up to eight passengers in its Lear Jets, King Airs and prop planes. Sixteen full- and part-time pilots are employed by Martinair.

Charters and rentals also are offered by **Hanover Aviation Co.**, 226-8359, **Dominion Aviation Services**, 271-7793, and by **Princess Vacations**, (800) 545-1300. Air ambulance specialists serving Richmond International include **Advanced Aeromedical Air Ambulance Service**, (800) 346-3556, **Advanced Air Ambulance**, (800) 633-3590 and **Air Response**, (800) 631-6565.

Ground Transportation

Groome Transportation offers limousine service to all parts of the Richmond metropolitan area with departures every 10 minutes or less. Groome provides hourly service to Petersburg, Fort Lee and Williamsburg and offers group rates and charter service to and from all parts of Virginia. Groome's vans and buses may be boarded in the area adjacent to baggage pickup. Groome has two telephone numbers: 222-7222 for pickup and schedule information and 222-7226 for charter information.

Approximately 30 independent taxi companies serve Richmond International Airport. Taxis also are located in the area adjacent to the baggage claim section of the airport.

Parking

More than 2,000 long-term and short-term parking spaces are available immediately adjacent to Richmond International's terminal building. In addition, two satellite parking lots handle 1,000 vehicles. A free shuttle service provides transportation between the satellite parking lots and the terminal building every 10 minutes. Convenient short-term metered parking is available in front of the terminal.

When you're in a rush to make a flight, look for the Valet Parking signs and spaces as you drive up to the terminal. Give the attendant your name, keys and flight information. You'll receive a receipt and be on your way. To save even more time, call the RIC Valet Parking Hotline, 226-3089, before your scheduled day of departure so that your receipt can be prepared in advance. When you arrive at the airport, just sign the receipt and give the attendant your keys. The fee for valet parking is $5 added to the $10 parking fee for the first day (and $1.50 per hour after 24 hours up to a maximum of $10 per day for additional days). Prepayment of valet and parking fees (by Visa or MasterCard) can be arranged by calling the Valet Parking Hotline — a helpful service, just in case you're low on cash when you return to Richmond.

Car Rentals

Six automobile rental agencies are located inside the baggage claim area of Richmond International Airport. All offer a variety of late-model cars. These rental agencies are:

Alamo	*222-5445*
Avis	*222-7416*
Budget	*222-5310*

Hertz	222-7228
National	222-7477
Thrifty	222-3200

Air Freight

Air cargo volume at Richmond International has grown at an average rate of almost 20 percent a year over the past decade. Richmond's air cargo growth far outpaces the nation as a whole, which has seen only about a 9 percent average annual increase over the same period. Richmond's growth as a distribution center and its strategic East Coast location have played an important part in the increase. Air freight services handled through Richmond International are provided by·

Airborne Express	(800) 962-7094
Beumon & Lawlivi (for Delta and United)	226-4233
Burlington Air Express	226-2675
CCX Express Cargo Service (for American)	226-7955
Continental Express	236-2827
DHL Worldwide	(800) 225-5345
Delta	222-3677
Emery Worldwide	(800) 443-6379
Federal Express	(800) 238-5355
Northwest	(800) 692-2746
United/United Express	226-4233
United Parcel Service	(800) 552-3900
U.S. Postal Service	226-0656

Other Airports

CHESTERFIELD COUNTY AIRPORT
748-1615

Chesterfield County Airport is a general aviation airport with a Federal Aviation Administration repair station. The airport offers a complete line of service including major repairs to airframes and engines. The airport serves corporate and general aircraft. Flight instruction, fueling and heated hangar space are available.

CHESTERFIELD COUNTY AIRPORT CHARTERS

Two aircraft charter firms are based at Chesterfield County Airport.

Air Chesterfield offers executive air charter service, sightseeing flights, aerial photography flights and priority air freight service. It also provides flight instruction and a ground school. Information is available by calling 748-8770.

Dominion Aviation Services, Inc., also based at the Chesterfield County Airport, offers charter flights leaving either the Chesterfield or Richmond International airports for almost any destination in the United States. Aircraft include everything from twin engine and jet prop aircraft. The phone number for information is 271-7793.

SUNDANCE AVIATION, INC.
798-6500

Sundance Aviation, located at the Hanover County Municipal Airport in the Industrial Airpark, offers certified flight instruction, contract flights, flight maintenance, fuel, hangar space and parking. It is located 2 miles off the Atlee-Elmont exit on I-95 N.

Inside
Media

Richmond is part of that magnificent Southern journalistic tradition that has produced some of the country's greatest editors, reporters and television commentators. It also is the home of Media General, a diversified communications company with major interests in metropolitan newspapers, weekly newspapers, broadcast and cable television, newsprint production and other operations in the United States and Mexico.

The city in recent years remained one of only a few in the nation with both morning and afternoon daily newspapers. That all changed in 1992 when the afternoon *Richmond News Leader* was combined with the morning *Richmond Times-Dispatch*. It was on the *News Leader's* pages that editorial writers Douglas Southall Freeman and James Jackson Kilpatrick and editorial cartoonist Jeff MacNelly first gained national attention, and it was as a reporter on the *News Leader* that television commentator Roger Mudd got his start. The *Times-Dispatch* editorial page was edited for many years by Pulitzer Prize-winning editor and historian Virginius Dabney. Paul Duke, originator and former host of "Washington Week in Review," is a native Richmonder and cut his teeth here with The Associated Press. Network weatherman Spencer Christian's first television job was here in Richmond.

One of the oldest African-American newspapers in the nation is the *Richmond Afro-American*, now in its second century of publication. Its beginnings go back to a weekly called *The Planet* that gained national prominence when it was edited from 1884 to 1929 by the illustrious John R. Mitchell, Jr. He fought courageously and indefatigably against Jim Crow laws and was responsible for forming the Mechanics Savings Bank of Richmond in 1902. The newspaper was sold in 1938 to Baltimore interests and at that time was renamed the *Richmond Afro-American* and the *Richmond Planet*.

Among the newest publications in the Richmond area is the Spanish-language newspaper *El Sol* that serves the area's growing Hispanic community.

Newspapers

RICHMOND TIMES-DISPATCH
333 E. Grace St.   *649-6000*

The *Times-Dispatch* is published daily and has a Sunday circulation that exceeds 250,000 copies. It bills itself as "Virginia's News Leader" and has correspondents and bureaus throughout Virginia, as well as a bureau in Washington, D.C. Its coverage of local and state political, business, sports, and general news is extensive. Its Monday edition carries an expanded business section called "Metro Business," it publishes weekly "PLUS" community news sections for Chesterfield, Henrico and Hanover counties and the Tri-Cities, and each Thursday it publishes a "Weekend" section devoted to upcoming cultural and arts programs and special events.

RICHMOND AFRO-AMERICAN
301 E. Clay St.   *649-8478*

Richmond has three weekly newspapers that circulate to primarily African-American audiences. The *Richmond Afro-American*, established more than 100 years ago with roots going back to the famous *Richmond Planet* as noted above, is the oldest. It is issued on Wednesdays, is distributed free and is published by the national Afro-American Newspaper Co.

RICHMOND FREE PRESS
101 W. Broad St.   *644-0496*

The *Richmond Free Press* is the city's newest African-American-owned newspaper. The weekly was launched by a group of influential local citizens in 1992 and is dedicated to high-quality coverage of local events and issues, especially those that "confront the African-American community." The newspaper has a full-size format, a circulation of about 28,000, is distributed at about 300 outlets, and is published on Thursdays.

THE VOICE
214 E. Clay St.   *644-9060*

This weekly African-American-owned tabloid is published on Wednesdays. It is distributed free of charge in Richmond and seven Southside Virginia counties and has a circulation of about 44,000 copies.

THE RICHMOND STATE
4914 Fitzhugh Ave., Ste. 212   *359-4500*

The Richmond State says it is "A Newspaper As Odd As Richmond" (which it describes as "weird, elegant, eccentric, offbeat, perverse, and intellectual all at once" and not like "every other McAmerica city"). Published weekly (except for one week in July, two weeks in August and one week in December), the journal is laid out in a style reminiscent of European newspapers of years gone by, including front-page advertising and

The State Capitol in the midst of Downtown Richmond.

Credit: Metro Richmond Convention and Visitors Center

notices. It carries highlights of weekly local news and an eclectic variety of analysis and opinion pieces covering current events, the arts, history, food, politics, religion, etc. The garden column is written by "C.Z. Guest, our garden writer from Manhattan." *The Richmond State* is available for free at distribution points within the center city, and by mail to subscribers in the suburbs and elsewhere (including the United Kingdom for which the newspaper posts a subscription rate of £50).

GOOCHLAND GAZETTE
2941 River Rd. W.
Goochland   556-3135

Published on Mondays, this weekly has a circulation of about 3,000. It serves the "horse country" of Goochland County, just to the west of the metro area, where many Richmond business executives live.

HERALD-PROGRESS
401 Air Park Rd.
Ashland   798-9031

This lively semiweekly, published twice weekly on Mondays and Thursdays, covers Hanover County. It usually consists of two sections and often has special sections.

MECHANICSVILLE LOCAL
988 Elm Dr. E.
Mechanicsville   746-1235

Published weekly, the *Mechanicsville Local* has a circulation of about 16,000 copies and is mailed to households in the 23111 ZIP code area of eastern Hanover County. It is distributed on Wednesdays.

THE VILLAGE MILL
3001 E. Boundary Ter.   744-1035

Published by the Brandermill Community Association, this full-size newspaper covers community news and serves the neighborhoods and businesses of Brandermill and Woodlake. It is published monthly and has a circulation of about 5,000 copies.

Specialized Publications

EL SOL
P. O. Box 36035
Richmond 23235   379-2799

The Richmond area has more than 12,000 Hispanic residents, including a large number in medical and other professions. *El Sol* was launched in 1992 by Yvonne Brenner, a former reporter for the *San Juan Star*, to serve this audience and Spanish-speaking residents across Virginia. *El Sol* first appeared in tabloid format and is now published monthly as a broadsheet. It is distributed free locally at the State Capitol, in coffee shops, at libraries, universities, certain restaurants and throughout Virginia at similar locations and by mail.

STYLE WEEKLY
1118 W. Main St.   358-0825

If there is an "in" publication in Richmond, this is it. *Style Weekly* used to call itself "The Cultural Guide To Richmond," and this it is, in the broadest sense of the word. In addition to thoroughly covering the arts and cultural scene, the weekly explores, analyzes and dissects all of the things that make Richmond tick and that sometime keep it from ticking. Its lively editorial content, classy display ads and classified personals appeal to an influential audience. A press run of 36,000 copies is parceled out every Tuesday to 250 free-distribution locations. They go fast. Avid readers of *Style Weekly* live in mortal fear they may miss a copy if they don't place priority on picking one up on the day of publication.

VIRGINIA CAPITOL CONNECTIONS
1001 E. Broad St., Ste. 225   *643-5554*

Published quarterly, *Capitol Connections* is devoted to state government issues and includes political commentary and cartoons.

VIRGINIA LAWYERS WEEKLY
106 N. Eighth St.   *783-0770*

Published every Monday, this newspaper includes digests of court cases decided the previous week and also includes news and commentary of interest to Virginia lawyers and law firms. The newspaper is mailed to more than 3,000 subscribers.

FOR KIDS' SAKE
1910 Byrd Ave., Ste. 106   *673-5203*

Published monthly, *For Kids' Sake* is a tabloid-size family newspaper that provides information on events, health and fun for school age children. It has a circulation of about 60,000 copies and is available free of charge at more than 200 locations.

INNSBROOK TODAY
4301 Dominion Blvd.
Glen Allen   *346-2782*

Published monthly, this magazine covers Innsbrook and Deep Run area news. It has 60,000-plus West End readers and is hand-delivered to every office and business in the area as well as to every home in Innsbrook's five neighborhoods.

NORTHSIDE MAGAZINE
P.O. Box 15119
Richmond 23227   *261-0588*

The *Northside Magazine* is published weekly in a tabloid newspaper format by Stone Arch Publications, Inc. Distributed free, it serves Richmond's North Side and parts of Henrico and Hanover counties. Circulation is about 25,000 copies. It cov-

ers neighborhood and community issues and is published the first of every week.

MATURE LIFE
22 E. Cary St.   *343-3000*

This is the official newspaper of the Capital Area Agency on Aging. It is published every other month and covers a wide range of news and information on services of interest to readers 60 and older in Richmond and seven surrounding counties. It has a circulation of about 38,000 copies.

LIFE STYLE
1118 W. Main St.   *358-0825*

This tabloid news magazine is published monthly in tabloid format by *Style Weekly* and carries consumer, health, financial and travel information and events listings of interest to the 50 and older audience (or, as *Life Style* puts it, "For People Who Weren't Born Yesterday"). Copies are available free at area locations.

NITE LIFE
12385 Gayton Rd.   *750-1201*

A monthly newspaper, *Nite Life* specializes in information about nighttime entertainment in Richmond.

MID-ATLANTIC SOCCER
1974 E. Parham Rd.   *(800) 899-8833*

Mid-Atlantic Soccer: Where the Kids are the Stars is published by Cadmus Publishing Group. It offers full-color coverage of the sport, plus an insert reporting on local news, all with a youth orientation. A major portion of the subscription fee goes to local soccer clubs.

OUT 'O THE BLUE REVIEW
P.O. Box 1117
Mechanicsville 23111   *783-1946*

This is a quarterly paper with music reviews, interviews, humor, and news and updates of the "Out o' The Blue Radio Revue" show. It is available only by subscription.

CATHOLIC VIRGINIAN
14 N. Laurel St.   358-3625

This is the newspaper of the Catholic Diocese of Richmond. It is published twice a month on Mondays and is mailed to 59,000 homes.

JEWISH NEWS
212 N. Gaskins Rd.   740-2000

This weekly is received by about 4,200 families on Fridays. It covers local Jewish events and Israeli and international Jewish topics.

VIRGINIA EPISCOPALIAN
110 W. Franklin St.   643-8451

This monthly newspaper is published by the Episcopal Diocese of Virginia. It contains diocesan, national and international news and commentary. Circulation is about 28,000 copies.

GOOD NEWS HERALD
1522 Rogers St.   780-0021

"Our editorial policy is to herald nothing but good news," says the masthead, "to spotlight positive citizen role models." Content features community personalities and is heavy on church news.

Magazines

RICHMOND METROPOLITAN MAGAZINE
2500 E. Parham Rd., Ste. 200   261-0034

This is Richmond's city magazine and features articles on the arts, entertainment, business, finance, health, local lifestyles and local personalities. Published nine times a year, it has an annual "Best and Worst" issue, and one issue each year is an annual "Newcomers Edition" that provides a broad base of information on housing, jobs,

health care, newcomers organizations, schools, other data and phone numbers of value to new residents. The magazine, with a circulation of about 25,000 copies, is privately owned and is available on newsstands or by subscription.

RICHMOND VENTURES
1407 Huguenot Rd.   378-8246

Published monthly, *Richmond Ventures* carries articles and information of interest to the small-business owner, entrepreneur and venture capitalist.

VIRGINIA BUSINESS
411 E. Franklin St., Ste. 105   649-6999

Edited and published in Richmond, this is Virginia's statewide business magazine. It is an influential and respected publication and has a monthly controlled circulation of more than 38,000 copies to business, professional and government leaders. The publisher is Media General Business Communications, Inc.

NEW VIRGINIA REVIEW
1306 E. Cary St.   782-1043

Richmond is home-base for a literary magazine, *New Virginia Review*. It is described under "Writers' Groups" in the Arts chapter of this guide.

Television

Richmond has three network affiliates, two independent stations, the public broadcasting operations of Central Virginia Educational Television (CVET) and two cable companies.

WTVR-TV CHANNEL 6
3301 W. Broad St.   254-3600

This was the first television station in the South and began broadcasting in 1948. It is the CBS affiliate and is owned by Roy H. Park Broadcasting of Virginia.

WRIC-TV CHANNEL 8

301 Arboretum Pl.　　　　*330-8888*

This is the ABC affiliate. Its operations date back to 1955, and it is owned by Young Broadcasting Inc.

WWBT-TV CHANNEL 12

5710 Midlothian Tnpk.　　　*230-1212*

An NBC affiliate, this channel is owned by Jefferson Pilot Broadcasting Co. It began broadcasting in 1956.

WCVE-TV CHANNEL 23
WCVW-TV CHANNEL 57

23 Sesame St.　　　　　*320-1301*

This is where you will find PBS programming plus locally produced shows. Both channels are operated by Central Virginia Education Television.

WRLH-TV CHANNEL 35

1925 Westmoreland St.　　　*358-3535*

An independent channel, WRLH-TV is owned by ACT III Broadcasting, a member of the Fox Network. The station has been on the air since 1982.

WZXK-TV CHANNEL 65

13 Mapleleaf Ct.
Ashland　　　　　　*550-1408*

This is an independent religious channel owned by Christel Broadcasting Inc. Its programming also is carried on channel 32 of Continental Cablevision and on channel 36 of Comcast Cablevision.

CONTINENTAL CABLEVISION

Richmond service:
918 N. Boulevard　　　　*355-7000*
Ashland, Hanover & Henrico service:
3914 Wistar Rd.　　　　*226-1900*

Continental Cablevision provides cable service to about 125,000 residents in Richmond and in Hanover, Henrico, Goochland and James City counties. Its more than 30 channels include these basics: C-SPAN, ESPN, Cable News Network, Arts and Entertainment, Black Entertainment, Financial News Network, MTV, Nickelodeon, and the Weather Channel. Premium movie channels, HBO and Cinemax and the Disney Channel are available for an additional fee. Also for additional fees Continental Cablevision offers digital cable audio services with stereo access to 30 radio stations across the country and connection services to the Virginia Voice for the Visually Handicapped. Its pay-per-view service includes major sports events, movies and special events. Senior citizen or multiple-installation discounts may be available, so be sure to inquire.

COMCAST CABLEVISION

6510 Iron Bridge Rd.　　　*743-1150*

Comcast serves more than 55,000 customers in Chesterfield County and offers a 37-channel "total preferred service." Also available is its channel basic service that includes local broadcast channels, selected cable channels such as C-SPAN and the Preview Channel. HBO, The Movie Channel, Cinemax, Showtime and the Disney Channel are available at additional cost. Pay-per-view channels also are available, as is Comcast's FM cable radio service.

Radio

Among morning drive shows, WRVA's Tim Timberlake-John Harding team ranks No. 1, followed by morning shows on WKHK, WCDX, WRVQ's Q-Morning Zoo and WTVR-FM. Overall, for the daily 18-hour period from 6 AM to midnight, country station WKHK and urban contemporary WCDX win the local Arbitron Radio Survey crown.

The area has four news/talk/sports radio stations that offer locally and nationally produced call-in programming. Blanquita Cullum, named one of the nation's "25 Most Important Talk Show Hosts" by *Talkers* magazine, launched her conservative, syndicated show here at WLEE in 1993. She moved her home base in 1995 to a studio in Washington, D.C., but still is carried by WLEE. A popular call-in show on WRVA is hosted by Doug Wilder, former governor of Virginia.

Formats change, but this is the way they stood as this guide book went to press:

WCDX-92.7 FM
(Urban Contemporary)   672-9300

WCVE-88.9 FM
(Public Radio)   320-1301

WDCE-90.1 FM
(Progressive Rock, Jazz, Info.)   289-8790

WDYL-92.1 FM
(Christian Music)   275-6161

WFTH-1590 AM
(Gospel)   233-0765

WGCV-1240 AM
(Gospel)   748-6161

WGGM-820 AM
(Christian Country, CNN News)   275-6161

WHCE-91.1 FM
(Educational, News)   328-4078

WKHK-95.3 FM
(Continuous Country)   330-9555

WKIK-104.7 FM
(Country Favorites)   345-1047

WLEE-1320 AM
(Call-in, Talk, ABC News)   675-0300

WLEE-96.5 FM
('70s Music)   330-3106

WMXB-103.7 FM
(Adult Contemporary)   560-1037

WPES-1430 AM
(Christian Inspirational)   798-1010

WPLZ-99.3 FM
(Urban Contemporary)   672-9300

WREJ-1540 AM
(Urban Contemporary Christian)   264-1540

WRVA-1140 AM
(News, Call-in, Talk, Info.)   576-3200

WRVH-910 AM
(Sports, Call-in, Talk)   780-3400

WRXL-102.1 FM
(Classic Rock, New Rock)   756-6400

WRVQ-94.5 FM
(Contemporary Hits)   756-6400

WSTK-1290 AM
('40s, '50s and '60s Hits)   768-1290

WSOJ-100.3 FM
(Adult Urban Contemporary)   768-0100

WTVR-1380 AM
(Big Bands, Sports, News)   355-3217

WTVR- 98.1 FM
(Beautiful Music)   355-3217

WVGO-106.5 FM
(Adult Rock)   330-3106

WXGI-950 AM
(Traditional Country)   233-7666

WYFJ-100.1 FM
(Sacred Music)   798-3248

Inside
Service Directory

Depending on the part of Greater Richmond in which you live, whom do you call to arrange gas, electric or cable television service? How do you get a building permit or dispose of hazardous waste? When are taxes due? How can you hook up with a newcomer's club?

This chapter provides some of the basic information you'll need to answer these questions and others. We've also listed telephone numbers of places you can call for complete details.

Automobiles

AUTO REGISTRATION
AND DRIVER'S LICENSES

2300 W. Broad St.   367-0538

New Virginia residents must visit the Department of Motor Vehicles (DMV) in person to obtain a driver's license, title, registration card, license plates and decals. In addition to the main office on W. Broad Street, DMV has offices on the north side of the James River at 5517 S. Laburnum Avenue, 9237 Quiocassin Road and at 8191 Brook Road, and south of the river at 10000 Courtview Lane, 11627 Midlothian Turnpike and at 4806 Old Midlothian Turnpike. Vehicle renewal registration can be handled by mail, and DMV accepts VISA and MasterCard for mail registration and in person at its Broad Street location.

State law requires that auto liability insurance be purchased before a vehicle may be registered. Otherwise a $400 uninsured motorist fee must be paid. Noncompliance with this requirement may result in revocation of the driver's license and of the privilege to register a motor vehicle in Virginia.

A driver's license is first issued for the number of years it will take that person to reach an age divisible by five, when a regular five-year cycle begins. Personalized and specialty plates are available, including those for a wide variety of colleges.

In addition to state registration, windshield decals must be purchased from the appropriate local jurisdiction. Information on local vehicle registration may be obtained by calling these telephone numbers: Richmond, 780-5700; Chesterfield, 748-1201; Hanover, 537-6050; Henrico, 672-4258.

Alcoholic Beverages

You can buy beer and wine by the case or bottle in grocery and convenient stores, at wine retailers and in other places licensed for "off-premise" sales. But the only places you can buy other alcoholic beverages by the bottle or case is at retail stores operated by the Department of Alcoholic Beverage Control (ABC), which regulates the sale of liquor, wine and beer in Virginia.

ABC stores, as everyone calls them, are conveniently located throughout the metropolitan area and sell distilled spirits, cordials and liqueurs and Virginia wines. Most are self-service, but some still are the kinds of package stores that were traditional in Virginia for many years, with a clerk behind a counter filling customer orders. You can use MasterCard and VISA credit cards for purchases of at least $15. The ABC Department also issues permits to bars, convenience stores, private clubs, restaurants and other establishments.

The legal age to purchase, consume or possess alcoholic beverages in Virginia is 21.

Building Permits and Plans

Chesterfield County	748-1057
Hanover County	537-6040
Henrico County	672-4360
City of Richmond	780-6950

Cable Television

Continental Cablevision serves Richmond, Hanover County and Henrico County. To order service in Hanover or Henrico, call 266-1900. The telephone number for repair service in these areas is 264-5048. In the City of Richmond, the telephone number for ordering service or repairs is 355-7000.

Chesterfield County is served by Comcast Cablevision. In the northern part of the county the number for service is 743-1150, and the number for repairs is 275-6789. In the southern (Chester) part of the county, the number for service is 796-2099 and the number for repairs is 748-6206.

Electric Utility

Virginia Power's telephone number for connections and disconnections in residential service for the Richmond metro area is 756-2010.

Fire, Police & Medical Emergencies

DIAL 911 FOR
ALL SUCH EMERGENCIES.

This is the universal fire, police and medical/ambulance number for the Richmond area. The enhanced 911 system is set up to help emergency response teams locate the address from which you are calling, but be prepared to give your street address just the same.

Gas Utilities

If you live in Richmond, Henrico County or the northern part of Chesterfield County your gas service will be provided by the Richmond Gas Utility, 644-3000. Gas service in most of Chesterfield County is supplied by Commonwealth Gas Service: (800) 543-8911 in the Midlothian area and 862-0600 in the Chesterfield Courthouse and Chester areas. In the Kings Charter area of Hanover County the number for Virginia Natural Gas is 798-3162.

Hazardous Wastes

To determine how to dispose of hazardous wastes such as antifreeze, explosives, motor oil, paint and other toxic household wastes call the state's Environmental Quality Waste Division at 762-4050. The National Response Center for pollution, toxic chemicals and oil spills

Consolidated bank&trustco.

Since 1903 Consolidated Bank & Trust has been providing "The Ability To Turn The Seemingly Impossible Into Glittering Realities."

**First and Marshall • P.O. Box 10046
Richmond, Virginia 23240 • (804) 771-5200
Member FDIC**

can be reached by dialing (800) 424-8802. If you want to recycle oil, call 367-6974, and for general questions about recycling call the Central Virginia Waste Management Authority at 359-8413.

Investment Firms

The Richmond area is home to a multitude of banks and firms offering a wide variety of investment services for both commercial and individual needs. Firms include:

BRANCH CABELL & CO.

919 E. Main St.   *225-1400*

Branch Cabell, established in 1904, enjoys an excellent reputation in Richmond's "Main Street" financial district and offers complete portfolio management and financial planning services.

A.G. EDWARDS AND SONS

1313 E. Main St.   *648-8800*

This firm's most noted credential is the five star award it received from *Kiplinger's Personal Finance* magazine. Founded in 1887, it is also one of the nation's oldest investment firms.

SCOTT & STRINGFELLOW INVESTMENT CORPORATION

901 E. Main St.   *643-1811*
901 Moorefield Park Dr.   *323-1012*

Scott & Stringfellow is the South's oldest member of the New York Stock Exchange. Headquartered in Richmond, it is a full-service regional brokerage, financial service and investment banking firm.

WHEAT FIRST BUTCHER SINGER

901 E. Byrd St.   *649-2311*

One of the largest financial services and investment banking firms headquartered outside New York City, Wheat today operates nearly 100 offices in about a dozen states. Richmond is the location of its home office.

Libraries

The Richmond area is endowed with a lot of great libraries — for research, audio tapes, videos, exhibits, seminars and, of course, for books and periodicals. The Richmond, Chesterfield County and Henrico County libraries have a number of branches, but the phone numbers for only the main libraries are given here.

VIRGINIA STATE LIBRARY

Reference Information	*786-8929*
Publications Information	*786-2311*

RICHMOND
PUBLIC LIBRARY (MAIN LIBRARY)

Literature and History Information	*780-4672*
Business, Science and Technology	*780-8223*
Art and Music	*780-4740*

CHESTERFIELD
COUNTY LIBRARY SYSTEM

Central Library	*748-1601*

PAMUNKEY REGIONAL
LIBRARY (HANOVER)

Ashland	*798-4072*
Hanover Courthouse	*537-6210*
Mechanicsville	*746-9615*

HENRICO COUNTY LIBRARY

Branch Info.	*222-2273*
Central Reference	*222-1318*

STATE LIBRARY
FOR THE VISUALLY
AND PHYSICALLY HANDICAPPED

395 Azalea Ave.	*371-3661*

In addition, there are extensive libraries at the University of Richmond, Virginia Commonwealth University, Randolph-Macon College, Virginia Union University and at area community colleges. Specialized libraries are at the Virginia Museum of Fine Arts (art and art history), the Virginia Historical Society (Virginia history and genealogi-

A couple pauses for a rest in Shockoe Slip.

cal collections), the Valentine Museum (Richmond history), the Museum of the Confederacy, the Edgar Allan Poe Museum and at the Black History Museum and Cultural Center.

Newcomers Clubs

A good way to meet people is through hobby and special interest groups. A list of these groups is published in the annual, early-August "Discover Richmond" section of the *Richmond Times-Dispatch* (single copies of this section are on sale throughout the year at the newspaper's front desk at 333 E. Grace Street).

In addition, two organizations are open to anyone who has moved to the Richmond area within the past two years: the Newcomers Club of Richmond, 378-8209 or 360-9627, and the New Virginians Club, 378-8859. There also are organizations such as the Chesterfield Welcome League, 739-7148, and Steel City Connection, open to natives of Pittsburgh or Steelers fans (write to 8300 Recreation Road, 23231).

Out-of-Town Newspapers

The most extensive variety of out-of-town newspapers (about 60, U.S. and foreign) is available at Books A Million, 9131 Midlothian Turnpike (272-1792). The Barnes & Noble Book Store in the Shops at Willow Lawn shopping center carries Sunday editions of many newspapers from major cities in the United States and abroad. *The New York Times*, *The Washington Post* and *The Wall Street Journal* are available at street-corner vending machines, which are plentiful, especially down-

town, and these newspapers also are sold at the Jefferson, Hyatt, Marriott and Omni hotels, at the State Capitol, at the Riverfront Plaza Sundry Shop and at certain chain drug and 7-Eleven stores. The Norfolk newspaper also is available at some of these locations and in vending machines.

Personal Property Taxes

CHESTERFIELD COUNTY
748-1201
Tax forms must be filed by March 1. Taxes are due June 5.

HANOVER COUNTY
537-6050
Tax forms must be filed by May 1. Taxes are due December 5.

HENRICO COUNTY
877-0747
Tax forms must be filed by March 15. Taxes due one-half on June 5, one-half on December 5.

CITY OF RICHMOND
780-5690
Taxes are billed during the period January 1 to March 31. Total payment is due May 1, although special arrangements can be made for partial payments.

Pet Licenses

We've used the heading "Pet Licenses" here because Richmond now requires licenses for cats as well as dogs. For information call:

Chesterfield County	751-4916
Hanover County	537-6050
Henrico County	672-4267
City of Richmond	780-5700

Public School Registration/Information

Chesterfield County	748-1405
Hanover County	752-6000
Henrico County	226-3600
City of Richmond	780-7710

Real Estate Taxes

In Chesterfield, Hanover and Henrico counties, one-half of real estate taxes are due June 5, and the balance is due December 5. In the City of Richmond real estate tax bills are due June 15. Information may be obtained by calling:

Chesterfield County	748-1201
Hanover County	537-6132
Henrico County	672-4267
City of Richmond	780-5700

Recycling Information

CENTRAL VIRGINIA WASTE MANAGEMENT AUTHORITY
359-8413

Senior Citizen Services

CAPITAL AREA AGENCY ON AGING
343-3000

The Capital Region Agency on Aging's services include congregate and home-delivered meals, a Foster Grandparents program, job training and employment, a senior discount card, weatherization and home repair assistance, certain health care services and volunteer opportunities.

Information and Referral

UNITED WAY SERVICES
275-2000

LONG-TERM CARE

OMBUDSMAN PROGRAM
(800) 552-3402

State Income Taxes

The deadline for filing individual state income tax returns is May 1. Call 367-8031 for information.

Support Services and Counseling

AIDS HOTLINE
(800) 533-4148

ALCOHOLICS ANONYMOUS
355-1212

AMERICAN RED CROSS
News of relatives in disaster areas   780-2250

ALZHEIMER'S DISEASE AND RELATED DISORDERS
320-HOPE

EMERGENCY SHELTER
782-9276

FAMILIES ANONYMOUS
323-4466

FAMILY CRISIS CENTER
282-4255

LEARNING DISABILITIES COUNCIL
748-5012

MEALS ON WHEELS
355-3603

MISSING CHILDREN:
Runaway Hotline	(800) 448-4663
Info Clearing House	(800) 822-4453

SALVATION ARMY
225-7470

TRAVELLERS AID
648-1767

YWCA WOMEN'S HOTLINE
| Richmond shelter | 643-0888 |
| Chesterfield shelter | 796-3066 |

An extensive list of telephone numbers of agencies and organizations offering support and counseling services in the Richmond area is carried under Community Service Numbers in the front of the white pages of the local telephone book.

Telephone Service

Bell Atlantic provides telephone service for almost all of the Greater Richmond area. Residential hookups can be arranged by calling 954-6222, and business service by calling 954-6219. Continental Telephone serves the Old Church part of Hanover County and service can be arranged by calling (800) 533-7610.

Tour Information

METROPOLITAN RICHMOND CONVENTION AND VISITORS BUREAU
782-2777

Trash Collection and Special Pickups

RICHMOND
North of James	780-6445
South of James	780-5051
Recycling Coordinator	780-6438

SURROUNDING COUNTIES
Chesterfield	748-1297
Henrico	261-8770
Hanover	537-6181

Virginia Lottery

You can access a 24-hour telephone to check on winning numbers by dialing 345-5825.

Volunteer Opportunities

If you're interested in volunteer work, the Volunteer Center of United Way Services at 771-5851 can put you in touch with about 50 groups ranging from museums and theater groups to social service, youth and health care organizations.

Voter Registration

To register to vote in Virginia you must be at least 17 years old and turn 18 by the next general election, you cannot be a convicted felon or judged to be mentally incompetent, and you must fill out an application under oath and register by early October, 30 days before the next general election that takes place in early November.

If you are physically unable to go to the registrar's office, it is possible to arrange for the registrar to come to your home. You will remain a registered voter as long as you vote at least once every four calendar years and you continue to live in the same precinct. If you change either your legal address or name you must notify your local registrar in writing or in person.

Information on voter registration is available by calling: Richmond, 780-5950; Chesterfield, 748-147; Hanover, 537-6080 (or 730-6080 for Ashland and Old Church); or Henrico, 672-4347.

Water and Sewer Hookups

City of Richmond	644-3000
Chesterfield County	748-1291
Hanover County	537-6024
Ashland	798-8650
Henrico County	672-4571

Other Useful Numbers

BEFORE YOU DIG
Buried Cable Information   (800) 552-7001

FISHING AND HUNTING LICENSES
367-1000

GO-FER SERVICES, INC.
674-0313

For personal errands, grocery shopping and delivery, gift basket and party platter delivery.

LOST BICYCLES

Chesterfield	748-1524
Hanover	730-6140
Henrico	672-4810

POISON CENTER
786-9123

POLLUTION, TOXIC CHEMICAL AND OIL SPILLS
(800) 424-8802

SOCIETY FOR THE PREVENTION OF CRUELTY TO ANIMALS (SPCA)
643-6785

TIME AND TEMPERATURE
844-3711

VAN AND CAR POOL INFORMATION
643-7433

WEATHER
268-1212

Index of Advertisers

ORDER FORM
Fast and Simple!

Mail to:
Insiders Guides®, Inc.
P.O. Drawer 2057
Manteo, NC 27954

Or:
for VISA or
Mastercard orders call
1-800-765-BOOK

Name _____

Address _____

City/State/Zip _____

Qty.	Title/Price	Shipping	Amount
	Insiders' Guide to Richmond/$14.95	$3.00	
	Insiders' Guide to Williamsburg/$12.95	$3.00	
	Insiders' Guide to Virginia's Blue Ridge/$14.95	$3.00	
	Insiders' Guide to Virginia's Chesapeake Bay/$14.95	$3.00	
	Insiders' Guide to Washington, DC/$14.95	$3.00	
	Insiders' Guide to North Carolina's Outer Banks/$14.95	$3.00	
	Insiders' Guide to Wilmington, NC/$14.95	$3.00	
	Insiders' Guide to North Carolina's Crystal Coast/$12.95	$3.00	
	Insiders' Guide to Charleston, SC/$12.95	$3.00	
	Insiders' Guide to Myrtle Beach/$14.95	$3.00	
	Insiders' Guide to Mississippi/$14.95	$3.00	
	Insiders' Guide to Boca Raton & the Palm Beaches/$14.95 (8/95)	$3.00	
	Insiders' Guide to Sarasota/Bradenton/$12.95	$3.00	
	Insiders' Guide to Northwest Florida/$14.95	$3.00	
	Insiders' Guide to Lexington, KY/$12.95	$3.00	
	Insiders' Guide to Louisville/$12.95	$3.00	
	Insiders' Guide to the Twin Cities/$12.95	$3.00	
	Insiders' Guide to Boulder/$12.95	$3.00	
	Insiders' Guide to Denver/$12.95	$3.00	
	Insiders' Guide to The Civil War (Eastern Theater)/$14.95	$3.00	
	Insiders' Guide to North Carolina's Mountains/$14.95	$3.00	
	Insiders' Guide to Atlanta/$14.95	$3.00	
	Insiders' Guide to Branson/$14.95 (12/95)	$3.00	
	Insiders' Guide to Cincinnati/$14.95 (9/95)	$3.00	
	Insiders' Guide to Tampa/St. Petersburg/$14.95 (12/95)	$3.00	

Payment in full (check or money order) must
accompany this order form.
Please allow 2 weeks for delivery.

N.C. residents add 6% sales tax _____

Total _____